MW00605491

A
SALEM
WITCH

A
SALEM
WITCH

The Trial,
Execution,
AND
Exoneration
OF

Rebecca Nurse

Daniel A. Gagnon

WESTHOLME
Yardley

Westholme Publishing, LLC
904 Edgewood Road
Yardley, Pennsylvania 19067
Visit our Web site at www.westholmepublishing.com

ISBN: 978-1-59416-367-8
Also available as an eBook.

Printed in the United States of America.

*To all who teach and preserve the history of
Danvers and Salem Village.*

O Christian Martyr! who for Truth could die,
When all about thee owned the hideous lie!
The world, redeemed from Superstition's sway,
Is breathing freer for thy sake to-day.
—*John Greenleaf Whittier, engraved on the Rebecca
Nurse Memorial in the Nurse Family Cemetery,
Danvers, Massachusetts*

Contents

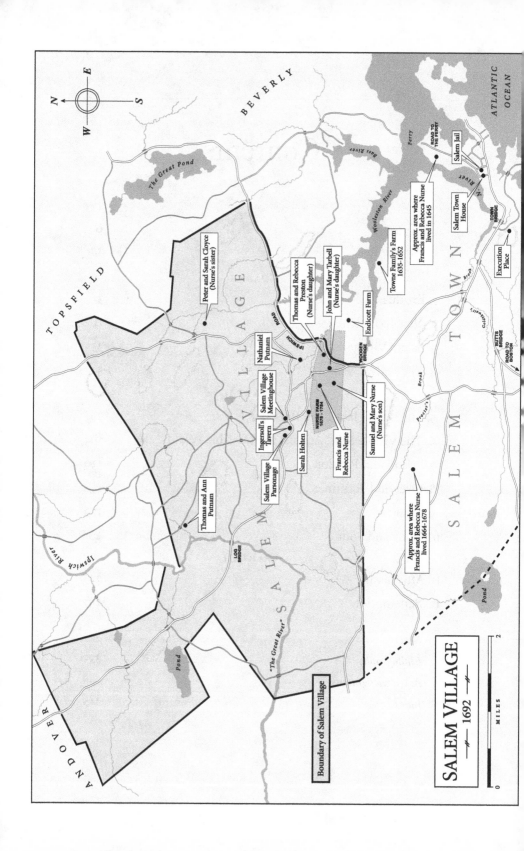

SALEM VILLAGE
— 1692 —

MILES

0   2

Boundary of Salem Village

ATLANTIC OCEAN

BEVERLY

TOPSFIELD

ANDOVER

SALEM VILLAGE

SALEM TOWN

The Great Pond

Ipswich River

"The Great River"

Pond

Pond

Bass River

Woolestan River

Forest River

LOG BRIDGE

IPSWICH ROAD

WOODEN BRIDGE

ROAD TO BOSTON

BUTTS BRIDGE

TOWN BRIDGE

ROAD TO THE FERRY

Ferry

Peter and Sarah Cloyce
(Nurse's sister)

Thomas and Rebecca Preston
(Nurse's daughter)

John and Mary Tarbell
(Nurse's daughter)

Nathaniel Putnam

Salem Village Meetinghouse

Ingersoll's Tavern

Salem Village Parsonage

Sarah Holten

Francis and Rebecca Nurse

Samuel and Mary Nurse
(Nurse's son)

NURSE 1678-1784

Endicott Farm

Towne Family's Farm
1635-1652

Approx. area where
Francis and Rebecca Nurse
lived in 1645

Salem Town House

Salem Jail

Execution Place

Approx. area where
Francis and Rebecca Nurse
lived 1664-1678

Thomas and Ann Putnam

Preface

LIKE MANY WRITERS investigating the 1692 Salem Village witch hunt, I was inspired by the actions of those innocents who died in the name of truth, and also by the sense of place associated with Salem Village. For many writers, it is a visit to Salem and the former Salem Village that first leads them to further examine the events of 1692 and the tragic history of those who were wrongfully killed. I am fortunate in that it was not a brief visit, but instead a lifetime thus far spent in the former Salem Village (present-day Danvers, Massachusetts) among the sites associated with 1692 that led me to undertake this project.

Among the seventeenth-century homes, stone foundations, and monuments associated with this dark episode of history, no victim of the witch hunt is remembered to the same extent as Rebecca Nurse. Her story is so compelling that it has been captured in dramatic productions, novels, history books, paintings, films, songs, the name of a rock band, and an academic team at the local middle school, to name only a few ways. Every American high school student who reads *The Crucible* is familiar with the broad strokes of her part in history.

Yet, previously there was no full-length scholarly biography of Rebecca Nurse. Prior to this project, the only monograph on Nurse's life was Charles S. Tapley's slim work *Rebecca Nurse: Saint but Witch Victim* (1930). A descendant of Nurse and a Danvers historian, Tapley drew primarily on the nineteenth-century secondary sources to construct a brief overview of Nurse's role in the trials, without either a full examination of her life before the witch hunt, or a discussion of her legacy after 1692—a legacy that has increased in significance since 1930.

This present volume seeks to remedy that gap in the historical scholarship of the 1692 Salem Village witch hunt. Nurse is probably the most well-known victim of the witch hunt today, because she maintained her innocence even though it cost her life, and she is the victim of 1692 who was most extensively memorialized throughout the subsequent centuries.

The Salem Village witch hunt is an event that is hard to comprehend in totality, with hundreds of people involved across a wide area, centered on Salem Village. The stories of individual people can be lost in larger historical examinations of events as complex as the witch hunt—which focus on an abstract discussion of ideology, imperialist conflicts, local politics, and religion. These discussions are important for our understanding of how such an event could occur, but the human element is often lost.

Examining the witch hunt through the life of one of its most well-known victims gives a more manageable perspective and clearer insight into what happened during the events of 1692 as a whole and brings forward the story of one of the most notable women in pre-Revolutionary American history, including how she was commemorated in the following centuries. This focus brings the narrative back to one of human tragedy, and it is easier to see this essential aspect of the witch hunt by focusing on the case of one woman, and how her life and the lives of her family members were affected by this event. Additionally, the chronology of a biography allows the reader to experience the witch hunt as it happened, unlike some historical works on the witch hunt that are arranged thematically or arranged based on the order the accused were put on trial, which distort the chain of events.[1]

As to the text, all dialogue from Rebecca Nurse and statements from those involved in the witch hunt come directly from court records or accounts written by observers of the events and are the original words, as recorded at the time. The language of quotations from original seventeenth-century documents is modernized for clarity and ease of reading. The (seemingly) strange spellings and grammar used in 1692, before the English language was standardized, can subconsciously distance the reader from the main actors of the witch hunt, separating the events from the present day and placing them in another imagined world. In reality, many themes of 1692 connect through the centuries to the present. Also, seeing spelling and grammar that to twenty-first-century readers appears "incorrect," the reader may mistakenly draw conclusions about the education and intelligence of the writer or speaker. Modernizing the language is meant to help the reader avoid these twenty-first-century presuppositions.

Along with the language, the dating system is also slightly modified for the modern reader. The Julian calendar (with the year beginning on March 25, and dates eleven days behind the current Gregorian calendar) was still used in seventeenth-century New England, or sometimes the two calendars were merged and dates between January and March of a certain year were listed as both years (for example, the beginning of the witch hunt took place in "1691/2"). Years in this text are noted as starting on the more familiar January 1.

Finally, in order to give a full account of the life of a seventeenth-century Puritan woman, much is also said about her husband, Francis Nurse, and other members of her family. As Massachusetts women at that time could not own property in their own name, and legal acts (such as wills, adoptions, etc.) were in their husband's name, Francis' name shows up exponentially more in the pre-1692 records than Rebecca's. This disadvantage is due to the society in which Rebecca Nurse lived, and the historical record suffers because of it. However, although her name is not on a deed or she is not listed as the legal guardian of an adopted child, one should not assume that she was not working alongside her husband on the farm or that she was not intimately involved in raising the child. These records that mention Francis Nurse reveal much about Rebecca's life.

Rebecca Nurse's story resonates for us today, as it has for those in previous centuries, and surely will for subsequent ones. It fills us with a desire for justice, and a respect for those who stand firm in the shadow of persecution. In the words of one local visitor to the Rebecca Nurse Memorial in 1900, "Perhaps the greatest incentive to ideal living in a changing world is the firmly held conviction that truth will finally vindicate itself. When this vindication becomes apparent, as in the case of one of the most striking martyrs of the Salem witchcraft, Rebecca Nurse, progress seems assured."[2] Let us work toward that vindication and use the past as a way to look to the future.

Introduction

THE EARLY SEVENTEENTH CENTURY was an age of upheaval and uncertainty. Rebecca Towne was born into a Puritan family in Great Yarmouth, England, in 1621, during the throes of the Reformation—a period of change not seen in Europe since the aftermath of the Fall of Rome. The relative stability of the medieval order in England began to see modernity gnaw away at the edges of its foundation, threatening the structure of society itself.

To escape this tumult of religious, political, and social strife, Rebecca and the Towne family traveled to America during the Great Puritan Migration to live with her coreligionists in the "New Jerusalem" of the Massachusetts Bay Colony. As one of the early settlers of Massachusetts living in Salem Town and then Salem Village (present-day Danvers, Mass.), her life was harsh and demanding. It was in Salem that she met and married Francis Nurse, with whom she lived for forty-seven years until she was killed.

There were challenges to overcome in establishing a household and a family on a barely explored continent, including fears of invasion by the French and Natives, illness, debts, and issues of village politics. Despite these challenges facing her and her community, she worked alongside her husband in developing a productive farm, raised eight natural and two adopted children, and received membership in the Salem Town church—confirming her status as a "visible saint" among the Puritans, and gaining the respect of those in the community.

Rebecca Nurse, following John Winthrop's dream of a "City Upon a Hill," came to the New World, only to be killed upon that hill when the

Puritan utopian experiment turned on its own saints. The accusation of witchcraft against her in March 1692 brought forth from historical obscurity the wife of a Puritan farmer in Salem Village to become a symbol of insistent innocence in a time of chaos and strife. Her life before 1692 was fairly ordinary for a first-generation Massachusetts Puritan, and it is for this reason that she is so significant. She gives us a view into how a regular person acted when confronted with one of the wildest, strangest, and most chaotic events in American history.

Throughout her ordeal, Nurse showed a calm unwavering faith in herself and her Christian religion despite strong pressure from the religious and political leaders of her day, and despite the certain pain that was inflicted on her spirit when she was accused of an unspeakable crime by her fellow villagers, who turned against one of their own who was previously accorded much respect in the church and society. From the first whispers against her through to the years after her death, Nurse's family fought persistently to prove her innocence, and later to posthumously clear her name.

While weaker men and women wavered and falsely confessed under pressure to the crime of witchcraft—the most serious crime a Puritan could commit, one which guaranteed the death of both body and soul—Rebecca Nurse stood firm as an example of an individual seeking true justice from her neighbors who were caught up in a zeitgeist of fear and suspicion.

THE 1692 WITCH HUNT that began in Salem Village and spread to the surrounding communities has been extensively researched like few other historical happenings. At least 172 people from across the region were accused of practicing witchcraft, 19 were hanged, one was pressed to death, and at least five died in the dungeon-like jails.[1] No other event in North American history prior to the American Revolution captures the imagination like the witch hunt in Salem Village. These events have been used by authors and playwrights over the centuries to teach readers and audiences lessons on religion, democracy, judicial independence, and the dangers of acting rashly when confronted by collective fears, both real and imagined. The witch hunt gives insight into the New England experience and the development of the soul of America.

Though all recognize the horror and suffering caused by the witch hunt, historiographical consensus on its cause—including what led to the accusations against Rebecca Nurse in March 1692—has not been reached.

The analysis of this event must recognize a confluence of diverse causes—as any hypothesis that claims one specific, overall cause of an event this complex is bound to fail.

Salem Village during Nurse's time was under intense outward pressure, including from Native American and French raiders, and interference from London. The stress of fighting what appeared to be a losing war against the Catholic French and pagan Natives set a scene where fear reigned.[2] Fear that some in the community might be secretly aiding the enemy, who was believed to be allied with the Devil, bubbled to the surface. The possibility that losing the war could wipe the Puritans off the map and destroy the "New Jerusalem" of Massachusetts, the Puritans' utopian project to refashion the world according to their faith, made it truly an existential conflict. If this possibility was not worrying enough, the English government's moves to limit Massachusetts' representative government and potentially force the colony to conform to the loathed Church of England, from which the Puritans had fled decades earlier, also threatened their way of life. As when all utopian experiments begin to falter, the community looks inward, worried that some among them might be bringing down the perfect goal of the new society.

These outside pressures combined with the inward pressures of many long-lasting local disputes and caused the community to rupture. This situation, combined with the universal belief that witchcraft was a real and true threat to Massachusetts society, led to the killing of innocents.

As to the case of Rebecca Nurse, it appears that the accusations were brought upon her through no real fault of her own. One historian describes her as "one of the most perplexing examples of those persons accused of witchcraft seemingly for no reason."[3] Other historians recognize this surprising and unlikely nature of her accusation, noting her "unblemished reputation," describing her as the "very model of Christian piety," and observing that she was "the most conspicuously innocent person of all those who died at Salem."[4] Her Puritanism was orthodox: she was a covenant member of the Salem Town church—the highest position that a woman could attain in the church, a visible saint according to Puritan theology. She was a most unlikely suspect to be conspiring with Satan.

Various reasons have been suggested as to why Nurse was accused of witchcraft, though none of these reasons alone is anywhere near strong enough to cause rational actors to wish death upon her, which a witchcraft accusation brought. What is clear is that she was first mentioned as a witch by one of the members of Thomas and Ann Putnam's household, which lay far across the village from the Nurse farm.

From the trial records, it appears that either Mercy Lewis or Mrs. Ann Putnam suggested Nurse's name to Ann Putnam Jr., after one of the latter's "fits," which were believed to be caused by witchcraft. The mystery of exactly who first mentioned Nurse's name in connection to witchcraft obscures the potential motive for the accusation, if any. This is the crucial gap in knowledge that prevents historians from pinpointing a direct cause for the unlikely charge against her. What is certain is that the accusations against her were baseless, impossible, and simply false. She was innocent, and maintained her innocence until the moment that she breathed her last.

Historians have several theories as to why Nurse was specifically accused, none of which is adequate. It is suggested that because a few of Nurse's siblings and nephews in Topsfield had a land dispute with Thomas and Ann Putnam's cousins in Salem Village, who lived along the disputed boundary with Topsfield, that it caused bad blood leading to the accusation against her.[5] But it seems unlikely that Thomas and Ann Putnam's family sought revenge on their cousins' behalf by targeting their cousins' opponents' pious old aunt who lived a distance away and had no role in the dispute. Of all her extended family, Nurse was the least connected to this issue, yet she was the first from the extended family to be accused. Also, the Putnams directly involved in the Topsfield dispute defended Nurse after she was accused, which further undermines the theory that the boundary dispute was the cause of the accusation.

In another theory, it is suggested that the Nurse family became too prosperous too fast while others were on the decline and therefore the accusation was caused by jealousy.[6] Despite the possible appearance of prosperity when they purchased a large Salem Village farm in 1678, the Nurse family was for many years barely scraping by financially, and owed a sizable mortgage on the land. They frequently fell behind on their taxes, a fact that the villagers were undoubtedly aware of because the tax debts were publicly acknowledged at town meetings.

A longstanding and influential theory concludes that factionalism within the Salem Village community pitted the Nurse family against the Putnam family over the issue of hiring Rev. Samuel Parris as the village minister in 1689, and that the two families lined up on different sides of a larger socioeconomic conflict between two east-west factions, which then explains the division between accusers and accused in 1692.[7] Recent scholarship has shown this theory to be quite limited, and this examination of the Nurse family's role in Salem Village prior to the witch hunt further refutes this factionalist framework, including the mistaken impression that the Nurse family long opposed Parris.[8]

The only example of someone in the Nurse family challenging Rev. Parris prior to 1692 was when Nurse's husband, Francis, only three months before the witch hunt, challenged Parris on one issue: the apparently fraudulent, and possibly illegal, change in the Salem Village parsonage's ownership from being property of the community to allegedly being given to Parris at a suspiciously called village meeting. The investigation of this possibly fraudulent act was supported by a majority of voters in Salem Village in 1691, and so Francis Nurse stood safely on the side of the majority during this confrontation with Parris and the small minority of the church members who still supported the minister after this suspicious act was uncovered.

This issue with Parris, though not the long-standing conflict usually described, likely contributed to the start of the witch hunt, as it made the minister and his supporters feel threatened and embattled right before the fits of the afflicted began. It was the two children in Parris' house that first had fits, a coincidence that cannot be ignored.

FOR CENTURIES THE DEBATE has continued as to whether those who claimed to be "afflicted" by witchcraft and appeared to suffer through frightening "fits" as if they were being tortured truly believed their accusations, or merely lied. Certainly the situation was unique for each of the afflicted accusers, with some likely suffering from mental health issues that possibly deluded them into believing the veracity of the supposed witchcraft, while the actions of others reveal them to be frauds and murderous liars. In Rebecca Nurse's case, fraud becomes apparent quite early on—possibly to bolster the accusations against such an unlikely suspect.

Once begun, the witch hunt spread like a fire through a crowded colonial town. Some writers describe the witch hunt as being mysterious and inexplicable, as being spread by the superstition of a previous century, or write it off as social hysteria of a bygone age—as if we today are so enlightened. Yet twenty-first-century readers have seen the spiraling embellishment of illogical false rumors online, have seen firsthand the assumed guilt of those accused of crimes whenever an accused person in handcuffs is shown on the nightly news, have seen headlines about doubt being raised over a prisoner's guilt years after they were executed for a crime, and have been given a glimpse into the mindset of the proponents of the witch hunt when in order to save a certain "way of life" those accused of causing "terror" are denied proper legal procedures—and in some instances tortured for false confessions and false evidence against their fellow accused. Of course, there are matters of degree in each situation, but to write off the spread of the witch hunt as the product of a time gone by, whose conditions could never be replicated, is to ignore the lessons that we can learn from this tragedy and apply to our own time. As Charles W. Upham wrote in the nineteenth century, "it would be wiser to direct our ridicule and reproaches to the delusions of our own times than to those of a previous age."[9]

However, one modern invention that was not present in 1692 is the so-called witchcraft of modern neo-paganism or nature-worshipping.[10] There is no connection between the modern Wiccan movement and the events of 1692, except that both may be used in the city of Salem to attract visitors. Furthermore, to wrongly suggest that elements of neo-paganism were present in 1692 obscures how tragic the witch hunt truly was: The innocents were accused of an impossible, nonexistent, imaginary crime—signing a contract with the Devil—that they could not have committed. No curses were cast, no bloody sacrament was actually consumed, no one really fought off ghosts, and no one walked on water. To claim that magic of some sort was committed is to believe—and give legitimacy to—the falsehoods and fantasies of the accusers.

ARTHUR MILLER WROTE that "Salem is one of the few dramas in history with a beginning, a middle, and an end."[11] However, he and most historians place the end of the story far too early—whether it is in the first months of 1693 when those still imprisoned after the witch hunt subsided were finally released, or in the early 1700s when the Massachusetts legislature reversed the convictions of many of those who were wrongfully killed. Such endpoints leave unexamined how the local community and descendants of the accused and their accusers coped with the tragedy in the following years, and how in the following centuries the victims were memorialized—a topic that sheds further light on our understanding of the witch hunt and those involved in it.

In 1885, Rebecca Nurse was the first person executed for witchcraft in the present-day United States to have a memorial erected to her memory, a large granite monument engraved with lines dedicated to her by a world-famous poet. A few years later, another granite monument was dedicated to those neighbors who supported her in 1692 after she was accused of witchcraft. After this was done, most other victims of the 1692 witch hunt did not receive similar memorials for more than a century, until the tercentennial of the witch hunt in 1992. This memorialization of Nurse also sheds light onto how the communities of Danvers, Massachusetts (formerly Salem Village), and the city of Salem (formerly Salem Town) first confronted their legacies of the witch hunt, and continue to do so today.

The legacy of Rebecca Nurse is the strongest of all those executed in 1692. In addition to her initial memorialization in the nineteenth century, her house and farm were purchased for preservation in 1907 by her descendants and local Danvers citizens, and it remains the only home of a victim of the witch hunt that is preserved and opened to the public. Her special legacy was clear during the tercentennial of the witch hunt in 1992, and clearly shown again on July 19, 2017, when on the 325th anniversary of her execution, hundreds of descendants, historians, and ordinary citizens descended on the Rebecca Nurse Homestead to honor her memory on a day proclaimed by the governor of Massachusetts to be "Rebecca Nurse Day."

Her story, of a clearly innocent woman accused of an impossible crime, betrayed by her community, and horribly killed, has been impressed on the American conscience. Though it took centuries to accomplish, Rebecca Nurse's legacy is remembered and finally redeemed.

Part I

ONE

EXODUS

This life's a voyage, the world's a sea
Where men are strangely tossed about;
Heaven's our port, steer thou that way:
There thou shall anchor safe no doubt.
—Inscription on a tombstone in the cemetery of St.
Nicholas Church, Great Yarmouth, England

ON FEBRUARY 21, 1621, cold water was poured over a baby in the stone font of St. Nicholas Church, in Great Yarmouth, England. Occurring at the end of Morning Prayer in the ancient church, her baptism was one in a continuum of such ceremonies celebrated on the site over the previous millennium. The vestmented priest—if he used the mandated Book of Common Prayer—announced to those present: "We receive this child into the Congregation of Christ's flock, and do sign her with the sign of the cross, in token that hereafter she shall not be ashamed to confess the faith of Christ crucified."[1] This baptism is the first historical record of Rebecca Towne of Great Yarmouth, better known later as Rebecca Nurse of Salem Village.[2]

Her hometown of Great Yarmouth lies on the eastern coast of England, at the mouth of the namesake River Yare. The ancient seaside town featured a market square surrounded by stone buildings, between which ran more than 150 narrow medieval alleys. These buildings were so tightly packed that only carts less than three and a half feet wide could pass these tight paths.[3] Near the central market lay the medieval castle, in the process of being demolished. Converted to a jail during the tumultuous preceding century, it kept prisoners criminal, political, and religious.[4]

The town was a little more than a mile from top to bottom, on a triangular peninsula: the short side faced north, the long eastern side faced the North Sea, and the western side was a quay facing the River Yare.[5] A wall of flint defended the northern and eastern sides, over a mile in length. Its ten gates and sixteen fortified towers reminded the inhabitants of the perils of living on the coast, across the narrow sea from their Catholic enemies in the Spanish Netherlands. In 1588, with the Spanish Armada off the coast, additional fortified mounds were built with cannons atop them and the city was garrisoned with soldiers to defend against a feared invasion.[6]

A sandy beach ran along the seaside eastern fortifications, and beyond that the sails of trading ships glided along the North Sea headed for Dutch ports. The sea was the lifeblood of Yarmouth, with fishing as a leading occupation, though it was also described as an enemy by one of Rebecca Towne's contemporaries, "The next enemy, though insensible, was the raging sea to the ocean east, which, from the first appearing of their buildings, has continually beaten upon them, and long since had in-rushed not only upon Yarmouth but also on the whole territories adjoining."[7] The changing tides posed a potent danger.

Towne and her parents lived in a stone dwelling, likely small, somewhere in this seaside town—the exact location is not known. She was the daughter of William and Joanna (Blessing) Towne, who wed at St. Nicholas Church in April 1620. William was born in 1599, and Joanna in 1595. William was a gardener, as was his father before him, though previously he served as an apprentice to a basket maker.[8] In those days, a gardener in eastern England was similar to a small-time farmer, and grew vegetables and beans for consumption. These crops became increasingly important during the previous generation when there was a grain shortage.[9]

After Rebecca, the Townes had seven more children: John (1623), Susan (1625), Edmond (1628), Jacob (1632), Mary (1634), Joseph (1639), and Sarah (1642).[10] Joseph and Sarah were not born until after the family arrived in Massachusetts. As the oldest daughter, Rebecca Towne spent her early years caring for her siblings, the youngest of whom was twenty-one years her junior. When not helping to raise the other children, her day consisted of housework and religious study—the foundation of a Puritan upbringing.

Born only five years after the death of William Shakespeare, Rebecca Towne lived during turbulent times for Yarmouth and for the entire Kingdom of England. Crops failed, the textile market faltered, and rising land prices forced farmers off their land. Additionally, the plague visited Yarmouth in 1579 and 1664. Common people struggled to support themselves and their families, so much so that the town of Yarmouth prohibited the poor from marrying unless they could prove that they were able to maintain a family.[11] Towne's parents married before this decree went into effect.

Towering over the low stone buildings was St. Nicholas Church, already five hundred years old at the time of Towne's baptism. Not even this grand and imposing structure was safe from occasional rising waters, for in 1287 the sea flowed right into the church itself.[12] But, most destructive to the church was not the ocean tide but new currents of thought in the years prior to Towne's birth, when the medieval Catholic Church that had united Western Europe for a millennium suddenly fractured.

In England, more than a century of religious turmoil began when King Henry VIII broke with the Catholic Church in 1534 so that he could attain an annulment and marry a different woman. He created the Church of England (also known as the Anglican Church) as a separate church with the monarch at the head instead of the pope. The king was now the head of both church and state. Conveniently, Parliament passed the Treasons Act of 1534 soon after this ecclesiastical split, which made it treasonous to deny royal supremacy over the church.[13]

Although Henry VIII separated from the Catholic Church, he kept most doctrine intact. Previously a chief opponent of Martin Luther and other Protestant reformers, he banned the printing of the Bible in English (to the dismay of Protestants), though it was difficult to enforce. The Six Articles, enacted in 1539, reinforced Catholic teaching against new Protestant ideas, and during Henry's reign radical Protestants were burned as heretics.

Subsequent English monarchs alternated between pro-Catholic and pro-Protestant leanings, however, and with the monarch as head of both church and state the religious dogma of the day was legally enforced. Edward VI (r. 1547–1553), who succeeded Henry, was raised Protestant, and during his reign Protestant reforms were made to the church. But Edward's successor, Mary I (r. 1553–1558), was Catholic. She undid many Protestant changes to the church, exiled prominent Puritans, and burned nearly three hundred Protestants as heretics. Next was Elizabeth I (r. 1558–1603), who steered England in a more Protestant direction and executed 183 Catholics, mostly priests. For ordinary Christians in Great Yarmouth, the official beliefs—which had remained fixed for a millennium—suddenly entered a period of continuous and sometimes radical change, and being caught with the wrong religious views could be fatal.

The Yarmouth area was a hotbed of radical Protestantism with a large contingent of Puritans, including the Towne Family.[14] "Puritan" was originally a pejorative term from Elizabethan times for religious radicals.[15] Puritanism was a variety of Reformed Protestantism that developed within the Church of England but was influenced by many Continental reformers, especially John Calvin. Most Puritans shared Martin Luther's belief that the papacy was the Antichrist, and they sought changes to the doctrine and liturgy of the Church of England that were far more radical and revolutionary than what any of the monarchs were willing to permit.[16]

The Puritans believed that baptism and the Lord's Supper were the only two valid sacraments, and they considered scripture to be the sole authority, refusing to recognize church tradition and hierarchy.[17] They desired each local church to be "congregational"—governed by its members who elected its ministers, with no bishops or higher authority than the local gathering of believers. Puritans believed that neither the English Reformation nor Luther's Reformation went far enough in radically reorienting Christianity—but even among themselves they had different ideas as to how far was far enough.[18] Puritans in general believed that the Church of England remained too connected to its Catholic roots.

The Towne family were Puritans, and their parish of St. Nicholas had preachers sympathetic to Puritanism, though the parish went through many changes during these tempestuous times. The religious shifts of St. Nicholas Church, site of Rebecca Towne's baptism, reveal the radical changes in religious belief during those years of uncertainty.

Christianity came to Yarmouth in the year 636, if not before, and the church building of Towne's time was consecrated in the year 1119. It was an elegant space for worship, as throughout the centuries wealthy parishioners willed money to the church for side chapels, altar decorations, valuable crucifixes, and other ornamentation. At one point the church reportedly had relics of Saints Nicholas, George, Margaret, and Maurice, along with a piece of the True Cross and a tiny piece of the Crown of Thorns.[19] It was an ornate and sacramental space, typical of the medieval church, and a far cry from the austerity of the Salem Village meetinghouse where she attended worship in her later days.

The Reformation radically altered the Townes' parish church of St. Nicholas. The building was stripped of all its images, paintings, and richly decorated altar.[20] One Yarmouth historian describes the demolition of all aspects of the building that resembled Catholicism, "Everything which, in the opinion of those in power, 'smelt of superstition' (which seemed to have embraced all articles of any value), was removed, and converted into money."[21] Side chapels were demolished, relics scattered, stained glass removed, vestments sold, and statues destroyed. To go a step further, the large engraved stone slabs atop tombs were removed and reused as doorsteps, and the churchwardens themselves took gravestones out of the cemetery and sent them to another town to be turned into grindstones for mills.[22] They ground away the history and tradition of their ancestors for their daily bread.

These changes were officially sanctioned, but this shifted in Rebecca Towne's lifetime when the monarchs made religious revisions moving away from the radical reformation hoped for by her and her family, and instead sought to return the Church of England to its Catholic counterpart. With the king as head of church and state, religious dissent was political dissent and the Puritans were persecuted by the monarchy. This is the primary reason that families such as the Townes left for New England.

James I (r. 1603–1625) declared that he would "make the Puritans conform, or harry them out of the land." In 1622, one year after Rebecca Towne's baptism, King James directed that only higher church officials could preach on topics such as "predestination, election, reprobation, or the universality, efficacy, resistibility or irresistibility of God's grace."[23] These were the topics where Puritans differed with the established church, and therefore the restriction was meant to silence their dissent on these key theological points.

Puritans in Yarmouth chafed at King James' restrictions, though the moves of the next monarch worried them even more. Charles I (r. 1625–1649) married the Catholic princess Henriette Marie of France. Now there was the real possibility that his son and successor might be raised Catholic like his mother. Since the defeat of the Spanish Armada, Protestantism was an important—if not defining—part of England's identity. Still today, the law prohibits a Catholic from inheriting the throne of the United Kingdom. Puritans were left to wonder whether the entire English Reformation might be undone.

King Charles selected William Laud to be Archbishop of Canterbury, the highest ranking clergyman in the Church of England, in 1633. Only two years later, the Townes left for Massachusetts, and Laud's reforms were a key reason why. Laud returned the liturgy to a previous generation's style of worship, with priests wearing traditional vestments and the parishioners required to stand for the recitation of the creed and the reading of the Gospels. Parishes were ordered to move their communion tables back against the east wall of the church and surround them with a rail. Communion was to be given only to those who knelt at the rail. This return to the traditional liturgy of the Eucharist appeared to the Puritans as a step back toward Roman Catholicism.[24]

Additionally, Puritans were suppressed and non-conforming Puritan clergy were forbidden to preach in English churches. In some instances Puritans formed associations, pooled their money, and hired "lecturers," former Puritan clergy who preached on Sunday afternoons and market days. The Townes likely attended unofficial services such as these somewhere in Yarmouth. Sunday afternoons became a particular bone of contention between the Puritans and the authorities when the official church encouraged recreation and the playing of games after Sunday church services.[25] The Puritans did not believe that the Sabbath was a day of rest or amusement, but rather a day of active worship and prayer.

A New England Puritan of Rebecca Towne's day described how these restrictions appeared to Puritans as the decline of the Church of England, "Instead of purging out Popery, a farther compliance was sought not only in vain idolatrous ceremonies, but also in profaning the Sabbath, and by proclamation throughout their parish churches, exasperating lewd and profane persons to celebrate the Sabbath like the heathen to Venus, Bacchus, and Ceres; in so much that the multitude of irreligious lascivious and popish affected persons spread the whole land like grasshoppers."[26] In the face of this plague, Towne and her family left for Massachusetts.

The suppression of Puritans further radicalized them politically and alienated them from the mainstream in England. Although modern readers likely have preconceptions of Puritans as conservative and traditional, as Calvinists the Puritans had more in common with the subversive extremists who stormed the Bastille in 1789 or the Winter Palace in 1917 than with any sort of traditional order. And like both above-mentioned groups, the English Puritans who remained in England went on to kill their own king and sought to entirely refashion their world in a new radically different image, breaking with the past.[27] But many Puritans, including Rebecca Towne and her family, left England for the New World in order to follow their beliefs and create a new society based on their radical vision.

Many settlers heading to the New World from England were young men seeking their fortunes, but the Puritans were exceptional in that whole families emigrated together, because their motives were primarily religious and not economic. Puritans saw moving to Massachusetts as a "voluntary banishment," and one contemporary of Rebecca Towne compared her fellow Puritan emigrants to John the Baptist who went out into the wilderness and warned others to "prepare the way of the Lord."[28]

The exact date of Towne's emigration and the ship on which she traveled are not known, though she likely left Yarmouth between April and

September 1635. Both of her father's parents passed away before 1630, so there was no prior generation to care for. Her brother John became an apprentice in Yarmouth on April 25, 1635, so the Towne family was presumably still in Yarmouth at that point. By September, her parents were cited by the authorities for missing communion, so they presumably departed before then.[29] Finally, judging from when the land was distributed in their Salem neighborhood, the Townes probably arrived in Salem no later than 1635.[30]

In 1635 alone, 3,000 Puritans immigrated to New England despite royal restrictions. For example, if one was of sufficient means to be taxed, they were forbidden to leave England without permission from the King's Privy Council. If one was too poor to be in that category, they needed a "certificate of conformity" from their local minister to prove that they were not a Puritan.[31] These restrictions might be a reason for the lack of contemporary documentation on when Towne left for New England: only those names of people who left *legally* were officially recorded.[32]

Between 1630 and 1643, 198 ships left old England for new, transporting about 21,200 people in the Puritan exodus.[33] Each ship carried around one hundred people or slightly more, and the passengers brought all supplies necessary for survival. In 1630 the first minister of the Salem church wrote back to those in England wishing to emigrate telling them what to bring, for there were no markets yet to buy provisions. He instructed them to bring meal for bread, malt for beer, wool, linen, and leather for shoes, all manner of tools, and "many other things which were better for you to think of there than to want them here."[34] Each person was also suggested to bring a year's worth of food for themselves. This long list of needed goods does not sound at all practical for the Puritan emigrants, most of whom were not wealthy. By 1635 Salem was slightly more established so Towne and her family needed to bring fewer goods than those on previous voyages.

Not all who ventured forth made it to the New World. The same year that the Townes probably left for Massachusetts, another Puritan ship making the journey was lost off the coast of present-day Maine. Ships needed to dodge pirates along the way, and some vessels nearly sank during the voyage due to leaks.[35] Some days, very little progress was made due to unfavorable winds, thereby extending the difficult journey.[36]

While previous vessels evaded Spanish warships on their trips, Rebecca Towne left after the war against Spain ended, though she likely saw foreign warships in the North Sea and English Channel before making it to the open seas.[37] Even more of a hazard to some emigrant ships were vessels from their own country's Royal Navy, whose crew could board ships and press—conscript on the spot—sailors into His Majesty's service, thereby leaving the Puritan ship with fewer sailors for the long ocean journey.[38]

Those traveling between England and Massachusetts also encountered stranger sights, such as sea monsters (or at least that is what they were believed to be). One later traveler described seeing a "sea-wonder" that was "called a calamorie." This encounter with a squid amazed the traveler, who commented on it having black ink inside of it instead of blood. Other sea monsters seen from ships bound for Massachusetts included "sea-horses," "sea-calves," and "torpedoes" (jellyfish). These jellyfish are described as strange creatures that were "better to behold than to handle, for it has this prodigious, yet clandestine quality, that if it be but touched or handled, the person touching it is presently benumbed, as a hand or leg, that is dead, and without feeling."[39] These strange sights were nothing that the Puritans from eastern England had encountered before.

Passengers were crowded, had no privacy, and sometimes had barely enough room to stand up. There were no ships designed to be ocean-going passenger vessels at this time, so the emigrants traveled on ships meant to carry freight, not people. On the long voyage many passengers became ill from scurvy and "infectious fevers," such as tuberculosis and smallpox.[40] One Puritan emigrant wrote that some passengers were terribly ill before even embarking on the ship yet were still determined to make the voyage, describing those "whose weak natures were so born down with disease that they could hardly crawl up the ship's side" to board the vessel in England.[41] Yet, they did not let these ailments prevent them from attempting the trip to the New World with their co-religionists. Those who were too ill to survive the journey and died en route had their bodies thrown overboard.[42]

In the face of these challenges, religious observance was kept during the voyage. According to Rev. Francis Higginson, one of Salem's first ministers, "We constantly served God morning and evening by reading and expounding a chapter [of scripture], singing, and prayer. And the Sabbath was solemnly kept by adding to the former, preaching twice and catechizing."[43] These rites of passage fostered a collective identity among the first generation of Puritans, who were refugees seeking not just a new physical home, but also a new spiritual one.

One morning, word spread throughout the ship: the Promised Land was in sight.

TWO

NEW JERUSALEM

Gather my Saints together unto me that have made a
Covenant with me by sacrifyce. Psa: 50:5
—Opening of the Salem church record book, 1629

THE SHIP, AFTER TRAVERSING SEVERAL THOUSAND MILES and diverse hazards, finally arrived. Cape Ann came into sight first, with its rolling
wooded hills and rocky beaches. Early travelers noted the abundance of
yellow flowers along the shore, with their reflections looking like yellow
paint poured into the sea.[1] This tableau concealed a hidden danger: there
were many rocks along the coast, and with no accurate charts by which
to navigate, ships ran the risk of disaster while the beautiful New World
lay just within grasp.[2] Avoiding these hidden hazards, the ship slipped
into Salem Harbor, and a few small buildings and wisps of smoke from
kitchen fires came into view.

Gov. John Winthrop, who completed a similar voyage in 1630 with a
great fleet of Puritan migrants, preached to his fellow travelers during his
voyage about the Puritans' mission in the New World and their covenant
with God. The Puritans believed that they replaced the Israelites as God's
chosen people, and that New England was their Promised Land.[3]
Winthrop said of their mission, "The Lord will be our God, and delight
and dwell among us, as His own people, and will command a blessing
upon us in all our ways. . . . We shall find that the God of Israel is among
us, when ten of us shall be able to resist a thousand of our enemies; when
He shall make us a praise and glory that men shall say of succeeding plantations, 'the Lord make it like that of New England.' For we must consider
that we shall be as a city upon a hill."[4] This new settlement was to serve

not just as an escape for Puritan souls that were constricted in England, but also as an example to inspire others to join the Puritan cause. This is the beginning of the belief in American exceptionalism.

Winthrop's sermon, however, also included a stark warning about what would happen should the Puritan project fail: "The eyes of all people are upon us. So that if we shall deal falsely with our God in this work we have undertaken, and so cause Him to withdraw His present help from us, we shall be made a story and by-word throughout the world. We shall open the mouths of enemies to speak evil of the ways of God, and all professors for God's sake. We shall shame the faces of many of God's worthy servants."[5] The stakes were high and, like all utopian experiments, Massachusetts struggled under the weight of these expectations.

It was at Salem that Winthrop landed, five years before Rebecca Towne. "Salem" was an ancient name for Jerusalem that means "peace."[6] The town—small as it was—served for a time as the chief city of the new Promised Land. For now, this New Jerusalem was merely a small seaside settlement on the edge of a dark, unexplored wilderness full of the Puritans' enemies, such as the pagan Natives and the Catholic French in Canada.

The primeval wilderness around Salem included ancient, towering trees among which lived wild mountain lions, wolves, bears, foxes, raccoons, "flying glowworms," and squirrels that "by a certain skin will fly from tree to tree."[7] The "roaring" of bears in the distance gave pause to those who strayed from settled villages, while smoke from Native fires rose ominously on the frontier horizon—a reminder that the Puritans were not alone.[8] In addition to perceived dangers in the woods, the New Englanders dealt with a new and inhospitable climate. The first settlers reported that the summers were hotter than in England, but most dangerously the winters were colder than back home.[9] Despite these hazards, they were able to worship as Puritans and it was here that they established their commonwealth.

By the time Rebecca Towne arrived in 1635, the construction of the Puritans' utopian project was well under way. All aspects of life revolved around their mission, which was in the words of one of Salem's first ministers, "to carry the gospel into those parts of the world, and to raise a bulwark against the kingdoms of the Antichrist which the Jesuits labor to rear up in all places of the world."[10] To do this, a government was needed.

The Colony of Massachusetts Bay in New England was effectively separated both religiously and politically from England. As King James I feared, there were neither bishops nor kings. Each town had its own Puritan congregational church that was independently governed. The civil government was based on the royal charter granted by Charles I in 1629. Massachusetts coined its own money, administered justice in its own name instead of in the king's name, and had an elected representative government. It was, in effect, a republic with only nominal allegiance to a king across the ocean.[11] Deputies to the General Court—the lower house of the legislature—were elected by all male church members, though this group was a minority of the population. The upper house of the legislature, the Council of Assistants, also served as the court of appeal and the only court with authority to try cases of life, limb, or banishment.

Massachusetts went so far as to refuse to fly the English flag, with its red-and-white cross of St. George.[12] Governor John Endicott, who became Rebecca Towne's neighbor across the river from Salem's Northfields, cut the red cross off of the flag with his sword because, as an iconoclastic Puritan, he believed that it was a popish symbol.[13] This particular action occurred during a time of swirling rumors that the king was going to revoke Massachusetts' charter and send loathed bishops from the Church of England to Massachusetts in order to rein in the Puritan religion.[14]

Endicott's rash action in cutting the flag was successful, for the English government relented and allowed the Salem militia to fly the king's coat of arms instead of the offensive English flag. This issue reveals the disconnect between Puritan Massachusetts and England, and it returned as a controversy as late as 1700, when witch trials judge Samuel Sewall resigned his militia commission over the return of the red-cross flag.[15]

In Salem, and other towns in the Bay Colony, local decisions were made by the town meeting, a gathering of all adult men in the town. Men could vote in town elections and be elected to town offices, regardless of whether they were church members.[16] To carry out the decisions of the local town meeting, a committee of selectmen was chosen to serve as the executive arm of the town government. With town meetings and independent self-governing churches, New England had the most representative institutions and the highest-developed civil society in all of English America. This government system was radically representative for the seventeenth century.[17]

REBECCA TOWNE AND HER FAMILY made their home in the Northfields area of Salem, along the Endicott River (now the Waters River). This area was across the North River from the town center, and reaching it required either a ferry ride or a long walk around to where the river narrowed and could be crossed. The center of Salem was the seaport, where fishing was a major trade.[18] Out in the more rural Northfields, there were farms with huts and small houses. Like their neighbors, the Townes' business was farming.

It is likely that the Townes moved onto their modest farm along the river soon after they arrived, though at this time deeds were not yet recorded.[19] The first record of their inhabitance is in 1640, when Rebecca Towne's father William was granted "a little neck of land right over against his house on the other side of the river."[20] Their farm was nine and a half acres in the shape of a right triangle, with the hypotenuse being the side along the riverbank.[21] This area has good, fertile soil, though the first few feet along the river are salty and sandy. The farm was located on a point near the confluence of the three tidal rivers that flowed out of what later became Salem Village. When the wind blows the right way, this point of land is surrounded by the sweet and salty stench of the sea.

Each day as Rebecca Towne tended the farm, the tide crested and fell in its never-ending rhythm. This coastal area is often banked with fog during the early morning, blotting out the view of the other side of the river. On clear days, small craft carrying people and goods floated by, and Governor Endicott's small sailing ship was a common sight.[22] While the setting was calming and beautiful in the summer, as the sun rose and sparkled off of the crystalline river, their house was weather-beaten in the winter, when the frigid wind whipped off the water, rattled doors and shutters, pierced cracks in windows, and rushed down primitive chimneys.

Where Rebecca Towne and her family lived was particularly susceptible to storm damage immediately after their arrival. At first, the settlers in Salem lived in wigwams, not too dissimilar to those of the Natives—though almost all of the Natives, the Naumkeag, were wiped out by disease prior to 1630, with only a few living near the outskirts of town by the time of Towne's arrival.[23] The "English wigwams" in which the settlers lived had a stone fireplace at one end, though they remained cramped and cold, and the huts leaked in heavy rains. Additionally, the wigwams' chimneys were made of wood, which could catch fire.[24]

If the Townes lived in one of these huts immediately after arriving, it was likely soon destroyed. In August 1635, the Great Hurricane struck Salem with a vengeance, and its gusts destroyed buildings and uprooted trees. Along with gales, the storm brought two twenty-foot-high tides, which inundated coastal lands and farms such as the Townes'. Elsewhere in New England, large ships were wrecked and the flooding was so severe that Natives along the coast climbed tall trees to avoid drowning.[25]

Over time, the Townes built a proper wooden house. The homes of these early settlers had a wooden frame with unpainted overlapping boards on the outside, and a roof of wooden shingles. Window openings were covered in oiled paper instead of glass, which was a luxury found in only the finest houses. Inside, the walls were whitewashed, and the brown wooden beams and floorboards were left exposed. Houses at this time typically had one ground floor room and one bedroom—the "chamber"—above it. The chimney was built on one side of the house, and both rooms had a fireplace for warmth.[26]

By 1642 eight people lived in the Townes' small home: Rebecca's parents William and Joanna, along with Rebecca and her siblings Edmund, Jacob, Mary, Joseph, and Sarah.[27] Elsewhere in Salem, Rebecca Towne had a widowed aunt, an uncle, and two sets of cousins.[28] Rebecca and the others in the Towne household spent most of their time out in the fields or in the ground-floor room of the house that served many purposes, primarily as a kitchen. Here the women cooked and did indoor work such as weaving. The focal point of the room was the enormous fireplace, with an opening as wide as eight or ten feet.[29]

The interior of these early homes was initially very sparsely furnished. Using the inventory of an estate of similar means from the 1640s as an example, the Townes likely had only a couple of chairs or stools, a trunk, and straw beds—maybe with bed frames, or maybe just straw bedding placed on the floor. For kitchenware, they likely had a frying pan, gridiron, skillet, a clay pot or two, a few wooden plates, wooden bowls, and a few spoons.[30]

To eat, the typical meal was of "hasty pudding," a mixture of cornmeal mush and milk, served with a piece of meat or fish and boiled vegetables. Pumpkins were a staple, so much so that "pumpkin" later became slang for a colonist who lived in eastern Massachusetts, an area nicknamed "pumpkinshire."[31] Baked beans and brown bread were common as well, and were baked in the oven—an opening in the back of the fireplace, which required one of the women in the family to stoop down over the fire to reach it. As women of the day wore long skirts, this was dangerous and they needed to ensure that the bottoms of their skirts avoided the flames licking around their shoes.[32]

In addition to work around their small houses, Massachusetts offered women more opportunities for work outside the home than in England—especially on farms. Farmers' wives were their partners in planting and gathering crops in the fields, and daughters worked alongside sons.[33] Towne likely accompanied her family when they brought their crops to the center of Salem to barter for other produce and products.[34] These market trips, along with attending religious services, were the main reasons for her to venture off the farm and into the town.

RELIGION WAS THE CENTER OF LIFE for Puritans. Historian Harry S. Stout writes that the Puritans "had willingly risked life and property to come to the wilderness so that they could sit on benches in drafty, gloomy barns for three to six hours on Sundays and hear the Word as it should be preached."[35] Persevering despite the inhospitable situation shows the strength of their beliefs, and they achieved their goal of worshipping as they saw fit despite many challenges.

The Sunday services were held in the meetinghouse, located at the main crossroads in the center of Salem. It was about an hour's walk from the Towne family's farm, and in the warm weather early settlers walked barefoot, only putting on their shoes when they arrived so as to prevent too much wear on their soles.[36] The building housing the religious services was called the "meetinghouse" because the word "church" referred to God's faithful elect—the group of people destined for heaven, the true believers who worshipped within—and not the building itself. Similarly, the Puritans were intentional about calling the Sabbath "the Lord's Day" instead of merely "Sunday" and referred to the twelve months by their numbers instead of using their names, which were created by the pagan ancient Romans.[37]

The Salem church was established in 1629, before the civil government, and Salem chose its first minister by ballot, the first use of the ballot in what became the United States.[38] Roger Williams was the minister in 1635 when the Townes most likely arrived in Salem. However, in October 1635 he was tried and convicted of heresy and sedition due to his unorthodox beliefs. He claimed, among other things, that the colony's charter and claim to Native American land were not legitimate, that all women needed to be veiled when in public, and that the Salem church should separate from the other Puritan churches because the others were not reformed enough. When the Salem church would not agree, he left the congregation. His wife did not, which led him to refuse to pray or say a blessing over a meal in her presence because she continued to attend the unregenerate services.[39] It did not take long for religious disputes to arise in the Promised Land.

On the Lord's Day, Towne's family was separated by sex and age in the meetinghouse. The women sat on one side, the men on the other, and children sat either in a special section at the rear or in galleries up above. In addition to Sunday services, there were also sermons on some Thursdays, known as "Lecture Day." The Sabbath services were a whole-day affair, with a lunch break before the second part of the sermon.[40] Sermons were very long because short sermons were seen as less reverent. Also, the thrifty New Englanders wanted to get their money's worth from the minister. One traveler voyaging through New England at this time witnessed a single prayer lasting two hours, during which the congregation was required to remain standing.[41]

There were issues, though, with some of the less pious Puritans leaving the service prematurely.[42] In addition to those who tried to sneak out, those who stayed behind behaved less than angelically sometimes. There were "tithing men" who patrolled the meetinghouse armed with long poles, woke slumberers, and kept order, especially in the children's section.[43] Even in the Promised Land there was chaff among the wheat.

In addition to unruly congregants, the church in the wild was not without its external problems. Many towns—including nearby Beverly—stored gunpowder and ammunition in the attic of the meetinghouse. Whenever there was a thunderstorm during meeting, those inside went streaming out for fear that the building might be struck by lightning, making fire and brimstone a little too real. Frigid weather also proved an issue, and sometimes it was so cold in meetinghouses that communion bread froze and rattled on the plate. The mood of the congregants of the Salem church was likely not warmed to prayer by the dead and bloody wolves' heads that hung on the outside of the meetinghouse. Wolves were a problem for farmers, so a bounty was paid for each wolf killed and the heads were hung on the meetinghouse.[44] Unlike the Israelites who first covenanted with God, the Puritans had the blood of wolves on their doorway instead of the blood of the lamb.

Behavior on the Sabbath was regulated outside of the meetinghouse as well, and profaning the Lord's Day was a serious offense. The Sabbath began at sundown Saturday night, at which point individuals were forbidden to stroll and play games outside, or congregate in taverns. One Boston man was set in the stocks for two hours due to his "lewd and unseemly behavior" on the Sabbath.[45] His crime was kissing his wife outside on the doorstep of his house. The fact that he just returned from a sea voyage and had not seen his wife for three years did not gain him any leniency in court. Strict Sabbath laws applied to children like Rebecca

Towne and her siblings as well as adults. There was even a debate among ministers over whether it was lawful to be born on the Sabbath, and whether such a daring child should be allowed baptism.[46] Although birth on the Sabbath was suspect, it was a common sight to see women exit the meetinghouse, sit on the ground outside and nurse their children.[47] There was no immodesty in nature's necessities.

In general, Puritan society had many laws to ensure their Promised Land did not drift from its spiritual purpose. Massachusetts was founded on high ideals and the law required high standards of behavior, but not all of the early settlers lived up to these expectations all of the time. The Essex County Quarterly Court has records of punishments meted out for eavesdropping, being "a common liar," selling a gun to the Natives, carelessness with fire, carrying fire and liquor into the woods at night, giving "contemptuous speeches," disbelief in infant baptism, gathering peas on the Sabbath, "naughty speeches," "being uncharitable to a poor man in distress," dancing, *profane* dancing, "wonton dalliance," and many instances of drunkenness.[48] Rebecca Towne steered clear of these pitfalls, and her name does not appear in any court records related to any alleged misconduct until 1692.

FOR ABOUT NINE YEARS Rebecca Towne lived with her parents and siblings along the riverbank, then around 1645 she married Francis Nurse and started her own family.[49] Rebecca and Francis were both about twenty-three years old at their marriage, which was typical for the time.[50] It is not known how they met, though as nearly the whole town attended the Sabbath services, it is quite likely that the meetinghouse was the scene of their first acquaintance.

Not much is known about Francis Nurse's beginnings. The first record of him in Salem, from 1640, is a rather unflattering mention in the Essex County Quarterly Court records: "Francis Nurse, a youth, for stealing of victuals & for suspicion of breaking [into] a house."[51] Since he was accused of stealing food, he was presumably in need of money. That Nurse was described as "a youth" reveals that he was less than twenty-one years old at the time, which supports his age being similar to Rebecca's. The printed record of the charge mentions that the original entry was partially crossed-out, though it's not clear precisely what that signifies.

Regardless of how Rebecca and Francis Nurse first met, courtship was formal and regulated. Although they could converse at public events such as Sunday meeting, young Puritans were not allowed to date or associate privately. Parents were very much involved in their children's marriage prospects, and as a young suitor Francis was courting Rebecca's parents as well as her.

According to the law, no man could marry before "he has obtained liberty and allowance from her parents."[52] It is of note that the law says "parents" not just "father." Marriage was a contract, and Francis Nurse needed to strike a deal, with the worth of Rebecca Towne's dowry openly discussed.[53] Though the dowry was negotiated, marriages in seventeenth-century Massachusetts were voluntary and likely included romance and love, as opposed to medieval marriages that were for business or political alliances, in which families arranged marriages sometimes without the consent of the couple to be wed.[54]

Once an agreement was reached, no engagement ring was given, but the betrothal was publicly announced.[55] This betrothal announcement was a longstanding Christian tradition, and the requirement was especially necessary in Massachusetts to protect against bigamy in the hope that if the person was known to be previously married someone would come forward and say so. There are reports of individuals marrying in Massachusetts despite already having spouses and families back in England, including one who the governor discovered had, in addition to the woman he lived with in Massachusetts, *two* wives left behind in England.[56] In previous ages, when one was less likely to leave the local community, such fraud was rare, for an individual's neighbors and fellow townspeople would know that he was already married. But these early Massachusetts settlers put an ocean between themselves and their pasts, breaking with their traditional communities to join a new one, not always with the salvation of their souls foremost in mind.

Short engagements were typical, with wedding preparations beginning soon after the agreement to marry. Just as engagement rings were not used, neither were wedding rings in the early years of the settlement, because they were seen as a Catholic tradition. By 1692 this view changed and women wore wedding rings, but men in North America did not wear wedding rings until the twentieth century.[57] The law forbid Puritan ministers from presiding over marriages—to prevent the impression that marriage was a sacrament, as the Catholics believed—and instead required that a magistrate officiate the ceremony.[58] Though, the minister was often invited to the gathering and led a prayer. At the celebration, gifts were not usually given to the bride, though sometimes a psalm book was given—a very Puritan gift. A psalm book came in handy, because at the celebration the gathered friends and family sang psalms between rounds of sack-posset, a thick spiced ale consumed on special occasions. This led to a more lubricated performance than at Sunday services.[59]

The marriage, though a civil affair, was announced at the service on the Lord's Day following the wedding. The newlyweds walked to the meetinghouse dressed in their finery along with the wedding party. This served as the public acknowledgment of their new marriage, since it was conducted privately.[60]

Rebecca Towne and Francis Nurse were now Goodman and Goodwife Nurse, for the titles "Mister" and "Mistress" were reserved for ministers, magistrates, and other distinguished persons.[61] They moved in together after their marriage, and began a new phase of their lives. Although the husband was given precedence in the family, Puritan wives were often very knowledgeable about the family's financial affairs and business, and often influenced family economic decisions.[62] Judge Samuel Sewall wrote in his diary that he put his wife in charge of the family's daily decisions, because she "had a better faculty than I at managing affairs."[63] The typical Puritan wife had her influence, but Puritan minister and writer Rev. Cotton Mather reminds us that she was not the head of the household: "Though she be . . . a Mistress, yet she owns that she has a master."[64]

The later segregation of "home" and "work" into separate spheres for the two sexes had not yet occurred, in part because in those days the home was also usually the site of work, especially on a farm.[65] Rebecca Nurse worked establishing and maintaining the household and as her husband's partner in the fields. She did this work in addition to bearing and raising eight children.

Nurse became a mother when her son John was born in 1645, and she later had seven more children: Rebecca (1647), Samuel (1649), Sarah (c. 1651), Mary (1659), Francis Jr. (1661), Elizabeth (1663), and Benjamin (1666).[66] First-generation women had on average 8.3 children, so Nurse's family size was typical.[67] It was desirous to have many children, especially in farming families that needed many hands to work the fields. Mather even writes of women who allegedly had more than thirty children, though that is likely an exaggeration.[68]

Childbirth in the seventeenth century could be a dreadful, potentially fatal experience. No medical professionals were present for births, only female friends and neighbors who themselves previously gave birth assisted in the process. These women had no formal training, though doctors of the time sometimes did not either.[69] In seventeenth-century Massachusetts, 2.5–3 percent of births ended in the death of the mother.[70]

To put this risk in perspective, the rate of maternal mortality in London around that time was 1.6–1.9 percent, and the current (2016) rate of maternal mortality in the Commonwealth of Massachusetts is 0.0058 percent.[71] Childbirth posed a true threat to the mother, but even that did not compare to the dangers the newborn confronted. It is estimated that in Salem as many as three out of every ten infants died.[72] Fortunately, all of Nurse's children lived to adulthood.

Rebecca and Francis Nurse began their family while they lived in Salem along the road to the Beverly ferry (present-day Bridge Street) near the home of Francis Skerry. It was long assumed, since at least 1867 when Salem historian Charles W. Upham was writing, that this was the only locale where Rebecca and Francis Nurse lived prior to moving to Salem Village in 1678.[73] They likely did live near the Beverly ferry for a while, but they then moved to a farm in the western part of Salem in 1664.[74]

While living near the ferry, Rebecca Nurse gave birth to her first seven children, but it is probable that both she and her husband were seriously ill at one point during the following years.[75] As to Francis Nurse, the records of the Essex County Quarterly Court show that he was discharged from required militia training in 1656, though the court record gives no reason why.[76] All men over sixteen were required to drill with the militia, unless they were doctors, ministers, students at Harvard College, or members of other exempt professions. Additionally, a county court could discharge a man "for bodily infirmity or other just cause."[77] Francis Nurse was about thirty-five, and did not qualify for any of the job-based exemptions, so illness is the probable reason.

Rebecca Nurse was ill around the same time. There is an eight-year gap between childbirths from 1651 to 1659. She had John in 1645, Rebecca in 1647, Samuel in 1649, and then Sarah around 1651. Then there is the large gap until Mary is born in 1659, Francis Jr. in 1661, Elizabeth in 1663, and Benjamin in 1666.[78] At first glance, this may appear to be a coincidence or a reflection of her husband's potential bad health alone, but during the witch hunt Rebecca Nurse mentioned a previous serious illness. In March 1692, she spoke of "fits that she formerly used to have," and in June 1692 two of her daughters said that she was "troubled with an infirmity of body for many years."[79] In a June 1692 petition to the court explaining a bodily abnormality of hers that was discovered, she states that it was due to "exceeding weaknesses, descending partly from an overture of nature and difficult exigences that hath befallen me in the times of my travails."[80] This is a description of a previous serious illness or injury, and "travails" was a term for childbirth.

In 1662, a few years after the illness, the Nurse family purchased their first parcel of land. Prior to this purchase, Francis Nurse twice asked the town for a land grant. In those days there was still land within the wide borders of Salem that was not claimed or settled and the town government was responsible for doling out this unsettled "common" land. Francis Nurse jointly requested land with Rebecca's father in 1647 and then by himself in 1661, but there is no evidence that any land was actually granted to him.[81] In 1662 the Nurse family finally purchased their first parcel, which was several acres of fields in Ryal Side, an area across the river from where Rebecca lived prior to marriage.[82] When they sold it five years later, the deed makes no mention of a house on the small piece of land but it does mention the growing of hay, so it probably served as extra land to cultivate but not as their residence.[83]

Finally, in 1664 the Salem selectmen granted Rebecca and Francis Nurse twenty acres for a farm. Although all the grants for farms given that day have a number of acres assigned to them, their exact sizes are not certain. At the end of the list of grants, the selectmen note that these petitioners were awarded such amounts of land "provided there be found at the place above mentioned so much land as will make them good after the first four old grants be made good."[84] The selectmen themselves did not even know how much land was there to be given out, and it is possible that the actual grant was less than the twenty acres mentioned.

In addition to the land grant's true size, its exact location is not entirely clear, but it appears that the general location of the farm was somewhere in the western reaches of Salem between the two east-west roads (present-day Lowell Street and Forest Street in Peabody), and near the brook (now named Proctor's Brook) which runs parallel to and in between these two roads.[85] One of the other landowners in the area was Emanuel Downing, whose son Sir George Downing is the namesake of Downing Street in London, the location of the prime minister's residence.[86]

Previously, the Nurse family grew hay in their fields in the Ryal Side and owned a few cows.[87] They continued as farmers on their new land, which was about seven miles from the center of town. Also, in 1677 along with several other men Francis Nurse jointly leased from the town government additional fields , which the family continued to farm for more than a decade.[88] When not farming in the winter months, Francis worked as a "traymaker," which was a woodworking trade.[89] Rebecca and Francis Nurse had land of their own, but continuous work was needed to establish a farm and raise their children.

DURING THE TIME that the Nurse family lived in this western part of Salem, the last of Rebecca's eight children, Benjamin, was born in 1666.[90] Much of Rebecca Nurse's life was spent raising and caring for her children in a harsh and dangerous environment on the edge of the wilderness, which affected all settlers' health but especially that of the young.

The average first-generation man (such as Francis Nurse) lived to be about seventy-two years old, and the average first-generation woman (such as Rebecca Nurse) lived to be about seventy-one years old, though some early settlers lived into their nineties and some even reached a hundred years of age. The life expectancy was significantly worse for the next generation, who braved the wilds of New England while still young. Most health issues were faced by the youngest children, and once age twenty was reached life expectancy drastically improved. For Rebecca Nurse's children's generation, if they made it to age twenty their life expectancy was about sixty-four years for men and sixty-two for women.[91]

Reverend Cotton Mather, as a writer and preacher famous both in his home of Boston and across the sea in England, was better off than most, but even his family suffered the death of children. He wrote, "The moans of your sick children may be stabs to your hearts and pierce and cut like daggers there."[92] He also warned children in a funeral sermon, "Children, go unto the burying-place; there you will see many a grave shorter than yourselves. 'Tis now upon computation found, that more than half the children of men die before they come to be seventeen years of age."[93] Apart from illness, records reveal that Puritan children faced many other hazards on the frontier, such as falling down wells or accidentally swallowing bullets.[94]

To heal children, mothers like Rebecca Nurse turned to home cures as well as professional medicine. There are claims that those later accused of witchcraft in Salem Village and elsewhere during the previous centuries were so accused because they practiced herb medicine, though this is not likely a cause of the accusation against Nurse or others in 1692.[95] The accused in 1692 practiced herb medicine because everyone did—even the "professional" doctors, most of whom had little to no training. Nurse's future neighbor in Salem Village, Zerubbabel Endicott, was a doctor and used all manner of herb and root concoctions to cure his patients, including cat's blood, "brains of a boar," and "hearts of dolphins."[96] In a similar vein, midwifery—when neighboring women gathered to aid an expectant mother in giving birth—was not more likely to make one subject of a witchcraft accusation in 1692.[97]

Care of children was regulated for the good of the community, and law mandated that they receive an education.[98] The Puritans saw a religious mission in this education, for they feared that Satan tried "to make it a means to persuade people from the use of learning altogether" to interfere with the passing down of the Puritan religion.[99] In the Puritan family, it was the mother who taught her children to read, and Rebecca Nurse educated her children well.[100] Robert Calef, a witness to the witch trials, later wrote of Nurse's "extraordinary care in educating her children, and setting them good examples."[101]

The literacy rate in Massachusetts was among the highest in the world and the ability to read was nearly universal, far higher than the 30 percent of the population in England that were literate.[102] Although the vast majority in Massachusetts could read, only roughly 60 percent of men and 30 percent of women could write.[103] Francis Nurse could read and write, but he sometimes signed documents with his "mark," a symbol of his woodworking trade instead of his name, which was a frequent practice of craftsmen.[104] It does not appear that Rebecca Nurse could write, since she signed documents with only a squiggle.[105]

WHILE MARRIED TO REBECCA, Francis Nurse had several appearances in court, primarily due to lawsuits. Such suits between neighbors were very common in the seventeenth century. In addition to his 1640 appearance in the court records, in 1642 he sued Elin Downing for "Defamation." Then in 1648 he was sued for "defaming Daniel Ray" along with Thomas Odingsells and was sentenced "to pay a fine or sit in the stocks." Next, in 1652 he was sued by Richard Waters "for impounding three cows and one heifer."[106] Waters lived next to Rebecca's parents, so this issue possibly involved cows wandering across property lines there.[107] Then in 1654 Francis Nurse sued Jonathan Porter and his wife Eunice for slander. Nurse won the case "and Eunice also made acknowledgment which the court accepted."[108] But, he returned to being a defendant in 1658 when the Town of Salem fined him for cutting down trees on the common land, and again that same year the selectmen voted to fine him "twenty shillings for his abusive carriage in the town meeting" during a debate about the upcoming year's town taxes.[109] Despite this litigious history, no harm was apparently done to his reputation for he continued to be appointed by the selectmen to survey land for the town and to settle land disputes, and he later went on to elected office in both Salem Town and Salem Village.[110]

Francis Nurse was elected one of the town constables, the local law enforcement officers, by a town meeting in November 1672, to serve in place
of John Southwick who died while in office.[111] As constable, Nurse carried
a black five-foot staff topped with brass that served as his symbol of office,
which he was required to take with him when discharging his official duties.[112] The constable's responsibilities included arresting people for
drunkenness, swearing, "Sabbath-breaking," or being "lying vagrant persons" or "night-walkers." He organized the town watch, announced upcoming elections, summoned coroner's juries if there was a suspicious
death, and gathered the "town rates"—local taxes. Interestingly, he may
not have even wanted the elected office, for so many people turned down
election as constable that Massachusetts passed a law that if anyone was
elected and declined to serve they would be fined.[113]

In addition to his time as constable, Francis Nurse served on trial and
grand juries. Jurors were paid for their time, and as will be seen the Nurse
family was in need of the money.[114] He sat on many juries for the Essex
County Quarterly Court, including serving on a grand jury alongside
John Hathorne and Bartholomew Gedney, judges at Rebecca Nurse's
witchcraft trial in 1692. Also, Francis Nurse and Gedney were chosen for
a committee to inventory the town's common land to pay the town's debt
to its minister, Rev. John Higginson.[115] These elections and appointments
show that Nurse retained the confidence of the community.

WHILE THE NURSE FAMILY lived on their farm and worked the land, their
children grew and married. Rebecca Nurse's daughter Rebecca married
Thomas Preston in 1669—a fateful choice, for in 1692 Thomas entered
the first legal accusation against an alleged witch. Later in 1669, daughter
Sarah married Michael Bowden in Topsfield. Rebecca's son John married
Elizabeth Smith in 1672, though she died in October 1673, ten days after
giving birth to Rebecca's grandson John Nurse Jr. Interestingly, in April
1677 Rebecca's son Samuel married Mary Smith, sister to John Nurse's
deceased wife, and a decade later Rebecca's son Benjamin married another
of the Smith sisters.[116]

There were also developments in the extended Towne family during
this time. Rebecca Nurse's parents sold their Northfields farm in November 1652, and moved to a partially cleared farm in Topsfield along the Ipswich River that they purchased the previous year.[117] William Towne,
Rebecca's father, died there in 1673, and Rebecca's mother Joanna and
brother Joseph continued to live on the farm after his death.[118] Rebecca's

brother Edmund married around 1652, Jacob married in 1657, and Joseph married in 1663. Rebecca's sister Mary married Isaac Easty around 1655 in Topsfield, and became a covenant member of the Topsfield church. Her sister Sarah married Edmund Bridges in 1660, but Edmund died in 1682 leaving her a widow with four children. She then married Peter Cloyce, either later in 1682 or in early 1683, who was her devoted husband during the witch hunt.[119]

IN ADDITION TO CHANGES IN THE FAMILY, there were significant political changes in Massachusetts and England around this time. In 1640 Charles I was beheaded in the aftermath of the English Civil War (sometimes referred to as the Puritan Revolution) by the Puritan-supported Parliamentary faction.[120] It was in Rebecca Nurse's hometown, the radical Puritan hotbed of Great Yarmouth, that Oliver Cromwell and his followers decided to kill King Charles. On July 9, 1642, not many years after she left, Yarmouth declared its support for Parliament and readied for war against its own king. The gates were reinforced, and the bridge over the River Yare was raised.[121] The Parliamentary faction in the war triumphed, the king was killed, and Oliver Cromwell ruled as a dictatorial Lord Protector.

During the civil war, Massachusetts made its loyalties to Parliament clear, and the General Court passed an act that those who supported the king's faction "shall be accounted as an offender of high nature against this commonwealth."[122] A minister of the Salem church, Rev. Hugh Peter, returned to England to fight against the king, showing solidarity between the Salem Puritans and their brothers and sisters remaining in England. Peter was even rumored to have been the hooded executioner who chopped off the king's head in front of the Palace of Whitehall (though this was an unfounded rumor).[123]

In 1660 Charles II returned to England and claimed his father's throne, ending the period of turmoil. Once Charles II restored the monarchy, Hugh Peter was put on trial before the House of Lords and died a cruel death: he was briefly hanged but was cut down before he died, and then the executioner strapped him to a table, disemboweled him while he still breathed, lit his removed organs on fire while he watched, and then cut his head off. For good measure the head of this former Salem minister was placed on a pole on London Bridge.[124] The new monarch was no friend of Puritanism, which was associated with the regicide of his father. The Restoration marks the decline of Puritanism in England, as the king reasserted the authority of the Church of England bishops over the congregations in England.

THOUGH THE PURITAN RELIGION withered back in England, in the distant outpost of Salem it continued and in 1672 Rebecca Nurse became a covenant member of the Salem church. This was the most important occasion for a Puritan, and only a small minority of the population was admitted as covenant members. Unlike the Catholic Church and the Church of England, which counted all of the baptized as members who had the potential for salvation, the Puritans did not. Only the select few who the church was convinced were predestined for heaven, the "visible saints," were allowed to become covenant members.[125] Only these members were allowed to receive the sacrament at the Lord's Supper, during which the elect broke bread and drank wine in memory of Christ's Last Supper.

Church membership was especially important for women at the time, because to gain membership they were judged on their own merits and given a level of respect and distinction entirely independent from their husbands.[126] Both men and women were spiritually equal in the covenant.[127] By the 1650s, most churches had a majority of female covenant members, and by 1692 Cotton Mather reported that women in Boston congregations outnumbered men by three or four to one. Faced with this disparity, he supposed that women might be more "Godly" than men and perhaps received more grace to make up for their sufferings in childbirth.[128] Nurse's status as a church member also meant that her children could be baptized into the church, thereby helping the souls of the next generation.[129]

There was a required process for attaining church membership, though no regard was given to wealth or social status—even servants and slaves could enter into the church covenant.[130] Nurse first met with the pastor to discuss her desire to join the covenant, and the elders then announced her candidacy. A time period was given for objections, and then the church members voted to admit her to the Salem church.[131] As part of the process, a person asking admittance to the church needed to relate a profound religious experience of "conversion," which could be an incremental experience or something as sudden as St. Paul's conversion on the road to Damascus.[132]

The entry in the Salem church records reads: "Goody Nurse having stood propounded a month and having no just exception made against her, but witnesses for her, she was admitted unto membership by confessing to the covenant and with the Church's consent after the usual manner."[133] The "usual manner" was a vote of the membership.

The ceremony itself involved reading the psalm at the beginning of the Salem church's covenant, "Gather my Saints together unto me that have made a Covenant with me by sacrifyce." Then Nurse swore to the covenant in the presence of the church members, promising to advance the gospel, shun idleness, live in lawful obedience to both church and commonwealth, and teach the faith to her children.[134]

Rebecca Nurse was now recognized as one of the select few, the visible saints proclaimed by God to live forever in Heaven. She had the full respect of the Salem church who voted her in and allowed her to take her place beside them at the Lord's Supper, and she was now more confident in her salvation at the Final Judgment. Nurse's status as a visible saint was recognized in 1677 when she was assigned a prominent seat in the meetinghouse next to Elizabeth Proctor, not far from the front.[135] Practicing her religion freely was the primary reason that Nurse and her family traversed the Atlantic, and with the admittance to church membership she now attained the highest possible status for a Puritan woman.

ALTHOUGH THE PURITANS believed that faith alone—not good works— gave one a place in heaven, Rebecca and Francis Nurse had a strong record of charity toward their neighbors. They adopted two children in need— in addition to the eight children they already had, and despite the family's financial troubles.

Sometime in the first half of 1674, Elizabeth Clungen left her four-year-old daughter (also named Elizabeth) at Rebecca Nurse's house, which was near the road leading out of town.[136] After she left the child, the court records state that the mother "went away out of this jurisdiction privately." Elizabeth was married to Thomas Clungen of Ipswich, who was either a sailor or a shipbuilder. Prior to leaving the child with Nurse on her way out of town, Elizabeth Clungen also left "some goods at the house of Richard Sibley."[137]

In June 1674, the court appointed two men, including witch trials judge John Hathorne's father, to inventory the goods left at Sibley's and decide their value. In November 1674, when it became apparent that Elizabeth Clungen was not returning, Francis Nurse went before the Essex County Quarterly Court in Salem and legally adopted the child. The record states that he "in charity took the child into his care and custody."[138] In seventeenth-century Massachusetts, it was the husband whose name was recorded for all the family's legal acts, though in reality a young child went into the mother's—Rebecca's—care.[139] The court also divided the inventoried Clungen goods, and "ordered" Francis Nurse to take them, "to remain in his hands for the use of the child," minus a portion given to Sibley "for house room and trouble about the goods." Nurse paid 17 shillings and 6 pence toward "debts owing from the [Clungen's] estate."[140]

This was not an ideal time for the Nurses to take another child into their care, for the Salem Town records state that the very month they adopted four-year-old Elizabeth Clungen, the Nurse family owed a debt of £8 s8 to the town. Instead of paying the debt in money, which was hard to come by for many in that time, Francis Nurse agreed to pay the town in wooden shingles, which were needed for the town house—the public building in the center of town that housed a school and was where town meetings and the county court met. He agreed to pay the debt within a fortnight, and the shingles were valued at 15 shillings per thousand or "as two indifferent men shall prize them." At the agreed-upon price, he needed to provide about 8,500 shingles to pay the debt, which appears impossible to accomplish in only two weeks' time. Unsurprisingly, the debt was not paid off in a fortnight. A little over two years later, in January 1677, there is an update on Nurse's debt in the town record book. He provided 4,200 shingles, six feet of wood, and fourteen days of work. Yet he still owed the town £1s10.[141]

As if taking in one needy child during this period of financial strain was not Christian enough, the Nurse family adopted yet another in June 1677, just five months after the above listing of their still-outstanding debt. The newest addition to the Nurse family was nineteen-year-old Samuel Southwick. Samuel's father, John Southwick, died in 1672 after an illness, and it was he who Francis Nurse was elected to replace as constable that year.[142] It is unclear what became of Samuel and his half-brother between their father's death in 1672 and Samuel Southwick's adoption by the Nurse family in 1677. As to other relatives, Southwick's grandparents were excommunicated from the Salem church in 1639 for being Quakers, and banished from Massachusetts in 1659.[143]

Despite themselves being persecuted in England, the Puritans did not support religious liberty for other groups. The Puritans established the colony as *their* Promised Land, and non-Puritans such as the Quakers were not welcome. On the subject of religious liberty, one Massachusetts Puritan said that members of other religions had "free liberty to keep away from us."[144] But after Charles II gained the throne, he forced the Puritans to tolerate the Quakers and in 1661 the Massachusetts General Court suspended enforcement of its anti-Quaker laws.[145]

Whereas previously in 1672 Francis Nurse was elected to take over John Southwick's duties as constable after he died, in 1677 he took over his duties as father. The court record states, "Samuel Southwick, son of

John Southwick, chose Francis Nurse as his guardian . . . which the court allowed."[146] It is interesting that instead of Samuel Southwick being assigned a guardian, the record states that he *chose* Francis. They likely knew each other previously, as the Southwick home was on the road between where the Nurse family lived and the center of Salem.[147] Nurse served as Southwick's guardian for only about two years—he was nineteen at the time of adoption, and the age of majority was twenty-one. Southwick and his half-brother John, who was adopted by a different family, retained their full inheritance of land and sold it when they came of age.[148]

It was claimed that this connection to the Southwicks led to the witchcraft accusations against Rebecca Nurse in 1692 due to the Southwick family's history of Quakerism, though this is unlikely.[149] Nurse's own religious orthodoxy was confirmed by her status as a church member, and Francis Nurse's views are seen in 1682 when he arrested a Quaker for spreading his beliefs.[150] Additionally, while there are examples of Quakers and Quaker sympathizers being accused of witchcraft in 1692, there are also examples of Quakers acting as accusers as well, so such a connection would not necessarily put Rebecca Nurse on a certain side of the witch hunt.[151] Last, Samuel Southwick's father was not a practicing Quaker and was respected in the community, as shown by his election as constable prior to his death.[152] That the community entrusted John Southwick to enforce the laws of the Puritan commonwealth shows that bias against his family had diminished.

THE 1670S WERE DIFFICULT for the Nurses, with financial troubles exacerbated by taking in two orphaned and abandoned children, but times were even worse for Massachusetts as a whole. In 1675 King Philip's War broke out between the Puritans and the Natives led by Massasoit's son King Philip, also known as Metacom, and the brutal struggle lasted until 1678. The colony was in turmoil, as battles raged along Massachusetts' western frontier, the south coast of the Plymouth Colony, and in and around present-day Rhode Island. About half of all towns in New England were attacked during the war, which was an existential conflict for both sides. King Philip's War was the defining event of a generation, a life-or-death struggle, a total war fought in homes, fields, New England towns, Native villages, and dark woods. It destroyed New England's economy, and it took over a century for household incomes to recover to their prewar levels.[153]

Salem was not immediately near the front, but the fear of attack was so great that a palisade wall was built on the inland side of the town for defense.[154] In June 1677 Francis Nurse was paid by the Salem militia committee "for fortification work," along with several other men.[155] It is probable that he worked on the palisade, even though the Nurses' farm lay well outside the defenses and remained unprotected. Her husband's fortification-building fortunately seems to be as close as Rebecca Nurse's immediate family got to the front lines, though her brother-in-law Isaac Easty volunteered for service in the war.[156]

In December 1675 a company of militia from Salem fought through the cold, wet swamps of Rhode Island to reach the Narragansett's island stronghold. The Nurse family likely knew many of these young Salem men drafted from nearby farms. Several men in this unit were later involved in the witch hunt, including Thomas Putnam Jr., whose family accused Rebecca Nurse of witchcraft in 1692.[157] At the great battle, the colonies of Massachusetts, Plymouth, and Connecticut each sent a thousand men for the assault on the Native camp. They waded through feet of frozen snow across a swamp and fought uphill to attack the Narragansett's stone fortress. During the battle, the Native settlement was burned, five hundred Natives died, and two hundred militiamen were either killed or missing.[158]

From expeditions such as this, horror stories of Native brutality filtered back to towns and farms along the coast. Obviously, these stories were one-sided and portrayed the Natives as savages while glossing over the brutality of the colonists. In reality, wartime abuses committed by the Natives were caused by the New Englanders' actions in the previous large-scale war, the 1637 Pequot War. During this earlier conflict, the European settlers had not spared Native women and children, so when King Philip's War broke out, the Natives adopted these same brutal tactics, slaughtering entire colonial families.[159]

During the war, there were reports that Natives in western Massachusetts peeled the skin off the dead bodies of militiamen and kicked around a dead New Englander's head like a soccer ball. One story recounted by New England prisoners was that the Natives cut a small hole in one prisoner's belly and pulled out his guts through the opening. Another tale was that Native women castrated captured militiamen and kept their body parts as souvenirs.[160] The Puritans long believed that the Natives' religion was Satanic, and stories such as these only furthered this view.

King Philip's War ended in Massachusetts when its namesake was killed in 1676 and his severed head was placed on a stick in Plymouth. But fighting with Natives and their French allies continued along the northern frontier in present-day New Hampshire and Maine until 1678.

Some defeated Natives relocated to northern New England and New France, awaiting an opportunity to once again confront the encroaching New Englanders. Such an occasion arrived in the years just before the witch hunt.[161]

WHILE THE WAR RAGED ELSEWHERE, a local death sparked a controversy that included several figures later prominent in the witch hunt. In 1676 Francis Nurse and son-in-law Thomas Preston were appointed to a coroner's jury to investigate the death of Jacob Goodall. In December 1675, while the Salem militiamen were fighting through the Rhode Island swamps, Goodall was working as a hired hand on Giles Corey's farm. John Proctor testified that Goodall appeared healthy at that time, though Thomas Putnam Jr. later wrote that Goodall "was almost a natural fool," so despite being physically healthy he was evidently mentally challenged in some way.[162]

One day, Goodall was taken home bruised, cut, and apparently beaten. A neighbor testified that on a previous occasion he saw Corey beat Goodall over one hundred times, to the point that the neighbor ran over to Corey and "told him he would knock him down" if he didn't stop beating Goodall.[163] John Proctor testified that Corey admitted this incident to him. Naturally, once Goodall died from his wounds suspicion fell on Giles Corey.

The coroners' jury found bruises and cuts on Goodall's arms and legs. In the end Corey was charged and found guilty of physical abuse, not murder, and only fined.[164] Corey died in 1692, crushed—not by the guilt of murdering his young mentally challenged neighbor—but instead by the stones placed upon his chest by Sheriff George Corwin for obstructing his trial for witchcraft.

In the spring of 1678, Rebecca and Francis Nurse departed their home in the western reaches of Salem Town for a farm in Salem Village, a community northwest and slightly inland from the center of the port town. This significant change in their lives set the stage for Rebecca Nurse's involvement in the witch hunt of 1692.

THREE

SALEM VILLAGE

But how can this be accomplished in a way of God when brother is against brother and neighbors against neighbors, all quarrelling and smiting one another? ... Will a righteous and holy God own contention and strife?
—Jeremiah Watts, describing Salem Village in a letter to Rev. George Burroughs, 1682

ON APRIL 29, 1678, FRANCIS NURSE signed a mortgage agreement to purchase a three-hundred-acre farm in Salem Village from Rev. James Allen of Boston.[1] Soon afterward, Rebecca and Francis moved their sizable family from the western part of Salem Town to their new farm in the village.[2] This homestead, still preserved today, was the family's home for generations. The move marked a material improvement for the family, though this move also led to Rebecca Nurse's involvement in the 1692 witch hunt.

Salem Village lay north of the Nurse family's previous farm and northwest of the center of Salem Town. It bordered the Town of Topsfield, where Rebecca Nurse's parents and siblings moved after they sold their riverbank farm in 1652. The village consisted of farms spread out between hills of varying heights, carved out by glaciers in a previous age, with large rocks and boulders strewn across the meadows and woodland.[3] Between the hills were lowlands cut by small streams that flooded in the spring and flowed into three tidal rivers, which then merged and meandered past the former Towne family farm before reaching the sea. The river stretched from Wilkins Pond and the Ipswich River in the west, across the commanding heights of Hathorne Hill, east through the village center with its meetinghouse, tavern, and watch house, over to the three rivers and the Ipswich Road near the edge of Gov. John Endicott's Orchard Farm. It was next to Orchard Farm and just south of the village center that the Nurse family established itself.

This section of the village had clear brooks that were originally traversed with "water horses," as the settlers called canoes. By the 1670s, there were paths through the woods and meadows between the farmhouses. Some trails were established cart paths, while others were marked only with blazes or cuts on trees.[4] The main country highway, the Ipswich Road, ran northward from Salem Town and forked near the southern edge of the Nurse farm. One road continued northeast onto Beverly and Ipswich, while the other road continued north past Rebecca and Francis Nurse's new farmhouse, then bent west through the village center and on to Andover.

Salem Village, rather than Salem Town, became the epicenter of the witch hunt in 1692. The village was a distinct community from Salem Town, but was essential to it. The villagers provided food for the ever-growing population, and hosted the roads between the port town and points north. The village was established in 1672, when the farmers received permission to construct their own meetinghouse, hire a minister, and establish a separate church from the Salem Town church.

This semi-autonomy was a long time coming for the villagers, who first made moves toward separation as early as 1666 when a group of farmers petitioned to hire their own minister, but the Salem town meeting refused.[5] The following year, several farmers signed a petition to the Massachusetts General Court seeking further autonomy, this time relating to the militia. The able-bodied men of the village, some of whom lived ten miles from the town center, were required to report for guard duty downtown, leaving their own families undefended. The General Court agreed and relieved the distant farmers of militia duty in Salem Town. The farmers established their own militia training field that Deacon Nathaniel Ingersoll later gave to the village as "a training place forever," and it remains town-owned land today.[6]

Salem Town was unwilling to grant the farmers further autonomy, because Salem had already lost much of its land to the newer towns of Beverly, Manchester, Marblehead, and Wenham.[7] Despite Salem Town's reluctance, the General Court allowed the village to establish a separate parish in 1672, once again primarily because of the distance between the village and the center of town. Although it developed as a separate community, politically the village remained a section of larger Salem, and did not yet gain total independence as the neighboring towns had.[8]

Along with its own parish, the village gained a degree of self-government, with its own village meeting—a periodic gathering of the men of Salem Village that served a similar role as a town meeting in an incorporated town. The main purpose of the village government was to levy taxes (known as "rates") to pay for the meetinghouse and the minister's salary, though most taxes and policies were still decided by the all-Salem selectmen and general all-Salem town meetings that included men from both Salem Village and Salem Town. In addition to the village meetings, a village committee was elected that had a role similar to the selectmen of a town. Francis Nurse was later elected to the village committee, which shows a level of respect from his new neighbors and fellow farmers who undoubtedly knew of his previous assignments and appointments in Salem Town.

While the village parish was formed in 1672, it was not a fully established church until it had a permanent ordained minister to celebrate the sacraments, and its own body of covenant members. The village had only nonordained ministers until 1689, so although it hosted services every Sunday, church members such as Rebecca Nurse needed to travel to the Salem Town church once a month to celebrate the sacrament of the Lord's Supper. This awkward inferior status was not resolved until Rev. Samuel Parris was ordained in 1689.[9]

The meetinghouse in the village center, where the villagers gathered each Lord's Day for worship with their neighbors and minister, was on Meetinghouse Lane, only half a mile from the Nurse farm.[10] The building was the antithesis of Nurse's childhood church of St. Nicholas in Yarmouth. Instead of the sacramental space of a stone medieval church, the village meetinghouse was simple, austere, and intentionally unadorned. From the outside, it was a square, unpainted building with a peaked roof of wooden shingles. There were several window openings, some with glass and some with only sliding shutters covering the openings. Inside, the building had plain white horsehair plaster walls, with exposed beams and rafters open up to the peaked roof. On the floor of the building were box pews, with an aisle down the center. Women sat on the east, men on the west, and slaves, servants, and children stood up above in the galleries. The pews below contained hard, uncushioned benches. Worship was not meant to be comfortable. Up front, a high pulpit was the focal point, with a wooden canopy above the pulpit to deflect the minister's voice down toward the congregation so that he was more clearly heard in the crowded building. The pulpit desk had a cushion on it, upon which the Holy Bible was placed.[11]

The temperature in the village meetinghouse was often uncomfortable, and unlike the Salem Town meetinghouse there was no stove for heat during the frigid winters.[12] On wintry Sabbaths the minister needed to break the ice in the christening bowl before children could be baptized.[13] To keep warm during services, foot warmers (a metal box containing hot coals brought from the farmer's hearth), blankets, and dogs were allowed in the pews.[14] In this bare, cold, and unheated building Nurse and family worshipped regularly.

While inside the meetinghouse, the faithful heard sermons on the church militant in its struggle against the Prince of Darkness and his legions, but their enemies were present in the temporal world as well as the spiritual. Especially in rural villages, fear of attack from Natives and wild animals was high. Worshippers attending Sunday meeting were required to be armed, but the firing of weapons was prohibited on the Lord's Day, unless firing at attacking enemies or wolves, so as to not spread false alarms or profane the Sabbath.[15]

Another reminder of the potential for attack on Salem Village was Watch-House Hill, just up the road at the end of Meetinghouse Lane, which featured a tall wooden tower on the highest point in the village center. Constructed in 1676 at the village crossroads, this strong structure built of logs served as a lookout tower and also as a fortified building that could be defended in case of attack.[16] Many villagers passed through its shadow on their way to the meetinghouse each Sunday.

Near the tower, at the crossroads of Meetinghouse Lane and the Andover Road, was Ingersoll's Ordinary, the village tavern. Deacon Nathaniel Ingersoll, veteran of King Philip's War, served rum, beer, and cider by the quart, and hot food between the two Sunday services.[17] The tavern was an important social place for the villagers to trade news and talk politics with their friends and neighbors. The Nurse farm was only a little ways down the road.

REBECCA AND FRANCIS NURSE's new farm was three hundred acres of fields, gentle hills, and streams. There was already a house on this site years before the Nurse family arrived, situated near a dirt path that led to the main road. The structure was described as a "farm house" in 1676, though a subsequent deed describes Francis Nurse as building the house in which they lived.[18] He may have used pieces from the previous structure to construct the newer house, which traditionally dates to 1678 when the Nurse family moved onto the farm. The house lies on a small rise in the land facing south, and originally included just two rooms, one stacked upon the other, made of hewn beams that framed white walls of horsehair plaster. The outside was covered with unpainted shingles and red-painted trim.[19]

Into this two-room house moved Rebecca and Francis Nurse, along with several of their children who lived there until they married and established households of their own.[20] Additionally, three of their children—Samuel Nurse, Mary (Nurse) Tarbell, and Rebecca (Nurse) Preston—built their own houses on other sections of the Nurse family's large farm. Preston's house still stands today.[21]

In April 1678, Rebecca and Francis Nurse began a twenty-one-year mortgage agreement for the farm, which neither lived to see completed.[22] The previous owner of the three hundred acres was Rev. James Allen, the prominent minister of the First Church of Boston who co-wrote a preface to one of Cotton Mather's books dealing with witchcraft, *Memorable Providences* (1689).[23] One month after Francis Nurse signed the mortgage agreement, Allen and his wife signed over the deed to him.[24] The Nurses were therefore the legal owners—as long as they adhered to the terms of the sale agreement and made their required payments.

The farm was originally known as the Bishop farm, because Townsend Bishop was first granted the land in 1636, and was the first settler to live there.[25] Bishop was a respected member of the community, but suspicion grew that he did not believe in infant baptism—a heresy to the Puritans— so he left town in 1646 due to persecution for his incorrect religious views.[26]

The farm had several different owners and tenants between then and 1678, including the Endicott family who lived on the neighboring Orchard Farm for many generations.[27] John Endicott Jr., named for his father the governor, owned the Bishop farm at his death in 1668. His widow Elizabeth later remarried, to Rev. James Allen from whom Francis Nurse bought the farm in 1678. Allen's wife Elizabeth died in 1673, making Allen the sole owner of the Bishop farm. However, Zerubbabel Endicott (brother of Allen's wife Elizabeth's first husband) claimed that he should have inherited the farm upon the passing of his brother, according to his father's wishes, instead of it going to Elizabeth's—and then to Allen's— control.[28] This began a series of legal disputes over the property that later embroiled the Nurse family.

Allen first sold the farm to Robert Sanford in 1674, who later repudiated the sale due to endless litigation with the farm's neighbors over its boundary lines, especially over a nineteen-acre tract of land that was also claimed by Nathaniel Putnam.[29] Prior to modern surveying technology, boundaries were marked out by paces and distances between natural landmarks that were vague and subject to interpretation.

It is suggested that the Nurse family knew of the previous boundary disputes, which is likely given how public and long-standing the issue was.[30] Allen did not include the nineteen acres disputed with Putnam in the sale to Francis Nurse, which lessened the risk for the Nurse family, and Allen states in the deed that he "was the true, lawful and sole owner of all the afore-bargained premises." Seeing as neighbor Zerubbabel Endicott had fenced in part of the land mentioned in the deed many years prior, this claim was quite contested. In the deed Allen also states that he "shall and will from time to time and at all times forever after, warrant and defend the above-granted premises . . . against all and every person and persons whatsoever, anyways lawfully claiming or demanding the sum or any part or parcel thereof."[31] This clause put the onus for defending the title of the land on Allen, instead of Francis Nurse, thereby making the purchase of a partially contested farm more palatable for the Nurse family.

In addition to Allen's promise to defend the claim to the land, the Nurse family negotiated a very advantageous payment deal with him. The purchase agreement committed them to pay £400, quite a large sum at the time, but the whole amount was not due in full until 1699. In addition to having twenty-one years to pay the full price, Rebecca and Francis Nurse were required to make only small annual interest payments in the meantime.[32]

Low interest payments and lack of a required large down payment meant that the Nurse family could use profit from farming to improve the farm and make it more productive, instead of needing to send most of their profit away to Allen. On top of this, the Nurse family received credit toward their final £400 balance for improvements they made to the farm. They did not have much capital to invest upfront, with their previously mentioned debts, but they did have many able-bodied sons and sons-in-law to work and improve the farm.

Another advantageous part of the purchase agreement for the Nurses was that if they were unable to pay the final sum they would be reimbursed for any improvements made to the farm over £150, which lessened the risk of investing time and money in improving the property. Also, if the Nurses were unable to pay the whole balance owed to Allen by 1699, any portion of the principal paid before then would count as the purchase of a proportional amount of the land. So, even in the worst-case scenario, the Nurse family was still guaranteed at least a portion of the farm.[33]

It was suggested by nineteenth-century historian Charles W. Upham that the success of the Nurse family in purchasing this farm "had awakened envy and jealousy among the neighbors."[34] It is hard for contemporary historians to determine how their neighbors felt, and there is really no recorded evidence as to the neighbors' opinions of the purchase. However, after Rebecca Nurse was accused of witchcraft many neighbors signed a petition and testified in support of her, showing that she was respected and well-liked in the neighborhood.[35]

As to potential jealousy among neighbors, it was clear from the houses built by three of Nurse's children on the farm that it was really the combined effort of four households that contributed to the purchase of the land, not just that of Francis and Rebecca. The Nurse family was in financial trouble prior to the purchase, with their aforementioned public debts to the town, and continued to owe debts after the purchase as well, including not keeping up with their annual payments to Allen. As will be seen, this subsequent financial trouble involved the courts, and therefore became public knowledge. They were unlikely candidates for financial envy.

One of the most common and persistent misconceptions of the 1692 witch hunt is that those accusing others of witchcraft gained their land upon their conviction, and therefore since the Nurse family owned land, Rebecca was more likely to be accused. This is simply not true.[36] First, such confiscation was prohibited by both Massachusetts and English law. Second, as a married woman, she did not herself technically own land or any personal belongings: all of the property of the household legally belonged to her husband.[37] Stealing land was not a motivation for lodging a witchcraft accusation against Rebecca Nurse, and there was no material gain for her accusers.

At the end of their first harvest season on their new farm, Rebecca and Francis Nurse hosted a double wedding on October 25, 1678.[38] Their daughter Elizabeth married Edward Russell, and their daughter Mary married John Tarbell. Russell lived in Salem Town with Elizabeth from their marriage in 1678 until 1685, at which time they moved to the nearby town of Reading. Tarbell grew up in Groton, west of Salem on the frontier. He lived there until the town was overrun by attacking Natives in 1676 during King Philip's War, during which Tarbell served in the militia.[39] After his marriage to Mary Nurse, he built a house on the Nurse family's three-hundred-acre farm, and later played an important role in the witch hunt and its aftermath.

This festive occasion inaugurated a new chapter in the lives of their daughters, but also in the lives of Rebecca and Francis Nurse. The double wedding and the first harvest on the large new farm gave them security in their approaching old age. Especially important for the aging couple was that their daughter Mary and husband John Tarbell, daughter Rebecca and husband Thomas Preston, and son Samuel and wife Mary now lived in nearby houses on the large farm.[40] These many hands allowed Rebecca and Francis Nurse to make good use of the land.

The new Nurse farm was also closer to Rebecca's mother and siblings. Rebecca's widowed mother Joanna lived in Topsfield until her death in 1683. William and Joanna Towne had no will, and so the court divided their belongings among their six children.[41] The sons received equal portions of the land, while the three daughters were given household goods. An inventory of Francis Nurse's belongings in 1694 shows that the Nurse family did not own many furnishings, and so this inheritance of household goods was probably significant for the family.[42]

To accept their inheritance, Rebecca's married sister Mary Easty and widowed sister Sarah Bridges (better known by her later married name, Sarah Cloyce) signed the probate document with their mark, but for some reason Rebecca did not sign for herself.[43] Instead Francis Nurse signed his mark "with the consent of Rebecca," as the record states.[44] The next time that Rebecca and her two sisters had their names mentioned in court papers was in 1692 when all three were accused of witchcraft.

WHILE THE NURSE FAMILY labored in their new fields, disputes about the farm's boundaries boiled. Land grants to settlers were often vague, and boundary markers were usually trees or large rocks. Ill-defined boundaries became an increasingly serious issue in the 1670s as coastal towns ran out of land, and existing plots were divided. In 1660, the average landholding in Salem Village was about 250 acres, but as farmers divided their land between multiple children, the average landholding in 1690 declined to 125 acres. As land became scarcer, there was an uptick in court cases (as if the Puritans were not already litigious enough) dealing with boundaries both between farms and between towns, which desired more land to grant their inhabitants.[45]

At home, Rebecca and Francis Nurse felt these new land pressures immediately after arriving on the farm. The land they purchased for £400 in 1678 was previously worth £116 in 1648 and £300 in 1674, showing a significant increase in value.[46] Although Allen was legally required to defend the title to the land that he sold to Francis Nurse, the Nurse family were the ones there on the ground, and were drawn into land disputes with neighbor Zerubbabel Endicott shortly after arriving. This ensuing series of land disputes has been used by legal historians as a case study on land law in seventeenth-century Massachusetts, and Salem historian Charles W. Upham describes it as "One of the most memorable and obstinately contested land-controversies known to our courts."[47]

Gov. John Endicott's 1632 grant for Orchard Farm, next door to the Nurse farm, was clearly defined on three sides, but not on the fourth, where it now bordered the Nurse property. The ensuing dispute—or series of disputes—has been viewed in two ways. One theory claims that the Nurse family's neighbor to the north, Nathaniel Putnam, took advantage of the vague border between Nurse and Endicott for his own personal gain, which is what Endicott claimed at the time.[48] A subsequent theory downplays the role of Nathaniel Putnam and claims that although Putnam appears frequently in the testimony of the Nurse-Endicott court cases, the issue truly was a boundary dispute based on vague and conflicting claims between the Nurse farm and Endicott's Orchard Farm.[49] However, neither of these theories puts the Nurse family at odds with Nathaniel Putnam, and according to the first theory their interests aligned.

Nathaniel Putnam was constantly expanding his landholdings, and of all the many Putnam names in the Registry of Deeds, his appeared most often until his death in 1700.[50] In April 1679, while the land dispute was in the courts, Putnam separately got into trouble for fencing in a portion of the town's common land as his own.[51] As regards the dispute in Salem Village, if the Allen/Nurse interpretation of the boundary won out, then one section of Endicott's land bordering Putnam's would be awkwardly almost separated from the rest of the Endicott farm. According to the theory that Putnam manipulated the dispute for his own gain, Putnam may have thought that such a situation would make Endicott more amenable to selling him the estranged parcel.[52]

In June 1678, only two months after he signed the purchase agreement with Allen, Francis Nurse was sued by Zerubbabel Endicott for cutting down trees that Endicott claimed were his. But Nurse, who had surveying experience from his appointments with the town to survey and lay out parcels of land, claimed "that he cut wood upon his land he bought of Mr. Allen."[53] The litigation had begun.

Although this lawsuit was between Endicott and Francis Nurse, Endicott directly accused Putnam of treachery during the trial. Then, Endicott proposed a rather hard-to-believe theory that what had been considered for decades as the northeast boundary marker of the farm was actually the southeast marker, thereby rotating the bounds of the Nurse farm 90 degrees so that it overlapped with most of the other neighboring farms, while giving Endicott the forty acres that he had claimed and fenced in. However, William Hathorne, father of witch trials judge John Hathorne, testified that the Endicotts knew that forty acres of Allen's land was on their side of the fence when they put it up. Further testimony revealed that when Allen showed Francis Nurse the bounds of the farm, most of the neighbors were also present and agreed with their interpretation, leaving Endicott alone in his odd theory.[54]

Whether there was malicious intent on the part of Putnam or Endicott, court testimony shows how truly confusing the disputed boundary was. John Hathorne testified that he previously saw a certain maple tree as a boundary marker. John Putnam Sr., himself involved in a boundary dispute with the Town of Topsfield, testified that thirty-five years earlier there had been a momentary worry that one of the Endicotts accidentally chopped down one of the boundary trees. Zerubbabel Endicott, the plaintiff, admitted the true vagaries of the boundary: "The honored court with the jury may be pleased to observe several improper words are used in the expression [of the bounds] by reason those men who were then the layers out of the land were (although plain-hearted, honest men) yet of little art and skill in mathematical, grammatical, or geometric rules and expressions."[55]

The 1678 trespass case was decided in Endicott's favor as well as the border issue—it was of course necessary to decide whose land it was in order to determine whether trespassing occurred. After several appeals, in October 1678 the General Court commissioned a survey of the land which temporarily settled the case.[56] This survey reawakened another dormant controversy, because it also included within the bounds of Allen's original land the 19 acres south of the Crane River that were previously disputed with Nathaniel Putnam. Allen did not sell this parcel to the Nurses, and so he now sued Putnam for the land. The Nurse family had no direct involvement in this dispute, since the land involved was disputed between Putnam and Allen, and it was not part of the farm that they purchased in 1678. After a series of appeals, the General Court agreed with Putnam, and caused the whole survey map of the Nurse Farm to be revised, further muddying the waters and prolonging the disagreements.[57]

In March 1683 the tables were turned and Francis Nurse sued Zerub-babel Endicott for trespass, though he dropped the suit. Three months later, in June 1683, Nurse sued Endicott for trespass again. During the trial, Nurse's sons-in-law Thomas Preston and John Tarbell testified that Endicott came onto the farm to chop down trees, carting away twenty-one trees on one occasion, and twenty-six on another.[58] Historian Charles W. Upham describes this scene as the "battle of the wilderness," and the court records reveal a tense standoff between the two sides in the woodland.[59]

Endicott hired several groups of men to take sleds and cut down the trees in the disputed land. Two of the hired men testified that while they were cutting, "Thomas Preston and John Tarbell came in a violent man-ner" and began emptying the logs from the hired men's sleds, claiming that the wood rightfully belonged to them.[60] Then, Francis Nurse arrived on the scene, and asked the men who hired them, to which Endicott—who also seems to have just arrived—answered that it was he who hired them. Samuel Nurse and Francis Nurse Jr. were also present, in what seems to be a crowded standoff. One can only imagine the ill-feeling and tempers that raged at the scene, over a dispute which by then was con-tested in various court cases for five years—or contested for decades, if the original Endicott inheritance dispute is taken into account.

Now that Endicott was cutting down trees on land that the Nurse fam-ily's deed described as belonging to them, Francis Nurse had little choice but to lodge the trespass suit. If he did not, and Endicott removed the trees without recourse, it would add to his claim of adverse possession. The county court sided with Endicott—even though this verdict contra-dicted a decision of the General Court, the highest court in the land, which the county court was not entitled to do.[61]

After a series of appeals, the General Court sided with Allen/Nurse, possibly in part because neither Endicott nor his attorney showed up.[62] Endicott was ill, and died soon afterward. Up to his death, Zerubbabel Endicott held fast to his claim not just to the border land, but to the entire Nurse farm, which Allen inherited at the death of Elizabeth Endicott Allen. When Zerubbabel Endicott's will was presented in 1684, he claimed that the entire Nurse farm remained part of *his* estate.[63]

After several cases were decided against Allen and the Nurse family, and in favor of Endicott, the Nurse farm was now less than the 300 acres Allen claimed it was when he sold it to them. So, in June 1684 Francis Nurse filed a complaint with Judge John Hathorne against Allen "for not making good" on the deal to sell 300 acres, since the courts decided the farm contained fewer acres.[64]

Nurse's lawsuit did not go forward and was instead settled out of court. The Nurse family sold forty-seven acres of the farm back to Allen for a price of £40, and forty-five of these forty-seven acres were located along the disputed boundary with the Endicotts.[65] At the end of their agreement, Nurse renounced his claim to the twenty-two acres of land that he believed he purchased from Allen in 1678, but were later determined to be Endicott's. Thomas Preston, John Tarbell, and Samuel Nurse—all of whom also built homes and maintained sections of the large farm—signed the agreement as witnesses. This agreement ended any further issues between Nurse and Allen, but lawsuits with the Endicotts continued.

Although this boundary dispute was acrimonious and long-lasting, it did not lead to the later witchcraft accusation against Rebecca Nurse. In 1692, Samuel Endicott, son of Zerubbabel (who claimed unto his grave that he was the rightful owner of the Nurse farm), signed the petition in support of Nurse after she was accused. Also, Nathaniel Putnam does not appear to have harbored ill-will against the Nurse family. He gave written testimony in defense of Rebecca Nurse at her witchcraft trial, despite the fact that his Putnam nieces were Nurse's main accusers.[66]

THE VAGARY OF BOUNDARY LINES affected not only personal real estate, but also towns and villages. There was a particularly heated border dispute between Salem Village and the Town of Topsfield, where Rebecca Nurse's siblings lived after 1652 when her parents sold their Northfields farm.[67] This dispute probably led to accusations of witchcraft against several Topsfield women in 1692, including Nurse's sister Mary (Towne) Easty. Although it was also long assumed that this dispute was a major factor in the accusation against Nurse, this is not likely.

In 1639 the land along the Ipswich River that later became part of Salem Village was given to the Town of Salem by the General Court, but in 1643 the General Court gave some of the same land to the Town of Ipswich, despite the fact that it had already been inhabited by farmers from Salem pursuant to their 1639 grant. To complicate matters, in 1658 the General Court created the Town of Topsfield out of the southern part of Ipswich, which included the disputed land. The Salem Villagers living on this land refused to pay ministry taxes to the Topsfield church, claiming that their land was rightfully in Salem Village, defying tax collectors and constables.[68]

Topsfield refused to recognize some of the land titles that had been given out by Salem in the disputed area, thereby throwing the ownership of some farmers' land into potential jeopardy.[69] Lawsuits were lodged with the courts, and tempers flared between Topsfield farmers and Salem Villagers out in the disputed fields and forests. The lawsuits continued until, according to one contemporary record, "a great deal of money and time has been spent at the law in a likely way of destroying and being destroyed one by another."[70] This dispute lasted from 1643 to 1728, and generations of families from both communities were involved.

Some of Rebecca Nurse's Towne family relatives lived on the Topsfield side of the disputed boundary, and they faced off against one branch of the Putnam family who resided on the Salem Village side of the contested line. In 1659, a joint boundary committee was established by Salem and Topsfield, and included members of the Howe, Towne, Easty, and Wilds families from Topsfield and the Putnam family of Salem Village.[71] All the Topsfield families mentioned above had at least one family member accused of witchcraft in 1692—one of whom was Mary Easty, Nurse's sister—and the branch of the Putnam family that lived near the disputed land included several of the accusers during the witch hunt.

As will be seen, the large extended Putnam family factors into many disputes in Salem Village—though sometimes Putnams can be found on opposing sides of the same issue. One seventeenth-century legal expert describes the Putnams as "notoriously litigious."[72] This is shown in the already discussed role of Nathaniel Putnam in the Endicott-Nurse boundary issue and in the Putnams' role here in the Topsfield dispute, and will be seen in the Putnams' role in the Salem Village ministry controversies and the role of Thomas Putnam Jr.'s family during the witch hunt in 1692.

One particular incident during the Topsfield dispute likely contributed to some of the accusations during the witch hunt, as it pitted one branch of the Putnam family against John Howe, whose sister-in-law Elizabeth Howe was later accused of witchcraft, and Isaac Easty Sr., the husband of Nurse's sister Mary, who was later accused of witchcraft, along with several of Nurse and Easty's Towne relatives. Jacob Towne and John Howe were both cutting trees in the woods along the disputed boundary. John Putnam Sr. witnessed this cutting on land that he believed to be his, but was alone and therefore outnumbered at the time. He left to get reinforcements.

Putnam later returned with several members of his family, and now the Putnams also began cutting trees in this disputed land. John Easty of Topsfield, along with Nurse's brother-in-law Isaac Easty Sr., nephew John Towne, and nephew Joseph Towne responded to the sound of trees being felled and confronted Putnam and his group. Putnam said to the Topsfield men, "I will keep cutting and carrying away from this land until next March." The Topsfield contingent asked him "What, by violence?" Putnam responded, "Aye, by violence. You may sue me: you know where I dwell," and then turned to his family members and told them to continue cutting trees, saying "Fall on."[73] The Topsfield men retreated, assumedly due to inferior numbers. The matter was far from over.

DURING THEIR YEARS in Salem Village, the Nurse family became an important part of the community. They were farmers in a village of farmers. Neighbors helped one another raise the frames of barns and houses, and worked together to clear the roads. Men gathered for village meetings, militia drills, and hunting parties, while women gathered for quilting parties, and all gathered for services on the Lord's Day.[74]

In the village, Ingersoll's tavern was the center of social life. Taverns of the day were also called "ordinaries" and "public houses," and Ingersoll's featured a tap room with a large fireplace, bare sanded floor, and many stools and chairs. There were also hooks on each side of the fireplace to hang firearms that villagers brought with them. Cider was usually the drink of choice, and in colonial times there was only one kind of cider: what we in the twenty-first century call "hard" cider. Beer, wine, whiskey, and rum were also common, and hot food was served.[75] Deacon Nathaniel Ingersoll and family ran the tavern, and later Rev. Samuel Parris' Native slave John Indian was hired out by Ingersoll to help in the tap room.[76]

Rebecca Nurse's husband and sons frequented Ingersoll's, both for social reasons and because village committees met there. It was in the tavern that the committee tasked with the contentious job of assigning seats in the meetinghouse met, and also where the militia elected its officers.[77] Business was transacted over pints, and news was shared along with local gossip. Francis Nurse continued to play an important official role in community affairs, as he previously did in Salem Town, and by now his and Rebecca's sons and sons-in-law were also active in village business.

Francis Nurse continued his litany of appearances on juries, including serving in November 1678.[78] That same month, he and sons John, Francis Jr., and Samuel swore oaths of allegiance to King Charles II before the Essex County Quarterly Court.[79] The Massachusetts General Court had received a letter from the king requiring all men aged sixteen and over to swear an oath of allegiance to him and His Majesty's Government and to renounce the Catholic Church—the Puritans would have been more than happy to do the latter.[80] Rebecca Nurse and her generation left England to escape the reach of the king and the Church of England, but over the following years royal interference in Massachusetts' affairs increased.

Now confirmed as a loyal subject, Francis Nurse continued to serve on juries and to survey land for the Town of Salem. In June 1682, he appears to have served again as a constable, for there is a record that he arrested Thomas Maule, a Quaker and general rabble-rouser who was later a critic of the witch hunt in the years after it ended.[81] Rebecca Nurse's son Samuel also served in public roles. In April 1684, he was chosen for the committee to renew the bounds around the village parsonage and meetinghouse land along with Thomas Putnam Sr., Nathaniel Putnam, and Nathaniel Ingersoll, three of the leading men in the village. Later that year, Samuel Nurse served on a committee to meet with Joseph Hutchinson and settle the bounds of the land Hutchinson gave the village for the meetinghouse.[82]

In one revealing case of public service, Francis Nurse and his sons did highway maintenance, beginning in 1683. Men who did highway work were paid by the town for their labor. Typically, the men from a certain neighborhood would get together to repair the public ways in their part of the town during certain seasons when less farm work was required. The men worked with oxen, pickaxes, and the like, digging up roots and rocks to ensure that the road was passable.[83]

In 1683, Samuel Nurse, Samuel Southwick, and Francis Nurse were paid for highway work along with several other men from the area. In 1684, Samuel Nurse was paid for one day of work, John Tarbell for four days, Thomas Preston for three days, and Francis Nurse for eight and a half days, a large number. The following year Samuel Nurse was paid for one day of highway work. In 1688, Francis Nurse was paid for four days of work, and paid for the work of his "boy" one day. His "boy" was a farmhand that he had working for him, since Nurse was around sixty-seven years old by this time. The record book reveals several other farmers who were similarly paid for the work of a hired hand in their household.[84]

The men of the Nurse family, and Francis in particular, likely worked so many days for the town repairing roads because they simply needed the money. Despite their advantageous mortgage terms, Francis and Rebecca Nurse fell behind on their annual payments. The farm's purchase was a smart way to improve their position and provide a livelihood for their children, but they were stretched by even the small required payments. In June 1684, Allen sued Francis Nurse for debt and won. Included in the court record is a list of the Nurses' annual payments to Allen. They were supposed to pay at least £7 annually for the first twelve years, and then £10 for the remaining nine years.[85] But in none of the first five years of the mortgage did they pay the required £7 in full.

There are a couple of other records that may point to financial need as well. In the summer of 1680, Francis Nurse had 40 shillings subtracted from his taxes in exchange for hiring out his bulls to the town for work. Also, in 1681 Nurse received £3 from the Salem selectmen for his work on the land surveying committee. It appears as though Nurse needed to press the selectmen for payment, since he was paid "provided he accepts thereof as full satisfaction."[86]

This financial trouble likely explains why Francis Nurse worked an unusual eight and a half days doing highway maintenance in 1684. The Nurse family's inability to pay their mortgage in full led Allen to sue Nurse for debt, right as Nurse sued him for not actually selling him 300 acres as promised. These suits led to the 1684 legal settlement with Allen in which the Nurse family sold back two sections of the farm for £40. One interesting side effect of this debt suit is that in order for Allen to win the suit, the court needed to confirm Allen's description of the farm's boundary and its size. Therefore, in a roundabout way, being sued for debt actually solidified the Nurse family's claim to the land disputed with the Endicotts.[87]

Financially, there were challenges for Rebecca and Francis Nurse, though by this time their children were mostly managing the farm. In 1681, Francis Nurse's estate was valued less for the village taxes than those of his son Samuel Nurse and sons-in-law John Tarbell and Thomas Preston, all of whom lived on sections of the farm.[88]

By 1684 THE NURSE FAMILY was so well-integrated into the village community that the voters elected Francis Nurse to the village committee.[89] The committee's chief job was to collect the annual tax for the ministry and meetinghouse, and all villagers were required to pay taxes to support the minister, regardless of whether they actually attended services.[90] This church was tax-supported by Salem Village and later the Town of Danvers until 1828, per Massachusetts law.[91] The issue of who to hire as the village minister was a long-simmering controversy that spanned decades. Francis Nurse now found himself in the middle of this imbroglio that one historian describes as "the most famous ministerial controversy in seventeenth-century Essex [County]," and this series of disputes contributed to the outbreak of the 1692 witch hunt.[92]

The village went through several ministers leading up to Rev. Samuel Parris' ordination in 1689, which finally established the village parish as an independent church, with its own members and a minister able to celebrate the sacraments. The village's first minister, Rev. James Bailey, was chosen in 1672 by a vote of the village.[93] In towns with fully established churches, like Salem Town, only the male covenant members—those visible saints who were believed to be going to heaven—were allowed to choose the minister, and the other potentially graceless inhabitants did not have a say in church affairs. However, since the village parish was not a fully established church until it had its own permanent ordained minister, the voters of the village decided on hiring ministers in the interim.[94] This practice was awkward and unusual, and heightened the ensuing controversies over the ministry.

Bailey was a young man, and received his degree from Harvard three years prior to becoming village minister in 1672.[95] His contract was renewed by vote in November 1673, but fourteen villagers refused to pay the tax to support the minister. This minority's dissent and refusal to pay required that the constable be brought in to attempt to compel payment, and the issue continued for the rest of Bailey's tenure in the village.[96] It was in the midst of this ministerial dispute that the Nurse family arrived in the village in 1678.

In 1679, some called for Bailey to be ordained and settled permanently as minister, which would formally establish the village parish as a full church. But an outspoken minority called for Bailey to be replaced, and there was a question raised about the manner in which the minister was chosen—by vote of the village meeting since the village congregation did not have its own separate membership yet.[97] The villagers asked the mother church in Salem to mediate, but it was unsuccessful and the issue was brought to the General Court.[98] The General Court ruled that the village should choose its minister by a vote of the householders, as it had been doing through the village meeting, until it became a fully established covenanted church, at which time only the church members would choose the minister.[99] But, by this time the village had already decided to abandon Bailey and search for a new minister.[100]

Although there were members of the Putnam family opposed to Bailey serving as minister, including the Nurses' neighbor Nathaniel Putnam, another branch of the Putnam family that became significant during the witch hunt supported him strongly. When Bailey moved to the village, he brought his wife Mary (Carr) Bailey and his wife's sister Ann Carr along with him. In November 1678, Ann Carr married Thomas Putnam Jr., son of the richest man in the village and a veteran of the brutal campaign against the Narragansett during King Philip's War.[101] Because they were relatives of Bailey, Thomas Putnam Jr. and Ann Putnam had a personal stake in the ministry dispute. Ann Putnam became particularly important during the witch hunt, as did her daughter Ann Jr. The man who replaced Bailey as minister, Rev. George Burroughs, was later accused of witchcraft by this family.[102]

In April 1680, the Nurse family's neighbor Nathaniel Putnam served on a search committee for a new minister that chose George Burroughs, a refugee from the wars with the French and Natives in Maine. Burroughs was voted in as minister in November 1680. The village soon after decided to build a parsonage for the minister, though it was made clear that while the minister had use of the parsonage during his term, it was owned by the village and belonged "to the inhabitants of this place and their successors forever."[103]

Burroughs' tenure was even more acrimonious than Bailey's. He had had a rough life during the frontier wars prior to his arrival in the village, and his poor luck continued as minister. His wife died in 1681, and he went into debt paying her funeral expenses. Taxes for the ministry were not all paid, as happened during Bailey's tenure, and his salary was in arrears. He eventually gave up trying to collect the £60 that the village owed him, and left the community. Soon after, several villagers to whom Burroughs owed money petitioned the Essex County Quarterly Court, and a public meeting was set up in April 1683 between Burroughs and the villagers to settle their accounts.[104]

John Putnam Sr., who was involved in the village boundary dispute with Rebecca Nurse's siblings in Topsfield, was one of Burroughs' supporters and previously loaned him money for his wife's funeral after the village stopped paying his salary.[105] Putnam even let Burroughs live in his house for nine months.[106] But, at the court-arranged meeting, John Putnam Sr.'s patience with Burroughs expired, and he joined the minister's opponents.

According to a deposition attested to by Nathaniel Ingersoll, while Burroughs was in the meetinghouse, the Essex County Marshal entered the building.[107] He spoke with John Putnam Sr., then approached Burroughs and read out a document accusing Burroughs of owing a debt to Putnam. Burroughs pointed out that he was in the middle of settling all his debts with the villagers that he could, but after John Putnam Sr. consulted with his brother Thomas Putnam Sr., they had Burroughs arrested on the spot for debt. In 1683 arresting a minister in a meetinghouse was extraordinary, but it pales in comparison to the events of 1692 when some of the same Putnams accused said minister of witchcraft and had him hanged.

It was into this mess that Francis Nurse entered the scene with his election to the village committee in January 1684. In September 1684, he served on a committee with Nathaniel Putnam and John Putnam Sr. to negotiate with Rev. Deodat Lawson about becoming the village's next minister.[108] Lawson's tenure was as sour and sad as those of the preceding ministers.

While the village—which by now surely had a reputation for infighting and disputes with ministers—was negotiating with Lawson, other issues boiled. The border issue with Topsfield was at the forefront, and there were also questions about the parsonage lands, which were donated by Joseph Holten, but now it was realized that the original deed could not be found. Additionally, during Francis Nurse's term on the village committee it was decided that the parsonage and the meetinghouse land needed to be surveyed and fenced, and that the meetinghouse needed interior work done. At the final meeting during Nurse's term on the committee in March 1685, a tax was agreed on to repair the meetinghouse, and a smaller tax was levied to pay Rev. Lawson's salary for the preceding year.[109]

Francis Nurse's term on the village committee ended, but in June 1685 he was elected to the important—and also controversial—position on the committee to reassign seats in the meetinghouse.[110] He was chosen along with Thomas Putnam Sr., John Putnam Sr., and three others. An appointment to the reseating committee was seen as a sign of high respect. For example, his fellow appointee Thomas Putnam Sr. was the wealthiest man in the village and a lieutenant in the militia, therefore making him an important personage. The meetinghouse seating committee met in Ingersoll's tavern, at the main crossroads in the village.[111]

The Puritans believed that appearance was very important, and since only a select few of the inhabitants were the visible saints chosen for heaven, all wanted to appear as though they were among the chosen ones. As one's seat in the meetinghouse—and therefore their adjudged status in the community—was very publicly known, it could cause ill feelings and jealousy.[112] Salem Village already had several long-running disputes, so the stakes were quite high.

The committee was ordered by the village meeting to assign seats giving regard "first to age, secondly to office, thirdly to rates [taxes paid]."[113] Those of a dignified age were assigned seats toward the front separated by sex, then the families of the minister, deacons, elected officials, magistrates, and militia officers were assigned rows behind the honorably aged. The remaining villagers were assigned seats according to wealth. The Puritan's Christian duty was to work for the Lord, and also to work for his or her own economic advancement. There was therefore a perceived connection between wealth and godliness, to the point that Rev. Cotton Mather went as far as to claim that one could not get to heaven without both piety and personal economic advancement on earth.[114] This set of beliefs, modified over the centuries, led to the contemporary American evangelical Christian belief known as the prosperity gospel.

The report of the 1685 meetinghouse seating committee is lost to history, so it is not known where Rebecca Nurse sat for services that year.[115] Toward the end of the decade she was assigned to the most prominent pew in the front row of the Salem Village meetinghouse, next to Mary Veren Putnam, widow of Thomas Putnam Sr. Upon Thomas Putnam Sr.'s death, he left Mary and her son Joseph most of his vast estate.[116] She was stepmother to Thomas Putnam Jr. and step-grandmother to Ann Putnam Jr., who played important roles in the 1692 witch hunt.

Having such an honored seat in the meetinghouse shows that Rebecca Nurse was perceived as a respectable, holy woman and that her family was perceived similarly. As to Nurse's children, Elizabeth was accepted as a covenant member of the Salem Town church in 1688, and seven of her children (Rebecca Nurse's grandchildren) were baptized there later that year.[117] Her son Samuel Nurse and his wife Mary became members of the village church in 1690, after it became its own independent church, along with her daughter Mary Tarbell and husband John Tarbell. Her sister Sarah Cloyce joined her husband Peter Cloyce as a member of the village church in 1690 as well.[118]

Rebecca Nurse's family contained several visible saints, which reflected positively on their mother. Many of her sons and daughters lived as her neighbors, and the others lived in neighboring towns. She was the matron of a large family, and well established in her new home of Salem Village. But, soon affairs in the village and in Massachusetts as a whole began to spiral out of control.

FOUR

THE FALL

Now, Tis a dismal Uncertainty and Ambiguity that we see ourselves placed in. Briefly, such is our case, That something must
be done out of hand. And indeed, our All is at the Stake; we are
beset with a Thousand perplexities and Entanglements.
—Rev. Cotton Mather, *The Present State of New England* (1690)

CONTROVERSIES AND SETBACKS wracked Massachusetts and Salem Village in the years leading up to the witch hunt, as a cloud formed over the
Puritans' Promised Land. Rebecca Nurse was directly involved in only
some of these upheavals, but crucially for her it has been argued that all
of these events contributed to either the outbreak of the witch hunt in
general, or the specific accusation of witchcraft against her in 1692.

In England, when King Charles II restored the monarchy in 1660 after
the chaos of civil war, he cracked down on those not conforming to the
Church of England, such as the Puritans. The Restoration ended all hope
of "purifying" the home country, and Puritanism in England shattered as
the Church of England, headed by the monarch and with its episcopal hierarchy, was reentrenched.[1] It was feared that this royal purge might come
to Massachusetts next.

Charles II died in 1685, and after his death those in Massachusetts
hoped that his successor would allow greater liberty for Puritans.[2] His
brother James II was proclaimed king in London in February 1685. As a
show of loyalty to the new monarch across the sea, the Massachusetts government ordered His Majesty to be proclaimed king in Boston as well.[3]
Samuel Sewall—a member of the Council of Assistants and a future witch
trials judge—was present for the ceremony, and his diary has an unin-

tentionally ominous entry for the major news of that day, "Monday April 20th. The King is proclaimed; eight companies, the troop, and several gentlemen on horseback assisting; three volleys and then cannons fired. This day a child falls upon a knife which ran through its cheek to the throat, of which inward wound it dies."[4] Though hopefully proclaimed in Boston, James II's reign would see the demise of Massachusetts as a nearly independent Puritan community.

LIFE CONTINUED in Salem Village, which had more than its share of local troubles. The disputed border between the village and Topsfield remained a serious issue, especially for several of Rebecca Nurse's siblings and nephews who lived near this contested boundary.

The next action in the dispute occurred before a judge. Rebecca Nurse's nephew Thomas Towne, nephews Joseph Towne and John Towne, brother-in-law Isaac Easty Sr., and nephew Isaac Easty Jr. sued John Putnam Sr. and some of his relatives over the previous incident when Putnam declared that he would continue to chop down trees in the disputed land "by violence" if necessary.[5] The suit was referred to a later court session but was never taken up, leaving the issue unresolved.

The Topsfield border dispute is far more complicated in how it relates to Rebecca Nurse later being accused of witchcraft than how it is usually described. On the one hand, the initial legal charge of witchcraft against Nurse in 1692 was made by Jonathan Putnam and Edward Putnam—the son and nephew of John Putnam Sr. who faced down the Townes with his feisty words in the forest.[6] This Putnam family link seems to imply a fairly straightforward connection between the Topsfield feud and the witchcraft accusation against Nurse.

But, John Putnam Sr., who actually owned the disputed land and confronted the Townes, supported Nurse after she was accused in 1692.[7] His son Jonathan Putnam, who filed the witchcraft charge against Nurse, also later signed a petition in her defense along with several other Putnam family members, and John Putnam Sr.'s brother Nathaniel Putnam separately entered testimony in defense of Nurse.[8] Only the family of Thomas Putnam Jr. and his brother Edward Putnam—nephews of John Putnam Sr. and members of the third branch of the Putnam family—testified against Nurse in 1692, but this branch was further removed from the Topsfield dispute.

Rebecca Nurse was quite possibly the least involved of the entire Towne family in the border issue. She never lived in Topsfield, nor is there evidence that her husband Francis or any of her children took part in this issue before she was accused.[9] Yet, Nurse was the first in her extended family to be accused of witchcraft. Her sister, sisters-in-law, and nieces in Topsfield were much more logical targets for the Putnams if they sought vengeance over this issue, therefore the Topsfield dispute is unlikely to be the main impetus behind the accusation against Nurse.

It is very likely that this dispute played a role in the later accusations against Nurse's sister Mary Easty in 1692, however, along with the accusations against several other Topsfield families. Easty's husband Isaac Easty Sr. had served as a Topsfield selectman, and he and their son Isaac Easty Jr. were involved in the lawsuit against the Putnams. Additionally, Easty lived right near her brother Thomas Towne, who was also involved in the lawsuit.[10] It was John Putnam Sr. who confronted several of Mary Easty's male relatives in the woods, and he lodged the formal accusation of witchcraft against Easty along with Thomas Putnam Jr. and several other village men. Accused in the same document as Easty were others from Topsfield that were involved in the dispute, including members of the Wilds and Hobbs families.[11]

AT THE BOSTON TOWN HOUSE in April 1685 there had been joy and celebration for the new king, but by July the mood turned to disdain and alarm as news arrived that the Crown had revoked Massachusetts' colonial charter, thereby ending its power of self-government. It was actually Charles II who voided Massachusetts' charter prior to his death, but news of the revocation did not arrive until after James II became king.[12] This loss of the charter meant the loss of the original mission of the colony, and in response ministers preached on the need to return to the founders' original vision of Massachusetts as a New Jerusalem.[13] It was feared that denying self-government to Puritan Massachusetts was the first step toward bringing the episcopal Church of England to New England.

With the loss of the charter and legal legitimacy, all of the land titles given out under the old charter by the Massachusetts government and the local towns were suddenly open to question. Did the Massachusetts farmers still own the land that they had toiled on for decades? Or was it all now the property of the king? Livelihoods were in question, and Massachusetts had a troubled future ahead.

The reign of James II, a Catholic who believed in supreme royal power, further alarmed the Puritan New Englanders. Less than a year after he became king, James prorogued Parliament and it never met again during his reign. Previously, as Duke of York and the proprietor of New York, James restricted rights in that colony and abolished its elected assembly. As king, he appointed military men to control England's colonies, and viewed the colonies as opportunities to make money for the Crown. James chose Sir Edmund Andros, a military officer who previously served as the despotic governor of New York, to rule Massachusetts and the rest of New England.[14]

In December 1685, on one of the darkest days of the year, the fifty-gun Royal Navy warship *Kingfisher* glided past the cannons of the Castle, the island fortress in Boston Harbor.[15] It docked at the end of one of Boston's main streets, and Sir Edmund Andros disembarked with a royal commission naming him as Captain General and Governor-in-Chief over His Majesty's Territory and Dominion of New England. Coming ashore behind him were two companies of English soldiers wearing bright red coats.[16] This was the first time that royal troops arrived in Massachusetts, whose militia fought without any help from England against the Natives during King Philip's War and during all previous conflicts.[17] Royal power had now arrived to bring order to this errant colony full of religious deviants from the Church of England.

Andros was sworn in as leader of the Dominion of New England at the town house that day, in a ceremony that marked the beginning of a dictatorial régime the likes of which Massachusetts had never seen.[18] Massachusetts as a political unit no longer existed: All of the English coastal colonies from present-day New Jersey to Maine had their charters revoked and were consolidated into the new Dominion, whose capital was Boston. Andros soon appointed a Dominion Council in place of the former elected Assistants, but he could make decisions without them, giving the royally appointed executive a new level of arbitrary power. Additionally, to further limit Massachusetts' representative government, property ownership was added as a requirement in order for men to be able to vote.[19]

Andros' actions and angry local reactions fit general themes that were later seen in the lead-up to the American Revolution. He began enforcing the Navigation Acts, which regulated trade between the English colonies to the benefit of England, and put smugglers on trial in special naval courts without juries, foreshadowing similar actions taken by the Crown in the 1760s and 1770s to enforce some of the same acts.[20] Also, Andros instituted new direct and indirect taxes, including special property taxes—quitrents—that needed to be paid to the central Dominion government, whereas previously landowners only needed to pay small local property taxes.[21]

These arbitrary taxes were unpopular and were resisted. In Boston, leading Puritan minister Rev. Increase Mather was arrested due to his opposition to the Dominion, and he later fled by ship for England disguised in a wig and white coat with the authorities in pursuit.[22] Rev. John Wise, the minister in Ipswich, was among those speaking out against Andros, and he referenced the Magna Carta to support their claim to traditional English rights. In response, Andros told Rev. Wise that all English rights were forfeited once the settlers left England, and that his only right was not to be sold as a slave.[23]

In 1687 several towns north of Salem Village refused to choose a tax collector to collect the money for Andros' régime. They claimed that they could only be taxed by their own elected representatives—and therefore there could be no fair taxation without representation. In response more than thirty men were arrested, including three former Assistants charged with sedition—one of whom was future witch trials judge and later critic of the trials Nathaniel Saltonstall.[24]

There were further abuses of the judicial system, including undermining the right of trial by jury. Instead of towns electing men to serve in the juror pool, as was done under the original charter, Andros' régime gave the county sheriff the power to choose whomever he wanted to serve on juries. Having the Andros-appointed sheriff choose jurors led to accusations of unfairly packed juries, subject to the whims of the régime. As Rev. Cotton Mather described it, "Foxes were made the administrators of justice to the poultry."[25] The assertion of the arbitrary power of the Crown for the first time in Massachusetts and the denial of traditional rights and liberties were shocking.

WHILE POLITICAL DISPUTES roiled Massachusetts, an unexpectedly significant argument with one of Rebecca Nurse's neighbors later proved consequential once she was accused of witchcraft in 1692. One day in the late spring of 1689, a group of pigs broke loose from Benjamin Holten's hog pen. These animals crossed the Crane Brook and tramped onto the Nurse farm, uprooting crops and snorting through the planted fields. Loose swine were a very serious problem for New England farmers because not only could swine destroy crops, but they were also truly dangerous and posed a serious risk to children and the elderly if they crossed paths.[26]

Upon discovering these errant swine, Rebecca Nurse went to the Holtens' house and complained to Benjamin Holten in the presence of his wife Sarah, who testified against Nurse in 1692. Only Sarah Holten's version of the events survives and, to little surprise since it was used against Nurse at her trial for witchcraft, it does not paint her in a good light. Sarah Holten described Nurse as "railing and scolding" Benjamin Holten and stated that "all we could say to her could in no way pacify her."[27] According to Holten, Nurse then called out to her son Benjamin Nurse to get his gun and shoot the pigs, presumably to stop the damage that they were causing.

Holten also claimed that the pigs were yoked, and that the Nurse family's "fence was down in several places," as a way to blame them for the incident.[28] According to the law at the time, in general it was the farmer's responsibility to fence in his fields so that stray cattle could not wander in. However, calves and swine were an exception to this rule, as the law recognized that they could "not be restrained by ordinary fences."[29] These animals were small and could squeeze between the rails, and therefore needed to be yoked.

This episode was later brought up during the witch hunt because Benjamin Holten became gravely ill and died not long after this argument with Rebecca Nurse. Wishing ill upon someone who later suffered harm could lead to suspicion that one used malefic magic to seek revenge.[30] Although Nurse was described as "railing and scolding" Benjamin Holten, at no point does Sarah Holten's testimony say that Nurse wished ill upon him before he became sick.[31] She only threatened to have her son shoot the pigs, and in this the Nurse family was well within their legal rights—though from Holten's testimony it is unclear if such action was taken or if it was merely threatened.[32]

In addition to the other controversies, arguments over the ministry continued to embroil Salem Village during the years before and after 1692. Francis Nurse, when he was on the village committee in 1684–1685, was involved in the hiring of Rev. Deodat Lawson as minister. But Lawson, like Rev. James Bailey and Rev. George Burroughs before him, did not last long in the village.

Some villagers initially sought to ordain Lawson as the permanent minister, and thereby formally establish the village congregation as a fully independent church. Rebecca Nurse's son-in-law John Tarbell supported Lawson's ordination, as did many Putnams.[33] However, the villagers were unable to come to an agreement, so the issue was arbitrated by Bartholomew Gedney and John Hathorne—local magistrates and later witch trial judges—along with other local officials and ministers.[34]

These men recommended that the villagers "desist, at present, from urging the ordination of the Rev. Mr. Lawson, till your spirits are better quieted and composed."[35] They also described the tense situation in the village: "We observe such uncharitable expressions and uncomely reflections tossed to and fro as look like the effects of settled prejudice and animosity."[36] Those on all sides of the previous disputes then joined together to search for a new minister.[37] In the end, the fateful choice was to hire Rev. Samuel Parris.

Parris' father and uncle were quite wealthy and involved in sugar plantations and the slave trade on Barbados. His father sent him to attend Harvard College, though Parris withdrew at the death of his father in 1673 and never graduated. Parris inherited a plantation in Barbados and moved to the island, but he returned to Massachusetts only a few years later and lived in Boston as a merchant. By 1686, due to declining fortunes and lawsuits for debt, Parris switched to pursuing a career in the ministry. It was a difficult job market for the not-graduated Parris, as there were few open positions, most ministers had college degrees, and an increasing number even had master's degrees. After a brief time preaching in Stow, Massachusetts, Parris began negotiating with Salem Village to become its new minister.[38]

Years of disputes made Salem Village an unattractive employer with a history of not fully paying its ministers, and Parris appears to have had no competition for the job. His negotiations with the village seem to show that he understood the previous issues and disputes. In particular, his knowledge of the terms of the previous contract with Lawson might mean that he spoke with Lawson about the position. Parris was a hard negotiator, and in the end received a better contract than Lawson.[39]

Francis Nurse and son-in-law John Tarbell were each elected by the village to serve on different successive special committees elected to hire Parris and negotiate to convince him to come to Salem Village. Several committees were needed to hire him, because Parris drove a hard bargain and the village needed to offer him more and more in order to secure his agreement to serve as minister.[40] It is likely that this negotiating role shows initial support for Parris by Francis Nurse and Tarbell, because if these members of the Nurse family opposed Parris it is unlikely that they would have agreed to serve on these committees whose goal was to offer concessions and entice Parris to agree to serve as minister.

On June 18, 1689, Parris' contract was approved and he was hired at an annual salary of £66.[41] Parris later wrote in a lawsuit that there had been "much agitation" among some of the villagers in a meeting prior to the vote when he was told of his final contract.[42] It is suggested that he may have expected the deed to the parsonage and the surrounding land, whereas the village gave Parris the use of the house, as previous ministers were given, but the village retained ownership over the building.[43]

In November 1689, Rev. Parris was formally ordained by Rev. Samuel Phillips of Rowley and Rev. John Hale of Beverly, who was later involved in the witch hunt. Ordination day was cold and windy, which caused Parris to give only an abbreviated sermon.[44] He preached on Joshua 5:9, "And the Lord said unto Joshua, This day I have rolled away the Reproach of Egypt from off you."[45] The village church was out of exile, and now fully established.

The church covenant, the agreement and set of beliefs written out at the founding of the church, shows a very negative view of the world, in contrast to John Winthrop's grand vision of a New Jerusalem five decades prior. The covenant mentions "renouncing all the van[ities] and idols of this present evil world."[46] What was in the 1630s a promised land had become an "evil" place to the true believers of Salem Village.[47]

The village church, formally the Church of Christ in Salem Village, was finally organized—seventeen years after it was given permission by the Salem Town church to do so. Rebecca Nurse's brother-in-law Peter Cloyce was among the original covenant members of the village church, and in the next four months he was soon joined by Nurse's sister Sarah Cloyce, son Samuel Nurse and wife Mary, and daughter Mary Tarbell and husband John.[48] Some historians have directly connected joining the village church during this time with supporting Parris as minister, and therefore these Nurse family church members were likely supporters of Parris.[49]

But, in a show of opposition only one month after Parris' ordination, thirty-eight families (outnumbering the covenant members) were not up-to-date in paying their taxes for the minister's salary, and the constable was brought in to collect payment.[50] Parris appears hurt by this nonpayment, and a few months later, while this nonpayment continued, he wrote in one of his sermons that although wicked men would "give 30 pieces of silver to be rid of Christ: they would not give half as much for his gracious presence and holy sermons."[51] None of the extended Nurse family was among the nonpayers.

Parris and his family—wife Elizabeth, son Thomas, daughter Elizabeth ("Betty"), and daughter Susannah, along with niece Abigail Williams—had moved into the parsonage earlier that year, after his contract was approved in June 1689. The Parris family also arrived with three slaves: two married Caribbean Indians—Tituba and John Indian—and also a Black boy.[52] The village parsonage was a two-story structure with five rooms, and its foundation can still be seen today.[53]

Parris began preaching in July 1689, and in the months before his formal ordination that November it appears as though he persuaded some in the village to transfer ownership of the parsonage to him—even though this was not in his contract.[54] This was an unusual request for the time, as ministers' contracts in most communities did not convey ownership of the parsonage to the minister.[55] None of the ministers who previously served in Salem Village was ever given ownership of the parsonage—they were merely allowed to live in it as part of their contract with the village, just as Parris' contract stipulated.[56]

It appears that some village men who became Parris' strongest supporters orchestrated a backroom vote in October 1689—or at least wrote such a vote into the village record book—whereby they transferred ownership of the parsonage to Parris.[57] This was one month before Parris was ordained, which usually meant that one would hold the position of minister in the community for life. But this conspiracy backfired, and when it was discovered in the months before the witch hunt it alienated many villagers who had not previously opposed Parris and shattered any sense of stability the village church had gained from finally becoming fully established.

IN MARCH 1687, Andros held an Anglican Good Friday service in Boston's South Meetinghouse, to the disgust of Massachusetts' Puritan ministers.[58] Under the Dominion, Andros reorganized the courts and government, appointing Anglicans to high posts.[59] There were now clergy in Boston who owed allegiance to the bishops of the Church of England, and Anglicans ruled over the Puritans' Promised Land. Rebecca Nurse and her co-religionists had traveled halfway around the world to a distant continent to practice their dearly held religious convictions and avoid the persecutions of crown and miter. Now, might the royal and ecclesiastical courts that punished the Puritans in England be established on the soil of their former Puritan commonwealth?

In 1688, James II's heir James Francis Edward, Prince of Wales, was born. In celebration, the cannons of the Castle in Boston Harbor fired, drums beat, and bells tolled in Boston. These noises were misconstrued and a confused panic began in the town because the ringing of bells was one of the ways to warn of severe fires.[60] For the Puritans, the situation was scarier still: the king's son and heir was to be raised Catholic. Now the Puritans faced the possibility of being subjects of a Catholic dynasty for years to come, which further inflamed political tensions against the new Dominion government. Back in London, some Protestant conspirators turned on their own king and invited a foreign Protestant power to invade England and depose James II to prevent a feared restoration of Catholicism in England.[61]

That same year, increased anti-Catholic sentiment led to witchcraft accusations against a Boston woman: Ann Glover, an Irish Catholic widow who was accused of witchcraft by children from the Goodwin family. There had been several prior instances of witchcraft accusations in colonial New England, but this 1688 case appears to presage some of the events of 1692. Those who claimed to have been hurt by the accused witch—four children, the oldest of whom was thirteen—acted similarly to how the first "afflicted" in Salem Village later acted: they claimed that the woman choked them without physically being present, and that the Irish woman's spirit came to them sometimes in the shape of an animal.[62] Last, the afflicted were examined by experienced physicians and diagnosed as bewitched, similar to how in 1692 a doctor gave credibility to the claims of witchcraft.[63] Parris was in Boston during this time and likely saw similarities to this case when fits began in Salem Village in 1692.[64]

In the end, Ann Glover was hanged, the first accused witch in Massachusetts to be executed since 1656. Glover is recognized by the Archdiocese of Boston as the first Catholic martyr in Massachusetts due to the anti-Catholic aspect of the accusations against her.[65] In addition to prejudice, mental illness probably contributed to the situation. Glover confessed to the crime, undoubtedly under pressure to do so, but one contemporary later wrote that in court "her answers were nonsense, and her behavior like that of one distracted" and that she was "a despised, crazy ill-conditioned old woman."[66]

Not only was Satan's army rising up, as it appeared when the alleged witch was discovered in Boston, but the armies of men were rising up as well. French pirates and privateers prowled the coast, and heavy taxes were imposed to fund wars against the French and the Natives.[67] In 1688, Andros sent a thousand men marching into Maine to build forts to defend against French and Native aggression, but the situation soon spiraled into a broader war across the frontier.[68]

In March 1689, Andros passed through Salem Town on his way back from commanding troops on the northern frontier and crossed paths with Rev. John Higginson, minister of Rebecca Nurse's church in Salem Town. Andros asked the minister for his views on the recent change in the law regarding land ownership. Higginson demurred, but Andros insisted that he answer. Higginson then said that he believed the land belonged not to the king, but instead to those in Massachusetts who had owned it for about sixty years. Andros was indignant at this answer, and after a strong reply he fumed, "Either you are subjects or you are rebels!"[69] Many in Massachusetts decided to be rebels.

A few weeks later, on April 18, 1689, two thousand militiamen flooded the streets of Boston. They arrested Andros along with twenty-four other Dominion officials, and forced the surrender of the Castle and the Royal Navy warship *Rose* in the harbor.[70] The uprising in Boston began as soon as word spread that the Protestant William of Orange (who was married to James II's Protestant daughter Mary) had successfully invaded England several months prior and deposed the Catholic James II. William and Mary now ruled England—and Massachusetts—as Protestant co-monarchs.[71]

After Andros was arrested in Boston, the Massachusetts government that had been elected in 1686—at the last election before the Dominion—was brought back to power.[72] From 1689 until a new charter from William and Mary arrived in the spring of 1692, Massachusetts was ruled by this provisional government, reelected each year. Thus, although the Puritans did not believe in a spiritual limbo, they found themselves in a political one with great uncertainty in the years leading up to the witch hunt.

Placing the colony in an even more precarious position, William and Mary soon declared war on France, because Louis XIV harbored James II and hoped to restore him to the English throne. The frontier skirmishes in New Hampshire and Maine were then transformed into a world war fought on four continents. The outbreak of the wider war caused an increase in fighting in North America, during the course of which Massachusetts soldiers reached as far north as the gates of Quebec, while the French and Natives penetrated as far south as Andover—the town next to Salem Village.

HISTORIANS HAVE long proposed that in addition to disputes between Salem Village and rival land claimants in Topsfield, factionalism between two rival groups *within* the village played a role in causing the witch hunt. It is also claimed that this factionalism directly led to the accusations against Rebecca Nurse. Despite several heated disputes in and around Salem Village during these years, it is not likely that two distinct long-standing factions actually existed as outlined in this theory, and the Nurse family did not play the role that historians have ascribed to them. However, at the very end of 1691 opposition to Parris swelled and the village was divided over the issue of whether he was illegally given ownership of the parsonage. Francis Nurse was among the village leaders who investigated and challenged this unlawful conveyance of the parsonage.

Historian Charles W. Upham, who wrote in the nineteenth century, described a particular intravillage conflict surrounding the ministry that lasted from the gathering of the Salem Village congregation in 1672 up through Parris' removal in 1697. This theory was expanded in Paul Boyer and Stephen Nissenbaum's *Salem Possessed* (1974), which claimed that there was a larger factional conflict between two distinct parties in the village that divided along economic, geographic, and political lines, and that this factional divide explains the cause of the witch hunt and explains who was accused during it. The two parties in this supposed protracted factional conflict were the Porter family's faction in the east of the village (which allegedly included the Nurse family) and the Putnam family's faction in the west.

There were many issues that supposedly divided these two factions. According to this framework, the Porter faction (in which the Nurse family is placed) allegedly lived in the eastern part of Salem Village along the boundary between agricultural Salem Village and commercial Salem Town, was economically improving compared to the Putnam faction because it was more connected to the commercial port town, opposed Parris, and was opposed to village independence. Meanwhile, the Putnam faction supposedly lived on the inland western side of the village farthest from Salem Town, was in economic decline because it was less connected to the port town, supported Parris, and sought independence for the village. This factionalism is claimed to have caused the witch hunt because most accusers in 1692 supposedly lived in the west of the village and most of the accused supposedly lived in the east. Therefore the witch hunt was allegedly the western Putnam faction striking back at the eastern Porter/Nurse faction through accusations of witchcraft.[73]

In the decades since this theory of factionalism was put forward, it has been partially refuted by other historians of the witch hunt. In particular, Richard Latner's research shows that the supposed pro-Parris faction was not in economic decline compared to the supposed anti-Parris bloc as was originally claimed, and Benjamin C. Ray revealed that there was no significant east-west split in accusations during the 1692 witch hunt, and therefore the claimed east-west factionalism is not the direct cause of the witchcraft accusations.[74] Though, of course, disputes and ill feelings in individual cases likely contributed to some of the nearly two hundred individual accusations lodged in 1692, both inside and outside the village.

The case of Rebecca Nurse and the role of the extended Nurse family prior to 1692 further challenge the factionalism theory. If the Nurse family's actions are thoroughly scrutinized, the evidence shows that they do not fit the category in which they were placed, and that they have many similarities with the Putnams on the above-mentioned issues that supposedly defined the two factions. Significantly, the Nurse family does not play the role that historians have long ascribed to it before 1692.

There are no indications that the Nurse family was more tied to the merchants in Salem Town or economically better off than the Putnam family. Before coming to the village, the Nurses were farmers in the western hinterlands of Salem Town—just as far from the commercial center as parts of Salem Village, in an area that was agricultural instead of commercial—and when the Nurse family moved to Salem Village, they—both Rebecca Nurse's immediate family and the extended family—were farmers, just as the Putnams were.[75] Additionally, the Nurse family was frequently in debt and behind on their taxes—not exactly signs of enviable economic success.

Regarding the issue of village independence, the Nurses and the Putnams—supposed rivals—were on the same side. Francis Nurse was one of the leaders of the village independence movement—something the Putnams strongly supported—and he was repeatedly chosen by the village to negotiate with Salem Town for more autonomy and long-desired independence, working alongside members of the Putnam family.[76] The desire for further autonomy and eventual village independence was a uniting factor, bringing together leaders from all parts of Salem Village—church members and non-church members, those from the east and those from the west—and therefore this issue did not cause a hostile divide in the village that led to the witch hunt.[77]

As to the Nurse family's view of Rev. Parris—another dispute that supposedly divided the village along the factional lines—there is no significant evidence that they opposed Parris as minister in general prior to 1692, only that in the final months before the witch hunt Francis Nurse served on the 1691 village committee that challenged the suspicious transfer of parsonage ownership to Parris.

Contrary to first appearances, the Nurse family also complicates the claim that most of the accusers in 1692 lived in the west of the village and most of the accused lived in the east. Rebecca Nurse's son-in-law Thomas

Preston lived on Nurse land in the eastern part of the village along the border with Salem Town and defended Nurse once she was accused of witchcraft.[78] Although he defends his mother-in-law in this instance, Preston was also one of the men who lodged the first legal accusation of witchcraft in 1692—against Tituba, Sarah Good, and Sarah Osborne—which makes him an accuser as well as a defender.[79] Two Putnams lodged this first legal accusation with Preston, and this group was a cross-section of the community that did not fit any factional divide.

One other way that the Nurse family has been incorrectly framed as long-time enemies of the Putnams relates to the farm boundary dispute. It is claimed that the Nurse family disputed land ownership with Nathaniel Putnam, but the Nurses' dispute was actually with the Endicotts, and Nathaniel Putnam was effectively an ally.[80] The Putnams and the Nurse family were not enemies prior to 1692, and these issues were unlikely to play a significant role in causing the accusation against Rebecca Nurse.

ALONG THE NORTHERN FRONTIER, the war continued. In addition to their religious differences with the Catholic French, the New Englanders continued to believe that the Natives were Satan's allies, as they had during previous conflicts. Rev. Cotton Mather wrote of the Natives, "the Indians, whose chief sagamores, are well-known unto some of our captives, to have been horrid sorcerers, and hellish conjurors, and such as conversed with demons."[81] This struggle was not just a war between men, but was believed to be a spiritual war for the survival of the last bastion of Puritanism.

Slowly but surely New England's enemies crept closer to Salem Village, as fear and paranoia traveled ahead of them. The village was along the main roads from Salem Town to points north, and refugees returning from the northern frontier traveled down these paths sharing stories of slaughter. These war stories spread, and were likely embellished—as rumors and word-of-mouth stories usually are—in the taverns of the village and Salem Town.[82]

As in King Philip's War, stories of frontier brutality alarmed New England. Tales spread that French soldiers smashed the skulls of traitors, and their Native allies scalped New Englanders, including one instance of a seven-year-old girl reportedly found scalped after a raid.[83] One New England official described Native atrocities against New Englanders in 1689: "Having killed 500 of them, roasting by slow fire more than 80 poor

Christians, whose warm blood they drink, and sometimes eat their flesh, laying their sucking infants to the bleeding veins of their captives."[84] Some stories are clearly embellished, but they were spread whether true or not and instilled great fear in the populace.

As the war continued there were isolated attacks on the outskirts of Salem. In 1690 John Bishop and Nicholas Reed were killed by Natives within the limits of Salem, and in 1691 so was Godfrey Shelton.[85] Only six months before the outbreak of the witch hunt, the towns in Essex County were ordered to post twenty-four scouts at all times on the northern frontier to guard against attacks.[86]

If the real threat of attack was not alarming enough, the rumor mill produced panics about potential attacks and conspiracies. A captured escaped slave told of a plan he made with a local man to spy for Massachusetts' enemies and prepare the way for an invasion force of three hundred French soldiers and five hundred Native warriors to cross the Merrimack River and attack several towns just north of Salem Village. The story was corroborated by another slave, who said their plan was to "destroy all the English and save none but the Negro and Indian servants and that the French would come with vessels and lay at the harbor that none should escape."[87] It was as if the New Englanders' worst fears of an unholy alliance conspiring against them had come to life.

Further attacks scarred New England and New York. In February 1690 French and Abenaki forces assaulted Schenectady, New York, massacring sixty people, slashing pregnant women, and bashing the skulls of children. That April, French and Natives attacked Salmon Falls, New Hampshire, killing and capturing between eighty and one hundred people. Soon after, they attacked settlements along Casco Bay in Maine, sending refugees to Salem and Boston telling horror stories of death, the burning of the towns, the unburied dead left to rot, and settlers that were kidnapped and taken to Quebec as prisoners.[88]

As the French and Native attacks continued, militia from Massachusetts—including men from Salem Village and Salem Town—were sent north to defend New England. Several village men were previously called up for duty, and the village church book notes that in 1690 three Village men were "killed at Casco" during the raids there.[89] The committee supervising Massachusetts' military expeditions included future witch trial judges John Richards and Samuel Sewall, along with Sir William Phips who became governor during the witch hunt.[90] Phips led an amphibious assault on the fortress capitol of New France: Quebec, a town perched on a cliff above the St. Lawrence River. The French easily repelled the New

Englanders, and the church in the lower town of Quebec was renamed Notre-Dame-de-la-Victoire to commemorate the victory of the Catholic French against their Puritan foes.

More than four hundred New Englanders died during the expedition, and Massachusetts was crippled by debt.[91] Phips soon left for England to request aid in the war against France. This hapless leader returned to Massachusetts in 1692 as royal governor, after Rebecca Nurse and dozens of others had already been accused of witchcraft—the crime of conspiring with the Devil, believed to be the French Catholics' and the Natives' most powerful ally.

The war hit home for Nurse in June 1691 when her youngest son Benjamin was called to militia duty on the northern frontier.[92] He was twenty-six, and his wife Tamsen was expecting their first child. The couple lived with Rebecca and Francis at the Nurse homestead or nearby. During wartime, the Massachusetts government conscripted only a portion of each town's militia, thereby leaving behind a portion for local defense.[93] Benjamin Nurse was one of the unlucky few ordered north, but he never went. Instead, Francis Nurse hired a substitute to serve in his son's place.

Hiring substitutes to avoid conscription was a legal practice in Massachusetts since at least 1675.[94] This practice continued in the United States after independence, and was not ended at the federal level until the Selective Service Act of 1917.[95] John Hadlock, whose farm was just north of the Nurse family's, was hired as Benjamin Nurse's substitute. On top of his military pay, Hadlock received two shillings sixpence per week from Francis Nurse. Hadlock collected part of this pay in December 1691, and the rest in early 1693 once his service was completed.[96]

Benjamin Nurse was safe at home when news spread in October 1691 of a French raid not far from the village. French forces crossed the Merrimack River and killed several people in Rowley and Haverhill, about twelve miles north of the Nurse farm.[97] Already refugees from the front had traveled to Salem and Boston down the Ipswich Road that ran through the Nurse farm, and now the enemy was frighteningly close.

ALTHOUGH THE WAR RAGED, the Nurse family and other villagers tended their fields much the same as before, not realizing what horror awaited them in 1692. Rebecca Nurse's children and their spouses began their own families, and she gained more grandchildren. By 1692, the Nurses, including the families of their three married daughters, consisted of thirty-four people living near Rebecca and Francis Nurse.[98]

Now that the next generation was well established, Francis Nurse officially divided the Nurse farm into sections and in January 1690 sold them to their son Samuel, and sons-in-law Thomas Preston and John Tarbell, who had lived on and tended these fields for over a decade but did not legally own them. These men were now required to pay their share of the annual mortgage payment for their sections of the land, lessening the burden on Rebecca and Francis Nurse. All three deeds transferring the land were signed by Francis in the presence of future witch trial judge John Hathorne.[99] According to village tax records for 1691, Samuel Nurse, Tarbell, and Preston now each owned estates valued at almost twice as much as that of Rebecca and Francis Nurse.[100]

The elderly couple retained ownership of the central section of the farm and continued to live in the original house. Although they passed a large portion of their land on to the next generation in 1690, Rebecca and Francis Nurse fell behind on rent payments in 1691 for fields in Salem Town that they had leased from the town since 1677, so they signed their lease (and the debt) over to their sons Benjamin and Samuel. Francis Nurse, despite being about seventy years old, worked on maintaining the town highways again in 1691, revealing that he still needed the wages paid to highway workers to make ends meet.[101]

Rebecca Nurse's family continued their public service in the village during these years. In April 1687 her son Samuel was elected to a committee to assess all of the estates in the village for tax purposes, in 1689 he was employed by the town government for highway work, and in 1690 became a "freeman" of the colony, giving him the right to vote for members of the Massachusetts government in Boston.[102] In September 1690, the village elected Nurse's son-in-law John Tarbell to the village committee, the highest elected position in Salem Village.[103] In 1691 the selectmen of Salem chose Francis Nurse to survey land and to be in Salem's pool of grand jurors.[104] This court experience was put to use in 1692.

DURING THE YEARS before the witch hunt, the farm boundary issue with the Endicotts flared up again. Sometime before May 1686 the Nurse family fenced in a piece of land that was still disputed. Samuel Endicott, son of Zerubbabel Endicott who fought the first round of lawsuits with the Nurse family, sued Samuel Nurse, John Tarbell, and Thomas Preston in June 1690 for cutting down trees and trespassing. In November 1690, Endicott sued Preston again for trespassing and detaining land.[105] Now that many of the western fields were owned by the next generation of the extended Nurse family, they were sued instead of Francis.

Endicott hired a surveyor to investigate the disputed boundary for use as evidence at trial. But, this plan backfired and the surveyor's testimony largely supported the Nurse family's claim to both title and possession of the land. Endicott lost both suits.[106]

Much had changed since this boundary dispute first began, and the extended Nurse family was in a much more secure position by 1690. One calculation places the value of the land that made up the Nurses' initial three-hundred-acre purchase—originally bought for £400—at between £560 and £900 in 1690 due to an increasing scarcity of land driving up its appreciation. By 1700, the fortunes of the Endicott family declined to the point that Samuel Endicott's brother Zerubbabel Jr. sold sections of Orchard Farm to Samuel Nurse and John Tarbell at below-market rates.[107]

THE FINAL and potentially the most significant controversy in Salem Village leading up to the witch hunt was the dispute over the ministry. It has been claimed that this dispute directly explains why in 1692 some villagers became accusers while others were accused.[108]

The Nurse family was long characterized by historians as Rev. Parris' opponents prior to 1692.[109] However, most of the evidence used to claim that the Nurse family opposed Parris is petitions from after 1692, when the Nurse family and others openly worked to remove Parris because he supported the witch hunt and testified against Rebecca Nurse and other innocent victims.[110] This misuse of later documents puts the cart before the horse, because it reflects the Nurse family's view from *after* the witch hunt, yet it is claimed that it shows their view *before* the witch hunt.[111]

As to the Nurse family's views on Parris before 1692, six members of the extended family—Rebecca Nurse's son Samuel Nurse and his wife Mary, daughter Mary Tarbell and husband John, sister Sarah Cloyce and her husband Peter—joined the village church after Parris became minister, and there is no evidence of them voicing opposition to Parris in any way prior to the witch hunt.[112] Francis Nurse and son-in-law Thomas Preston also served on two of the committees that persuaded Parris to come to the village.[113] But, in 1692 Parris supported the accusations against many of the innocent victims, including those against Rebecca, and harassed the families of some of the accused in the village, such as the extended Nurse family.[114] A 1697 petition by Samuel Nurse, John Tarbell, and others who opposed Parris after 1692 clearly connects their later opposition to Parris' leading role in the witch hunt. After listing actions that Parris took during the witch hunt, they state that he "has been the beginner and procurer of the sorest afflictions, not of this village only, but to this whole country, that ever did befall them."[115]

The only evidence from before the witch hunt that historians have presented to claim that Rebecca and Francis Nurse were anti-Parris is that Rebecca never transferred her church membership from the Salem Town church to the village church after it was formally established in 1689 and that Francis was elected to the village committee in the fall of 1691 that challenged the suspicious conveyance of the parsonage to Parris.[116] As to Rebecca not transferring church membership, no surviving documents shed light on her reason for this. Perhaps since she was a seventy-one-year-old who had been attending the Salem Town church for about fifty-five years she simply wished to stay a member of her original church. Also, she attended weekly services with Rev. Parris and the Salem Village church, so not officially transferring church membership was not a boycott.[117]

As to Francis Nurse and the 1691 village committee, they challenged Parris not in general, but instead initially only on the issue of parsonage ownership, which exploded into a controversy mere months before the first accusations of witchcraft began in Salem Village. Parris and his strongest supporters may have held a grudge against Francis for his actions upholding the law and the previous votes of the village, but it was not part of any long-running opposition to Parris on the part of the Nurse family.

During the fall and winter of 1690–1691, there were two special committees chosen by village meetings—one in October 1690 that was comprised of Francis Nurse, Nathaniel Putnam, and John Putnam Sr., and one in January 1691 that included Francis Nurse, Daniel Andrew, Joseph Porter, Joseph Hutchinson, and Thomas Putnam Jr.—to investigate the deed to the parsonage and associated fields that were previously given to the village, but for which the deed was apparently lost as early as 1685.[118]

During 1691, many in the village discovered the October 1689 entry in the village record book that allegedly gave Parris ownership of the parsonage—despite a prior vote prohibiting ownership of the parsonage from ever being transferred to any village minister and requiring that it remain village property. This October 1689 vote recorded in the village record book was irregular: the entry with the alleged vote has no warrant written before it in the record book, nor is there a signature from the clerk attesting to the results. It is not clear who was in possession of the record book at that time, or who wrote the entry.[119] Parris believed that he legally owned the parsonage during the disputes after 1692, presumably based on this October 1689 recorded vote.[120] It is unclear how this suspicious vote came to light, but it is likely that it was uncovered by the committee elected in January 1691 to investigate the legal ownership of the parsonage upon which Francis Nurse served.[121]

In the fall of 1691, as the autumnal skies turned to gray and bright leaves fell off the trees, these new revelations that Salem Village had been dispossessed of the parsonage swirled. Meanwhile, long-standing opposition to Parris by some other villagers had continued since his ordination, and during the year from July 1690 to June 1691 more than £18 of Parris' £66 salary was unpaid.[122] Also, from mid-1690 through the end of 1691 no Salem Village men and only eight women became members of the village church, showing a decline in support from previous years, and none joined between the end of August 1691 and the beginning of the witch hunt in February 1692.[123] It was during that fall and winter that the parsonage issue was at the forefront.

A village meeting for October 16, 1691, was called by the outgoing village committee—that included John Tarbell, Nathaniel Putnam, and Jonathan Putnam—to elect a new village committee and decide on the ministry taxes for that year. On the last Sunday before this meeting, Parris made a plea to the church members that he was nearly out of firewood.[124] Parris was responsible for providing his own firewood according to his contract, but perhaps he meant to show that he was affected by the lack of payment the previous year as an attempt to influence the upcoming village meeting.[125] If it was, he failed.

At the October 16 meeting, Francis Nurse was elected to the village committee along with Joseph Porter, Joseph Hutchinson, Daniel Andrew, and Joseph Putnam. These were all of the men who served on the second committee investigating the parsonage deed, except Thomas Putnam Jr.— whose wife and daughter accused Rebecca Nurse of witchcraft only a few months later. At the first village meeting called by this new committee, the issue of the parsonage ownership was at the forefront, and these men's previous work investigating the parsonage ownership was a key reason why the voters chose them for the village committee.[126]

However, like the Nurse family, these men did not necessarily oppose Parris in general previously. For example, none of the five men on the 1691 village committee were on the list of non-payers of the ministry tax in 1689, which is used by some historians to gauge opposition to Parris.[127] Their opposition was confined to this one malicious deception: the suspicious conveyance of the parsonage.

After this new village committee was chosen at the October 1691 village meeting, someone present made a motion to order the village committee to renew the tax to pay the minister, as was required each year, but this motion was voted down by a majority of the villagers present.[128] It was therefore a majority of the whole village meeting that decided not to collect Parris' salary, not just the village committee on which Nurse served. At the next meeting, the first called by the new village committee, the parsonage ownership was the primary issue on the agenda.

After sunset on November 2, 1691, seventeen church members gathered at the parsonage to meet with Parris. There was a rift forming between a majority of voters in the village who were upset about the suspicious transfer of the parsonage, and Parris, who was supported on this issue by only a small minority in the village. According to the church record book, Parris told the gathered church members, "I have not much to trouble you with now; but you know what Committee, the last town-meeting here, were chosen; and what they have done, or intend to do, it may be [that you know] better than I. But you see I have hardly any wood to burn."[129] After the meeting, Parris wrote the words he had just spoken into the church record book in the chilly upstairs study of the parsonage.

At this church meeting in the parsonage, only seventeen of the twenty-seven male church members attended and the meeting was an hour and a half late to start, which can hardly be seen as a show of support and solidarity for their minister. Those present voted to send a delegation to request that the village committee raise a tax to support the minister. On November 10, the church members met again to hear the report of the messengers, but only three other church members showed up along with Parris, one of whom was Thomas Putnam Jr.[130] It is noteworthy that so few church members attended these meetings that dealt with a near-existential crisis for their pastor.

The situation grew even colder at the next meeting of the church members on November 18 at Nathaniel Putnam's house, near the Nurse farm.[131] At the meeting, Parris chastised the church members who were present (the record does not say how many were there that day) for their lack of attendance at previous church meetings. Then, those present voted to sue the village committee for not collecting taxes (even though it was a majority of the voters at the last village meeting that decided not to collect the tax, not a vote of the committee). During these discussions, the church record book notes that "the Pastor desired the brethren that care might be taken that he might not be destitute of wood," and Parris told the group that he "had scarce wood enough to burn till the morrow, and prayed that some care might be taken."[132] As the wind became frosty and knocked the brown leaves from the trees, Parris' situation became even more cold and desperate.

The blowback from the suspicious attempt to transfer the parsonage ownership was strong, and the minister became increasingly isolated. Parris' deteriorating mood can be seen in his sermons, which deal with betrayal and fighting enemies. On November 22 Parris preached on Psalm 110: "The Lord said unto my Lord, sit thou at my right hand until I make thine enemies a footstool."[133] Parris' sermons between November 1691 and February 1692, the crucial months leading into the witch hunt, contained the overarching theme of war between the church and Satan.[134] Even before the setback over the parsonage ownership, Judas Iscariot and betrayal had long been common themes in Parris' sermons, and he also focused on the lower points of Jesus' life in a series of sermons on the life of Christ preached during the years leading up to 1692.[135] As the fall days grew darker, the recent challenge by the majority vote at the village meeting could only exacerbate Parris' fear of betrayal.

The controversy reached new heights in the following weeks. The village record book has a warrant for a village meeting called for December 1, 1691. The warrant, signed by Francis Nurse and the other members of the village committee, announced that the meeting's purpose was "to consider of a vote in the book on the 10 of October 1689 wherein our right in the ministry house and land seems to be impaired and made void: also to consider about our ministry house and two acres of land given to Mr. Parris."[136] Additionally, the village meeting would again debate payment to Parris, this time either "by voluntary contributions or by subscription," since levying a tax was voted down at the previous meeting.[137] Finally, the meeting also was to examine a vote approving Parris' original contract that occurred in June 1689, but for which there was no warrant in the record book, like the meeting with the contested parsonage vote.

There is no entry in the village record book recording the results of this crucial December meeting, nor is there any mention of this meeting in the village church book, which jumps from an entry dated November 18, 1691, to one dated March 27, 1692, in the midst of the witch hunt. It is therefore uncertain if this December meeting actually occurred, though there is a later deposition that seems to describe this meeting and it deals with Parris' contract in a way that logically fits here in the chain of events.[138]

The later deposition that possibly describes this village meeting was written in 1697 by three men—Joseph Porter, Daniel Andrew, and Joseph Putnam—who were on the 1691 village committee with Francis Nurse (who died prior to the writing of the deposition). The document describes a village meeting during which a group of villagers "desired those things [that] concerned Mr. Parris and the people might be read, and accordingly it was. And the entry, that some call a salary, being read, there arose a difference among the people." The page of the village record book that was read was the June 1689 contract with Parris—a topic on the warrant for the December meeting—which gave Parris the *use* of the parsonage but not ownership. After hearing the contract read, some at the village meeting "replied that they believed that Mr. Parris would not comply with the entry." Then, one villager suggested that Parris be called to the village meeting, and the minister subsequently arrived. The June 1689 contract was again read in Parris' presence, and the deposition records Parris' response: "His answer was as follows: 'He never heard or knew anything of it, neither could or would he take up with it, or any part of it.'" The deposition then notes that Parris called the villagers who wrote the contract "knaves and cheaters."[139]

Nathaniel Putnam, a founding member of the village church, the first to sign the church covenant right under Parris' own signature, and in whose home the village church met that November, was the moderator of the village meeting that day. After Parris' last comment, Putnam declared, "Sir, then there is only proposals on both sides, and no agreement between you and the people." Parris replied, "No more, there is not; for I am free from the people, and the people free from me."[140] After this announcement, the village meeting ended. There was no longer a contract for the village government to pay Parris' salary, yet as the ordained permanent minister he remained the pastor of the village church and could only be removed by a vote of the church members.

Parris' overzealous supporters' plan to secretly dispossess Salem Village and give him ownership of the parsonage backfired, and now it was unclear who actually owned the house in which he lived. Significant portions of the village now opposed Parris continuing as minister under his contract, as the village meeting votes show. Support for Parris continued to dwindle, as is seen in a significant drop in baptisms and applications for church membership following November 1691.[141] If his previous statements about being out of firewood were true, the Parris family was also on the verge of freezing to death.

As the winter days darkened and the temperature dropped, Parris spent the frigid winter with no certain income or firewood supply, huddled in the parsonage with his family. It was in this anxious, desperate, and uncomfortable parsonage that Betty Parris and Abigail Williams began having strange fits and soon became the first to allegedly be afflicted by witchcraft in Salem Village.

Part II

FIVE

THE DEVIL HATH BEEN RAISED

Farewell, happy fields,
Where joy forever dwells! Hail, horrors! hail,
Infernal World! and thou, profoundest Hell,
Receive thy new possessor—one who brings
A mind not to be changed by place or time.
The mind is its own place, and in itself
Can make a Heaven of Hell, a Hell of Heaven!
—John Milton, *Paradise Lost* (1667)

REV. SAMUEL PARRIS FACED THE CROWDED, cold meetinghouse. "Christ has placed His Church in this world, as in a sea, and suffers many storms and tempests to threaten its shipwreck," he declared.[1] Parris' voice was absorbed by the rapt audience that huddled against the cruel cold that day. He later cut his afternoon sermon short due to the inhospitable temperature in the meetinghouse.[2] It was the first Sabbath of 1692, and the villagers attended the service as they did each Sunday, not knowing what evil the new year would bring to their little community.

Sometime between January 16 and 19, it began. Betty Parris and Abigail Williams suddenly became ill and had seizure-like fits.[3] Nine-year-old Betty Parris was the minister's daughter. Eleven-year-old Williams is described as Parris' niece, and although she lived with the Parris family her true relationship to the family is unclear. In the seventeenth century, "niece" was a more generic term for a familial relationship.[4]

These two girls climbed into holes, crawled under furniture, and struck "sundry odd postures and antic gestures, uttering foolish, ridiculous speeches, which neither they themselves nor any others could make sense of."[5] They folded themselves into contortions that were nearly impossible for a human being to accomplish. One witness wrote, "Their motions in their fits are preternatural, both as to the manner, which is so strange as a well person could not screw their body into; and as to the violence also it is preternatural, being much beyond the ordinary force of the same person when they are in their right mind."[6] Rev. John Hale of Beverly added, "These children were bitten and pinched by invisible agents; their arms, necks, and backs turned this way and that way, and returned back again, so as it was impossible for them to do of themselves, and beyond the power of any epileptic fits, or natural disease to affect. Sometimes they were taken dumb, their mouths stopped, their throats choked, their limbs wracked and tormented so as might move a heart of stone."[7] They appeared to suffer in frightening ways.

The two girls' fits continued, interrupting the daily routine in the parsonage. The other children of the Parris household, Thomas (age ten) and Susannah (age three), were never mentioned as having fits or being unwell. It appears that only Betty Parris and Abigail Williams acted in this way.[8] Parris, his wife Elizabeth, the other children, and the family's Native slaves Tituba and John Indian could only watch in fright as the terrifying fits continued.

A MESSENGER GALLOPED down the Ipswich Road that ran through the Nurse farm, headed for Boston. He carried a letter from Rev. George Burroughs, the former village minister who now preached in Maine. Burroughs' message described horrific slaughter on the frontier: "Pillars of smoke, the raging and merciless flames, the insults of the heathen enemy, shouting, hacking (not having regard to the earnest supplication of men, women, or children, with sharp cries and bitter tears in the most humble manner), and dragging away others."[9] Burroughs attributed this hell on earth to divine retribution.

On the snowy morning of January 25, the Puritan minister of York, Maine, Rev. Shubael Dummer, started his day as any other. As he walked out his door to greet the day and began to mount his horse, there was a bang and he dropped dead on the ground. Neighbors heard the gunshot and ran to the fortified blockhouses in the town. Many did not make it in time. The French and Abenaki warriors killed fifty men, women, and children in their first charge into the town.[10]

Devout Puritans believed that Satan was "daily walking to and fro compassing the Earth" and constantly searching for "a new way to stop (if it were possible) this work of reformation."[11] None would have wondered why York's Puritan minister—the leader of their one true faith—was the first victim in a war against the French Catholics and Abenaki pagans. Rev. Dummer, though, had been unwilling to return French and Abenaki prisoners of war after previous battles, which is why he was the Abenaki's first target. His lifeless body was stripped and hacked apart.[12]

News of this tragedy traveled fast—it reached Boston the next day, and Salem Village probably around the same time.[13] The tales of horror shocked those in Massachusetts, and the Salem Town church collected money for the survivors.[14] The bloodbath at York was frightening, yet more terrors were to come.

In THE VILLAGE, Abigail Williams' and Betty Parris' fits continued as the winter weather howled outside. Rev. Parris initially thought that these members of his household were possessed, and he tried to treat the fits with prayer and fasting. For weeks, Betty Parris' and Williams' frightening fits continued, but Rev. Parris initially attempted to keep it within the walls of his own home. Writing two months later, he stated that it "was several weeks before such hellish operations as witchcraft was suspected."[15] Parris' attempt to quietly help the girls without mention of witchcraft at this early stage casts doubt on the theory that the witch hunt was a conspiracy orchestrated by Rev. Parris and others from the start.[16]

After weeks of fear and worry, Parris called multiple doctors to examine the suffering children. According to Rev. Hale of Beverly, these many doctors ruled out "epileptic fits" as a cause of their symptoms, among other possibilities.[17] The actions of the two girls did not fit with any known ailments, and once a medical explanation was eliminated by this congress of doctors they looked for alternative explanations.

Hale later wrote, "At length one physician gave his opinion, that they were under an Evil Hand. This the neighbors quickly took up, and concluded that they were bewitched."[18] This "one physician" is traditionally considered to be Dr. William Griggs, the local doctor.[19] It appeared that Satan no longer dwelled only on the frontier, the blood-drenched borderlands between the Puritans, the Catholic French, and the pagan Natives, between the light of the City upon a Hill and the perceived darkness of the wooded north. Now, Satan dwelt in Salem Village—and in the minister's house, no less.

IN THE SEVENTEENTH CENTURY, a "witch" was not the same as the Hollywood image of a witch in American culture today, and has no connection to the recent Wiccan movement of alternative spirituality, which is a recently invented tradition. In terms of language, "witch" was a word that applied to both men and women in early modern times, though the vast majority of suspected witches in seventeenth-century New England were women.[20]

A witch was a person believed to have signed a written contract with the Devil. This contract was an agreement whereby the person transferred his or her allegiance from God to Satan, and agreed to do his bidding and join him in his war against the Kingdom of Heaven and Christ's church on earth. The supposed witches were believed to have access to the Devil's preternatural powers to help him or her in his war against God, but also for the witch to use in his or her own personal life—perhaps to gain the witch earthly success, or to exact revenge on a neighbor who had mistreated him or her in the past. It was believed that the powers given to a witch allowed him or her to torture, pinch, prick, bruise, convulse, and choke their victims, in addition to causing disease and killing them.[21]

A witch was also thought able to appear as a "specter"—an apparition of the witch that appeared at locations different than where the witch actually was. This belief in specters proved particularly important during the witch hunt, because it was used to discredit all alibis. Even if an accused person had witnesses verifying their whereabouts when one of the afflicted claimed that they were being harmed by witchcraft, such an alibi was meaningless because the witch did not need to be physically present in order to do witchcraft—he or she could have sent their specter to do it. Additionally, it was soon assumed that the Devil could only appear in the shape of witches—those who consented for him to use his or her shape—and not in the shape of innocent persons.[22] Therefore, if someone saw a specter of a neighbor, it meant that the neighbor must necessarily be a witch in order for that specter to exist. Since the accusers were believed to be telling the truth, such claims of seeing one's specter were considered strong evidence that the accused was a witch.

Contrary to how they are often portrayed, witch hunts are a modern phenomenon, and more of a product of modern fears and anxieties than medieval superstitions. Parliament did not make witchcraft a capital crime in England until 1542, after the Reformation was under way and only one year before the scientific revolution began when Nicolaus Copernicus published his heliocentric theory. Although the contemporary reader likely scoffs at belief in witchcraft, this belief crossed all levels of seventeenth-century society, including well-educated scientists and philosophers in addition to the masses in Europe, North America, and beyond. The codification of witchcraft into the laws of many European states, both Catholic and Protestant, reveals the wide extent of this belief in diabolical magic.[23]

Back in England, intellectuals from all backgrounds believed in witchcraft. Sir Francis Bacon, whose skeptical methodology and writings on inductive reasoning led to the development of the scientific method, believed that witchcraft could be used as evidence in an empirical scientific sense, and he sought to scientifically study how witches manipulated nature.[24] In addition to his intellectual pursuits, Bacon served as Attorney General of England under James I who markedly changed English witchcraft law. Similarly, Sir Robert Boyle, the scientific luminary who is known as the first modern chemist, publicly discussed his belief in witchcraft at least as late as 1678.[25]

Although alleged spectral magic believed to be done by witches is likely seen by the modern reader as superstition, it was connected with the development of modern science. Rather than a conflict between belief in witchcraft and belief in science, belief in witchcraft was for some in the seventeenth century a scientific belief.

Rev. Cotton Mather, one of the leading ministers of Boston who is often faulted for his strong belief in spectral evidence, was a medical student prior to becoming a minister, and historian Sarah Rivett describes Mather's use of empiricism when examining the actions of the afflicted accusers as being in accord with the methods of the leading scientific thinkers of the day.[26] Rivett also notes that in the preface of Mather's *Memorable Providences Relating to Witchcraft and Possessions* (1689) he directly references Sir Robert Boyle's empiricist methods for scientifically ascertaining the truth.

Mather believed that the so-called invisible world of specters could be examined and explained through observation and controlled experimentation—the foundation of modern science. Mather's beliefs and methods for trying to prove spectral affliction aligned with many of Boyle's methods of experimental physiology, and Mather ran experiments such as the touch test—during which an afflicted person touched an accuser who then invariably had an immediate fit. He noted how when the eyes of the accused rested on the afflicted they immediately had a fit. The admission and examination of spectral evidence began as science but quickly devolved into poor science. Rivett notes, "It remains modernity's shadow that unchecked inquiry can lead to bad science as well as bad religion, each with its accompanying tendencies towards violent domination."[27] It is easy to look dismissively upon those who attempted to use spectral evidence in a scientific manner, but in an age in which all sorts of natural phenomena that once seemed magical were being explored and accepted as science, it is only logical that witchcraft was approached this way too.

In fact, scholars who denied the existence of witchcraft suffered ridicule from their fellow academics. In 1669, John Wagstaffe of Oxford University published *The Question of Witchcraft Debated, or a Discourse Against Their Opinions that Affirm Witches*.[28] In response, other scholars published pamphlets attacking Wagstaffe's claim that witchcraft did not exist, and Wagstaffe was himself accused of witchcraft. His career over, Wagstaffe drank himself to death.[29]

English monarchs likewise believed in witchcraft. In particular, James I amplified this fear, and his actions later affected those accused of witchcraft in Salem Village in 1692. Previously, as king of Scotland, he had authorized torture to produce confessions from those accused of witchcraft. In England, witchcraft accusations and trials increased with his ascension to the English throne in 1603. The following year James I had Parliament pass a new stricter law against witchcraft, the one under which all subsequent accused witches in England were prosecuted and the one that was used in Massachusetts in 1692. The 1604 Witchcraft Act called for execution by hanging for anyone convicted of malefic witchcraft, and added the idea of a witch's pact with the Devil into law.[30] Once the idea of a pact with the Devil was codified, an accused witch could be legally convicted with far less evidence, whereas previously an accused witch could only be convicted if a jury was convinced that the accused used witchcraft to commit murder. This significant change led to an increased number of accusations and trials.

After the middle of the seventeenth century, the witchcraft panic abated on the Continent, where trials were conducted primarily by professional inquisitors away from the public eye. In England, however, the frenzy continued a little while longer because the English justice system had one feature that many trials on the Continent lacked: the publicity and sensationalism of a public jury trial.[31] English witch trials were public spectacles that further fanned the flames of fear, as is later seen in Massachusetts. In 1682—a decade before the Salem Village witch hunt—the last execution for witchcraft in England occurred at Devon, ending a period of time in English history when approximately 500 people were tried for witchcraft, and 112 executed.[32]

Excluding the 1692 witch hunt, 93 persons were accused of witchcraft in New England during the seventeenth century.[33] From the 1650s on there was a strong unwillingness by the Massachusetts authorities to prosecute or even believe these accusations. That changed in 1692.

ON FEBRUARY 25, 1692, the day after Dr. Griggs diagnosed the two girls as afflicted by something evil, Rev. Parris was out of town attending a sermon at another church. In his absence, Mary Sibley—Parris' neighbor and a village church member—went over to the parsonage with an idea of her own. She instructed Parris' slaves Tituba and John Indian to bake a "witch cake."[34]

This English white magic concoction supposedly would reveal whoever was using evil powers to harm the afflicted. It consisted of a loaf of rye bread, with an unusual ingredient: the urine of the afflicted girls. Those present then fed this creation to the Parris' dog, and upon the cake being eaten the identity of the witch was supposed to be revealed. This was the closest thing to witchcraft done in Salem Village in 1692, and it was done by a church member under the minister's own roof.[35] Despite this scheme, Sibley was herself never accused of witchcraft.

Initially after the doctor's diagnosis, the afflicted did not accuse anyone of causing their fits, though, they soon became a public spectacle. Many in the village, Salem Town, and surrounding towns went to see the girls in their fits, but Rebecca Nurse did not.[36] When later asked about not visiting the afflicted, Nurse said that she had not thought it wise to visit because she feared that some of her own previous "fits"—health issues—from which she suffered earlier in life might be reawakened.[37]

Friends and neighbors of the Parris family frequently visited the parsonage to see the afflicted girls. It is likely that Thomas and Ann Putnam were among those who visited as they were friends and supporters of Parris. Their daughter, Ann Putnam Jr., later stated that the day of the witch cake she had fits and was visited by a specter that tortured her "most grievously" and tried to get her to sign the Devil's book. Likewise, Elizabeth Hubbard—niece of Dr. Griggs who diagnosed the sufferers as being afflicted—began to have strange and wild fits.[38] Putnam and Hubbard lived in other parts of the village, away from the parsonage in the village center. The affliction was spreading.

REV. PARRIS, who probably felt overwhelmed and helpless to stop the continuing fits of his daughter and niece, invited some neighboring ministers and "worthy gentlemen from Salem" to visit the parsonage and observe the two girls on February 26, the day after the witch cake incident.[39] Rev. Hale of Beverly was among those present. Although no records mention the names of the others, it is supposed that the group also included Rev. Nicholas Noyes of Salem Town and Stephen Sewall of Salem Town, who later became the clerk of the witch trials court.[40] The gentlemen interviewed Tituba, who confessed that she baked the witch cake. Hale records that she also claimed that "her [former] mistress in her own country was a witch," but "she said that she herself was not a witch."[41] It is interesting that Tituba mentions her former owner in the Caribbean, but not Sibley who taught her the witch cake method. Sibley was found out soon enough.

Despite Tituba denying that she was a witch, the gathered group now suspected her of afflicting the two girls in the Parris household. Parris' friends concluded, like Dr. Griggs, that the fits of the afflicted were probably caused by something unnatural and "feared the hand of Satan was in them." Their advice to Parris was to "sit still and wait upon the Providence of God to see what time might discover."[42] They did not act on their suspicions, but others did.

Ann Putnam Jr. later reported that on February 27 a specter appeared to her again to torture her and that "she told me her name was Sarah Good and then she did prick me and pinch me most grievously." The specter then allegedly tried to get her to sign the Devil's book and become a witch also. Elizabeth Hubbard later claimed that while she was walking to the house of her uncle Dr. Griggs that same day, Sarah Good transformed into a wolf and followed her as she walked across the village. Hubbard also claimed that Sarah Osborne, another village woman, tormented her that day by "pricking and pinching" her "most dreadfully."[43] Hubbard's accusations were particularly important because the previously afflicted girls were too young to legally testify, but Hubbard, age seventeen, was old enough and her accusation bore legal weight.[44]

The next few days saw further fits by the four afflicted, and as they screamed and convulsed the weather took a turn for the worse. Storms in Boston prevented the governor from attending the Sabbath service, and elsewhere in New England there was a storm of rain and lightning that "destroyed many cattle in the meadows, carried away some houses, and washed away in many places the very land with the English grain sown in it."[45] In Salem Village, the combination of heavy rains and high tide caused the rivers to flow backward, inundating low-lying fields and turning the freshwater streams to saltwater.

It was on February 29, a dark day with lightning flashes and booming thunder, that the screams and contortions of Ann Putnam Jr., Elizabeth Hubbard, Betty Parris, and Abigail Williams reached such a pitch that four men in the village decided to act on the words of these four young women. They trekked through the savage storm and down the flooded paths to Salem Town to lodge the first formal accusations of witchcraft.

IN THOSE DAYS, to report suspicion of a crime an individual would make a formal accusation to a local justice of the peace, also called a magistrate. In the case where a child was the victim of a crime, the complaint could be filed by an adult. Once a formal complaint was made, the magistrate issued an arrest warrant that required the accused person to be brought to a preliminary hearing before the local magistrates. Normally, those who filed legal criminal accusations needed to post a bond to show that they were serious with following through on the charges. It is not known why, but this procedure was not followed for witchcraft accusations in 1692.[46] Forgoing the bond requirement likely increased the number of accusations made, because the accusers could file complaints with no strings attached.

The first three formal accusations of witchcraft, against Sarah Good, Sarah Osborne, and Tituba, had no inkling of village factionalism. Four men filed the accusations because the early afflicted accusers—who were women and minors—had no legal standing to do so themselves.[47] The four men who filed the complaints were Thomas Putnam (father of Ann Jr.), Edward Putnam (uncle and neighbor of Ann Jr.), Joseph Hutchinson, and Thomas Preston (Rebecca Nurse's son-in-law)—who never could have guessed how the evil of the witch hunt would later affect his own family. In a perhaps surprising way, these accusations were a show of unity from men who came from three different families from different areas of the village. But this unity was soon fractured, as seen when Thomas Putnam and Edward Putnam later testified against Rebecca Nurse, while Hutchinson and Preston defended her.

The arrest warrants issued by the magistrates state that the four men "made complaint on behalf of Their Majesties" against Sarah Good, Sarah Osborne, and Tituba for "suspicion of witchcraft, by them committed, and thereby much injury done."[48] Many more warrants would follow.

THE NEXT MORNING, March 1, the weather cleared.[49] Although the first witchcraft accusations are seen as very significant by historians today, to

those in 1692 at first they looked no different than other isolated witchcraft accusations in New England history. Rev. John Higginson, Rebecca
Nurse's minister in Salem Town, later wrote that at this point the incident
"was very small, and looked at first as an ordinary case which had fallen
out before at several times in other places, and would be quickly over."[50]
In prior instances of New England witchcraft accusations, only one or
two people were accused. But the preliminary hearings of the first three
accused in 1692 showed that something much different was happening
in Salem Village.

The three women were arrested and taken to Ingersoll's tavern and
then to their hearings in the Salem Village meetinghouse, presided over
by magistrates John Hathorne and Jonathan Corwin who rode in from
Salem Town.[51] Rebecca Nurse did not attend, but it is highly likely that
Francis Nurse and her sons were there, because a village town meeting
was scheduled for right after the hearing and Francis was required to
make a report on his negotiations with Salem Town for greater village autonomy.[52] Also, since son-in-law Thomas Preston was among those who
filed the formal accusations, he presumably attended the hearings.

Sarah Good, Sarah Osborne, and Tituba were each easy targets for a
witchcraft accusation, because all three women had details in their past
that made them more suspicious to their neighbors.[53] Tituba was a Native
slave from Barbados, not originally a Puritan, and was the domestic slave
in Rev. Parris' household where the first two afflicted girls began acting
strangely.[54] Sarah Good was a middle-aged woman and a pipe-smoker,
who had a tempestuous relationship with her husband, William Good.
The Goods did not have a home of their own, and Sarah was a beggar
who went door to door. On at least one occasion she was heard suspiciously muttering while walking away from the parsonage after asking for
alms.[55] Sarah Osborne was an older sickly woman who, after her first husband died, scandalously married her servant. There was also a disputed
inheritance between Osborne and the children she had with her first husband.[56]

At the three women's hearings, the afflicted wailed, accused the women
of hurting them, contorted themselves, claimed to see specters, and
claimed that these women were causing them the great pains that they
appeared to be having. Magistrate John Hathorne recorded that the accusers were "dreadfully tortured and tormented."[57] Sarah Good professed
her innocence, and there was not yet any substantiated evidence that
witchcraft had been committed. But Good then changed tactics and
claimed before the magistrates and crowd that it was Sarah Osborne who

committed witchcraft against the children, as a way to deflect suspicion away from herself. As historian Bernard Rosenthal notes, in effect, at that moment, Good became an accuser and there was now legal testimony from an adult corroborating the accusations from the young accusers against Osborne.[58]

At the end of her hearing, Good was sent to jail to await trial, along with an infant baby in her arms. On her way to the jail in Ipswich, the guard reported that Good "leapt off her horse three times," denied the charges against her, "continued railing against the magistrate, and she endeavored to kill herself."[59] The guards then brought Osborne forward. She denied any knowledge of witchcraft, but she too was sent to jail to await trial.[60]

Tituba's actions during her hearing, and during her second interrogation the next day, were significant for the witch hunt as a whole, and for Rebecca Nurse's case in particular. During Tituba's public hearing in the meetinghouse she painted a wild tale of mysterious figures that she said she saw come to the parsonage to afflict Betty Parris and Abigail Williams. Tituba first began by denying everything, including that she had ever hurt the two girls, but by the end of her two hearings she corroborated nearly all that she and the other women were accused of.[61] Tituba falsely confessed to witchcraft and admitted to hurting both Betty Parris and Abigail Williams, though claiming that she was pressured to do so by the other alleged witches. Moreover, instead of just pinching and pricking the afflicted, Tituba said that Osborne and Good wanted her to kill Ann Putnam Jr.[62] This confession lent credibility to the accusations.

Tituba's is a striking confession from one who initially said that she was innocent. Rev. Hale wrote that when Tituba was questioned she had wounds on her body, which were attributed to the Devil.[63] One contemporary critic of the witch hunt later claimed that Rev. Parris "did beat her and otherways abuse her" into confessing.[64] In general, she seems to have made up her confession as she went along based on the questions the magistrates asked, and simply told them what they seemed to want to hear.[65] As a slave who knew that she was in front of important men, telling them what they wanted to hear might have been a self-preservation measure.

Tituba went on to mention fantastic spiritual creatures, including one that was "sometimes like a hog and sometimes like a great dog," along with red cats and black cats that asked her to serve Satan. She claimed that she and other witches "ride upon sticks" and said that she had seen "a thing with a head like a woman with two legs and wings"—at which point Abigail Williams chimed in that she too had seen this weird amalgamation, and that it transformed into Sarah Osborne.[66] It was noted that Tituba's statements matched up almost exactly with the accusations made by the four afflicted accusers.[67]

Tituba's false statements began a disturbing pattern of people falsely confessing to a crime that was imaginary. In total fifty-five persons falsely confessed to witchcraft in 1692, and each one seemingly added legitimacy to the erroneous process.[68] Rev. Hale later noted their importance: "The success of Tituba's confession encouraged those in authority to examine others who were suspected, and the event was, that more confessed themselves guilty of the crimes they were suspected for. And thus was this matter driven on."[69] The crowd of villagers and spectators from other towns that crammed in the pews and galleries of the meetinghouse heard the frightening description of alleged witchcraft, saw the fits of the afflicted accusers, and heard a member of the minister's own household confess to using witchcraft to hurt the very children that she was supposed to care for. It was now hard for them to doubt that something evil gathered in Salem Village.

Significantly for Rebecca Nurse, as part of her confession Tituba described a wider Satanic plot that included "four women" besides her who "sometimes hurt the children" and a "tall man of Boston" with black clothes and white hair who joined them. Later, when privately questioned by the magistrates, she upped the number of yet-to-be-caught witches to nine.[70] Tituba's claim that there were still more witches to be identified is an important turning point and all but ensured that more accusations would follow.[71] Tituba named Sarah Good and Sarah Osborne as two of the witches, but that left two other women yet unaccounted for in the village, and one man in Boston who appeared to be their leader—or even the Devil himself. The crowd was faced with the possibility that two of their friends, neighbors, or family members might be among the unidentified witches—perhaps they were even gathered in that very meetinghouse.

Walking by the meetinghouse later that night, three men heard a "strange noise not usually heard," the sound of which came closer, closer, and closer to them in the dark night so that they were "affrighted" by it. When they moved toward the noise they saw an "unusual beast" lying on the ground which vanished, and in its place appeared to them the three accused women who were sent to jail in chains earlier that day.[72] It was not just young women seeing specters, but grown men too. Only time would tell whose specter would be seen next.

In the days following Tituba's hearing, she took the accusations up another notch by claiming that witchcraft killed Rev. Deodat Lawson's wife and daughter years earlier when he was the village minister.[73] The idea that people were murdered by witchcraft, along with her claim that there were at least two other still unidentified witches in the village, heightened fear in the community.

Throughout the village, the public hearings and Tituba's confession were the talk of the town. Rebecca Nurse, though she did not attend the hearings, heard reports of them, presumably from her husband and children.[74]

Although three accused witches were in custody, the accusers' fits continued unabated. In response, Parris invited other ministers to his house to pray on March 11. The witchcraft—according to Tituba—was widespread, and therefore one minister alone could not confront such a threat. The ministers prayed with the afflicted, during which the victims seemed calm, but as soon as the prayers ended and the spiritual defense was gone they broke out into fits anew.[75] A private day of fasting was also held at the parsonage, and then later a day of fasting for the whole village. There were also days of "public humiliation" held in the village and at other neighboring churches to make amends for whatever sin caused witchcraft to be let loose in Massachusetts.[76]

Rev. Cotton Mather in Boston even offered to take the afflicted into his home to isolate them, and to pray and fast with them. In 1688 when children in the Goodwin family in Boston appeared to be afflicted and then accused Ann Glover of witchcraft, Mather took those children in and they eventually recovered, likely due to being in a different environment. However, Mather's similar offer in 1692 was declined.[77] Although the afflicted were not sent to Boston, Parris did send his afflicted daughter Betty to live with Stephen Sewall's family in Salem Town, where she recovered and no longer played a role in the witch hunt.[78] Her recovery shows that if the other afflicted accusers had left the village and were isolated from one another, the witch hunt could have taken a very different course.

It is curious that Parris sent his daughter out of the village, but not his niece Abigail Williams.[79] By inviting ministers, doctors, and others into the parsonage yet not removing all of the afflicted accusers from the community, word of their afflictions continued to spread. Because the afflicted stayed in contact, it allowed those who genuinely believed in their affliction to reinforce this belief in one another.[80] The three afflicted who remained in Salem Village continued to have fits, even more villagers claimed to be afflicted, and soon yet another witch was named.

On March 12, Ann Putnam Jr. claimed that she saw the specter of Martha Corey. This accusation against Corey was soon added to by newly afflicted Mary Warren, the twenty-year-old servant of John Proctor.[81] Corey was a member of the village church and the third wife of Giles Corey, who was previously suspected of murdering his mentally challenged neighbor, Jacob Goodell. Francis Nurse and son-in-law Thomas Preston served on the coroner's jury for the investigation in 1676.[82] In the past Giles Corey was also accused of stealing from Judge Jonathan Corwin's father, setting fire to John Proctor's house, and allegedly sending invisible horses to chase a neighbor off of his farm.[83] Before her life with Giles Corey, Martha had her own history that inspired gossip: while married to her previous husband in Salem Town she had given birth to a mixed-race son.[84]

The Sabbath service on March 13 was interrupted by outbursts from those who claimed to be afflicted, which now included middle-aged Bethshua Pope, who sensationally claimed to have been struck totally blind during the service and clasped her hands over her eyes so tight that her arms could not be pried from her face.[85] At home after the service, Ann Putnam Jr. told her family that during her fits she saw a new, yet-to-be-identified specter. The "apparition" was vaguely familiar to her, and she later testified that "she did not know what her name was then, though I knew where she used to sit in our meetinghouse." Several of those present in the Putnams' house suggested names to Ann Jr. before she identified the specter: it was Rebecca Nurse.[86]

HISTORIANS AND WRITERS have been puzzled for centuries as to what caused the fits that began with two girls in the parsonage and then spread to seventy individuals of different ages and backgrounds, from several different communities.[87] With such varied cases, one must assume that there were a variety of factors that caused the fits.

Of all the witchcraft accusers throughout New England history who were considered to be "possessed" or "afflicted," 86 percent were women.[88] There were also many male accusers during this period, but few men ever claimed to be "afflicted" as the accusers in 1692 were. Of all of the allegedly "possessed" or "afflicted" accusers in New England from 1620 to 1725, 69 percent were between the ages of ten and twenty-nine and 68 percent were single.[89] In 1692 the main afflicted accusers were single young women, which fits this trend. It was primarily women accusing women during the 1692 witch hunt—though they needed their husbands or male family members to file the legal paperwork.

Many theories have been suggested to explain what caused the fits that the afflicted accusers appeared to suffer in 1692, and these theories tend to fall into two categories: mental or physical illness (therefore meaning that the fits and symptoms of the afflicted were genuine), or intentional deception (in which case the fits and symptoms were faked). The original outbreak was likely based on mental illness, but as the case against Rebecca Nurse progressed, her accusers used intentional deception and fraudulent evidence.

As to mental illness as a cause of the fits, some writers such as Marion L. Starkey claim that the actions of all of the afflicted can be explained by "hysteria," while most scholars view mental illness as playing a role for some of the accusers but not fully explaining the fits of all of the allegedly afflicted accusers.[90] Emerson W. Baker notes that conversion disorder is likely the cause of some of the initial fits.[91] This disorder was first discovered by Sigmund Freud, and it describes a condition when mental stress and anxiety are converted into physical symptoms. Stress can be converted into physical symptoms as common as nail-biting, knots in the stomach, and sweaty palms, or as severe as debilitating motor and verbal tics, blindness, numbness, paralysis, and fits.[92]

There are several sources of stress that may have caused the disorder. Of the twenty-four young female afflicted accusers in 1692 who were over the age of sixteen but still single, seventeen had lost at least one parent.[93] Moreover, afflicted accusers Abigail Hobbs, Mercy Lewis, Susannah Sheldon, and Sarah Churchill were war refugees from the frontier who witnessed atrocities—Lewis, Churchill, and Sheldon's parents were brutally killed by Natives—and they may have suffered from posttraumatic stress disorder.[94] Historian Peter Charles Hoffer describes several of these early afflicted accusers as "emotional tinderboxes" due to what they previously suffered.[95]

Those in Rev. Parris' household were also under stress, for the family did not have enough wood to fully heat the house and the family was not even sure who owned their home. The children likely saw this stress in their parents, which led them to be the first afflicted. As if wartime atrocities and freezing families were not enough, the addition of sermons about war between Satan and the church that Parris began preaching at the end of 1691, and an outbreak of smallpox in 1691—a frightening and incurable illness—surely heightened tensions.[96]

Along with the above stressors, Hoffer also proposes that some of the accusers suffered from psychological effects stemming from child abuse, and in the cases of the older teenage accusers such as Mercy Lewis, potentially sexual abuse. However, there is simply not enough evidence to make this determination with confidence.[97] In particular, Hoffer suggests that perhaps Betty Parris, one of the first to have fits, was an abused child. Her actions fit the broad symptoms of emotional maltreatment syndrome, which affects those suffering from verbal abuse. Separating her from the abusive environment would have stopped the syndrome's symptoms, and she did indeed recover once she was sent to live with Stephen Sewall and freed from the parsonage environment.[98] But, after the witch hunt she returned home and there is no record of the fits recurring, as would occur when one returns to the environment that previously caused the symptoms.

Conversion disorder, or rather its symptoms, can on occasion spread to others who do not have the illness through a condition colloquially called "mass hysteria," though now more commonly termed mass psychogenic illness. Essentially, other people in close proximity to the one who is originally ill begin to act similarly, as if they had the same condition, often assuming that it was somehow contagious or caused by an environmental factor that they assume they were also exposed to. Though not fully understood, half of recent known cases occurred in schools, and the majority of victims were young women—which fits the demographics of the early afflicted in 1692. Such an epidemic often begins among higher social groups and moves downward, and Baker points out that the first two afflicted in 1692 were the daughter and niece of the minister, who could be perceived as having the highest social status in Salem Village. He also notes that those afflicted soon afterward were Ann Putnam Jr. and Mrs. Ann Putnam, members of a leading village family, and Mary Walcott, whose father was the leader of the village militia.[99]

The most famous recent example of mass psychogenic illness occurred at a school in Le Roy, New York, in 2011. In total eighteen individuals suffered from fit-like symptoms, and in a crowded room the cry from one of the sufferers would set off the others and cause them to come down in fits.[100] An even more recent case occurred during the winter of 2012–2013 at the Essex Agricultural High School ("Essex Aggie") in Danvers, Massachusetts, and the North Shore Technical High School in neighboring Middleton, Massachusetts, both regional public technical high schools. This case is interesting because both schools are in the area formerly known as Salem Village, and Essex Aggie—where most of the students who exhibited symptoms attended—is near the former site of Thomas and Ann Putnam's farm.

In this instance, one student had a vocal disorder, including vocal tics and hiccups, that spread to more and more students, until about two dozen showed symptoms. The affected were between the ages of fifteen and eighteen, and all but one were female.[101] The Massachusetts Department of Public Health investigated and ruled out any environment factors, and after searching through medical records found no common factors that could cause the symptoms.[102] Although the state did not officially determine what caused the symptoms, it is suggested that it was mass psychogenic illness, and that this temporary mental illness spread the symptoms when there was no physical reason—nor prior psychological disorder—that caused them in the students other than the initial one who had a vocal tic.[103]

One aspect of such outbreaks is that attention on the sufferers can exacerbate the symptoms. During the Essex Aggie incident the media were essentially stonewalled by both town and state health officials: media reports were questioned and little information was released in an attempt to downplay and minimize coverage of the event in the hope that decreasing attention would help the students recover more quickly.[104] But, the previous Le Roy incident was widely reported in all forms of media, with television trucks parked along the town's main street, and the victims appearing on national television with their symptoms broadcast to the world.[105] Such attention not only worsened symptoms, but spread them: viewing news stories on Facebook about the sufferers led to the reawakening of past trauma for a thirty-six-year-old nurse who came down with nearly identical fits despite never having been in direct contact with the original sufferers.

The afflicted accusers in 1692 were put through the seventeenth-century equivalent of a media circus when they appeared before crowded meetinghouses and courtrooms in front of neighbors and visitors who traveled miles to see them. These crowds provided the afflicted in 1692 not just with harmful excessive attention but also with reinforcement that the symptoms were real, as the crowd believed. If those in 1692 did suffer from conversion disorder, these repeated appearances in front of crowds likely made their symptoms worse and longer-lasting.

In addition to mental illness as a possible explanation for the fits in 1692, scholars have suggested various physical medical explanations—none of which sufficiently explains the fits of the afflicted. These theories have been rebutted over the decades, yet often still appear in publications and television programs about the witch hunt. One theory that continues to linger despite being discredited among historians decades ago is the hypothesis that the ergot fungus grew on grain in Salem Village and when it was ingested it could give the eater LSD-like hallucinations. This theory was effectively rebutted only eight months after it was first published in 1976, because neither the causes nor most of the symptoms of ergotism were present in Salem Village in 1692.[106] Encephalitis, Lyme disease, and epilepsy have also been suggested as possible causes of the initial symptoms of the afflicted.[107]

While mental illness may explain the initial fits of some of the first few afflicted accusers, it does not explain all of the claimed afflictions in 1692, and there are numerous instances of lying and fraud by the accusers. The strongest piece of evidence that undermines the possibility that conversion disorder or physical illness caused *all* of the afflictions is the very convenient timing of the fits. In many instances the fits seemed to come and go on cue, such as when one of the accused crossed the threshold into a room or when the verdict was announced at Rebecca Nurse's trial. After these outbursts the afflicted accusers returned to appearing quite normal. Also, some accusers' alleged afflictions immediately stopped when the person named as their tormenter confessed, which seems intentional.[108] Witch hunt critic Thomas Brattle wrote in 1692, "Many of these afflicted persons, who have scores of strange fits in a day, yet in the intervals are hale and hearty, robust and lusty, as though nothing had afflicted them."[109] Historian Peter Charles Hoffer notes that "hysteria" does not just appear and then disappear when convenient, as happened to some of the afflicted in 1692.[110]

Several witnesses describe open fraud occurring later in 1692, and after Rebecca Nurse's arrest her family gathered testimony impugning the credibility of several of her accusers. At Nurse's trial one of her accusers was caught in a clear act of fraud that was later reported to the court.[111] These and yet more examples of fraud become readily apparent in the case of Nurse, which means that neither mental nor physical illness can explain the totality of the fits.

THE PUTNAMS invited Martha Corey over to talk with Ann Putnam Jr. about Putnam's accusation against her before any legal action was taken. They either gave the recently named witch the benefit of the doubt because she was a church member, or they set a trap. Corey voyaged north to Thomas and Ann Putnam's house by the Ipswich River in the western fields of the village.

The moment that Corey stepped through the door of the Putnams' house, Ann Jr. convulsed, her hands and feet bending in bizarre poses. She screamed at Corey that she was the one doing this to her. Ann writhed on the floor and appeared as though she was being choked. She accused Corey of witchcraft to her face, at which point Putnam's tongue shot out of her mouth, stretched to its maximum, and then her teeth clamped down on her tongue, as if trying to silence her. Once she started to recover, she took a few steps toward Corey and then fell down as if she was blinded. The Putnams' maid Mercy Lewis—a refugee from the wars in the north—soon fell into fits as well. To those present, the cause of the fits appeared clear: Martha Corey used witchcraft against Ann Putnam Jr. and Mercy Lewis.[112]

Once those present at the Putnams' house saw the fits after Corey crossed the threshold, she was doomed. On March 19 a warrant was issued for Corey's arrest.[113] Tituba previously claimed publicly that she had at least four confederates, and with the accusation against Corey it now appeared that three were discovered. That left at least one more.

REBECCA NURSE had already been named once by Ann Putnam Jr., and all in the village were on the lookout for at least one more witch believed still at large. Now, in the Putnams' home on the far side of the village from the Nurse farm, her mother Mrs. Ann Putnam claimed that Nurse's specter afflicted her too.

Mrs. Putnam previously witnessed many tragedies in her family. Years prior, her brother John Carr of Salisbury became very ill and slowly lost his mind—which some had attributed to witchcraft. She suffered through the deaths of her sister Mary Bailey—wife of the first village minister Rev. James Bailey—and her children, and also the deaths of her other sister Sarah Baker and several of her children. Most traumatically, Mrs. Putnam's infant daughter Sarah died in 1689 at only two months old.[114] Now in 1692 her daughter Ann Jr. was afflicted, but it was the Putnams who brought death and suffering to other families in the village.

Mrs. Putnam laid down on her bed on March 18 to take a rest after caring for Ann Jr. during her fits. While lying there, she later claimed that she saw the specter of Martha Corey appear to her. Mrs. Putnam alleged that she was "almost pressed to death" while lying on the bed. The next day, Corey's specter returned along with Nurse's specter, and according to Putnam "they both did torture me a great many times this day with such tortures as no tongue can express."[115]

Maybe it was seeing her daughter have fits that led her to have her own, perhaps reawakening old memories of the tragedies that earlier came to pass on her family. Or, as historian Marilynne K. Roach notes, the first two adult women who claimed to be afflicted—Mrs. Bethshua Pope and Mrs. Ann Putnam—both had one thing in common: they were in the early stages of pregnancy.[116] Perhaps there was an underlying physiological cause at play as well.

The same day that Mrs. Putnam allegedly saw Nurse's specter, Nurse's name was on the lips of other accusers in the village as well. As the solid freeze of winter thawed, ice melted and pooled in the paths, and the ground shifted and settled, a visitor came to the village from Boston. On March 19, Rev. Deodat Lawson, a former village minister, arrived and stayed at Ingersoll's tavern. He had heard that Tituba told the magistrates that witchcraft killed his wife and daughter years earlier, and he came to see what he could discover.[117] That evening, after Lawson established himself at the tavern, he had a visitor.

Seventeen-year-old Mary Walcott came to Ingersoll's to speak with Lawson. As she stood right inside the door of the tavern with the visiting minister, she recoiled and screamed about her wrist. Lawson used a candle to shine light on her wrist and later wrote that he "saw apparently the marks of teeth both upper and lower set, on each side of her wrist."[118] It seems very convenient that before Lawson even left Ingersoll's after putting down his belongings an accuser sought him out and showed him alleged evidence of witchcraft.

Later that evening, Lawson visited Rev. Parris at home along with Hannah Ingersoll, wife of the tavern-keeper. While with Parris and family in the parsonage, Lawson saw Abigail Williams have "a grievous fit; she was at first hurried with violence to and fro in the room (though Mrs. Ingersoll endeavored to hold her), sometimes making as if she would fly, stretching up her arms as high as she could, and crying 'whish, whish, whish!' several times."[119] Then, the third accusation against Nurse was uttered in the presence of the Parris family and the visiting minister.

Lawson writes that Williams next said, "There is Goodwife Nurse! Do you not see her!" Williams went on to tell those gathered that Nurse offered her "The book," but then Williams yelled "I won't, I won't, I won't take it, I do not know what book it is. I am sure it is none of God's book, it is the Devil's book, for aught I know." Immediately after she said this, Williams "ran into the fire, and began to throw fire brands about the house; and ran against the back, as if she would run up [the] chimney, and, as they said, she had attempted to go into the fire in other [previous] fits."[120] It was better to burn in the fireplace than sign the Devil's book and burn for all eternity.

The following day, Lawson gave the sermon for the Sabbath services in the village meetinghouse. Nurse was not present due to illness, as she had been suffering from a stomach ailment for some time.[121] Lawson began the morning service with an opening prayer, during which several of the afflicted had "sore fits," convulsing in the meetinghouse. Next a psalm was sung, and as Lawson rose from his seat to read the scripture passage on which he was to preach, Abigail Williams cried out "Name your text!" Lawson continued and read the text, at which point Williams exclaimed, "It's a long text!" In addition to Williams' impudent outbursts, soon after Lawson began his sermon Mrs. Bethshua Pope yelled, "Now there is enough of that!"[122]

During the afternoon session when Lawson was outlining the doctrine portion of his sermon, Williams again interrupted, "I know no doctrine you mentioned. If you named any, I have forgotten it."[123] The uproar and fits prevented the Salem Villagers from worshipping in peace. Since Nurse later appeared to be up-to-date-on who was afflicted, it is quite likely that her family reported back to her at home what they witnessed in the meetinghouse that morning.[124]

The accusations against Nurse took an even more public turn on March 21 at Martha Corey's post-arrest hearing. At the hearing, before a meetinghouse that was crowded with Nurse's friends and neighbors, Ann Putnam Jr. announced that "she saw the shape of Goodw[ife] C[orey] and she thought Goodw[ife] N[urse] praying at the same time to the Devil, she was not sure it was Goodw[ife] N[urse], she thought it was."[125] The whole village now knew that Nurse was suspected of being a witch along with the others.

At the hearing, Corey claimed that the accusers were "distracted" or mentally unstable. Magistrate John Hathorne responded, "You charge these children with distraction: It is a note of distraction when persons vary in a minute, but these fix upon you, this is not the manner of distraction."[126] Hathorne has a point here, their behavior is coordinated and targeted on Corey, instead of random fits.[127] Between their fits, Hathorne said of the afflicted accusers, "Do you not see these children and women are rational and sober as their neighbors?" In the end Corey was sent to jail to await trial, but not before she asked the judges, "Can an innocent person be guilty?"[128]

Mrs. Ann Putnam claimed that Nurse's specter came to her again the next day, March 22. Putnam stated, "The apparition of Rebecca Nurse did again set upon [me] in a most dreadful manner very early in the morning as soon as it was well light and now she appeared to me only in her shift and brought a little red book in her hand, urging me vehemently to write in her book." She continued, "because I would not yield to her hellish temptations she threatened to tear my soul out of my body, blasphemously denying the blessed God and the power of the Lord Jesus Christ to save my soul, and denying several places of scripture which I told her of to repel her hellish temptations and for near two hours together at this time the apparition of Rebecca Nurse did tempt and torture me before she left me as if indeed she would have killed me."[129] Rebecca Nurse, a visible saint presumed to be destined for heaven, was now allegedly luring Mrs. Putnam to deny Christ.

ON MARCH 22 OR 23, Peter Cloyce (Rebecca Nurse's brother-in-law), along with Salem selectman Daniel Andrew, Salem selectman Israel Porter, and his wife Elizabeth Hathorne Porter (the sister of magistrate John Hathorne) traveled up the dirt path to visit Nurse.[130] She was sick in bed, laying in the plain first floor room of the farmhouse. These friends gathered next to her along with the members of her household, in this dimly lit room on a dark late winter day, with light from the flickering fire enlivening the somber scene.

The visitors later stated that they were "desired to go to Goodman Nurse's house to speak with his wife and to tell her that several of the afflicted persons mentioned her."[131] It is interesting that Francis Nurse or her children did not just tell her themselves. This meeting was clearly intentionally planned by Francis. Perhaps he was already planning a defense for his wife and thought it best for her to hear the news from these respected friends who could serve as witnesses to attest to her first reaction when she heard that she was accused. This is exactly what they did when they wrote down Rebecca Nurse's reactions in a document later submitted to the court.

The visitors reported that they found Nurse in "a weak and low condition," because she had been ill for "almost a week." She had a stomach condition of some kind, and was described as "pale-faced." The friends asked her how she had been doing, and "she said she blessed God for it" because during her quiet time at home "she had more of His presence in this sickness than sometime she have had, but not as much as she desired." In a positive spirit, she said that "she would with the Apostles press forward" and quoted "many other places of scripture for the like purpose."[132]

Then, "on her own accord she began to speak of the affliction that was amongst them and in particular of Mr. Parris' family, and how she was grieved for them though she had not been to see them, by reason of fits that she formerly used to have, for people said it was awful to behold" the afflicted. She continued, saying that "she pitied them with all her heart, and went to God for them." She was very sympathetic toward the suffering of the afflicted, though "she said she heard that there were persons spoken of that were as innocent as she was she believed, and after much to this purpose, we told her we heard that she was spoken of also."[133]

After hearing this, Nurse said "if it be so, the will of the Lord be done," and sat a while silently "being at it were amazed." Then she turned and told those gathered, "Well, as to this thing I am as innocent as the child unborn. But, surely, what sin has God found out in me unrepented of that He should lay such an affliction upon me in my old age?"[134]

The friends concluded their visit, judging by Nurse's responses that she did not know the horrible news that she had been accused until the moment they told her.

ON MARCH 23, possibly at the same time that Rebecca Nurse's friends gathered around her in the Nurse family's first floor room, Rev. Lawson went to visit Thomas and Ann Putnam's family. Lawson and Thomas Putnam found Mrs. Putnam lying on her bed after apparently suffering from a fit. She invited Lawson to pray with her and her husband while she was feeling well enough, even though she said that the specter she saw forbade her from praying. Lawson notes that the prayer began as any other, "but after a little time, [Mrs. Putnam] was taken with a fit: yet continued silent, and seemed to be asleep." Then, "when prayer was done, her husband going to her, found her in a fit; he took her off the bed, to sit her on his knees; but at first she was so stiff, she could not be bended; but she afterwards sat down; but quickly began to strive violently with her arms and legs."[135] She then appeared to converse with a specter—allegedly that of Nurse.

Mrs. Putnam reportedly referenced a passage of scripture and shouted, "Goodwife Nurse be gone! Be gone! Be gone! Are you not ashamed, a woman of your profession [of faith], to afflict a poor creature so? What hurt did I ever do you in my life! You have but two years to live, and then the Devil will torment your soul, for this your name is blotted out of God's Book, and it shall never be put in God's Book again, be gone for shame, are you not afraid of that which is coming upon you?" She then continued, "I know, I know, what will make you afraid; the wrath of an angry God, I am sure that will make you afraid; be gone, do not torment me, I know what you would have . . . but it is out of your reach; it is clothed with the white robes of Christ's Righteousness."[136] Putnam, with her eyes shut, then began a scriptural debate with the specter that must have impressed Rev. Lawson, but the specter allegedly denied the existence of whichever text Mrs. Putnam referenced.

Putnam then claimed that if the text was read the specter would not be able to exist, but then "she was sorely afflicted; her mouth drawn to one side, and her body strained for about a minute." Regaining composure somewhat, she announced, "I will tell, I will tell, it is, it is, it is! . . . It is the third chapter of the Revelations." Lawson later wrote that he was reluctant to read the passage because he did not want to involve himself and holy scripture in such diabolical activities as were apparently happening, but eventually he read it: "And write unto the Angel of the Church which is at Sardis, These things saith he that hath the seven Spirits of God, and the seven stars, I know thy works: for thou hast a name that thou livest, but thou art dead." As he reached the end of this first verse, about a church that appeared to live but was really dead on the inside, Putnam suddenly opened her eyes and recovered.[137]

Putnam claimed that the next day she was "again afflicted by the apparitions of Rebecca Nurse and Martha Corey, but chiefly by Rebecca Nurse." Across the village, Abigail Williams also claimed to be tormented by Nurse's specter, and around this time Elizabeth Hubbard likewise claimed to see Nurse's shape.[138] These accusations were in addition to Ann Putnam Jr.'s prior mentions of Nurse's specter.

Edward Putnam and Jonathan Putnam were possibly also present for the scene with Mrs. Putnam, her husband, and Lawson—the minister wrote that there were other "spectators" present—and later that day, March 23, these two men traveled into Salem Town.[139] They met with magistrates Jonathan Corwin and John Hathorne to file a legal complaint against Nurse for practicing witchcraft.[140] They likely met with the magistrates in one of their homes, conducting their business in the front room of the house. Again, no bond was required from the accusers.

A warrant was issued that evening calling for Rebecca Nurse to be arrested and brought to Ingersoll's tavern by 8 o'clock the next morning. The warrant, written in Hathorne's hand, reads:

To the Marshall of Essex or his deputy:
     There being complaint this day made before us by Edward Putnam and Jonathan Putnam, yeomen, both of Salem Village, against Rebecca Nurse, the wife of Francis Nurse of Salem Village,

for vehement suspicion of having committed sundry acts of witchcraft and thereby having done much hurt and injury to the bodies of Ann Putnam, the wife of Thomas Putnam of Salem Village, Ann Putnam, the daughter of said Thomas Putnam, & Abigail Williams &c.

You are therefore in Their Majesties' names hereby required to apprehend and bring before us Rebecca Nurse, the wife of Francis Nurse of Salem Village, tomorrow about eight of the clock in the forenoon at the house of Lt. Nathaniel Ingersoll in Salem Village, in order to her examination relating to the above said premises and hereof you are not to fail.
Salem, March the 23d 1692
John Hathorne
Jonathan Corwin Assistants[141]

Rebecca Nurse, at home in her sickbed, nodded off to sleep unaware of the transaction taking place at the magistrate's house in Salem Town.

SIX

THE VISIBLE SAINT AGAINST THE INVISIBLE WORLD

I can say before my Eternal Father I am innocent, and God will clear my innocency.—Rebecca Nurse, at her post-arrest hearing, March 24, 1692

EARLY ON THE MORNING OF MARCH 24, there was a rap on the front door of the Nurse house. Francis Nurse, or perhaps one of the family's adult children, opened the heavy and windowless wooden front door, swinging on its iron hinges. The door opened inward, into the dark entranceway of the house, causing the unknowing opener to squint against the morning light.

Standing on the large flat stone in front of the door was George Herrick, holding his black staff of office as marshal of Essex County, along with the constable and several other men.[1] They came for Rebecca Nurse.

Marshal Herrick read out the warrant to those present, which presumably included Francis and those children still living at home, announcing his duty to take Rebecca into custody "in Their Majesties' names."[2] One must imagine their outrage that their mother—a woman quite old and ill—was pulled from her warm bed, thrust out into the cold March air, and then marched along like a common criminal down the muddy roads of the village.

The Nurse family's later actions show that they went to all lengths to support their dear wife and mother, and it is likely that they followed the marshal and Rebecca Nurse as they trudged through the spring mud to Ingersoll's tavern in the center of the village.[3]

Marshal Herrick wrote his description of the arrest at the bottom of the warrant after the deed was done: "March 24th 1692 I have apprehended the body of Rebecca Nurse and brought her to the house of Lieut. Nathaniel Ingersoll where she is in custody."[4] It is a calm and unfeeling report as required from an officer of the law, one which nonetheless minimizes the trauma of that day.

NURSE WAS NOT a likely suspect for witchcraft in 1692 because of her respectable life and status as a visible saint, but also because of her demographics. Her respectable life was noted in the trial documents and by a contemporary chronicler of the trials. Her reputation was very different from those of the previously accused women, all of whom had something in their pasts that made them susceptible to the witchcraft accusation.

In one trial document, Nurse's neighbor to the north, Nathaniel Putnam (who was involved along with the Endicotts in the farm boundary dispute), stated: "Her life and conversation has been according to her profession [of faith] and she has brought up a great family of children and educated [them] well so that there is in some of them apparent signs of godliness."[5] Robert Calef, a chronicler of the trials whose *More Wonders of the Invisible World* was published in 1700, wrote of Nurse, "The testimonials of her Christian behavior, both in the course of her life, and at her death, and her extraordinary care in educating her children, and setting them good examples, etc., under the hands of many, are so numerous, that for brevity are here omitted."[6] This description is significant, because religious and devout wives were much respected in Puritan society.[7] Whereas the previously accused had shaky reputations, Nurse's was impeccable.

That Nurse, who was a full member of the Salem Town church—a visible saint, who was destined for heaven and believed to be filled with God's grace—was accused of witchcraft was shocking. Her accusation raised questions about the status of other church members as well. Nurse's was therefore a watershed case, though as the witch hunt continued, even a minister was not safe from the noose.

As to Nurse's demographics, being a woman put her at a marked disadvantage. Carol F. Karlsen notes in her examination of the role of gender in New England witch hunts, "The history of witchcraft is primarily the history of women," and she relates that between 1620 and 1725, 344 persons were accused of witchcraft in New England, and of those whose sex is known, 78 percent were women.[8]

During the Salem Village witch hunt, of the 185 accused of witchcraft mentioned by name in the records, more than three-fourths were female, in keeping with the larger trend of accusations in New England. Nurse was therefore far more susceptible to a witchcraft charge than a man in a similar situation. However, the Salem Village witch hunt is noteworthy for the relatively high number of men executed (six, including Giles Corey who was pressed to death), compared to other witchcraft "outbreaks" (as Karlsen terms the events) in early colonial New England.[9]

Although women made up most of the accused and executed, Nurse's age made her an outlier. The great majority of those accused were middle-aged or younger, not older women like Nurse (despite what the Hollywood stereotype of witches may lead one to believe). Of those accused of witchcraft in New England from 1620 to 1725, middle-aged women (aged forty to fifty-nine) were more likely to be accused of witchcraft than older women (aged over sixty). Only 18 percent of all accused women were over sixty, as Nurse was. But, once accused, older women in the Salem Village witch hunt were more likely to be tried, convicted, and executed than middle-aged women.[10]

In addition to age, Nurse's economic situation makes her a less likely victim. Most women accused of witchcraft in New England had come to control land and property—an unusual occurrence for women—due to inheritance, most often caused by a lack of male relatives.[11] Nurse does not fit this category. Her husband was still alive and she had many male heirs to inherit the property if he died, so there was no chance at the time of her controlling property on her own. Plus, her husband had already deeded most of the farm over to the next generation.

John Putnam Demos' investigation of the backgrounds of witchcraft suspects similarly shows that Nurse's is not a typical case. He found nine traits that define the "typical" accused witch, and of these nine traits Nurse fits only two: she was female, and of English Puritan background. The other seven traits do not apply to her: middle aged, married with few or no children, frequent conflict with family members, previously accused of committing crimes, practiced a medical vocation, was of low social position, and "was abrasive in style, contentious in character."[12] Nurse is an outlier among those accused of witchcraft in New England.

THE MARSHAL TOOK Rebecca Nurse to Ingersoll's tavern by eight o'clock, as the arrest warrant required. She remained (likely in an upstairs room) with her hands bound for almost two hours, because her hearing was scheduled for ten o'clock.[13]

At some point while they were at Ingersoll's, the constable ordered "drink and cake," and the marshal's "attendants" ordered drink, all of which was charged to the Massachusetts government. Ingersoll also later charged the government for Marshal Herrick keeping his horse there, eating supper, and staying over one night.[14]

Magistrates John Hathorne and Jonathan Corwin rode in from Salem Town for the hearing, wearing their dark suits. These black riders rode along the country road that ran through the Nurse farm, and within sight of the Nurse family's house perched on its slope, its now empty windows staring at them. The magistrates left their horses at Ingersoll's barn and entered the tavern.

It was decided that the tavern could by no means accommodate the gathered crowd, and the hearing was moved to the meetinghouse. The size of the crowd was enormous, especially considering that it was almost planting season and nearly all of the villagers were farmers who needed to prepare their fields at this time of the year.[15] In a commonwealth where plays and theaters were illegal, the hearings and trials of 1692 were the greatest show the villagers had ever seen.[16] In addition to the many villagers and spectators from nearby towns, Rev. John Hale of Beverly and Rev. Deodat Lawson (the former village minister, now minister in Boston) were present. Lawson later wrote a description of the beginning of the witch hunt, including Nurse's hearing, that was published only a few weeks later.

The two magistrates entered the meetinghouse and sat behind a table at the front of the room, wearing their black robes of office and facing the gathered masses. The meetinghouse had a large communion table that was used once a month for Sacrament Sunday, when the saints gathered around it to celebrate the Lord's Supper. On this day, it was used as the judges' bench, and there was no communion to be had. Opposite them, the crowd—including many accusers—sat in pews, stood in doorways, crowded into galleries above, and gathered outside around open windows.[17]

Before the hearing even began the magistrates made several prejudicial errors that empowered the accusers' case against Nurse—mistakes that were committed at the other initial hearings as well. The accusers should have been brought into the hearing one by one, as was the usual protocol for witnesses at initial hearings, so that the accusers could not hear one another's testimony and align their stories, or cause chaos from their combined fits. Also, the public should not have been allowed in, as initial hearings were customarily done in private.[18] Allowing the public to see the accusers having fits all together and screaming at the accused damned them in the court of public opinion long before any trial came.

Nurse was led through the main entrance of the meetinghouse by Marshal Herrick and the guards, facing the two magistrates as she walked down the center aisle through a canyon of eyes—some with fear and contempt, and some showing sympathy for an old woman suffering through such an ordeal.

She walked by the prominent pew where she sat during Sunday services. Nurse had crossed the Atlantic and had forsaken her native home to be counted among the saints of the New Jerusalem, but now her faith and her many good works no longer mattered. The spell of suspicion was cast.

As it was a meetinghouse and not a proper courtroom, there was no bar at the front for the accused to stand at. Instead, Nurse was led into the front pew and told to stand leaning on the wooden front wall of the box pew, in place of a bar. Though the pew had a bench just behind her that must have seemed tantalizingly close to the elderly Nurse, weak and frail from age and illness, she was required to stand for the entirety of the hearing.[19]

There she stood, seven or eight feet from the magistrates, with one guard on either side of her—ready to grab her hands should the feeble and ailing grandmother attempt to harm anyone.[20]

Once all were in place, the hearing began with a prayer by Rev. Hale of Beverly.[21] Then, Nurse's warrant was read, naming the charge against her as "having committed sundry acts of witchcraft and thereby done much hurt and injury" to Mrs. Ann Putnam, Ann Putnam Jr., and Abigail Williams.[22] The three above-named were present, along with several other afflicted accusers.

THE WITCH-HUNT BEGAN with just two afflicted girls—Rev. Samuel Parris' daughter Betty (age nine) and niece Abigail Williams (age eleven). Now, however, the accusers counted among them women of all ages and stages of life. Those present included two married women, Mrs. Ann Putnam (thirty-one) and Mrs. Bethshua Pope (in her thirties, the aunt of Benjamin Franklin); three unmarried women who were old enough to be referred to as "grown persons" by the magistrates, Elizabeth Hubbard (age seventeen, and niece of Dr. Griggs), Mercy Lewis (age seventeen, maid in the Putnam household), and Mary Walcott (age seventeen, who lived close to the parsonage and was a Putnam cousin); along with Mary Warren (age twenty); and also two younger girls, Ann Putnam Jr. (age twelve) and Abigail Williams.[23] There were also at least three afflicted persons who were not present and had not joined in the accusations against Nurse: Betty Parris (the first of the afflicted), "an Ancient woman named Goodall," and Sarah Bibber (age thirty-six) who later joined the accusations against Nurse and whose fraud was exposed at Nurse's trial in June.[24]

This was not a circle of children accusing adults of witchcraft, as the episode was portrayed in some early histories of the witch hunt. By this point, it was primarily married and unmarried women, who were well past the age of reason and had received some level of education, accusing fellow women. In total, 38 percent of the afflicted accusers were women over the age of twenty, 44 percent were "single-women" between the ages of sixteen and twenty years old, and only 18 percent were under sixteen years old.[25]

Whereas the actions of a group of children can be more easily written off as being nonsensical antics, the actions of rational adults accusing other adults is far scarier, and shows how universally accepted the belief in witchcraft was by those in all stages of life.

The role of respected adults in leveling witchcraft accusations is primarily shown in Mrs. Putnam's actions on this day. Although it was her twelve-year-old daughter who apparently first accused Nurse (after the other members of the Putnam household suggested names to her), it was Mrs. Putnam who appeared as the primary accuser at Nurse's hearing and submitted written evidence against her in the following weeks. She became the star witness of the hearing due to her sensational carrying-on and convulsing during testimony, and she later claimed that she was "several times afflicted in the morning by the apparition of Rebecca Nurse" even before the hearing began.[26]

AFTER THE WARRANT WAS READ, the accused was typically given the opportunity to reply to the charges.[27] From the written record, it is unclear if Nurse had this opportunity, or if she did whether she used it, because the transcript of her hearing begins with Hathorne questioning the accusers, instead of with a statement by Nurse.[28] Rev. Parris took the official notes of what was said at the hearing, furiously writing to keep up with the pace of events, and stopping periodically to wet the quill with his mouth.

However, the Nurse family later accused Parris of "not rendering to the world so fair if true an account of what he wrote on examination of the accused."[29] He likely left out some of what Rebecca Nurse said in her defense. All court reporters in 1692 were effectively working for the prosecution, and therefore unlikely to be sympathetic to the defendants.[30]

According to Parris' official transcript, Hathorne began the hearing by asking an unnamed accuser, "What do you say? Have you seen this woman hurt you?"[31] The accuser responded, "Yes, she beat me this morning." Hathorne then asked Abigail Williams, "Abigail, have you been hurt by this woman?" She replied, "Yes." After Williams' answer, Ann Jr. had "a grievous fit" and "cried out that [Nurse] hurt her."

Once Ann Putnam Jr. composed herself, Hathorne turned to Nurse, "Goody Nurse, here are two, Ann Putnam the child and Abigail Williams, who complain of you hurting them. What do you say to it?" She replied, speaking apparently for the first time, "I can say before my Eternal Father I am innocent, and God will clear my innocency." Hathorne, seeming struck by her language, responded more sympathetically, "Here is never a one in the assembly but desires it, but if you be guilty pray God discover you."

Henry Kenny, a village farmer and relative of accuser Mercy Lewis, suddenly rose up from the crowd in the meetinghouse and began to speak. Allowing the interruption, Hathorne asked, "Goodman Kenny, what do you say?" The record summarizes Kenny's testimony, stating that "he entered his complaint and further said that since this Nurse came into the [meeting]house he was seized twice with an amazed condition."

Hathorne then said to Nurse, "Here are not only these [referring to the younger accusers], but here is the wife of Mr. Thomas Putnam who accuses you by credible information and that both of tempting her to iniquity and of greatly hurting her."

"I am innocent and clear, and have not been out of doors these eight or nine days."

Hathorne called on Deacon Edward Putnam, brother of Thomas, "Mr. Putnam, give in what you have to say." Edward Putnam then spoke as a witness against Nurse. From the next question Hathorne asks, it is clear that his testimony related to Nurse allegedly hurting one of the afflicted, most likely his niece (and neighbor) Ann Putnam Jr. The next day he submitted a written deposition that was later used at Nurse's trial. In the document, which is probably similar to what he said at the hearing, he states that "Ann Putnam Jr. was bitten by Rebecca Nurse, as she said."[32]

After Edward Putnam spoke, Hathorne asked, "Is this true Goody Nurse?"[33]

"I never afflicted no child in my life."

"You see these accuse you. Is it true?"

"No."

Hathorne continues his questioning, though after Nurse's repeated denials he asks in seemingly a more open and neutral way, "Are you an innocent person relating to this witchcraft?"

But before she could answer, Mrs. Putnam screamed at Rebecca Nurse from the crowd, "Did you not bring the Black Man with you?! Did you not tempt God and die?! How often have you eaten and drunk your own damnation?!"

This shocking outburst struck to the heart of Nurse's status as a visible saint. Mrs. Putnam references 1 Corinthians 11:29: "For he that eateth and drinketh unworthily, eateth and drinketh damnation to himself, not discerning the Lord's body." She is implying that Nurse is not worthy of her status as a visible saint who shared in the communion table, because she is in league with the Devil. In later months, Nurse and others were accused of participating in diabolical sacraments mocking the Lord's Supper with Satan himself, and this remark could foreshadow those accusations.

Hathorne, surprised into forgetting about his previous question and interpreting Mrs. Putnam's exclamation as a legitimate question, turned to Nurse, "What do you say to them?" "Oh Lord help me...," she uttered, shaken by the outburst. Then, Nurse spread her hands out toward heaven as if she was praying. As soon as she did this the accusers fell down into wild fits, or as Parris writes: "the afflicted were grievously vexed." They claimed the Devil was present in the room, whispering in Nurse's ear, and pointed to fluttering brightly colored spectral birds they claimed were zooming around the austere meetinghouse. None in the audience could see these spectral sights, which Rev. Cotton Mather later described as "wonders of the invisible world."[34]

After the scene calmed down, Hathorne asked Nurse rhetorically, "Do you not see what a solemn condition these [the accusers] are in? When your hands are loose the persons are afflicted."[35] Hathorne believed that Nurse's actions directly caused the accusers' fits.

Next, Mary Walcott and Elizabeth Hubbard accused Nurse of tormenting them. They previously testified that they saw Nurse's specter, but never previously accused her of hurting them. Walcott screamed and claimed that she was bitten by Nurse's specter. She came forward and showed her wrist with teeth marks on it.[36]

After the two women spoke their part, Hathorne said, "Here are these two grown persons who now accuse you. What say you? Do you not see these afflicted persons, and hear them accuse you?"[37] It is of note that to the magistrate these two seventeen-year-olds were then considered to be "grown persons," and his differentiating them from the younger girls seems to be so as to give their testimony more credence than Ann Putnam Jr.'s.

Nurse replied, "The Lord knows I have not hurt them. I am an innocent person."

Hathorne continued, calling attention to her status as a visible saint, "It is very awful to all to see these agonies, and you, an old professor [of the faith], thus charged with contracting with the Devil by the effects of it, and yet to see you stand here with dry eyes when there are so many wet!" By this point, evidently some in the crowd teared up at witnessing the fits of the accusers. Also, there was an old folk belief that a witch could not cry, so Hathorne's comment was fishing for circumstantial signs of guilt.[38]

"You do not know my heart," she insisted.[39]

Hathorne then admitted that he was not entirely confident in the credibility of spectral evidence, and asked about the accusers' claims of specters associating with Nurse, "What uncertainty there may be in apparitions I know not, yet this with me strikes hard upon you, that you are at this very present charged with familiar spirits, this is your bodily person they speak to, they say now they see these familiar spirits come to your bodily person. Now what do you say to that?"

"I have none sir."

He again asked her to confess, and then asked essentially the same question, "If you have confessed and give glory to God, I pray God clear you if you be innocent, and if you are guilty discover you. And therefore give me an upright answer: Have you any familiarity with these spirits?"

"No, I have none but with God alone."

Hathorne's repeated questions searched for a confession, his goal throughout the hearing. A confession was the most credible evidence against a witchcraft suspect, because witchcraft was a charge that otherwise lacked the hard evidence of more earthly crimes.

Next, he changed his line of questioning completely, and inquired about her illness: "How came you sick? For there is an odd discourse in the mouths of many."

"I am sick to my stomach," she replied.

"Have you no wounds?"

"None but old age."

The afflicted accusers previously claimed that they fought back against Nurse's specter, and his question was a way to see if she had bodily wounds that were incurred when the accusers fought her alleged appari-tion.[40]

Hathorne then restated the evidence against her, continuing his pat-tern of acting like a prosecutor, "You do know whether you are guilty and have familiarity with the Devil, and now when you are here present to see such a thing as these testify a black man is whispering in your ear and [spectral] birds about you. What do you say to it?"[41]

"It is false. I am clear."

Her repeated denials again had an effect on Hathorne. He next asked a reaching question, while almost conceding that Nurse might be inno-cent, "Possibly you may apprehend that you are no witch, but have you not been led aside by temptations that way?"

"I have not."

"What a sad thing it is that a church member here and now, and others of Salem, should be thus accused and charged."

Just as Hathorne made this remark (and appeared to ease up the pres-sure of his questions), Mrs. Bethshua Pope convulsed and yelled. Her fit caused a cascading effect of fits from the other accusers, as the wailing and gnashing of teeth spread through the meetinghouse.

After order was restored, Hathorne began again, asking questions in a more pointed way than before this round of fits. The actions of the ac-cusers affected his questioning throughout the hearing, and the accusers became the most violent whenever he began to moderate his questioning or adopt a more sympathetic tone toward Nurse.

"Tell us, have you not had visible appearances, more than what is com-mon in nature?"

"I have none, nor never had in my life."

Hathorne then asked her a dangerously loaded question, "Do you think these [accusers] suffer voluntarily or involuntarily?"

Depending on Nurse's answer, she could be accused of doubting the veracity of the accusers' fits if she said they behaved in such a way volun-tarily, yet if she responded that they were involuntary such a statement could also be used against her because how could she know if they were true fits unless she was the one causing them?

All she said was "I cannot tell."

"That is strange, everyone can judge," Hathorne replied, trying to draw an answer out of her.

"I must be silent."

Next, the magistrate set another trap, "They accuse you of hurting them, and if you think it is but by design, you must look upon them as murderers." They could be viewed as murderers if their accusations were false because the crime of witchcraft carried the death penalty.

"I cannot tell what to think of it."

This answer seems to have struck many at the examination as odd, and to those in the crowd her answer does leave open the possibility that she might think they were murderers. There appears to be a disruption in the written record at this point. Nurse was then asked the same question again. Parris wrote that the question "was somewhat insisted on."

"I do not think so," she replied.

Parris recorded that her lack of a previous precise answer was because "She did not understand aright what was said."[42] Nurse, in her old age and infirm condition, was hard of hearing, which contributed to the misunderstanding. The afflicted drew upon this as a weakness of hers and claimed that she could not hear because Satan—"the black man"—was whispering in her ear.[43]

Hathorne continued on the same point, "Well then, give in an answer now: do you think these suffer against their wills or not?"

"I do not think these suffer against their wills."

Hathorne began a new line of questioning, drawing attention to the fact that she never visited the accusers, potentially to make her appear unsympathetic, "Why did you never visit these afflicted persons?"[44]

"Because I was afraid I should have fits too."

Following her response about the fits, the accusers reminded the crowd just what their fits looked like, and Rev. Parris noted that the accusers then fell into fits "abundantly and very frequently."

Hathorne, referencing these fits they just saw, again asked Nurse's opinion of why the accusers react to her words in such a way. "Is it not an unaccountable case that when you are examined these persons are afflicted?"

"I have got nobody to look to but God," replied Nurse, after which Parris noted that she moved her hands slightly while speaking, and "again upon stirring her hands the afflicted persons were seized with violent fits of torture."

Rev. Lawson later wrote that Nurse's "motions did produce like effects as to biting, pinching, bruising, tormenting, at their breasts, by her leaning." And at one point during their fits, the accusers bent over backward to the point that it looked "as if their backs were broken."[45] Just as a previous comment by Hathorne revealed that he believed the cause and effect between her motions and the fits, here Lawson's language betrays the same belief.

"Do you believe these afflicted persons are bewitched?," Hathorne then asked.[46]

"I do think they are."

The fits of the girls convinced a great many people, and it should not be surprising that Nurse believed they were afflicted by *something*—just not by her. Though she continued to maintain her own innocence to the last, she was not a doubter that witchcraft existed and appeared to be present in the village. The fits of the accusers were too fantastic to be explained any other way at that point.

Once again acting like a prosecutor, Hathorne brought up the case of Tituba, who previously confessed to practicing witchcraft, in an attempt to get Nurse to confirm that an image of her, if not her bodily person, attacked the accusers. "When this witchcraft came upon the stage there was no suspicion of Tituba. . . . She professed much love to that child Betty Parris, but it was her apparition that did the mischief, and why should you not also be guilty, for your apparition does hurt also?"

"Would you have me belie myself?" Nurse reproachfully asked Hathorne. She would admit no such thing, because Tituba said not just that the Devil used her shape but that she was guilty of witchcraft.

After Nurse said this, her head drooped to one side, presumably due to exhaustion after standing throughout this grueling interrogation. After spending the previous days bedridden with illness, the physically drained (though mentally sharp) Rebecca Nurse had stood for quite a length of time while firmly insisting on her innocence in the face of Hathorne's loaded questions and traps.

When her head listed to one side, Elizabeth Hubbard's head mimicked it, rolling to the exact same position. As the crowd watched this movement with amazement, Abigail Williams screamed, "Set up Goody Nurse's neck—the maid's [Hubbard's] neck will be broken!" At this point, some in the meetinghouse—presumably the guards—grabbed Nurse's head and thrust it upright. As they moved her head, Elizabeth Hubbard's head likewise moved up and returned to a normal position.

At one point, Mrs. Ann Putnam fell into a wild fit as the eyes of the village looked on. Rev. Lawson wrote that she suddenly lost all her strength, and that "she could hardly move hand or foot."[47] Meanwhile, more and more of the accusers fell into fits. The accusers claimed that they saw Nurse riding outside the meetinghouse with the Devil himself, when she was clearly standing against the pew, struggling to remain standing before a perplexed crowd of spectators and the writhing accusers.

Lawson writes that he was "a little distance" from the meetinghouse as this cascade of fits happened, but that he nevertheless heard the "hideous screech and noise." He also relates the fear caused by so many of the other accusers joining in on the fits, "some that were within told me the whole assembly was struck with consternation, and they were afraid, that those that sat next to them were under the influence of witch-craft."[48] Neighbors looked around and saw people that they knew all their lives shrieking, contorting, and bending over backward to gruesome angles. No one knew who might be next to be afflicted—or accused.

Eventually, due to the great disorder and terror caused by the scene, the magistrates allowed Thomas Putnam to carry Mrs. Ann Putnam out of the meetinghouse, and as soon as she passed the threshold, she suddenly regained her composure and her fits ended. She later testified in writing about the scene, "The honored magistrates gave my husband leave to carry me out of the meetinghouse, and as soon as I was carried out of the meetinghouse doors it pleased Almighty God, for his free grace and mercy sake to deliver me out of the paws of the roaring lions and the jaws of those tearing bears that ever since that time they have no power to afflict me."[49]

Once Nurse's neck was forcibly straightened and the pandemonium subsided, Magistrates Hathorne and Corwin directed Rev. Parris to read observations that he took down during Mrs. Putnam's previous fits. His notes do not seem to have survived, but there is a deposition attested to by Mrs. Putnam (though written by Thomas Putnam) submitted either later that day or the next day, for it mentions her conduct at the hearing in addition to previous fits.[50] It is likely that this description of previous fits, noted by date, is similar to that which Parris read aloud through his ink-stained teeth.

Mrs. Putnam mentions that Nurse's specter first appeared to her on March 19 along with Martha Corey's specter, and she stated: "they both did torture me a great many times this day with such tortures as no tongue can express."[51] The next day was Sunday and no specters appeared, and then, according to her testimony, on March 21 only Corey bothered her, with Nurse's specter returning on March 22. On that day the deposition states that Nurse's specter tried to get Mrs. Putnam to sign the Devil's book, denied God and Jesus' power to save Putnam's soul, and then tortured Putnam for two hours as if she was trying to kill her. Putnam claimed that on March 23, both Corey and Nurse's specters returned, and on the morning of March 24, before Nurse's hearing, Nurse's specter tortured her several times.

After Rev. Parris read his notes about Mrs. Ann Putnam's fits, Hathorne asked Nurse, "What do you think of this?"[52]

"I cannot help it, the Devil may appear in my shape."[53]

Her final remark is very significant. Perhaps she stated this because after witnessing the fits—the screaming, wailing, claims of spectral attacks, and the wounds presented as evidence—she was awed into believing at least some of it was credible affliction, potentially by the Devil using her guise. It was traditionally believed that the Devil in his tricks could impersonate anyone—saints and sinners alike—and so this is not an admission of guilt.

Although Hathorne admitted earlier during the hearing that he was unsure of how valid spectral evidence was, as the witch hunt continued the witch trials court operated under the belief that the devil could only appear in one's shape if they were guilty—in which case, Nurse's response could later be interpreted as nearly an admission of guilt, even though it was not intended to be so. Such a belief was in contrast to traditional Puritan (and other Christian) theology and in contrast to the recommendations given to the court by leading ministers that June.[54] This later belief by the court that if one's specter was seen one was automatically guilty was insurmountable for defendants, and since no others could see the alleged specter there was no way to disprove what an accuser allegedly saw. Once accused, guilt was assumed and there was no way out.

After Nurse's answer, Rev. Parris' written account of the hearing ends. On the back of the transcript, he wrote: "This is a true account of the sum of her examination, but by reason of great noises by the afflicted and many speakers many things are pretermitted [omitted]."[55] The noise, calamity, and uproars during the hearing made it difficult for recorders to keep up, especially when using a quill pen that did not write quickly and needed to be continuously re-inked. Other records from 1692 suffer similar omissions. In this case, it means that some of what Nurse said is likely lost to history, and known only to those who were present.

As mentioned above, the Nurse family later accused Parris of not accurately transcribing what was said at the hearing, likely omitting some of the defense testimony.[56] One piece of defense evidence that was probably entered at the hearing but was not recorded by Rev. Parris is the statement by Daniel Andrew, Peter Cloyce, Israel Porter, and Elizabeth (Hathorne) Porter, magistrate John Hathorne's sister. In this document, they recounted their visit to Rebecca Nurse at home and her reaction when first told that she was named as a witch. The document describes Nurse as appearing innocent and unknowing of the alleged witchcraft.

Above their signatures at the end of the document, Daniel Andrew and Peter Cloyce wrote that "to the substance of what is above, we, if called there to, are ready to testify on oath." It was given to the magistrates, and their offer to testify refers to Nurse's hearing.[57] Two months later, Nurse's defender Daniel Andrew was accused of witchcraft and forced to flee.

At the end of her hearing, magistrates Hathorne and Corwin found the evidence against Nurse to be sufficient. They ordered the guards to take her to the Salem jail to await further trial. Their official order reads: "Upon hearing the aforesaid, and seeing what we then did see, together with the charges of the persons then present, we committed Rebecca Nurse, the wife of Francis Nurse of Salem Village, unto Their Majesties' Jail in Salem, as per mittimus then given out, in order to further examination."[58] Rebecca Nurse, like Sarah Good, Sarah Osborne, and Martha Corey before her, was bound with rope, and later irons.[59]

Thus the doleful procession of constables made its slow return journey to Salem Town to deposit Nurse in jail to await trial along with the other accused. They traveled along muddy paths still strewn with dead leaves from the fall mixed into the mud caused by spring rains, and passed spectators who turned out along the way to see an accused witch in the flesh.[60]

Nurse and the guards went down the same muddy country road by which the officials arrived that morning, and slowly wound their way through the bare fields of her farm, still brown and dead from winter, where she and Francis worked for years to gain success in this life and the next. She also passed by the homes of several of her children, whose houses were within sight of the main road. Her daughter Rebecca Preston's husband, Thomas Preston, had filed the first legal complaint of witchcraft in 1692 against Tituba, Good, and Osborne, which began the witch hunt in February.[61] One can only imagine his thoughts as the accusations now struck his own family.

This melancholy trip was the last time Rebecca Nurse saw her home.

BACK AT THE MEETINGHOUSE, the crowd broke for lunch and ventured up the road to Ingersoll's tavern where the magistrates ate. An expense report shows that the government paid for the magistrates' "Drink and Entertainment" in addition to the charge of stabling their horses for the day.[62] While at Ingersoll's, they conducted a second hearing for an accused person, four- or five-year-old Dorothy Good, daughter of already accused Sarah Good.[63] Neither church members nor small children were above suspicion.

That afternoon, the magistrates and many villagers returned to the meetinghouse for the Lecture Day sermon. Undoubtedly, they chatted to each other about the scene they had witnessed in that same hall earlier that morning. Rev. Lawson, the village's former minister, gave the sermon that day. Francis Nurse served on the committee that hired him as the village minister in 1684.[64]

Lawson's sermon was fiery as he urged the villagers on against the army of darkness, though he also cautioned against false accusations and premature conclusions. While Nurse's somber procession of guards headed toward Salem Town and she left the village for the last time, Rev. Lawson stood before her neighbors and declared war on Satan's servants: "Satan is representing his infernal forces, and the devils seem to come armed, mustering amongst us. I am this day commanded to call and cry an alarm unto you: ARM, ARM, ARM! Handle your arms, see that you are fixed and in a readiness, as faithful soldiers under the Captain of our salvation. ... Let us admit no parley, give no quarter; let none of Satan's forces and furies be more vigilant to hurt us than we are to resist and repress them."[65] His voice echoed through the meetinghouse, a building intentionally designed to carry the excited sermons of the minister.

Then, addressing magistrates Hathorne and Corwin (who stayed for the sermon), he continued, "Do all that in you lies to check and rebuke Satan; endeavoring, by all ways and means that are according to the rule of God, to discover his instruments in these horrid operations ... and the cause that seems to be so dark, as you know not how to determine it, do your utmost, in the use of all regular means, search it out."[66]

Lawson roused the villagers to arms against their perceived enemy. The first salvos of a spiritual war were fired, and now the prosecution of the war lay in the hands of the judiciary and the government. Rebecca Nurse, who previously heard many similarly fiery sermons on the conflict between good and evil from that same pulpit, was now perceived as being on the opposing side of her neighbors in that great battle. Soon, she was also on the opposite side of some of these villagers in court, on trial for her life.

SEVEN

PRISON AND PETITION

No one alive knows or is able to express what I have suffered
since I came into this place.
—Description of the Salem jail by a prisoner in 1682

THE SALEM JAIL WAS AN INHOSPITABLE, barbaric place for any human
being to live, and especially so for someone ill and elderly like Rebecca
Nurse. She spent her days in this muddy and unfurnished building not
far from Salem's North River, braced against the freezing nights and en-
during the filthy days.[1]

The jail was a small austere wooden structure of twenty feet by twenty
feet. Daylight filtered in through the iron bars on the window openings, and
the front door bore a lock to confine the prisoners and their specters within.
Beyond the bars, a prison yard was visible, surrounded by a fence to contain
the accused—if they were ever allowed outside. William Dounton, the jail
keeper, was in charge of the prisoners. A member of the Salem Town church,
he previously shared the sacrament of the Lord's Supper with Nurse but now
kept his fellow church member chained in the dungeon-like jail.[2]

Cold was the chief worry during the frigid March nights. Although
this jail was fairly new, it had only one brick fireplace for the prisoners to
huddle around for warmth.[3] The previous jail building was infamous for
its brutal winter conditions, and the new structure was not significantly
different. During the winter of 1684, magistrate John Hathorne feared
that two horse thieves kept in jail would freeze to death, so he arranged
for them to self-exile themselves. They departed for Barbados as inden-
tured servants.[4]

In addition to the brutal weather, the prisoners experienced inhumane filth. Job Tookey, a prisoner testifying before the Essex County Quarterly Court in 1682 (who was also accused of witchcraft in 1692), described the jail as "a sad dolesome place." He added, "No one alive knows or is able to express what I have suffered since I came into this place; and still daily do being almost poisoned with the stink of my own dung and the stink of the prison, having never had so much as a minute's time to take the air since I came into this dolesome place."[5] In 1679 Thomas Gratchell described the previous jail building in a letter to the Essex County Quarterly Court as "A noisome place not fit for a Christian man to breathe in."[6] Since the jail was near the river, large water rats scurried through murky puddles of excrement on the floor and darted between the prisoners.[7] As all the nearby jails in 1692 filled well past capacity with the huddled, unfortunate accused, the conditions were even filthier than those described by the prisoners during previous years.

Disease in jails was so common that there was even a disease named "gaol [jail] fever"—a severe form of typhus carried by lice that spread easily in crowded, dirty jail conditions.[8] At the end of 1692, the mother of a middle-aged woman confined in the Salem jail wrote to the government, "Some have died already in prison, and others have been dangerously sick, and how soon others [might also be], and among them my poor child by the difficulties of this confinement may be sick and die, God only knows."[9] The filthy and crowded conditions accelerated the spread of disease, while malnourishment made the prisoners even more vulnerable.

That fall, several men petitioned the government on behalf of their family members imprisoned in the Salem jail and noted the prisoners' hunger, "The distressed conditions of our wives and relations in prison at Salem who are a company of poor distressed creatures as full of inward grief and trouble as they are able to bear up in life withal, and besides that the aggravation of outward troubles and hardships they undergo: wants of food."[10] Dirty, dung-covered, and starving, these innocent people would have looked (and smelled) more and more like a caricature of the old unkempt witch with every passing day.

In addition to the filth and lack of food, in some situations the other prisoners themselves made the jail unbearable. Keeping those who later falsely confessed to witchcraft in the same large jail room as those who maintained their innocence led the false confessors to pressure and harass prisoners like Nurse with the goal of getting them to falsely confess too. One accused prisoner later wrote that in the Salem jail she was "hurried out of my senses" by two of the false confessors, who "cried out against me charging me with witchcraft [over] the space of four days mocking me and spitting in my face saying they knew me to be an old witch and if I would not confess it I should very speedily be hanged."[11] This prisoner broke under pressure and falsely confessed simply in order to stop the harassment.

Ordinarily, prisoners were only kept in jail for brief periods of time. It was very rare for imprisonment to be a sentence ordered by a court; instead, it was usually a temporary condition until one's case was tried.[12] Bail was not allowed for witchcraft or other capital crimes under the colony's laws, so all the accused remained confined.[13] In 1692 some waited almost a year before being brought before a court.

On the same day that the magistrates sent Nurse to the jail, they also sent little Dorothy Good, the four- or five-year-old daughter of Sarah Good. At Dorothy's hearing, the afflicted fell into fits whenever this little girl looked at them, and one of the afflicted even showed teeth marks on her arm—as was done at Nurse's hearing—and claimed that Good's specter bit her.[14] This poor child lived through the witch hunt but spent seven or eight months in jail and subsequently lost her mind from the trauma. With her mother confined in the Boston jail, Dorothy was motherless and had only Nurse and the other prisoners of the Salem jail to care for her in the harsh conditions.[15] Accusations continued, as more and more of Nurse's neighbors joined her behind the dismal dark walls, waiting for their day in court.

WHILE REBECCA NURSE was imprisoned in Salem Town, back in Salem Village Mrs. Ann Putnam had no fits for almost two weeks. According to Rev. Deodat Lawson, "some others" of the afflicted also saw Nurse's specter less frequently after she was imprisoned.[16] This change lent further credibility to the claim that Nurse was the cause of their fits.

Although some of the accusers saw their conditions improve after Nurse was jailed, Ann Putnam Jr. did not. Edward Putnam, Ann Jr.'s uncle, claimed that the day after Nurse's hearing, she "was bitten by Rebecca Nurse." He also stated that around 2 P.M. that day, Ann Putnam Jr. "was struck with [Nurse's] chain, the mark being in a kind of round ring and three strokes across the ring. She had six blows with a chain in the space of half an hour and she had one remarkable one with six strokes across her arm. I saw the mark both of bite and chain."[17] This claim that Nurse hit her with a chain was a new kind of accusation, and was related to Nurse's physical body now being chained in the Salem jail.

These chain marks are part of a significant shift in the accusations against Nurse and others in 1692. Early in the witch hunt, the alleged harm from witchcraft was primarily invisible and only the afflicted accusers' claimed reactions to spectral torment were visible as they screamed and thrashed around in their fits. The afflicted claimed to see spirits that ordinary people could not and offered no evidence other than their word and their strange behavior. However, with Nurse's case the accusations soon began to include an increasing amount of false physical evidence. No longer can so-called hysteria, conversion disorder, or other psychological conditions explain the entirety of the accusers' actions, as they might explain the genesis of the terror. From here on, fraud becomes increasingly evident—and this faked evidence proved fatal to the accused.

For example, at Nurse's hearing the previous day in the crowded meetinghouse Mary Walcott screamed and claimed that Nurse's specter bit her. She then presented her wrist and, according to Lawson, those present saw the bite marks on Walcott's skin.[18] If there was an alleged bite mark and upon examination there truly appeared to be teeth marks on her arm, then there must have been an actual bite (or someone pressed something in the shape of teeth against her arm to create the mark). Did Walcott bite herself on purpose to create a mark to frame Nurse? Did one of the other accusers next to Walcott bite her without her expecting it, leading to the surprised scream and the production of a genuine bite mark that Walcott then falsely attributed to Nurse? It cannot be known for sure if this instance is conspiracy among the accusers, or Walcott's action alone. But, it is an example of obviously false and forged evidence—*someone* bit her arm (or intentionally pressed something against it) in order for teeth-like marks to be present, and it was falsely claimed to be Nurse's fault.

Writing in 1700, Robert Calef described incidences of alleged biting during the witch hunt: "The accusers are said to have suffered much by biting . . . but such as had not such bewitched eyes have seen the accusers bite themselves, and then complain of the accused. It has also been seen when the accused, instead of having such a set of teeth [to match the imprint], has not one in his head."[19] Calef describes clear fraud. Also, his point about the accused person not even having teeth to cause the bite is interesting in regards to Nurse, because at the time an elderly woman like her was unlikely to have any teeth left. Although it is probably exaggerated, when Edward Ward wrote of Boston in 1699 he recounted that the odds were "ten to one" that a woman had lost all of her teeth before marrying age in her early to mid-twenties, never mind at Nurse's age of seventy-one.[20]

Rev. Lawson relates other instances that can be read as early examples of false physical evidence, and also of conspiracy among the accusers, which is examined by historian Bernard Rosenthal.[21] Lawson wrote in a narrative that he later published with the sermon he gave the day of Nurse's arrest, "Some of the afflicted, as they were striving in their fits, in open court, have (by invisible means) had their wrists bound fast together with a real cord, so as it could hardly be taken off without cutting. Some afflicted have been found with their arms tied, and hanged upon a hook, from whence others have been forced to take them down that they might not expire in that posture."[22] No hallucination or nervous twitch can cause a rope to magically tie itself around the accuser's hand: it was done intentionally. Also, Lawson's comments reveal a conspiracy, because it does not seem possible for an accuser to get into these situations on her own. The accusers must have worked together to orchestrate these deceptions.[23]

In addition to examples of fraud and conspiracy in Lawson's narrative that accompanied his sermon, historian Peter Charles Hoffer takes note of signs of coordination in Lawson's better-known other account of the early phase of the witch hunt, *A Brief and True Narrative of Some Remarkable Passages Relating to Sundry Persons Afflicted by Witchcraft, in Salem Village* (1692).[24] For example, in this account Lawson wrote of the accusers, "They did in the assembly mutually cure each other, even with a touch of their hand, when strangled, and otherwise tortured." As soon as one of the other accusers put their hand on the person having a fit, their fit suddenly stopped as if by command. Additionally, Lawson records, "They did also foretell when another's fit was a-coming, and would say, 'look to her, she will have a fit presently,' which fell out accordingly, as many can bear witness, that heard and saw it."[25] Hoffer sees these statements as examples of some accusers directing the fits of others.[26]

Returning to Edward Putnam and Ann Putnam Jr.'s claims about Nurse hitting her with a chain, this situation is also a clear example of faked evidence and potential conspiracy. Salem historian Charles W. Upham seizes upon Ann Putnam Jr.'s claim about being hit by a chain as the most damning evidence of her lying, and proof that her actions were driven by lies rather than any delusion. Writing in the nineteenth century, Upham states that the incident with the supposed chain marks "makes it more difficult to palliate her conduct on the supposition of partial insanity. . . . It is hard to avoid the conclusion that Ann Putnam [Jr.] was guilty of elaborate falsehood and studied trick."[27] She used premeditated lying and deceit to support her false accusation of witchcraft against Rebecca Nurse.

In this incident with Ann Putnam Jr. and the alleged chain attack described above, Edward Putnam later swore to the truthfulness of his testimony in court. Is he lying when he said "I saw the mark both of bite and chain" on the arm of his niece? Perhaps Ann Putnam Jr. willfully bit her arm and then showed it to her uncle and claimed it as evidence to deceive him. Additionally, if there really was a chain mark on her arm—in this case the testimony describes a series of six different chain marks appearing in the space of half an hour—either she or someone else was intentionally pressing a chain (or chain-like object) against her arm in several different instances in order to create misleading marks to deceive her uncle.

It seems incredible that Edward Putnam did not notice little Ann repeatedly leaving his presence, someone else hitting her (or her hitting herself) with a chain-like object hard enough to leave a mark, then her reentering the room to show him the marks, over and over, six times in half an hour, and not wonder why it only happened when she was out of sight. Or, maybe Edward Putnam, deacon of the Salem Village church, made the whole thing up and swore on God's name to a lie in order to further some conspiracy. As previously noted, there is no strong motive for him—or the other members of the Putnam family—to lie and frame Nurse specifically. Whether Ann Putnam Jr. lied to her uncle, or her uncle was conspiring and lied to the court, a willful and malicious deception occurred, which was used as evidence against Nurse.

Writing in the 1760s, Massachusetts Royal Governor Thomas Hutchinson shared a similar interpretation as Upham of the obvious instances of fraud. He wrote in his *History of the Province of Massachusetts Bay*, "There are a great number of persons who are willing to suppose the accusers to have been under bodily disorders which affected their imaginations. This is kind and charitable, but seems to be winking the truth out of sight. A little attention must force conviction that the whole was a scene of fraud and imposture."[28] While the reasons for the afflicted accusers' initial fits are unclear and historians continue to debate and investigate whether their fits began as symptoms of mental illness or as intentional lies, it is clear that fraud and lies appeared quite quickly after the witch hunt began. Fraud appeared early on in Nurse's case, and became even more egregious at her trial in June.

THE SABBATH FOLLOWING Nurse's arrest, March 27, was Easter Sunday according to Catholics and Anglicans. Although the Puritans did not mark this occasion, it happened to be the monthly Sacrament Sunday at the village church.[29] On this occasion, Rev. Samuel Parris delivered a sermon related to the accusations against Nurse and the others during the preceding month. Parris writes that the sermon was "Occasioned by dreadful witchcraft broke[n] out here a few weeks past, and one member of this church, and another of Salem upon public examination by civil authority vehemently suspected for she-witches, and upon it committed."[30] His sermon was an attempt to unite the congregation behind him in the face of the perceived threat, but it backfired.

That morning, Rev. Parris climbed the pulpit in front of the villagers sitting in the meetinghouse—the very place where a few days prior the accusers wailed, Nurse was sent off to jail, and Rev. Lawson preached his rallying cry. Those facing Parris in the pews were a combination of accusers, bystanders, and friends and relatives of the accused. Parris began by reading John 6:70, in which Jesus reveals that one of the apostles will betray him: "Have I not chosen you twelve, & one of you is a Devil."[31] To the congregation's surprise, Nurse's sister Sarah Cloyce rose in her pew.

The scripture passage relating that one of Christ's chosen ones, a visible saint, was instead a devil in disguise was a clear enough allusion to the accusation against Nurse. Cloyce could not bear to hear her own minister compare her innocent sister to Judas, and as soon as Parris read the text she stood up, exited her pew, walked out the front door of the meetinghouse with her back to Rev. Parris, and according to one account, "flung the door after her violently, to the amazement of the congregation."[32] Another source describes the slammed door slightly more mildly, blaming nature: "The wind shutting the door forcibly, gave occasion to some to suppose she went out in anger."[33] Regardless of which version is more accurate, the villagers in the pews saw Sarah Cloyce abruptly leave the service and heard the slam of the door reverberate around the bare rafters of the meetinghouse. This scene was not forgotten.

Parris then continued his sermon, drawing clear lines between the community and those accused of witchcraft: "We are either saints or devils, the scripture gives us no medium." He also declared, "There are such devils in the Church: Not only sinners but notorious sinners; sinners more like to the Devil than others. So here in Christ's little Church."[34] Parris does not discuss the *possibility* of witches (devils) being present, but instead states that there *are* witches, accepting their presence as fact.[35] Furthermore, although only five people were accused of witchcraft at this point, Parris engaged in wild speculation and announced the possibility that there were many more witches yet to be caught: "Christ knows how many devils [are] amongst us: whether one, or ten, or 20 and also who they are."[36] The irresponsible suggestion that there could be so many more witches yet to be caught only heightened the fear at this early stage of the witch hunt.

In this sermon, Parris also expressed the belief that the Devil could not impersonate the innocent—a belief that had fatal consequences in 1692. Parris taught, "The Devil would represent the best saints as devils if he could, but it is not easy to imagine that his power is of such extent to the hazard of the Church."[37] This belief meant that in effect when the accusers (who were believed to be speaking the truth as to what they saw) claimed to see a person's specter, the accused person must be guilty. Parris is the first person from Salem Village to publicly declare this fateful belief, which was later adopted by the witchcraft court and caused an insurmountable assumption of guilt for the accused.

Cloyce's disruption and defiance toward Rev. Parris that morning placed much attention on her—a very dangerous thing at such a time of suspicion. Two accusers later claimed that on the day that she "ran out of the meetinghouse from the Sacrament in a great rage," she met the Devil at the door and "made a curtsy, and at that time set her hand to his book," signifying that she was a witch.[38] Cloyce leaving the service on Sacrament Sunday meant that she, a church member, did not receive the Lord's Supper, a fact not lost on the accusers. Lawson recounts that several of the accusers later claimed that Cloyce forsook the Lord's Supper with the village church to celebrate a satanic sacrament outside with "red bread and drink."[39] This was only the beginning of the reaction against Cloyce.

Later that same day Mary Sibley, who had instructed John Indian and Tituba to bake the witch cake several weeks prior, was brought before the gathered church members. Of all those involved in the witch hunt, Sibley had done the closest thing to witchcraft, which Parris described as "going to the Devil for help against the Devil." Parris further denounced her and said of her experiment with the witch cake: "By this means (it seems) the Devil hath been raised amongst us, and his rage is vehement and terrible, and when he shall be silenced, the Lord only knows."[40] Sibley apologized to her fellow church members for her actions, and was forgiven. She was never charged with witchcraft, while respected church member Rebecca Nurse—who was never connected to any supposed magic charms—lay in jail, and soon her sister Sarah Cloyce, also a church member, joined her.

THE FOLLOWING DAY, March 28, was Rebecca Nurse's fourth in jail, still with no trial date set. Back in the village, her family prepared her defense.

Nurse's son Samuel and son-in-law John Tarbell went to Thomas and Ann Putnam's house to gather information. The more than three-mile journey to this remote corner of the village took the two men past the home of the widow Sarah Holten and her pigs, down the Andover Road past Ingersoll's tavern and the watchtower, alongside the village militia training field, and down a rural country path until they eventually reached the fields along the banks of the Ipswich River, under the looming shadow of Hathorne Hill. Here, the Putnams lived.

This journey was a dangerous one. It was after Martha Corey paid a visit to this house exactly two weeks prior—and Ann Putnam Jr. screamed as she crossed the threshold—that she was arrested on charges of witchcraft. Samuel Nurse and Tarbell, the relatives of an accused witch, were now themselves potential targets for accusations.

Ann Putnam Jr. was a significant figure in 1692: she was involved in cases against sixty-nine people, including thirteen who would be executed. Together, four members of the Putnam household—Thomas Putnam Jr., Ann Putnam Sr., Ann Putnam Jr., and Mercy Lewis—were responsible for more than 160 accusations.[41] As to Nurse's case, of the eighteen surviving depositions against her, ten were signed by one or more members of the extended Putnam family.[42] Members of this family played a pivotal role in the witch hunt.

There is clear evidence that Ann Putnam Jr. lied and made false accusations, though there is also the possibility that her initial fits were caused by previous trauma, before her actions changed to fraud. Three years earlier, when she was only nine years old, she watched her six-week-old sister Sarah die a frightening death.[43] It was horrific, and Ann later testified that her little sister had fits in which it appeared as though the infant was "whipped" to death.[44] Witnessing her little sister die in such a cruel manner likely left a lasting impression on the child.

Thomas Putnam and his uncle Nathaniel Putnam (the Nurse family's neighbor) were the village's largest landholders, and both Thomas and Mrs. Ann Putnam were members of the village church.[45] Accusations made by members of Thomas Putnam's household and charges filed by him or his relatives were taken seriously. From the documents that Putnam entered as evidence, it appears that he believed that his family was attacked by real witchcraft.[46] Additionally, Putnam wrote a letter to the magistrates later that spring in which he seems to believe that his daughter was a prophet of sorts.[47] These were the people that Samuel Nurse and Tarbell went to speak with.

From the two men's testimony, they were apparently allowed to visit and ask questions of the Putnam family and their servant Mercy Lewis.

Although ill-will between these families is taken for granted by many historians, it is important to note that the Putnam family was willing not just to talk with the Nurse family emissaries but even allowed themselves to be questioned. Had there truly been a sharp grudge between the families prior to the witch hunt, one would assume that the Nurse contingent would not have been welcome to pay a visit to the Putnams in this way.

After arriving, Tarbell asked the Putnams several questions while trying to collect evidence about the initial accusation against Nurse and the circumstances leading up to it. He wrote his account of that day in testimony submitted to the court. Tarbell wrote that "upon discourse of many things" he "asked them some questions and, among others, I asked this question: whether the girl that was afflicted [Ann Putnam Jr.] did first speak of Goody Nurse before others mentioned her to her." Ann Jr. does not seem to have been present, because her family answers the question, "They said she told them she saw the apparition of a pale-faced woman that sat in her grandmother's seat [in the meetinghouse] but did not know her name."[48] Nurse and Ann Jr.'s grandmother, as two of the most respected older women in the village of good Christian reputation, had a prominent pew in the meetinghouse reflecting this status. But this respect, and acknowledged Christian behavior, was not enough to save her from being accused.

It is interesting that the Putnam women claimed that Ann Jr. saw an image of Nurse but did not know her name. If the Nurses were sworn enemies to the Putnams, as was long suggested, surely Ann Jr. would have heard Nurse's name before, likely from her parents' complaints. This lack of familiarity with Nurse casts further doubt on the theory that she was accused because of factional village disputes.

Tarbell then asked, "But who was it that told her it was Goody Nurse?" He received no clear answer. Mercy Lewis, the Putnams' servant and another one of the afflicted, said it was Mrs. Putnam that identified the alleged vision as Nurse. In turn, Mrs. Putnam claimed that Lewis first said that it was Nurse. Tarbell writes that the two women "turned it upon one another saying 'it was you,' and 'it was you that told her'" without any clear conclusion.[49]

Ann Jr.'s initial accusation, in which she claimed to see someone who sat in the same pew as her grandmother, does not necessarily point to Nurse. Several women sat with Ann Jr.'s grandmother on the long and crowded bench in the meetinghouse. Why then was Nurse's name suggested for the specter and not one of the other women, presumably all of whom were elderly and would have fit the description she reported? It is not possible to confirm the motive for accusing Nurse without knowing exactly who it was that first accused her—whoever told Ann Jr. that the specter she claimed to see was that of Rebecca Nurse.

Additionally, if it was known which person first accused Nurse of witchcraft, it might have been easier for Samuel Nurse and Tarbell to evaluate what caused the accusation, and it might inform how the family could best prepare evidence for her defense. Since no conclusion was reached, modern historians are left with conflicting theories and ideas as to why someone in the Putnam household accused Rebecca Nurse. As the two men departed the Putnams' house they were probably similarly puzzled. The one piece of information that they gleaned was that Nurse's name was first mentioned back when only Ann Jr. was having fits, and before Mrs. Putnam or Mercy Lewis reported any fits.

Samuel Nurse and Tarbell began their more than three-mile journey home, passing by Ingersoll's tavern at the village center again. That day at Ingersoll's the arrests of Nurse and the other accused was the topic of conversation. Among those sitting in the barroom were twenty-six-year-old William Rayment Jr. of Beverly and twenty-seven-year-old Daniel Elliott of Salem Village, who both took part in this discussion and later entered testimony to the court about it.[50]

Rayment mentioned that Elizabeth Proctor was recently accused, to which "Goody Ingersoll replied that she did not believe it." Also present at Ingersoll's were "some of the afflicted persons." At the mentioning of Proctor, "one or more of them cried out 'there is Goody Proctor,' 'there is Goody Proctor, old witch! I'll have her hang!'" What happened next is particularly interesting for historians trying to decipher the reasons for the witchcraft accusations. Rayment recounts that after this outburst, "Goody Ingersoll sharply reproved" the afflicted, after which "they then seemed to make a jest of it." Elliott recounts that after Hannah Ingersoll chastised the afflicted, one of them "said that she did it for sport, for they must have some sport."[51]

It is unclear which of the accusers were at Ingersoll's that day, or which of them claimed that the accusation against Proctor was merely "sport." Meanwhile, Nurse spent another cold night in the Salem jail, weak and ill.

THE LAST FEW DAYS of March brought further accusations, and March 31 was a public fast day for the sufferings of the afflicted. One particularly fantastic accusation lodged by Abigail Williams regarding the fast day involved Rebecca Nurse.

Williams claimed that Nurse's "apparition" came to her and hurt her while she was at home that day. While this spectral attack allegedly occurred in the parsonage, Williams claimed that forty more witches entered the house to hold an evil mock communion service in her presence.[52] Satan's legions were allegedly now in the minister's home, whose ownership was still contested.

Nurse was accused of participating in this mock communion rite in the parsonage, during which the witches allegedly consumed "red bread and red drink" that appeared to be real flesh and real blood.[53] Williams said of the mock sacrament, "They said it was our blood, and that they had it twice that day."[54] She also mentioned Nurse's sister Sarah Cloyce— not just as being present, but also serving as the deacon who distributed the evil sacrament. According to Lawson's accounts of her fits, Williams at one point cried out, "Oh Goodwife Cloyce, I did not think to see you here!" and then said "Is this a time to receive the Sacrament? You ran away on the Lord's Day and scorned to receive it in the meetinghouse, and is this a time to receive it? I wonder at you!"[55] Cloyce's defiant exit that previous Sunday had made a clear impression on the accusers.

The next day, April 1, the Putnams' servant Mercy Lewis added more details to the description of the witches allegedly profaning the parsonage. Lawson recounts Lewis as staunchly rebuking the witches when she claimed to be confronted with this evil sacrament: "They did eat red bread like man's flesh, and would have had her eat some, but she would not; but turned away her head, and spit at them, and said, 'I will not eat, I will not drink, it is blood,' etc. She said, 'that is not the bread of life, that is not the water of life; Christ gives the bread of life, I will have none of it!'"[56] In this passage, Lewis appears as the heroic defender of the faith against the unseen enemy in Rev. Parris' absence, quite certainly how she wanted Rev. Lawson (who recorded her words and actions) to think of her.

Lewis also described to Lawson an apocalyptic vision she said she had that same day. "Mercy Lewis aforesaid saw in her fit a white man and was with him in a glorious place, which had no candles nor sun, yet was full of light and brightness; where was a great multitude in white glittering robes and they sang the song in the fifth of Revelation the ninth verse, and the 110 Psalm and the 149 Psalm; and she said with herself, 'How long shall I stay here? Let me be along with you.' She was loth to leave this place, and grieved that she could tarry no longer."[57]

The verse of Revelation that Lewis mentions reads: "And they sung a new song, saying, Thou art worthy to take the book, and to open the seals thereof, because thou wast killed, and hast redeemed us to God by thy blood out of every kindred, and tongue, and people, and nation."[58] The mentioned book is the Book of Life, in which are inscribed the names of all who will be redeemed at the Final Judgment. This book is the exact opposite of the Devil's book in which the accused witches allegedly signed their names. Those whose names are written in the Devil's book are the souls that will not be redeemed.

The alleged vision implies that Mercy Lewis was chosen by God to stand in the light of heaven with the saints, again described in a way so as to boost her religious credentials. Also, such an apocalyptic vision—complete with singing the song from the Book of Revelation—implies that the end of days was near in Salem Village.

Around the same day that Mercy Lewis allegedly had her visions, twenty-three-year-old Stephen Bittford later claimed that he had a vision of his own. He stated that he awoke and saw the spirit of Nurse along with the spirits of John and Elizabeth Proctor standing in his bedroom. He recounted that he suddenly had "a very great pain" in his neck and could not move his head.[59]

Having one's specter seen with Nurse's was now considered strong evidence against an accused person. A legal complaint of witchcraft against Elizabeth Proctor was made on April 4 along with a complaint of witchcraft against Nurse's sister Sarah Cloyce, whose actions that fateful morning in the meetinghouse still echoed in the minds of the accusers.[60]

ON APRIL 11, Deputy Governor Thomas Danforth, along with four other members of the Council of Assistants—James Russell, Isaac Addington, Samuel Appleton, and Samuel Sewall—rode into Salem Town and entered the meetinghouse, the earthly home of Rebecca Nurse's parish the Salem Town church.[61] The Assistants were the upper house of the legislature, which doubled as the highest court in the colony and the only court that tried cases of life and limb.[62] The governor, Simon Bradstreet, did not attend and remained in Boston because he was elderly and infirm.[63]

Instead of bringing the newly accused before only the two local magistrates as was done previously, the out-of-town members of the Council of Assistants joined the local Assistants John Hathorne and Jonathan Corwin for the hearings of the recently arrested. News of the witchcraft accusations in Salem Village spread far and wide, and the issue was viewed by the council as being so serious that it required their intervention. The alleged witches were no longer seen as a threat to Salem Village alone, but as a threat to the whole besieged Puritan commonwealth.[64]

Deputy Governor Danforth, who presided over the hearings that day, was a strong proponent of traditional Massachusetts rights and liberties and a skeptic of the witch hunt. (This is entirely counter to how play-wright Arthur Miller portrays him in *The Crucible*, which uses his name for a composite character that does not resemble the actual historical figure.) As historian Emerson W. Baker notes, Danforth and the council could have put an end to the witch hunt at this session, or at least inhibited the fast flow of accusations.[65] As the highest governing body in the colony (excepting the absent governor) they had broad authority to decide the legitimacy of the accusations and the process for handling them.

Later in 1692, Danforth was listed as a leading opponent of the witch hunt, along with Governor Bradstreet.[66] Danforth and the other Assistants had been hesitant over the previous decades to allow accused witches to be convicted. The magistrates' skepticism began in 1656 when Ann Hibbens of Boston, the widow of a magistrate and the sister of a former governor, was found guilty of witchcraft by a jury when she was tried before the Assistants. However, the Assistants refused to accept the jury's guilty verdict, and the case was then sent to the General Court. The delegates of the General Court, which in addition to being the lower house of the legislature settled appeals from the Assistants, found Hibbens guilty and she was hanged.[67]

Though it might seem strange to modern American readers that the houses of the legislature (both the Assistants and the General Court) also acted as judicial courts, this was the traditional English constitutional system in which there was no clear separation of powers between the highest legislative and judicial bodies. In England and subsequently the United Kingdom, the House of Lords, the upper chamber of Parliament, was also the highest court of appeal until constitutional reform in 2009.[68]

In the Hibbens case, the Assistants showed caution in rejecting the verdict, but were simply overruled by the lower house of the legislature. The Assistants believed that a great injustice was done, and thereafter inhibited convictions for witchcraft. Only one person was hanged for witchcraft between 1656 and 1692, Ann Glover of Boston, who falsely confessed to the crime and was executed in 1688.[69] In light of this tradition of skepticism and the insisted upon innocence of the accused, there was a strong chance that the witch hunt would end here.

Assistant Samuel Sewall noted the large crowd at the hearings in Salem Town that morning, which probably accounts for why the council chose to convene in the Salem Town meetinghouse instead of in the smaller town house where the county court usually met.[70] Though Rebecca Nurse was confined and chained in the Salem jail a few streets away, as she had been for nineteen days, she was present in the testimony of the accusers and allegedly present in spectral form.

The council conducted the hearings of several of the accused that day, including Nurse's sister Sarah Cloyce. The guards brought the prisoners to the meetinghouse by 11 A.M., and the proceedings began with a prayer by Rev. Nicholas Noyes, one of the ministers of the Salem Town church.[71] As Nurse's sister stood before the council and the gathered crowd, the afflicted broke out into fits, similar to what occurred at Nurse's hearing. But, Cloyce struck a much sharper tone than the elderly and ill Nurse did at her hearing.

John Indian, husband of Tituba, now claimed to be among the afflicted and was the first of Cloyce's accusers to testify that day. At one point during his testimony, Cloyce interrupted,

"When did I hurt you?"

"A great many times."

"Oh, you are a grievous liar!"[72]

Later in the hearing, Mary Walcott accused Cloyce of appearing to her with a book and hurting her "sometimes in company with Goody Nurse and Goody Corey, and a great many that I do not know." The council record states that as Walcott finished saying this "she fell into a fit again." Accuser Benjamin Gould also mentioned Nurse, and said "that he had seen Goodman Corey and his wife, Proctor and his wife, Goody Cloyce, Goody Nurse, and Goody Griggs [the wife of the doctor] in his chamber last Thursday night."[73] Here again the recently accused were connected to Nurse in an attempt to tie them to her assumed guilt.

The council questioned Abigail Williams, who testified about the witches' Sabbath she claimed to witness a week earlier in the parsonage, when forty witches allegedly assembled and drank the blood of the afflicted in a mockery of the Christian sacrament. Mercy Lewis added to this description of the black mass, by alleging that a "fine, grave man" was also present—potentially the Devil, because "he made all the witches tremble." Williams then mentioned that she also saw this powerful man at Ingersoll's tavern, along with specters of "Goody Cloyce, Goody Nurse, Goody Corey, and Goody Good." This claim appeared to overwhelm Cloyce, for according to the council record, "Cloyce asked for water. And sat down as one seized with a dying fainting fit; and several of the afflicted fell into fits, and some of them cried out 'Oh! Her spirit is gone to prison to her sister Nurse!'"[74] That night Cloyce and the other accused joined

Nurse in the Salem jail. The council ordered them held to await future trials.

In appearance, the gathered Assistants acted no differently than Hathorne and Corwin did previously, and by accepting the evidence against the accused and ordering them to jail, the highest political authorities in the colony gave the witch hunt a stamp of approval.[75] But historian Bernard Rosenthal suggests that Governor Bradstreet may have simultaneously worked behind the scenes to prevent the witchcraft accusations from ever reaching a grand jury or going to trial—potentially with the hope that the fear would subside.[76]

Usually the grand jury phase of the prosecution took place soon after the initial hearings, but not in April 1692.[77] The interim government had the authority to put the accused on trial and execute them, but took no action to begin the next stages of prosecution.[78] This is in sharp contrast to the actions of the new royal government that took power in May and immediately made arrangements to try the suspects as quickly as possible. Since they were later noted as opponents of the trials, it is quite plausible that perhaps the elderly Governor Bradstreet and Deputy Governor Danforth prevented the proceedings from moving on to their next stages because they were skeptical of the accusations.[79] In the end, the trials were merely delayed, while more and more accusations were filed.

THE NEXT MORNING, April 12, a new period of Nurse's imprisonment began. The council ordered that Nurse, her sister Sarah Cloyce, Martha Corey, little Dorothy Good, Elizabeth Proctor, and John Proctor be transferred from the Salem jail to the Boston jail, where several other accused from Salem Village already languished.[80]

The turnkey gathered the prisoners, and their convoy left the jail on horseback, escorted by Marshal George Herrick and other guards.[81] The prison column traveled through the town center, probably drawing a crowd of spectators. After leaving the bounds of Salem, the prisoners and guards followed rough roads on a winding fifteen-mile journey to the ferry at Boston Harbor, which took most of the day.[82] They passed the glistening ponds on the outskirts of Lynn, crossed the Saugus River, and voyaged on past Rumney Marsh. From there they rode around Powderhorn Hill, looming as a mountain among the marshes, and continued on until they reached the ferry landing at Winnisimmet, a small coastal village on the banks of the Mystic River that included Native dwellings among the New Englanders' houses.[83]

In those days, relatives sometimes accompanied prisoners while they were transported and rode with them. Perhaps some members of Nurse's and Sarah Cloyce's family also traveled with their loved ones, since Giles Corey accompanied his accused wife Martha that day as far as the ferry.[84] Corey did not take the ferry across due to lack of money, but he was accused of witchcraft soon afterward, and next time his ferry fare was paid by the marshal.

Across the confluence of rivers lay Boston. It was practically an island, with only a thin neck connecting Boston's South End to Roxbury on the mainland. It was a town of wooden and stone buildings ringed by docks, with three hills towering above the settlement.[85] The first two hills, Copps Hill and Fort Hill, were along the harbor and fortified with timberworks and artillery, and the third rise was Beacon Hill.[86] Governor John Winthrop first set a beacon upon the hill in the 1630s to warn Bostonians in case of an invasion by England during an early dispute over the colony's charter.[87] The Massachusetts government later supplemented the beacon with "loud babbling guns" perched atop the hill.[88] When fired, the sound from these cannon rattled the houses below and reverberated across the harbor and rivers to warn neighboring towns of an impending attack on the capital of the commonwealth. As war raged on the northern frontier against the French and their Native allies, fears of invasion remained high in 1692.

Nurse, the other prisoners, and the guards embarked on the ferry and floated out onto the Mystic River and then passed by the mouth of the Charles River—that King Charles I had humbly named after himself decades earlier.[89] As their small craft traversed the wide harbor they passed large ships from ports across the world, and yet more ships being built in shipyards.[90] The ferry sailed past the North Battery, a pier with a fortified position of earth and timber at the end with several cannon.[91] Although one war lived in the spiritual world, this was a reminder that another war was very real.

The ferry disembarked at the end of one of the main streets in Boston, in a neighborhood of merchants' counting houses along the wharfs.[92] The commotion of cargo being unloaded, carts rolling by, seagulls blaring, and fish-criers hawking their wares was a stark contrast to quiet Salem Village.[93] Even in this early age, six thousand people crammed into this metropolis of New England, a town of one thousand houses wedged up against one another, that one traveler compared to the buildings of London that also had no space between them.[94] Around these tightly packed buildings the town had streets paved with pebble stone that doubled as open, stinking sewers.[95] The stench of this filth intermixed with the smells of fish and sea to greet Nurse and the others.

The prisoners traveled another mile and a half to the jail. As they passed down one of the widest and busiest streets in Boston they undoubtedly attracted attention. After the meeting of the Council of Assistants in Salem Town, the out-of-town Assistants returned to their homes, spreading the word about the Salem "witches" throughout the colony.[96] One can only speculate how the spreading of gossip embellished and warped the story of the accused and the afflicted inhabitants of Salem Village by the time it reached the ears of common people in Boston—as if the actual allegations were not sensational enough. In addition to local gossip, the stories of Nurse, Sarah Cloyce, and others involved in the witch hunt were enshrined in print. Rev. Lawson spent a month in Salem Village writing down observations, which he published after he returned to Boston the first week of April. The magistrates "revised and corrected" Lawson's account prior to publication, and that day Nurse passed by the bookshop in Boston where the book was sold.[97]

Nurse and the other prisoners continued their travel through Boston under the interrogating eyes of the locals. The prisoners passed through North Square, the location of the North Meetinghouse where Rev. Cotton Mather and his father Rev. Increase Mather preached. Just before reaching the jail, they passed by the Boston Town House, seat of the Massachusetts government, and in the square nearby were the town stocks and whipping post.[98] Finally, Nurse and the others arrived at Prison Lane, a residential street one block long with the jail and jailer's house about halfway down the street.[99] At the end of Prison Lane the upward slope of Beacon Hill appeared, with the signal tower at the top. No light shone forth on that day.

The jail was a bleak, stone structure with one large common room where prisoners spent most of their days, and a fenced-in yard where they could get a breath of fresh air. Off the common room were hallways leading to small cells divided by wooden walls in which the prisoners spent their nights. A prisoner in the 1750s wrote that the hallway leading to these cells reminded him "of the dark valley of the shadow of death."[100] These cells were sopping wet when it rained, sometimes with five or six inches of standing water on the ground.[101] The muddy floor was covered in wood shavings to soak up the rainwater and bodily fluids.[102] The jail was rundown when Nurse arrived, and later that spring jailer John Arnold purchased nails, boards, and locks to repair both the jailer's house and the jail.[103]

Prisoners were first kept in chains, that could weigh eight pounds, and later in full shackles. It was believed that iron shackles would prevent the accused from sending their specters out from the jail to attack the afflicted.[104] The Boston jail also had a collection of leglocks, handlocks, neck irons, and iron rods with sliding shackles if needed.[105]

Surviving descriptions of the Boston jail describe it as hell on earth. The son of another elderly woman (of roughly Nurse's age) who was in the Boston jail wrote to the General Court that the jail was "stinking," and asked that his elderly mother "may not forever lie in such misery, wherein her life is made more afflictive to her than death."[106] There were other prisoners in jail in addition to those accused of witchcraft, and the residents were described by a Royal Navy officer imprisoned in 1692 as "witches, villains, negroes," and murderers.[107] A visitor to the Boston jail in 1686—before it was filled past capacity as it was in 1692—described it as "the grave of the living. . . 'tis a house of meager looks, and ill smells: for lice, drink, and tobacco are the compound: or if you will 'tis the suburbs of Hell; and the persons much the same as there." He describes the prisoners wearing ragged "thread-bare" clothing, and wrote of the sight of the poor souls confined in the terrible conditions, "Tis a spectacle of more pity than executions are."[108] This evil place was Nurse's new home and, with no trial date set, it was not clear how many months she would suffer within its walls.

WHILE REBECCA NURSE and the other accused languished in jail, the witch hunt gathered more speed. Despite her lying in chains miles away, the afflicted in Salem Village continued to yell and scream Nurse's name.

On April 12, Marshal George Herrick and several others went to the parsonage to receive a written report from Rev. Parris. However, he was not yet finished writing it because he was continuously interrupted by the fits of members of his household, and the chaos spilled into his upstairs study. The marshal sat down in the parsonage to wait for Parris to finish writing, and was then caught in the middle of the afflicted's fits. Abigail Williams told the marshal that a specter sat in his lap, John Indian claimed that John Proctor's specter was riding on the back of the reverend's dog, and then according to Parris' notes John Indian yelled, "Goody Cloyce, oh you old witch!" and began thrashing in "a violent fit that three men and the marshal could not without exceeding difficulty hold him." Just as Parris finished his report and read it to the marshal—who was probably in a hurry to leave this house of horrors—Mary Walcott, who oddly was "knitting and well-composed" during all of the previous chaos and disorder that permeated the parsonage that night, suddenly screamed that she saw John and Elizabeth Proctor, Martha Corey, Dorothy Good, Sarah Cloyce, and Rebecca Nurse.[109]

The next day, Abigail Williams had a fit and said that Nurse tried to force her to sign the Devil's book. Additionally, Williams claimed that because of Nurse she was "almost choked, and tempted to leap into the fire." Around the same time, Constable John Putnam Jr., a weaver, spread a rumor about Nurse's mother, Joanna Towne. In his own testimony to the court later that spring, he was vague about what he said and only admitted that he "reported something which I had heard concerning the mother of Rebecca Nurse, Mary Easty, and Sarah Cloyce." However, in a separate document submitted to the court, Mrs. Ann Putnam reveals the yarn that John Putnam Jr. spun: "John Putnam had said it was no wonder they were witches for their mother was so before them."[110] This is the only time such a claim was made, and there is no evidence that Nurse's mother was ever formally accused of witchcraft during her lifetime.

After making this comment about Nurse's mother, John Putnam Jr. claimed that he "was taken with a strange kind of fits."[111] Worse yet, his testimony states that his two-month-old daughter also suffered "strange and violent fits, which did most grievously affright us, acting much like to the poor and bewitched persons when we thought they would have died." Two days later, the child "departed this life by a cruel and violent death, being enough to pierce a stony heart."[112] These strange, unfortunate coincidences were used as yet more evidence against Nurse and Sarah Cloyce. Soon, Mary Easty was caught in the crosshairs too.

ON APRIL 18, warrants were sworn out against Giles Corey of Salem Town, Abigail Hobbs of Topsfield, and Bridget Bishop of Salem Town. One more notable person was mentioned in the warrant: Mary Warren, one of Nurse's accusers at her initial hearing, was now herself accused of witchcraft.[113]

Eighteen-year-old Mary Warren was a servant and one of the afflicted accusers present at Nurse's hearing in March, but her fits stopped once her master John Proctor (who did not believe that she was truly afflicted by witchcraft) threatened to beat her, and he may have followed through on that threat.[114] Warren later said that Proctor was angry that she accused people of witchcraft that he believed to be plainly innocent.[115] Proctor made this threat of corporal punishment in the wake of Nurse's initial hearing, and so it was Nurse whose innocence he was sure of. According to Salem villager Samuel Sibley, on the day after Nurse's hearing Proctor said to him about Warren and the other accusers, "If they were let alone so we should all be devils and witches quickly, they should rather be had to the whipping post." Proctor also reportedly threatened to "thresh the Devil out of" Warren.[116] Proctor believed that the accusations of the afflicted were merely misbehavior, not affliction from witchcraft, and therefore thought that their actions could be corrected by the disciplinary measures used at the time.

Warren's fits stopped after this threatened (or actual) beating. At some point in the days after her fits stopped, she reportedly said that the accusers "did but dissemble" in making their accusations, meaning that their accusations were false.[117] Warren was a threat to the accusers, because she could bring down the entire witch hunt, with serious consequences for them. Bearing false witness in a felony case was itself a felony, and if caught perjuring themselves with accusations of witchcraft that carried the death penalty, the false accusers could be executed.[118] In the words of magistrate John Hathorne at Nurse's hearing, causing an innocent person's death through a false accusation would make the accusers "murderers."[119]

Soon after Warren's statement, the accusers turned on her with a response that historian Emerson W. Baker describes as "quite calculated."[120] Warren was accused of witchcraft, brought before the magistrates on April 19, and claimed at the start of this hearing that she was innocent. Now she was on the other side, and the assumption of guilt that burdened all of the accused pressed down upon this former accuser. By the end of her hearing she fell into fits again, falsely confessed to witchcraft, and then her fits stopped.[121] The other accusers succeeded in circling the wagons and prevented Warren from undermining their position.

Warren was examined several more times over the month following her arrest. She claimed that after she signed the Devil's book she saw Nurse, Sarah Cloyce, and Dorothy Good most often out of the accused. But when Warren was in jail, she told her fellow prisoners a completely different story. On May 4, she told them that the magistrates "might as well examine Keysar's daughter" and "take notice of what she said as well as [what] any of the afflicted persons [said]." George Keysar's daughter, Hannah, evidently had some mental issues, and was described as "distracted for many years." Warren also told the other prisoners, "when I was afflicted I thought I saw the apparition of a hundred persons" and said that "her head was distempered so that she could not tell what she said, and the said Mary told us that when she was well again she could not say that she saw any of the apparitions at the time aforesaid."[122] Warren's statements imply that she did indeed suffer genuine mental episodes during her fits, but she still knew that the "affliction" was not caused by witchcraft and therefore lied when she knowingly accused innocent people of a capital crime.

On May 13, Warren returned to being an accuser and testified against Abigail Soames at her hearing, despite previously admitting to the other prisoners that her accusations were false. After the proceeding, she claimed that Nurse's specter along with those of Rev. George Burroughs and John Proctor attacked her and that Burroughs' specter bit her. One document states that this bite mark "was seen by many"—another example of the accusers using false evidence. Warren also claimed that Burroughs later appeared in her cell and summoned several witches, including Nurse and Elizabeth Proctor, who told her that "they were deacons, and would have had her eat some of their sweet bread and wine, and asking what wine it was one of them said it was blood and better than our wine."[123] Despite her shifting story and claims that the witchcraft accusations were not true, Warren went on to be a grand jury and trial witness for the capital crime of witchcraft against sixteen of the accused, including several who were killed in part due to her testimony.[124]

ELSEWHERE IN THE VILLAGE, on April 21 one man believed that he went toe-to-toe with the Devil's minions. Benjamin Hutchinson, foster son of tavern keeper Nathaniel Ingersoll, was outside the tavern around 11 A.M. when Abigail Williams said that she saw the specter of Rev. George Burroughs, one of the village's previous ministers.[125] If a church member with a spotless reputation like Rebecca Nurse could be accused of witchcraft, it was only a small step to next accuse a minister.

Williams claimed that Burroughs' specter confessed to murdering his two deceased wives, in addition to killing the wife of Rev. Lawson. Further, she said that Burroughs' specter was standing in the roadway watching them right at that very moment! Hutchinson threw his pitchfork at the spot where Williams said the specter stood, just as Williams fell into "a little fit," before she recovered and claimed that Hutchinson succeeded in tearing the minister's spectral coat, but not in injuring him. Hutchinson and Williams then went into Ingersoll's, where Williams claimed to see Burroughs' specter yet again in the great room of the tavern. Hutchinson drew his rapier and attempted to stab the spectral presbyter, but was told that he missed. Then Williams said that there was also a spectral cat, which he subsequently attempted to stab—with success, according to Williams.[126]

Soon after, the villagers gathered for the Lecture Day sermon down the road in the meetinghouse, and around 4 P.M. after the service some villagers returned to Ingersoll's. Hutchinson and Williams reentered the tavern along with Mary Walcott, and suddenly the spectral duel began anew. Walcott and Williams yelled out in the barroom that a specter of Deliverance Hobbs bit Walcott on the foot from under the table. They then claimed that the specters of Deliverance and William Hobbs were now standing at the edge of the table, so Hutchinson again drew his rapier and, according to his later testimony, "stabbed Goody Hobbs on the side as Abigail Williams and Mary Walcott said."[127]

Walcott and Williams then shouted that the room was now full of invisible witches. Hutchinson again stabbed and slashed at the air hoping to wound the invisible foes, and twenty-seven-year-old Eli Putnam joined him with his sword and swung away at the air in the barroom.[128] It is not clear what most of the other villagers thought of this scene (and opinions were likely influenced by how many pints had passed across the bar), but since Eli Putnam suddenly jumped in next to Hutchinson to join the fight, the accusers were apparently successful in getting others to believe that there was indeed a spectral battle occurring, even though no one else could see the supposed enemies.

The afflicted accusers soon declared victory and announced that the two men killed "a great black woman . . . and an Indian that came with her, for the floor is covered with blood." Of course, none but the two accusers could see these alleged casualties or the spectral blood. If the alleged specters in the tavern were not startling enough, Walcott and Williams turned around and looked through the pane-glass window toward Whipple Hill. On the hill they "said they saw a great company" of specters.[129] It appeared as though, rather than on the plains of Armageddon, the forces of evil had chosen Salem Village for their final battle. Hutchinson and Putnam reportedly won the battle of the barroom, but the imagined enemy remained strong, and frighteningly close by.

AWAY FROM the spectral duels, the evil of the witch hunt again touched Rebecca Nurse's family. Her sister Mary Easty was arrested on April 21, along with several others. The following morning, before Easty and the other recently arrested had their hearings, the afflicted accusers described another alleged convocation of witches outside the parsonage. Those who falsely confessed to witchcraft in later days added yet more details of this described gathering. According to the accusers, there was a blast of a trumpet, which signaled the witches to gather.[130] They claimed that all of the witches from the area flew in on poles and then had a picnic of bread and cheese in the parsonage pasture.[131]

Deliverance Hobbs, accused alongside Mary Easty, later falsely confessed to witchcraft and testified on two different occasions that she saw Nurse's specter. In one instance, she said that she saw Nurse's specter along with several of the other imprisoned women outside in the field receiving the evil sacrament of "red bread and red wine like blood" from Rev. Burroughs. She claimed that Burroughs then gave a sermon, and "pressed them to bewitch all in the Village, telling them they should do it gradually and not all at once, assuring them that they should prevail."[132]

According to one of the other false confessors, the Devil himself appeared in the pasture and opened "a great book," which his followers set "their hands and seals to" thereby agreeing to "afflict persons and to overcome the Kingdom of Christ, and set up the Devil's Kingdom." One of the afflicted also testified that she "heard them talk of throwing down the kingdom of Christ and setting up the Devil on his throne." William Barker, one of the false confessors, added in another court record that "Satan's design was to set up his own worship, [and] abolish all the churches in the country." He also said that Satan's army of 150 spectral swordsmen mustered in the parsonage pasture near the meetinghouse on that day to accomplish this goal.[133]

As the invisible satanic supper allegedly convened in the pasture, Hathorne and Corwin conducted hearings for Mary Easty and the other recently arrested in the meetinghouse. The building was so crowded that day and so many people were outside gathered around the windows that they blocked the openings to the point that the accusers could not see the accused across the room because not enough sunlight entered the dim building.[134]

These hearings continued despite the Devil's forces supposedly massing across the road, but the specters' supposed presence did disrupt the hearings. Rev. John Hale of Beverly reported that at one point those in the dark meetinghouse suddenly "heard in the air the sound of a trumpet," just like the one that allegedly announced the witch meeting. He writes that some individuals went to search for whoever blew the horn, but "upon all enquiry it could not be found that any mortal man did sound it."[135] This mystery did nothing to quell the villagers' fears.

As soon as the guards brought Mary Easty into the shadowy meeting-house, the afflicted accusers "fell into fits."[136] Easty was fifty-eight years old, and the mother of nine children.[137] She, like Nurse, was convincing in her claims of innocence, to the point that the magistrates appeared skeptical of the accusation against her and asked the accusers, "Are you certain this is the woman?"[138] But the wild actions of the accusers returned the judges to harder questioning, similar to how they were influenced by the accusers' fits at Nurse's hearing in March. Mary Easty and the other accused were ordered to the Salem jail, and the prisoners and guards passed by the Nurse house on their way to Salem Town.

The next day, the magistrates questioned Deliverance Hobbs (arrested the same day as Mary Easty) for a second time, after she confessed to witch-craft at her hearing the previous day. Part of the evidence against her at her first hearing was a wound in her side that was connected to the claim that Hutchinson stabbed her specter in Ingersoll's tavern. During her sec-ond interrogation, Hobbs told the authorities that she was a "Covenant Witch" (just as one might be a covenant member of the Puritan church), and she went on to further describe the spectral scene in the field next to the parsonage.[139] She claimed specifically that Nurse was not only present there (despite being in the Boston jail) but that Nurse was also one of the women who distributed the evil sacrament to the assembled witches.

Those who falsely confessed to witchcraft were often examined mul-tiple times in order to pry more evidence from them. Hobbs was ques-tioned again on May 3, at which point she once again mentioned Nurse as a fellow witch.[140] Whatever her motive was for falsely confessing to witchcraft—for it was too early to know whether falsely confessing would prolong her life, or dramatically shorten it—tying herself to previously accused Nurse added credibility to her "confession." Hobbs went on to make an important appearance at Nurse's eventual trial.

BACK IN BOSTON, the capital was busy preparing for Election Day. In con-trast to Satan's swordsmen gathering in Salem Village, on April 25 there was a large militia demonstration on Boston Common near the jail. At the conclusion, just as darkness arrived, former Salem Village minister Rev. Deodat Lawson read a prayer, and then all eight companies fired a volley in salute.[141] Echoing through the town streets, this loud boom was audible to Rebecca Nurse and the other prisoners in the nearby jail, and this noise was followed by the sounds of the militiamen marching off to drink and commiserate at nearby taverns.

Election Day was on May 3, and a few men from Salem Village attended. On that day, the deputies of the General Court and the freemen of the colony met at the Boston Town House in the square near the jail. All freemen of the colony could vote in person for the officers of the colony, such as the governor, and many eligible voters travelled miles to cast their vote.[142] The holiday was a social occasion as well as a political one, with many gatherings taking place after the official business was done.[143] Nurse's son Samuel was a freeman, but it is not known if he was in Boston that day.[144] The freemen reelected Governor Simon Bradstreet in what was the last time Massachusetts elected its own governor until the American Revolution. Down the street in the jail, nothing changed.

One of the Salem Village men in Boston for the election, John Willard, found himself accused of witchcraft due to an odd exchange that day. Several men from the village and former village minister Rev. Lawson met up for lunch that noon. The elderly Bray Wilkins later claimed that during lunch with these men John Willard, who was married to his granddaughter, gave him a strange look.[145] According to eighty-one-year-old Wilkins, this chance glance made him unable to "dine, nor eat anything. I cannot express the misery I was in for my water was suddenly stopped, and I had no benefit of nature, but was like a man on a rack."[146] For twelve days, until Willard was arrested on May 16, the elderly Wilkins claimed to remain in this condition, unable to urinate at all.

Once Willard was arrested, Wilkins later stated that his condition became the opposite, and suddenly he could not stop continuously urinating. He testified, "I was vexed with a flowing of water, so that it was hard to keep myself dry."[147] Dr. William Griggs confirmed that Wilkins' illness was supernatural, just as he originally diagnosed the afflicted as being harmed by witchcraft at the start of the witch hunt.[148] The actual cause of this irregularity was possibly a urinary tract stone or an inflamed prostate.[149]

In the following days, Susannah Sheldon accused Willard of traversing Salem's North River on some sort of flying saucer and landing in Salem Town by the bridge near to where the executions later took place.[150] This was a strange claim, but many stranger ones followed.

AWAY FROM THE Election Day revelers, Nurse remained chained. More and more newly accused filled the jail alongside her, while others simply could not survive the terrible conditions. Given the squalor and refuse in which Nurse lived and how ill she was when arrested, it is a wonder that she was able to survive this period of confinement as the days lengthened and the crowded jail room grew hotter.

On May 10, Sarah Osborne died in the Boston jail. Osborne, Sarah Good, Good's infant daughter, and Tituba were the first to be sent to the Boston jail on March 7, and had lived there for two full months.[151] Like Nurse, Osborne was ill when she was accused of witchcraft. Her condition worsened in the grimy and dismal conditions of the jail. Her death is the first of the witch hunt that is recorded, but unfortunately far from the last.

When Sarah Good arrived in the Boston jail in early March she brought in her arms a four-month-old infant.[152] Not much is known of the child, except that it spent part of its short life living in the putrid dungeon with the other prisoners, and soon died. In a petition written after the witch hunt ended, Good's husband wrote of the infant, "a sucking child died in prison before the mother's execution."[153] The child was in jail for almost a full month before the governor and council ordered prison keeper John Arnold to buy extra blankets for the infant. The child therefore lasted at least one month in the Boston jail, and died sometime before June 2 when its death is mentioned in court testimony.[154]

In the cramped quarters of the jail's common room, Nurse was likely present to witness this tragedy. As if the death of an infant was not traumatic enough for Sarah Good, after word of the infant's death reached Salem Village, accuser Susannah Sheldon claimed on June 2 that she had a dream in which Good told her that she intentionally killed her own child to "give it to the Devil."[155] There was no mercy to be found.

In June, Roger Toothaker—who was younger and healthier than Nurse—also died in jail. He was only fifty-eight, compared to Nurse who was seventy-one and ill.[156] In addition to being younger, Toothaker had been in jail for less than one month, whereas Nurse had been imprisoned almost three months by that time.[157] Amazingly, Nurse, especially in her frail and sick condition, survived imprisonment in such a horrible place.

As if the situation was not already miserable, the guards crammed more and more prisoners into the jail. On April 28 a mysterious prisoner named Samuel Passanauton joined Nurse and the others. The jail record describes him only as "an Indian" and states that he remained there for eight weeks.[158] It is unclear where he was from or what crime he was accused of committing, as those accused of other (non-witchcraft) crimes were also in the jail at the time.[159]

Four days later, Nurse and the others were joined by four more people sent down from Salem Town accused of witchcraft. Among these was

Lydia Dustin of Reading, an eighty-year-old woman with a "crooked back" who died in jail during the spring of 1693. Another of these prisoners was fourteen-year-old Sarah Morey, who was of a tender age and her mother later stated that "imprisonment was more to our damage than I can think of, know, or can speak."[160] The jail was killing innocents and ruining lives.

On either May 8 or 9, four more individuals accused of witchcraft entered the Boston Jail, including Rev. George Burroughs of Wells, Maine (and formerly of Salem Village).[161] The magistrates sent another group down from Salem Town on May 12, including Giles Corey of Salem Town, and Nathaniel Putnam's slave Mary Black of Salem Village, who lived on the farm next to the Nurse family.[162] The stone jail was jammed with alleged witches.

These prisoners, and those who continued to be sent down from Salem that spring and summer, reveal how the witch hunt had progressed since Nurse was accused. Three individuals were accused in February, and three in March (including Nurse). Then, twenty-two were accused in April as the witch hunt spread rapidly.[163] Additionally, once church members Nurse and Martha Corey were accused in March, individuals of all social classes and degrees of respectability were open to accusations, even those with political and religious influence. On the same day in April, Salem selectman and very wealthy ship-owner Philip English was accused, along with former Salem Village minister and Harvard graduate Rev. George Burroughs. In May, selectman Daniel Andrew was also accused but fled arrest. In the words of one prosecutor, "The afflicted spare no person of what quality so ever."[164]

In Burroughs' case, he was the minister of a precarious frontier town. After requests for reinforcements due to substantiated fears of French and Native attacks, in early May a detachment of soldiers arrived. But, instead of securing the town and defending the population, they had been given a direct order from the Council of Assistants to arrest Burroughs.[165] The soldiers brought the reverend in chains all the way from Maine to Salem Town, and left Wells vulnerable without any further reinforcements. In a truly bizarre scene, a minister was now in the Boston jail chained along with church member Rebecca Nurse.

In early May, two more of the commonwealth's enemies, this time of a more worldly sort, were imprisoned in the jail. François le Barre and François Blang, listed as "of Canada, prisoners of war," joined the alleged witches and others in the dank dungeon. There is another entry nine days later that notes one "Charles François" as a prisoner.[166] Judging from his

French name, he is presumably another prisoner of war, but there is no identifying information listed alongside his name in the record.

To those in Massachusetts, the worldly war against the French and Natives and the religious war against the alleged witches were connected. Rev. Cotton Mather later wrote that he heard from "one who was executed at Salem for witchcraft" that French Canadians and Natives were also present at the alleged witch meetings, "to concert their methods for ruining New England."[167] Now in the Boston jail New England's supposed spiritual and temporal enemies languished together.

In addition to the influx of inmates, visitors were also allowed into the jail, and Nurse's family visited her. Her son Samuel stated in a petition to the government after the trials that the Nurse family "spent much time and made many journeys to Boston and Salem and other places in order to have vindicated her innocency." He also noted that they paid for her charges so that she would receive food while in jail, for which each prisoner—not the government—was responsible for paying. Mary Easty's husband Isaac also later recounted that while she was in jail he "provided maintenance for her at my own cost and charge [and] went twice a week to provide for her what she needed." Easty joined Nurse in the Boston jail later that month.[168] An entry in the Salem Village church book also mentions that Peter Cloyce was often visiting his wife, Nurse's sister Sarah, when she was in jail.[169] Without families bringing them supplies and food, the lives of Nurse and her sisters would have been even more miserable.

THAT SPRING, events in the village continued to spiral out of control. John Willard remained on the run from his arrest warrant, and old man Wilkins still could not stop wetting himself. At the hearing for newly accused Alice Parker, accuser Mercy Lewis' tongue turned black—not from telling lies, but rather from sticking it out too far during a fit. Parker told her that her tongue would be blacker yet when she died.[170] John Indian, tending bar at Ingersoll's tavern, showed visitors scars on his arm that he claimed were from witchcraft, though the scars appeared to have been caused prior to the witch hunt.[171] One night, Elizar Keysar saw large glowing jellyfish float down his chimney. He called for his maid, who looked up the chimney and also saw them, but when his wife looked she did not see anything. On another occasion, a man from Newbury recounted that years earlier he saw Susannah Martin turn a dog into a beer keg.[172] Most strangely, one man at Ipswich believed that his horse was ill due to some spectral means, so he stuck a lit pipe into the horse's rear end in an attempt to somehow cure it. Due to what appears to be some poorly timed flatulence, the flame increased and nearly lit his barn on fire.[173]

The witch hunt greatly disturbed daily life in the village. Accusations interrupted planting and cultivating in the spring and summer and continued through harvest season, which—in addition to drought—led to a scarcity of food and provisions.[174] The villagers were too caught up in attending the exciting hearings and fighting imaginary specters to farm. The fruits of their planting died on the vine, not harvested due to the distraction of the Devil coming to Salem Village.

Also during this time, George Jacobs Sr. called his servant Sarah Churchill a "bitch witch," and fired her because her fits were getting in the way of her housework. Unsurprisingly, he was accused and arrested not long after.[175] More surprisingly, Jacobs' granddaughter Margaret was accused as well and she falsely confessed. Pressured by the accusers who told her that she would hang if she did not confess, she did and then testified against her own grandfather—which cost him his life.[176]

At his hearing, Jacobs said that the Devil could take anyone's shape—even the innocent—and therefore just because the accusers claimed to see Jacobs' image did not mean he was guilty. Hathorne rebuked him, "not without their consent," revealing a strong belief in the validity of spectral evidence. This exchange shows a difference since Nurse's hearing in May when Hathorne cautiously said, "What uncertainty there may be in apparitions I know not."[177] Hathorne had by now made up his mind and believed that such claims of specters were damning evidence.[178]

While shadows of suspicion spread over the chaotic village, Nurse's husband Francis and the rest of her family took action. In addition to visiting her in jail, the Nurse family worked on a strategy for her legal defense. The first step toward preparing a defense was when John Tarbell and Samuel Nurse previously visited the Putnams' house in March and questioned the women of the household about which of them first accused Rebecca Nurse.

In ordinary times, if a woman was accused of witchcraft, her husband could file a countersuit of defamation on her behalf, and usually win.[179] But, 1692 was no ordinary time. Had Francis Nurse filed such a suit he would have found himself before Hathorne, Corwin, and a jury of his neighbors. As Rebecca Nurse's post-arrest hearing showed, such a suit would have been futile because the accusations were widely believed.

Next, Francis Nurse and family gathered support for Rebecca from friends and neighbors in the form of a petition. The document notes Francis Nurse as its author, and it was probably signed over a period of time, since the names are written in different colored ink. The signatures were collected between Rebecca's arrest on March 24 and May 13, when one of the signers—Daniel Andrew—was accused of witchcraft and fled arrest.[180] The petition reads:

> We whose names are hereunto subscribed being desired by Goodman Nurse to declare what we know concerning his wife's conversation for time past: We can testify to all whom it may concern that we have known her for many years and according to our observation her life and conversation was according to her profession [of faith] and we never had any cause or grounds to suspect her of any such thing as she is now accused of.

Israel Porter	Samuel Sibley
Elizabeth Porter	Hepzibah Rea
Edward Bishop Sr.	Daniel Andrew
Hannah Bishop	Sarah Andrew
Joshua Rea	Jonathan Putnam
Sarah Rea	Lydia Putnam
Sarah Leach	Walter Phillips Sr.
John Putnam Sr.	Nathaniel Felton Sr.
Rebecca Putnam	Margaret Phillips
Joseph Hutchinson Sr.	Tabitha Phillips
Leada Hutchinson	Joseph Holten Junior
Joseph Holten Sr.	Samuel Endicott
Sarah Holten	Elizabeth Buxton
Benjamin Putnam	Samuel Aborn Sr.
Sarah Putnam	Isaack Cooke
Job Swinnerton	Elisabeth Cooke
Esther Swinnerton	William Osborne
Joseph Herrick Sr.	Hannah Osborne
Daniel Rea	Joseph Putnam
Sarah Putnam[181]	

The thirty-nine names on this petition reveal much about where many of the inhabitants of Salem Village stood during the witch hunt and further dispels several commonly held misconceptions about whether certain disputes in the village led to Rebecca Nurse being accused of witchcraft. The signers are a crosscut of the community and do not divide directly along any factional lines. Nurse's supporters include one of the men who signed the initial legal complaint against her, the father of one of her accusers, many Putnams—including those involved in the Topsfield dispute—and the Endicott with whom they had the boundary issue. Therefore, the Topsfield dispute and the farm boundary issue could not have been leading causes of Nurse being accused.

Elizabeth (Hathorne) Porter, who visited Nurse with her husband Israel Porter and Peter Cloyce before Nurse was arrested, signed the petition. She was magistrate John Hathorne's sister, and supported Nurse even though her brother decided that there was enough evidence to hold Nurse for trial. Daniel and Hepzibah Rea registered their support as well, despite their own daughter Jemima claiming that Nurse afflicted her.[182]

Several of the Holtens—Joseph Holten Sr., Sarah Holten, and Joseph Holten Jr.—signed in support of Nurse, despite another family member accusing Nurse of witchcraft. The name "Sarah Holten" is on this petition and also appears in testimony against Nurse at her trial that claimed Nurse used witchcraft to kill Benjamin Holten (who was Joseph Sr. and Sarah's son, and Joseph Jr.'s brother). It was previously suggested that perhaps Sarah Holten changed her mind partway through the witch hunt and switched from defending to accusing Nurse, but this is unlikely. More likely is that the two Sarah Holtens are different people, since both Benjamin Holten's mother and wife were named Sarah. The Sarah Holten who later entered the accusation against Nurse at trial is clearly Benjamin's wife.[183] The Sarah Holten who signed this petition is presumably the elder Sarah Holten, Benjamin's mother, because her name and her husband's are right below each other and their names are in the same handwriting on the petition.[184] These two women reveal how one family could have divergent opinions on the witchcraft accusations with Benjamin Holten's wife and his mother on opposite sides at Nurse's trial.

As to the large Putnam family, seven signed in support of Nurse, including John Sr. and Rebecca Putnam, the heads of a significant branch of the family. John Putnam Sr. was the uncle of Thomas Putnam Jr. and served as a deputy to the General Court until 1692.[185] He was the Putnam most involved in the Topsfield feud against Nurse's siblings, but since he signed in support of Nurse it is unlikely that the Topsfield issue was a significant factor in why she was accused of witchcraft. Thomas Putnam's other uncle, Nathaniel Putnam, entered a similar piece of testimony on behalf of Nurse.[186] He also was a deputy to the General Court, and his son Benjamin defended Nurse.[187] Jonathan Putnam, one of the men who filed the legal accusation against Nurse in March, also signed the petition.[188] In the weeks since he rode into Salem Town to accuse Nurse of witchcraft he must have had a change of heart.

Twenty-two-year-old Joseph Putnam signed the petition for Nurse and became an opponent of the witch hunt in general, even though his half-brother was Thomas Putnam Jr., husband of Mrs. Ann Putnam and father of Ann Jr. who were some of the most prolific accusers. Joseph Putnam showed his opposition to Rev. Parris by not attending the village church and had his newborn baptized in the Salem Town church instead. For six months, he reportedly kept his horses saddled and at the ready both night and day in order to escape should he or one of his household be accused. Joseph Putnam was also constantly armed to resist any arrest attempt.[189]

Samuel Endicott, grandson of Governor John Endicott and son of Zerubbabel Endicott, who was involved in the boundary feud with the Nurse family and Nathaniel Putnam, continued to press his family's land claims. Yet, he signed the petition for Nurse, showing that his positive opinion of her overrode the frustration of the land dispute. Nathaniel Putnam, whose support was mentioned above, was the third party involved in the dispute. Therefore the Nurse-Endicott boundary issue was not a factor in the witchcraft accusation against Nurse.

Another noteworthy signer was Samuel Sibley. His wife, Mary Sibley, was an early believer that the alleged witchcraft was real, and she organized the baking of the witch cake in February as counter magic against the believed witchcraft. Samuel Sibley was apparently more skeptical, at least in regard to the accusations against Nurse.

Unfortunately, once one of the signers of the petition, Daniel Andrew, was accused of witchcraft the petition was possibly not as influential—despite the long list of well-known and respected people who signed it. Andrew was accused on May 14 along with his sister Rebecca Jacobs and brother-in-law George Jacobs Jr., only days after George Jacobs Sr. was arrested. Daniel Andrew fled the charge and escaped arrest.[190]

Signing the petition was a courageous act by Nurse's supporters. As they saw their friends, neighbors, and family members accused, the signers would have been safest to keep their heads down and not turn against the tide of suspicion. They must have been quite sure of Nurse's innocence in order to take the risk of associating their name with hers.

ON MAY 14, the sounds of drumming and marching feet echoed off the stone walls of the Boston jail. A crowd gathered at the end of Prison Lane, in front of the Boston Town House. Eight companies of militia marched by as an honor guard for Rev. Increase Mather and Sir William Phips, the new royal governor of Their Majesties' Province of Massachusetts-Bay.

Both men arrived from England that evening aboard a thirty-six-gun Royal Navy warship, with the new provincial charter in hand.[191] There was new authority in Massachusetts, and cannons floating in the harbor to back it up.

Phips previously commanded the disastrous 1690 attack on Quebec, but as royal governor he became a key figure in the witch hunt. His biographers, Emerson W. Baker and John G. Reid, note in the beginning of their study of Phips' life that some previous historians characterize Phips merely as "a simpleton whose proximity to major processes and prominent individuals entitles him to be regarded best as the Forrest Gump of Anglo-America in the 1690s, caught up in events he could not understand, or at worst as a clown whose freakish rise through the social ranks made him an ultimately ludicrous figure."[192] Although Baker and Reid's work further complicates this narrative and raises new questions, Phips remains a man who was out of his depth as a military leader in 1690 when he led the New England fleet against Quebec and also out of his depth as royal governor during the witch hunt, when he made a decision that cost Rebecca Nurse her life.

Phips grew up in one of the easternmost frontier outposts in Maine. He was likely illiterate and did not have the refined manners of a Puritan gentleman, often resorting to crude language and threats. Years earlier he got into a bar fight in Boston and told the constable who came to arrest him that he "did not care a turd for the governor, for he had more power than he had," and on a separate occasion he told two Boston constables to "kiss his arse."[193] This rogue was now Massachusetts' first royal governor—whether drunk tavern dwellers acknowledged his authority or not.

The parade of militia and local dignitaries arrived at the town house, illuminated by candles, at the end of the dark street that the jail was on. The swearing-in ceremony was cut short, however, as the sunset marked the start of the Sabbath. Rather than infringe on the Lord's Day and continue the official reading of the commission and the firing of volleys, all present departed while the eight militia companies escorted their new commander Governor Phips and Rev. Increase Mather back to their homes.[194]

On Monday, after the Sabbath was over, Bostonians and militia once again passed by the jail on their way to Town House Square. Eight militia companies from Boston and two from Charlestown escorted Sir William Phips and the members of the Council of Assistants to the town house to resume the ceremony.[195] Rev. James Allen, previous owner of the Nurse farm and minister of Boston's First Church, began the occasion with a prayer. The new charter was read, as were commissions for all of the new royally appointed officers of the Massachusetts government. Drums rolled, and the militia fired volleys that echoed off of the Boston jail.[196]

Phips, the first royal governor of Massachusetts, bore many of the same political and military titles as General Thomas Gage, appointed Massachusetts' last royal governor in 1774. In addition to his position as governor—formally, "Captain General and Governor in Chief over Their Majesties' Province of Massachusetts-Bay in New England"—Phips was also commissioned a far-reaching military role in charge of all the armed forces in New England as "Their Majesties' Lieutenant and Commander in Chief of the militia forces, forts . . . within Their Majesties' several colonies of Connecticut, Rhode Island and Providence Plantations, the Narragansett Country or King's Province, and the Province of New Hampshire."[197] As governor he inherited the supposed war against the witches, and as commander-in-chief of all New England he inherited the war against the French and Natives.

In order to accept his royal commission, Phips was required to swear an oath affirming that he was not Catholic—because Catholics could not hold public office in either England or New England. Although many of the Assistants were present to witness Phips' oath, Corwin and Hathorne were not. It is not clear why they were absent, for no hearings took place that day in Salem Town or Salem Village.[198] After Phips denounced the "Church of Rome," he officially assumed office as Governor of Massachusetts-Bay, a province that now included the former Plymouth Colony, present-day Maine, Nova Scotia, and (in theory) the part of Quebec south of the St. Lawrence River including the Gaspé Peninsula.[199]

The prisoners in the stone jail momentarily became old news as Boston gossip turned to politics and the calling of a new General Court. At least some of the elite reacted with optimism to Phips' arrival, despite the new charter curtailing representative government. Rev. Cotton Mather wrote, "Sir William Phips, at last being dropped, as it were, from the Machine of Heaven, was an instrument for easing the distresses of the land."[200] It was later under the authority of Phips' government that Nurse and the other accused witches were put on trial.

The arrival of Gov. Phips had one immediate effect on Nurse's life: one of the governor's first orders was that all those accused of witchcraft were to be put into extra irons to restrain them, and the jailer's bill to the government shows that the following week he purchased ten sets of shackles for the prisoners. These irons were in addition to the eight-pound chains they were already in, because the authorities wanted to make it even harder for the accused to continue to afflict their accusers back in Salem

Village.[201] As if the jail was not miserable enough, the weak and ailing Nurse now could barely move, struggling under a pile of irons.

IN SALEM VILLAGE, Nurse's family received good news for the first time in a long while: on May 18 Nurse's sister Mary Easty was released from the Salem jail. All of her accusers, except the Putnams' maid Mercy Lewis, were no longer sure that Easty was the person afflicting them.[202] One can only imagine the joyful reunion that occurred when she was freed and returned home to her family in Topsfield. Easty's release probably gave hope to both the Nurse and Cloyce families who had loved ones in a similar situation.

But less than forty-eight hours later, the witch hunt again closed in around Easty. One could not escape so easily after being named as a witch. On May 20, the accusers changed their stories again and claimed that Easty afflicted them. Constable John Putnam Jr. and Benjamin Hutchinson (who dueled the specters at Ingersoll's tavern) entered a complaint on behalf of Ann Putnam Jr., Mercy Lewis, Mary Walcott, and Abigail Williams. Marshal Herrick arrested Easty again late that night.[203] Her brief gasp of freedom and reunion with her family was over, forever.

BACK IN BOSTON, yet more prisoners accused of witchcraft joined Rebecca Nurse in the overcrowded jail. Four arrived on May 19, and seven more arrived on May 23, including Nurse's sister Mary Easty.[204] The last additions to the jail while Nurse remained there were several more "Frenchmen" who arrived on May 29.[205] The prison was brimming with the commonwealth's enemies.

Down the street from the jail at the Boston Town House, the wheels of the new government began to turn, and its initial focus was on military matters and the witch hunt. On May 23 Gov. Phips gave his order to purchase the extra irons for the prisoners, but Their Majesties' Province of Massachusetts-Bay did not have the money to purchase them. The government was strapped for cash due to the expenses of both the spiritual and temporal wars that it waged. Assistant Samuel Sewall loaned the government money out of his own pocket so that it could continue to function.[206]

The next day, the governor and council met, with both Hathorne and Corwin present. They appointed sheriffs and other civil and judicial officers, and also announced that the first General Court would be held on June 8.[207] After making these decisions, Gov. Phips took his first significant action regarding the witch hunt. On May 27 he established a Court of

Oyer and Terminer to conduct the witchcraft trials. "Oyer" and "Terminer" are French legal terms for "to hear" and "to determine," and this type of court was erected in special situations when a regular court system was not available or qualified for a certain incident. In this case, a regular court system for the new province had not yet been established.

Nurse first felt the force of the new court when guards came to move her and several other prisoners back to the Salem jail to await trial. On May 31, newly appointed prosecutor Thomas Newton wrote a letter to Secretary of the Province Isaac Addington ordering the transfer. Newton wanted the prisoners sent "post-haste" so that they would be in Salem Town for the first sitting of the court on June 2.[208] The letter is countersigned by William Stoughton, lieutenant governor and newly appointed chief justice of the court.

Earlier that day Newton went to Salem Village along with members of the Council of Assistants to witness firsthand one of the hearings in the meetinghouse. He described the scene in his letter to Addington: "All this day I have beheld the most strange things, scarce credible but to the spectators." He also notes how the fits of the accusers disrupted the legal process at the hearing, "The afflicted persons cannot readily give their testimonies, being struck dumb and senseless for a season at the name of the accused."[209] His conclusion after witnessing the hearing was that the trials would be very time consuming, and that it would be a while before all the requested prisoners could be tried.

On the morning of June 1, Nurse left the horrid stone jail in Boston that had been her home for seven weeks.[210] Guards led the prisoners bound for their fate in Salem Town out of the jail for the long trek north. Previously, all trials for capital crimes took place in Boston, but the Court of Oyer and Terminer sat in Salem Town instead. This was simply a matter of logistics because the majority of witnesses for both the defense and the prosecution resided in Salem Village, Salem Town, or nearby. It would have been a serious burden for all involved to travel to Boston for each trial.

The guards led the prisoners down the street, past the town house, and back to the docks. They then crossed the harbor, where the governor's warship bobbed on the waves, and the prisoners began the slow trek back to Salem Town along the winding dirt roads. Nurse's group of prisoners heading to Salem Town passed another group of accused being escorted south on the road to Boston.[211] As Nurse and the other prisoners traveled north, slowly the beacon on the hill disappeared from sight on the horizon behind them.

The interior of St. Nicholas Church, Great Yarmouth, England, from a nineteenth-century postcard. Rebecca Towne (Nurse) was baptized here on February 21, 1621. (*Author*)

The Rebecca Nurse House, where Nurse lived in Salem Village during the witch hunt. The house and farm were purchased by Danvers citizens led by Sarah E. Hunt in 1907 to ensure its preservation, and it is now the non-profit Rebecca Nurse Homestead Museum. It is the only home of a victim of the witch hunt that is preserved and open to the public. (*Author/Danvers Alarm List Company*)

The house where Benjamin and Sarah Holten lived in 1689, prior to Benjamin's early death after his pigs escaped and destroyed crops on the Nurse Farm. Sarah Holten later testified against Nurse at her trial. This house, which still stands, is known primarily as the Samuel Holten House after the Patriot leader who served in the Continental Congress, the Congress of the Confederation, and the U.S. Congress. (*Frank Cousins, Courtesy of the Phillips Library*)

The foundation of the Salem Village Parsonage, where Reverend Samuel Parris lived in 1692 and whose ownership was disputed in the years before the witch hunt. Today, the site is preserved by the Town of Danvers and is open to the public. (*Author*)

Exterior and interior photos of the reproduction of the 1678 Salem Village Meetinghouse that is part of the Rebecca Nurse Homestead Museum in Danvers, Massachusetts. The reproduction meetinghouse was built from the original specifications for the PBS film *Three Sovereigns for Sarah* (1985) about Rebecca Nurse and her sisters Mary Easty and Sarah Cloyce during the witch hunt. (*Author/Danvers Alarm List Company*)

Nathaniel Ingersoll's tavern in Salem Village. The tavern, or ordinary, is where Reverend Deodat Lawson stayed when he came to Salem Village during the first weeks of the witch hunt and where Rebecca Nurse was briefly imprisoned the morning of her arrest. Additionally, the magistrates ate and drank at Ingersoll's between conducting hearings in the meeting-house down the road, and even conducted some hearings in the taproom of the tavern. It is a private home today. (*Author*)

In April 1692, it was alleged that a gathering of witches took place in the fields near the Salem Village Parsonage, and that the alleged witches flew on poles to the meeting where they partook in an evil communion rite. Rebecca Nurse was accused of serving as a deacon at one of these evil sacraments, where allegedly the participants drank real blood and ate real flesh in a mockery of the Christian sacrament. This woodcut is from *The History of Witches and Wizards: Giving a True Account of all their Tryals in England, Scotland, Swedeland, France, and New England; With their Confession and Condemnation* (1720). (*Wellcome Collection*)

William Stoughton, right, served as lieutenant governor of Massachusetts and the chief justice of the Court of Oyer and Terminer in 1692. Samuel Sewall, left, served in the upper house of the Massachusetts legislature—the Council of Assistants—and as a judge on the Court of Oyer and Terminer in 1692. Unlike the other judges, in 1697 Sewall publicly repented for his role in the witch hunt. (*Danvers Archival Center*)

At Rebecca Nurse's trial, Sarah Bibber had a fit and claimed that Nurse's specter stabbed her with pins. She showed the court the pins and a wound as evidence. However, Nurse's daughter-in-law Sarah (Craggen) Nurse revealed to the court that she saw Bibber take the pins off of her clothes and stab herself with them. The pins pictured here, now in the Essex County Superior Court's law library, are allegedly pins used by accusers during the trials, but might simply be pins that were used to clip the documents together. (*Frank Cousins, Courtesy of the Phillips Library*)

The death warrant for Rebecca Nurse, Sarah Good, Susanna Martin, Elizabeth Howe, and Sarah Wilds, who were all executed on July 19, 1692. Chief Justice William Stoughton signed the bottom and sealed the top corner with red wax. (*Boston Public Library*)

Proctor's Ledge, the small rise below what is today known as Gallows Hill, was the most likely execution spot in 1692. A memorial at the base of the ledge was dedicated in 2017 for the 325th anniversary of the witch-hunt. The executions are believed to have taken place not where the memorial is, but rather at the top of the ledge above the memorial, shown here. (*Author*)

Descendents and Danvers community leaders around the Rebecca Nurse Memorial in the Nurse Family Cemetery at the monument's dedication on July 30, 1885. Prior to the dedication, Reverend Charles B. Rice (sitting front left, with hat in his right hand) led a service at the First Church of Danvers (formerly known as the Church of Christ in Salem Village). The pine trees in the background remain today. (*Danvers Archival Center*)

A view of the crowd at the Rebecca Nurse Homestead in 2017 for the 325th anniversary of Nurse's execution. July 19, 2017, was declared "Rebecca Nurse Day" in the Commonwealth of Massachusetts to honor the anniversary. (*Ronald A. Gagnon*)

The Salem Village Witchcraft Victims Memorial, located across from the site of the former Salem Village Meetinghouse in Danvers, Masachusetts. The memorial was erected through community donations in 1992 for the tercentennial of the witch hunt, and contains statements of innocence by those killed, including a quote by Rebecca Nurse. (*Author*)

EIGHT

OYER AND TERMINER

Tituba: "The Devil came and bid me serve him. . . there was a tall man of Boston. . ."
Hathorne: "What clothes doth the man go in?"
Tituba: "He goes in black clothes, a tall man with white hair."
—Tituba's questioning before the magistrates on March 1, 1692

CHIEF JUSTICE WILLIAM STOUGHTON, sitting between the other black-robed judges, called out Thomas Newton's name. He rose and faced the judges' bench.

Newton was an English lawyer who lived in Boston, but on this day he was in Salem Town to be sworn in as Their Majesties' Attorney General. Newton previously served as the prosecutor in New York for an oyer and terminer court investigating a rebellion related to the 1689 revolt in Boston against the Dominion regime.

As attorney general in 1692, he prosecuted the witchcraft trials in June and July, including that of Rebecca Nurse, before he was promoted to a different position. He wrote the indictments against the accused, determined the order of trials, and argued the prosecution's case at trial. Having a trained lawyer as the prosecutor further weighed the scales against Nurse and the other accused who were not allowed professional counsel.[1]

Newton stood before the court and swore, "I, Thomas Newton, being appointed to perform the office of Their Majesties' Attorney-General in the prosecution of several persons to be indicted and tried before Their Majesties' Justices of Oyer and Terminer now sitting . . . do swear, that according to my best skill, I will act truly and faithfully on Their Majesties' behalf, as to Law and Justice do pertain, without any favor of affection. So help me God."[2] With a court sitting in Salem Town and an attorney general to prosecute the cases, the grand jury sessions and trials of the accused began.

Nurse's case moved on to the grand jury stage on June 3, the day after Newton's swearing in. Typically, multiple cases were brought before the grand jury on the same day, and later there were often multiple trials held on the same day. This was common English practice, since many courts only met in session quarterly or occasionally. The Oyer and Terminer Court sat in session for several days at a time with a few weeks between each of its four sessions. Nurse appeared before the grand jury in the court's first session at the beginning of June, and her trial was on June 29 in the court's second session.

In Continental Europe, which followed Roman law, professional judges and inquisitors ran the legal system, sometimes behind closed doors. In contrast, English justice was done by common people: the jurors selected for particular trials were not professionals. This method of justice based on the judgment of ordinary men in theory ensured a fair process, and in England fewer than one quarter of all defendants in witchcraft cases went to the gallows, which is roughly half the conviction rate as on the Continent.[3] Very similarly to England, Massachusetts had only a 26 percent conviction rate for those accused of witchcraft prior to 1692.[4]

The three-part English judicial process required many people to be persuaded by the evidence in order for one to be found guilty of a crime. First, the two magistrates at Rebecca Nurse's initial hearing in March needed to be convinced that there was enough credible evidence of her guilt to hold her in prison and move the process on to its following stages. Then at the grand jury session—where her case headed next— an eighteen-man grand jury had to endorse the charges against her before being put to trial.[5] Next, the twelve-man jury at her public trial needed to find her guilty in order for her to be convicted of a crime. Even if the jurors found one guilty of witchcraft through—in the words on one legal historian—their "stupidity or malice," the trial judges could still refuse to accept a guilty verdict from the jury if the judges themselves had doubts, which occurred previously in Massachusetts.[6]

Although the witch trials court is frequently portrayed in popular culture as a kangaroo court organized by a mob led by fiery ministers, this is not shown in the documents from the trials. According to Bernard Rosenthal, general editor of the authoritative collection of the trial documents from 1692, "Although popular images are those of a society in the grips of 'hysteria,' there is nothing in the judicial attention to order and detail to suggest the legal authorities behaved that way. Certainly there were disruptions in the court by the 'afflicted,' but these disturbances did not change the orderly bureaucratic handling of the cases."[7]

The calm, deliberate way in which the judicial system murdered the innocent accused is far more frightening than if the accused had been simply killed by a mob. It is expected that mob justice is senseless and wrong, but it is not expected that the established legal system is. The witch trials court was an organized, legal, and publicly accepted judicial process with many procedural safeguards—primarily the need to convince such a large number of jurors and magistrates of guilt in order to attain conviction—that was supported at the highest levels of the Massachusetts government.

This killing of innocents occurred in what was potentially the most educated society of the time, with a court that had several judges who earned university degrees—hardly a den of ignorance.[8] It occurred in one of the most democratic societies of the time, which had a history of representative government and of opposing arbitrary rule. Also, the jurors were no longer chosen according to any religious qualification (as the new charter stipulated).[9] Despite these characteristics of Massachusetts society, the witch hunt was still able to happen, and innocents were killed. This is the true horror story of 1692.

EXAMINING THE STATUS and membership of the Court of Oyer and Terminer is important for understanding how the court acted and how it was viewed by the local residents of Salem Village and Salem Town. According to one interpretation, the Oyer and Terminer Court was technically illegal because only the General Court had the power to legislate law courts into existence, and a new General Court had not yet convened under the new charter.[10] However, other historians note that Governor William Phips established the court on a temporary and emergency basis using the royal prerogative powers granted to him as royal governor, the representative of Their Majesties.[11] None challenged the court's legitimacy at the time, nor in petitions for redress submitted to the Massachusetts government after the witch hunt ended.

Governor Phips believed that the situation was too dire to wait for the legislature to act and create a permanent court system—it did not do so until November 1692, six months later.[12] Public order was Phips' main concern when he assumed office as royal governor. He was responsible for the security of New England, and witchcraft appeared to seriously threaten it, as another witch hunt broke out in Connecticut at the same time.[13] Phips justified establishing the emergency court in a letter to the Privy Council in England that October: "The loud cries and clamors of the friends of the afflicted people with the advice of the Deputy Governor and many others prevailed with me to give a Commission of Oyer and Terminer for discovering what witchcraft might be at the bottom or whether it were not a possession. The chief judge in this Commission was the Deputy Governor and the rest were persons of the best prudence and figure that could then be pitched upon."[14] Here Phips also described the first intervention on the course of the witch hunt by newly appointed Lieutenant Governor William Stoughton. It was his first of many.

Another reason Phips gave for acting quickly in establishing the emergency court is that he claimed to have the prisoners' best interests at heart. His written order that formally established the court states that he acted "Upon consideration that there are so many criminal offenders now in custody, some whereof have [remained] long and many inconveniences attending the throngs of the jails at this hot season of the year; there being no judicatories and courts of justice yet established."[15] Those in jail, like Rebecca Nurse, had already waited months for a trial, and the approaching hot weather increased the risks of death in jail. Though, the establishment of the Oyer and Terminer Court, with its perfect conviction rate, simply raised the prisoners' chances of death even higher.

The court was empowered by Phips' order "To enquire of, hear and determine for this time according to the law and custom of England, and of this Their Majesties' Province, all and all manner of crimes and offences had made, done or perpetrated within the Counties of Suffolk, Essex, Middlesex and either of them."[16] The counties named reveals how far the witch-hunt spread since February, and in total twenty-two towns other than Salem were involved in the witch hunt.[17]

That Phips' order instructed the court to operate "According to the law and custom of England" is significant, because English law differed from Massachusetts law and provided fewer rights to the accused. This wording was needed because the laws passed under the previous Massachusetts charter were no longer in effect now that there was a new royal charter and provincial government. It was not until June 8 that the General Court met and officially revived the old colonial laws from the first charter government.[18]

True to Phips' directive, the court followed the English Witchcraft Act of 1604, enacted by King James I before elderly Rebecca Nurse was even born.[19] By following English precedent, which ignored the rights and liberties that Massachusetts guaranteed its inhabitants, acts such as confiscation of movable goods—but not land—and torture of prisoners to exert confession were permitted.[20] Nurse, as a woman, did not technically own property—it was all held in her husband Francis' name—so the issue of confiscation did not apply to her case, and she was not subject to torture as several others were that summer.

As to the justices of the Court of Oyer and Terminer, they were the elites of the province. The judges appointed by Phips were Lt. Governor and Chief Justice of the Court William Stoughton of Dorchester, John Richards of Dorchester, Nathaniel Saltonstall of Haverhill, Wait-Still Winthrop of Boston (grandson of Governor John Winthrop), Bartholomew Gedney of Salem Town, Samuel Sewall of Boston, John Hathorne of Salem Town, Jonathan Corwin of Salem Town, and Peter Sergeant of Boston.[21]

These men were all respected gentlemen in the province, and several were leaders in the Massachusetts militia: Sewall was a captain, Saltonstall, Richards, and Gedney were majors (Stoughton was also a major prior to becoming lieutenant governor), and Winthrop was a major-general and commander-in-chief of the Massachusetts military.[22] All previously served as magistrates at various times, and many had served as Assistants. This prior judicial experience was their prime qualification for sitting on the new court. A few of the judges had even presided over previous witch trials.[23] In the words of one historian, "No more experienced or distinguished court could have been assembled anywhere in English America."[24] In addition to the judges, Stephen Sewall of Salem Town (Judge Samuel Sewall's brother) was appointed as clerk of the court.[25]

Of the judges, Chief Justice William Stoughton was the pivotal figure. His portrait shows him as an older man with white hair, wearing a black suit and cloak. He rode into Salem Town to preside over the court, and he arguably had more influence on the court than any other person in 1692. It was he, the tall dark-robed man sent from Boston, who held Nurse's and the other prisoners' fates in his hands.

Stoughton was born in England, but grew up in Dorchester, Massachusetts. He graduated from Harvard in 1650 with a divinity degree and then returned to England around the time of the English Civil War and Oliver Cromwell's dictatorship. He received a master's degree from Oxford—in an age when most in England could not even write their names.[26] He attained further academic honor when he was awarded a fellowship at Oxford, but he lost his fellowship in 1660 with the restoration of the monarchy that ushered in the return of anti-Puritan laws.[27] Faced with this discrimination, Stoughton returned to Massachusetts where he served as a judge, among other public offices.

As a judge of the witchcraft court, Stoughton was awed by the accusers' fits, and reportedly he later stated that "when he sat in judgement, he had the fear of God before his eyes."[28] He acted under the assumption that the accusers' afflictions were genuine and that witchcraft threatened New England. Stoughton—and therefore the court's—readiness to believe the accusations against Nurse and others tipped the scales of justice against the accused. The court's actions in 1692 went contrary to the skepticism toward witchcraft accusations that was engrained in the Massachusetts magistrates over the previous decades.

In the preceding years, several witchcraft cases (with both men and women charged) came before the Assistants, the only court empowered to try capital crimes in Massachusetts prior to 1692. The Assistants were generally cautious with witchcraft charges, and showed a reluctance to convict and execute. This tradition of skepticism dated back almost four decades to the trial of Ann Hibbens in 1656. During the thirty years prior to 1692, fourteen individuals were accused of witchcraft with only one, Goody Glover of Boston (who "confessed"), executed.[29]

In 1681, Gedney, Richards, Saltonstall, and Stoughton were among the judges presiding over the acquittal of accused witch Mary Hale. In 1683, Gedney and Stoughton presided over the acquittal of accused witch Mary Webster. That same year, Stoughton also presided over the trial of accused witch James Fuller. The accused was found not guilty of witch-craft but was sentenced to a whipping for bragging that he prayed to the Devil.[30] With these judges' prior skepticism in witchcraft cases, the hard-nosed and merciless prosecution that followed in 1692 is a significant change.

One potential reason for the judges' hardline approach in 1692 is that for political reasons they could not afford to appear soft on witchcraft. Several of the judges had previously served the hated Dominion govern-ment, which forsook the old New England system of representative gov-ernment and replaced it with an arbitrary government based on royal power. As a magistrate under the Dominion, Stoughton put down a tax protest in Essex County, during which residents clamored that there should be no taxation without representation.[31] His role in these events was unpopular and would have been hard for locals to forget.

Although Stoughton and some of the other magistrates who sup-ported the Dominion jumped ship when the tide turned in 1689, their association with the regime that undermined the traditional ways of the Puritan New Jerusalem may have hurt their local credibility. In 1692 they could show their loyalty to the Puritan way by purging the witches from the Promised Land. As witch-hunters, they could now appear as defending New Jerusalem in the spiritual realm, just as they tried to defend Massachusetts in the temporal world as the military leaders of the province.[32] These men were doing quite poorly in their military defense of Massachusetts at this time, and could now place the blame for their defeats on witchcraft instead of their mismanagement.[33] Historian Mary Beth Norton writes that the judges "quickly became invested in believing in the reputed witches' guilt, in large part because they needed to believe that they themselves were *not* guilty of causing New England's current woes."[34] The judges were unable to defeat Satan and his soldiers in Maine, so they instead fought him in the courtroom.

The judges of the court were also compromised in other ways that may have led them astray from justice. Historian Emerson W. Baker points out that several of those involved in the Oyer and Terminer Court proceedings had serious conflicts of interest. Judge Corwin's child was thought to be afflicted back when the accusations first began, and therefore he was not an impartial judge in the cases. Rev. Samuel Parris, whose daughter and niece were the first to appear afflicted, served as a court recorder. Thomas Putnam had been the village clerk for years and served as an official court recorder and wrote many of the depositions presented by the prosecution in court, presumably because those entering evidence were themselves unable to write.[35] He wrote more depositions for the grand juries than anyone else—more than 120—and also adjusted them for use at the trials afterward.[36] However, he was far from a neutral scribe: three members of his household were among the afflicted accusers, he himself entered legal complaints of witchcraft against thirty-five persons, and he personally testified against seventeen of the accused.[37]

In addition to the judges' and court recorders' flaws, the establishment of the special court before the establishment of a regular judicial system may have caused its own complications. According to one legal historian, the creation of the Oyer and Terminer Court may have actually led to even more witchcraft accusations. Since the arrival of Governor Phips with the new charter, the courts established under the old charter expired, but the legislature had not yet created a new regular court system. It could have been seen that the most efficient way for one to settle their neighborly disputes was now to couch the accusations in supernatural language and go before the Oyer and Terminer Court, instead of waiting to bring a case forward once the new court system was established.[38] This theory would only cover accusations lodged after the court was established in May, and of course it assumes a rather shallow view of people willing to deceive and lie in order to have their unrelated disputes heard—but, it was a witch hunt after all.

The number of people who claimed to be victims of witchcraft increased over the subsequent months, with a total of about seventy-five people that claimed to be afflicted (not including those who also falsely confessed to witchcraft).[39] As to the number of accused, when the court was commissioned on May 27 there were forty-two accused persons, but by the time it actually met in June there were at least seventy-one accused persons.[40] These accusations continued to spread outward from their start in Salem Village. On May 28, the day after Phips commissioned the court, arrest warrants were issued for accused witches from Andover, Marblehead, Reading, Topsfield, Boston, Salem Town, Rumney Marsh, Billerica, Wenham, and Charlestown.[41] There was no end in sight.

BEFORE THE TRIALS BEGAN, skepticism of the spectral evidence used in the initial hearings was expressed by one of the foremost ministers in the province, Rev. Cotton Mather. John Richards, a newly appointed judge of the Oyer and Terminer Court, asked Mather for advice on how to deal with spectral evidence, the accusers' claims of seeing and being harmed by specters that were invisible to everyone else. This query reveals how even an experienced magistrate such as Richards needed advice when it came to the quite extraordinary witchcraft charges in 1692, and it also shows a divide emerging between the ambitious court and a more hesitant clergy—though, later in the year Mather publicly wrote in support of the court and seemingly contradicted what he told Richards in private.

Supposed acts of witchcraft did not leave behind physical evidence that other crimes such as a murder or robbery would, and often there were no direct witnesses. To the modern reader, it is clear that the reason for this is that witchcraft is not real—so of course there would be no credible evidence. But, to the seventeenth-century thinker this lack of physical evidence was only a minor stumbling block: witchcraft was a preternatural crime and therefore it seemed logical that it would leave behind very different types of evidence compared to more worldly crimes.

One legal text consulted by the court in 1692 was Michael Dalton's *Countrey Justice* (1661). In this book, Dalton advised local magistrates that when dealing with potential witchcraft, "the Justices of the Peace may not always expect direct evidence, seeing all [the witches'] works are the works of darkness."[42] The judges therefore were left with only indirect evidence, primarily alleged spectral evidence. But, the use of such evidence was not without controversy—and rightly so, for it comes down to the word of the accuser against that of the accused.

On major issues of the day, the magistrates occasionally consulted with the leading ministers of Boston, since they were the most educated men in the colony. Also, though all political power rested with the civil government, the ministers' social power was used to smooth over especially divisive issues facing Massachusetts.[43] Certainly the witch trials in general—and the rules of evidence in particular—could become one such divisive issue. But, in contrast to previous instances when the ministers and magistrates worked hand-in-glove, the court did not follow Mather's advice and later disregarded the advice of other ministers as well.

Mather wrote in response to Richards, "It is very certain that the devils have sometimes represented the shapes of persons not only innocent, but also very virtuous, though I believe that the just God then ordinarily provides a way for the speedy vindication of the persons thus abused."[44] Here Mather states a belief that witches can use the spectral shapes of even a "virtuous" person as a trick, and therefore just because an accuser claimed to see the specter of an accused person does not mean that the accused are guilty. But, he also expects that the innocence of such an accused person would be revealed through the process.

Mather's opinion is here expressed privately and his caution is not the view that the court took. Previously in May Judge Hathorne expressed his belief in the accuracy of spectral evidence—despite his initial uncertainty about spectral evidence's infallibility at Nurse's hearing in March—and Stoughton's court followed a strong belief in the validity of spectral evidence.[45]

PREPARATIONS FOR THE next stage of Rebecca Nurse's prosecution began before the grand jury even met. On May 30, Chief Justice Stoughton sent a warrant to High Sheriff George Corwin to gather jurors. With the arrival of Phips and the new charter, George Corwin, twenty-six years old, was selected as the first High Sheriff of Essex County, the head law enforcement officer in the area. Two of the Oyer and Terminer judges (Jonathan Corwin and Wait-Still Winthrop) were his uncles, and Judge Bartholomew Gedney was his father-in-law.[46] Corwin was ordered "to return eighteen honest and lawful men of your bailiwick to serve upon the

Grand Enquest [grand jury], and forty-eight alike honest and lawful men to serve upon the Jury of Trials at the said Court; hereof fail not."[47] Only twelve men of the forty-eight summoned served at each trial, which means that it was probably not the same jurors who decided each case, but all eighteen members of the grand jury served at all the grand jury hearings at that session of the court.

Next in the preparations, beginning on May 31 several accusers appeared before Hathorne and Corwin and swore an oath that their previously submitted written testimony was truthful. Once sworn to, these documents could be presented by Attorney General Newton to the grand jury as evidence for the prosecution, and each would then be sworn to a second time before the grand jurors. This swearing of evidence on May 31 likely occurred in the Salem Village meetinghouse, or perhaps at Ingersoll's tavern.[48]

Mrs. Ann Putnam's previous deposition, from after Nurse's initial hearing, was read before Hathorne and Corwin, during which she claimed, "At the same moment that I was hearing my evidence read aloud by the magistrates to take my oath I was again re-assaulted and tortured by my aforementioned tormenter Rebecca Nurse."[49] Now Nurse's specter was allegedly obstructing the judicial process.

Also present for the taking of testimony was Attorney General Newton. On June 1, the magistrates interviewed falsely confessed witches Abigail Hobbs, Deliverance Hobbs, and Mary Warren in the presence of Newton. Warren—the accuser-turned-accused-turned-accuser—deposed that while she was in the Salem jail the specters of Nurse, Rev. George Burroughs, and others appeared to her and tried to persuade her to take part in the witches' sacrament. Later, during questioning by the magistrates, the false confessors alleged that Nurse's specter appeared and harassed them. The note written by Attorney General Newton at the bottom of the court record states, "Memorandum: That at the time of her taking this deposition, Goody Nurse appeared in the room and afflicted the deponent Mary, and Deliverance Hobbs, as they attested, and also almost choked Abigail Hobbs as also testified."[50] The attorney general's note does not equivocate or express any doubt as to the three women's claims, which shows that he believed the accusers when they said Nurse's specter was there attacking them.

Constable John Putnam Jr.—who previously spread a rumor about Nurse's mother being a witch and then blamed the death of his young child on Nurse, Mary Easty, and Sarah Cloyce—informed witnesses to appear the next day for Nurse's grand jury hearing. Putnam gathered witnesses by authority of a summons written by court clerk Stephen Sewall. The order reads: "To Abigail Williams, Ann Putnam [Jr.], Mercy Lewis, Elizabeth Hubbard, Mary Walcott, Ann Putnam Sr., Susannah Sheldon: We command that they and every of them, all excuses set aside, appear before Their Majesties' Justices of the Court of Oyer and Terminer held this present Thursday, being 2 June, at eight of the clock in the morning, to testify the truth of what they know upon certain indictments exhibited at our Court on behalf of Our Sovereigns against Rebecca Nurse."[51] The accusers did not miss their appointment.

ON JUNE 1, as Nurse's prison column crossed Boston Harbor and then wound its way along the roads back to Salem Town, the Oyer and Terminer Court began its work. While Nurse and the prisoners were in transit, so were most of the newly appointed justices. Several came from Boston and Dorchester, and they traveled some of the same roads as the prisoners to be in Salem Town for the first sitting of the court the next morning. That the majority of judges came from out-of-town is significant for how the court was viewed by locals in the village and Salem Town.

Historians have noted that the courts in seventeenth-century Massachusetts were ordinarily a way for the local community to resolve disputes and air differences, with the goal of correcting an error and restoring the transgressor to their place in the community after correction was made.[52] But beginning during the Dominion era in the later 1680s, individuals no longer turned to the courts to resolve local tensions because under the Dominion regime there was less local control over who was chosen as jurors. Previously, each town elected freemen to serve in the pool of potential jurors for different court sessions, but the Dominion empowered the sheriff (who was appointed from Boston) to pick jurors as he saw fit. Additionally, the magistrates were no longer the local elders who lived in the communities they arbitrated in, but could be from other areas.[53]

In 1692, the Oyer and Terminer Court was similarly alien and imposed from Boston. The jurors were chosen by the sheriff who reported to the Boston government instead of to the local community, and most of the judges came from outside the local area. This was a new style of court, and its mission was not to allow a process for transgressors to be restored to their place in the community. Instead, its mission was to purge an imagined enemy from its midst.[54]

THE OYER AND TERMINER COURT sat for the first time at the Salem Town House on June 2, 1692. The activity of the day commenced when a surgeon and jury searched several prisoners for witches' marks in the Salem jail.[55] It was believed that the Devil marked those who owed allegiance to him, and that some witches suckled imps from these spots. The prisoners were strip-searched in the attempt to discover any abnormal marks, such as dead skin, a discolored area, a three-dimensional spot, or anything else that seemed unusual, and the examiners often pierced the spots with pins to see how the prisoner reacted.[56] This was probably the most humiliating part of the judicial process.

Dalton's *Countrey Justice* recommended physical searches of the accused witches and noted that examiners should look for "Some big or little teat upon their body, and in some secret place, where he [the Devil] sucks them. And besides their sucking, the Devil leaves other marks upon their body, sometimes like a blue spot, or red spot, like a flea-biting; sometimes the flesh sunk in, and hollow, (all which for a time may be covered, yea taken away, but will come again in their old form). And these the Devil's marks be insensible, and being pricked will not bleed, and be often in their secretest parts, and therefore require diligent and careful search."[57] Nurse's examiners were indeed quite diligent.

At 10 A.M., Nurse, Bridget Bishop, Sarah Good, Susannah Martin, Alice Parker, and Elizabeth Proctor were examined. They were later examined again before suppertime to see if there were any noticeable changes to their bodies, which could be suspicious. A jury of nine women assigned by Sheriff Corwin searched Nurse and the other female prisoners. These women worked with a surgeon, John Barton.[58] It is not clear if the male surgeon was actually present in the room for the examination or if he merely consulted with the female examiners and received their report.[59]

At this first examination, the female jury reported that on the bodies of Nurse, Bishop, and Proctor they "discovered a preternatural excrescence of the flesh between the pudendum and anus much like to teats and not usual in women, and much unlike to the other three that have been searched by us, and that they were in all three women near the same place."[60] Even the most private of places was not off-limits to the investigators. One possible theory put forward for the abnormality the investigators state they found on Nurse's body is a dropped womb.[61] Nurse told the examiners that the mark they found was related to difficulties experienced during childbirth, which could support this theory.[62]

Rev. John Hale of Beverly later wrote of the weight that supposed witches' marks carried as evidence: "if found, these were accounted a presumption at least of guilt in those that had them."[63] But in the fall of 1692 Thomas Brattle, a critic of the witch hunt, pointed out that everyone likely has some sort of spot on their skin somewhere on their body that is not regular, and therefore the prisoners were set up to fail, "The jury brought in that [on] such or such a place there was a preternatural excrescence. And I wonder what person there is, whether man or woman, of whom it cannot be said but that, in some part of their body or other, there is a preternatural excrescence. The term is a very general and inclusive term."[64] All of the women examined with Nurse that day—except for pregnant Elizabeth Proctor—were hanged before the summer was out.

After this first physical examination, the guards brought Bridget Bishop to face the grand jury at the Salem Town House. Out of all the prisoners, the attorney general chose to try Bishop first. She was not the first person accused, but it has been suggested that her case was brought forth first because there was the strongest case for conviction.[65] Rev. Cotton Mather, who in his letter to Judge Richards previously urged caution in dealing with spectral evidence, wrote of the overwhelming popular opinion against Bishop, "There was little occasion to prove the witchcraft, it being evident and notorious to all beholders."[66] Mather rode to Salem Town to attend her trial and see her conviction in person.

Attorney General Newton's choice to try Bishop first is interesting, because her case is not actually the one with the strongest case for conviction. The false confessors would have been the easiest cases for the prosecution to begin with, instead of one who maintained her innocence as Bishop did. Those who falsely confessed would have had few—if any—defenders, and their swift convictions would have given legitimacy to the court and solidified popular support of the witch hunt, while accomplishing Gov. Phips' goal of trying the prisoners quickly. This did not happen, and the 1692 witch trials are the only ones in the history of Western civilization in which the confessors were not executed.[67] Instead, those tried before the court maintained their innocence until their dying breaths, brought in defense witnesses to dispute the wild accusations, and cast doubts on the credibility of the evidence and the accusers. The accused individuals' pushback against the charges further fractured the community and eventually led opinion to turn against the court.

The guards brought Bishop into the Salem Town House to face the grand jury. The eighteen grand jurors approved indictments against her for afflicting Mercy Lewis, Abigail Williams, Elizabeth Hubbard, Ann Put-

nam Jr., and Mary Walcott.[68] Next, she was arraigned and put on trial before a twelve-man trial jury. The judges of the court present that day likely
included Chief Justice William Stoughton, Samuel Sewall, John Hathorne,
Bartholomew Gedney, John Richards, and Nathaniel Saltonstall.[69] Though
Bishop maintained her innocence, the jury found her guilty.[70]

After Bishop's grand jury session and trial, Nurse's case was up next.
First, though, she and the other accused were once again physically examined by the jury of women at 4 P.M. that day.[71] Bishop, though already
found guilty, was apparently examined again with the other female accused. She presumably recounted to the other prisoners the story of her
grand jury session and trial. It was now clear to all that the word of the
village accusers was enough evidence to condemn an innocent person to
death.

At this second physical examination, the jury of women found different
results for Nurse than previously. Their report states, "instead of the excrescence within mentioned it appears only as a dry skin without sense . . .
that that piece of flesh of Goodwife Nurse's formerly seen is gone and only
a dry skin nearer to the anus [remains]."[72] This apparent change could
have been interpreted as even more suspicious.[73] As to the official results
of the physical exam, one historian's study of the signatures and "marks"—
unique symbols in place of a signature drawn by those who could not write
their name—led to a suggestion that some were forged.[74] Nurse later stated
to the court that at least one of the women disagreed with the others over
the allegedly suspicious nature of the spot in question.[75]

Nurse was scheduled to have her grand jury hearing the same day as
the physical examinations, according to the date specified on the subpoena for witnesses.[76] However, it appears that there was not enough time
remaining in the day. Instead, several witnesses submitted testimony to
the court in preparation for a grand jury session the next day.

Mrs. Putnam submitted new testimony at this time against Nurse, including new accusations even more startling than her previous ones. Her
deposition states that on the previous day, when Nurse was in transit between jails, "the apparition of Rebecca Nurse did again fall upon me and
almost choke me and she told me that now she was come out of prison
she had the power to afflict me and that now she would afflict me all this
day long and would kill me if she could."[77] Nurse's natural body being
out of jail allegedly gave her specter the opportunity to roam and attack
Mrs. Putnam for the first time since her imprisonment.

Mrs. Putnam's deposition further states that Nurse "told me that she
had killed Benjamin Holten and John Fuller and Rebecca Shepard, and

she also told me that she and her sister Cloyce and Edward Bishop's wife of Salem Village had killed young John Putnam's child because young John Putnam had said it was no wonder they were witches for their mother was so before them and because they could not avenge themselves on him they did kill his child."[78] Putnam's accusation against Nurse changes from using witchcraft to harm the afflicted to using witchcraft to commit serial murder.

As Mrs. Putnam's testimony continued so did the new accusations, and they became more personal. Putnam claimed, "Immediately there did appear to me six children in winding sheets which called me aunt, which did most grievously affright me, and they told me that they were my sister Baker's children of Boston and that Goody Nurse and Mistress Cary of Charlestown and an old deaf woman at Boston had murdered them, and charged me to go and tell these things to the magistrates or else they would tear me to pieces for their blood did cry out for vengeance. Also there did appear to me my own sister Bailey and three of her children in winding sheets and told me that Goody Nurse had murdered them."[79] After suffering through the deaths of many family members taken before their time, Mrs. Putnam now blamed Nurse for these tragedies.

THE NEXT MORNING, June 3, Rebecca Nurse awoke in the Salem jail knowing that her grand jury hearing was at hand. Prisoners and their guards, who carried their staffs of office and were led by the young Sheriff Corwin, processed through downtown Salem from the jail to the town house. On their way, they passed the Salem Town meetinghouse, home of the church where Nurse was declared a visible saint two decades prior and where she shared the Lord's Supper with some of those who now claimed that she was a servant of Satan.

The column turned right at the meetinghouse, and continued up Town House Lane. On one side of the street was the house of Rev. Nicholas Noyes, junior minister of the Salem Town church and proponent of the witch hunt, while on the other side was a house owned by Bridget Bishop, the first condemned to die during the witch hunt. In the middle of the road stood the town house where the grand jury waited.

The building was two stories tall with a grammar school on the ground floor and an assembly space on the second floor for town meetings and sessions of the county court. The exterior of the building had clapboard on the outside walls, and white plaster on the furnished inside. Unlike the cold village meetinghouse where Nurse was first questioned, this structure had two chimneys, unneeded on a June day, built by Nurse's supporter Daniel Andrew who was now himself accused of witchcraft. In another difference from the village meetinghouse, the Salem Town House had large glass windows to let the light flow in on the proceedings.[80]

Nurse entered the building and climbed up the stairs to the assembly hall, where her accusers and the grand jury waited. It is not clear if there were also spectators present for the grand jury proceedings, or if they were conducted behind closed doors.[81] The names of the grand jury members are lost to history except for that of foreman John Ruck, a Salem Town merchant, who signed the bottom of each indictment.[82]

Chief Justice Stoughton administered the oaths to the grand jurors and then withdrew from the courtroom, because grand juries were not presided over by judges.[83] During the hearing both the prosecution and the defense could call witnesses. A witness who entered a deposition—written testimony—for the prosecution's side would be present while it was read aloud and then swore an oath that the document contained the truth.[84] The witness had also previously sworn to the document's truthfulness before the magistrates.[85] It is important to note that only the prosecution evidence was sworn to under oath, and defense witnesses were prohibited from swearing their testimony under oath until 1702.[86] This discrepancy gave defense evidence less weight in the eyes of the court, since the witness was not swearing upon penalty of perjury that it was true.

For each alleged crime that the prisoner was accused of committing, the attorney general drew up an indictment on behalf of Their Majesties and presented it to the grand jury. A separate indictment of witchcraft was drawn up against the accused for each alleged victim. Evidence for both sides was presented, and most likely the attorney general directly argued his case against Nurse before the grand jury and presented the sworn depositions from the accusers. The eighteen grand jurors together could respond to an indictment in two ways: They could endorse the indictment by accepting it as "*billa vera*" (a "true bill") thereby sending the charge to trial, or they could reject it by returning it "*ignoramus*" thereby dropping the charge.[87] Next, a trial was convened either the same day, as in the case of Bishop, or weeks later, depending on the schedule of the court sessions and the strategy of the attorney general.[88]

Nurse's grand jury session began with the reading of the indictments against her. She was indicted on four charges, each for allegedly afflicting a different person. The four afflicted mentioned in the indictments were Ann Putnam Jr., Mary Walcott, Elizabeth Hubbard, and Abigail Williams.

For a reason that is not clear, the attorney general did not enter an indictment against Nurse for allegedly afflicting Mrs. Putnam, despite Mrs. Putnam being one of her earliest and most vocal accusers.

All of the indictments were written according to the same formula, with names and dates filled in on a pre-written form. Below is the first indictment against Nurse, for afflicting Ann Putnam Jr. The italic words are filled in on the form for this specific indictment:

> Anno Regni Regis et Reginæ et Mariæ Nunc: Angliæ &ᶜ Quarto: Essex ss
> The Jurors for our Sovereign Lord & Lady the King & Queen present that *Rebecca Nurse the wife of Francis Nurse Sr. of Salem Village in the County of Essex, husbandman,* the *four & twentieth* Day of *March* in the *fourth* year of the Reign of our Sovereign Lord & Lady William & Mary by the Grace of God of England, Scotland, France, & Ireland, King & Queen, Defenders of the Faith, &ᶜ and divers other days & times as well before as after certaine detestable arts called witchcraft & Sorceries: wickedly & feloniously hath used Practised, & Exercised at & within the Township of Salem in the County of Essex aforesaid in upon & against one: *Ann Putnam Junior of Salem Village aforesaid in the County aforesaid, singlewoman,* by which said wicked arts the said *Ann Putnam Junior* the *said four & twentieth* Day of *March* in the *fourth* year abovesaid and divers other days & times as well before as after, was and is hurt, tortured, Afflicted, consumed, Pined, wasted & tormented against the peace of our said Sovereign Lord and Lady the King & Queen and against the form of the Statute in that case made & Provided.[89]

At the bottom of each indictment, Attorney General Newton wrote the names of the witnesses to be called for that charge. The above indictment for afflicting Ann Putnam Jr. lists Ann Putnam Jr., Mary Walcott, and Abigail Hubbard as witnesses.

The attorney general did not base indictments on the written depositions entered to the court as evidence. Instead, the indictments were based on spectral evidence of alleged acts that occurred at the initial hearings of the accused, which is why Nurse's indictments list March 24 as the date of the supposed crimes.[90] Capital charges needed two witnesses, and with the crowds present at the initial hearings the number of witnesses to the accusers' claimed afflictions was more than sufficient.[91] In Nurse's case, Hathorne and Corwin could be considered witnesses to Nurse's alleged crime of committing witchcraft at her hearing because the accusers' fits happened in front of their eyes.[92] Once an accused person attended their initial post-arrest hearing and the accusers reacted in front of the magistrates, there was enough evidence to indict—and to convict.

After the four indictments were read, evidence was presented against and for Nurse. The report from the physical examination was read to the jury, and the previous day the women who conducted the examination signed their report and swore to its accuracy before the judges at Bishop's trial. Also read to the court was the account of Nurse's initial hearing, as recorded by Rev. Parris.[93] This report details how every slight movement of her head and hands supposedly caused the afflicted to writhe and scream, and also includes Nurse's ambiguous answers—due to her being hard of hearing and ill—to some questions that Hathorne asked her.

Next, the prosecution entered the written evidence from the supposed victims and witnesses to Nurse's alleged witchcraft. Mrs. Putnam appeared before the grand jury while the clerk read out a deposition that she originally submitted on March 24, the day of Nurse's hearing, and to which she previously swore on May 31.[94] In the deposition, Putnam catalogued a litany of accusations against Nurse, including that Nurse's shape first appeared to her on March 18, that Nurse's specter tried to force her to sign the Devil's book, and that Nurse's specter denied the validity of scripture. Putnam also described how she needed to be carried out of Nurse's hearing because of her fit—allegedly caused by spectral torture. Strictly speaking, this testimony does not relate to the charges against Nurse, which were for afflicting Ann Putnam Jr., Mary Walcott, Elizabeth Hubbard, and Abigail Williams. Mrs. Putnam's testimony does not describe her witnessing any of these four individuals being afflicted by Nurse, and only mentions Nurse allegedly afflicting her.

Next, Abigail Williams presented testimony that she swore to on May 31. This evidence, unlike Mrs. Putnam's statements, directly related to an indictment since one charge was specifically for Nurse allegedly afflicting Williams. The statement was read aloud in the presence of the court, and Williams "owned her testimony" to be true before the court. Williams alleged that Nurse's apparition came to her many times beginning on March 15, and that she was "pulled violently and often pinched and almost choked and tempted sometime to leap into the fire" by Nurse's specter. Williams also testified that she saw Nurse's specter at a witch Sabbath sitting at a place of honor next to a man "with a high-crowned hat," and that Nurse's specter allegedly admitted that Nurse "committed several murders together with her sister Cloyce."[95] This murder accusation is similar to the testimony that Mrs. Putnam had submitted the day before.

Admitting this testimony from Williams, aged eleven, and later admitting testimony from Ann Putnam Jr., aged thirteen, was quite unusual because ordinarily one needed to be fourteen in order to testify in a capital felony case. Historian Tony Fells posits that this fact reveals how the testimony of these two girls was believed so genuinely by the court that they looked the other way about this age requirement.[96]

Elizabeth Hubbard entered testimony as well, in which she claimed that she first saw Nurse's apparition on March 20, and that during Nurse's hearing on March 24 her specter "hurt me most grievously," and "if she did but look upon me, she would strike me down or almost choke me."[97] Last, she alleged that Nurse's specter also afflicted Mrs. Putnam, Ann Putnam Jr., Abigail Williams, and Mary Walcott.

In further testimony, Ann Putnam Jr.—despite her young age—deposed that she was afflicted by a specter beginning on March 13, but did not immediately know whose image it was except that the specter was of the same woman who sat with her grandmother in the meetinghouse. Most of the deposition mentions how she was "grievously tortured" by Nurse during her hearing on March 24.[98] Additionally, Putnam claimed that she witnessed Nurse's specter hurt Mary Walcott, Elisabeth Hubbard, and Abigail Williams, who were mentioned in the other indictments, and also Mercy Lewis.

Mary Walcott swore to what was probably the only other piece of evidence for the prosecution. Walcott's deposition states that she first saw the apparition of Nurse on March 20, but that it did not hurt her until Nurse's hearing on March 24.[99] She claimed that at the hearing, Nurse's specter "most grievously afflicted her," and also that Nurse's specter admitted to killing Benjamin Holten, John Harrod, and Rebecca Shepard—echoing Mrs. Putnam and Abigail Williams' claims of spectral murder. Walcott also claimed that she witnessed Nurse's specter harm the other three afflicted mentioned in the indictments, along with Mercy Lewis.

To foreman John Ruck, the several accusations of Nurse committing spectral murder were very significant, because his own daughter was allegedly killed by spectral murder committed by Rev. George Burroughs. Ruck was the father of Sarah (Ruck) Burroughs, Rev. Burroughs' deceased second wife.[100] There were allegations that Burroughs did not treat Sarah well, and refused to let her write to her father.[101] Burroughs was previously accused of murdering her by Ann Putnam Jr., who claimed on May 9 that she saw specters of Burroughs' dead first and second wives in a very similar way to how at Nurse's grand jury session multiple accusers swore before Ruck that Nurse allegedly committed murder through witchcraft.[102]

Although there is no direct evidence of Ruck being biased against Nurse specifically, the claim that his daughter was killed by one of the other accused could not have remained out of his mind as similar accusations against Nurse were read aloud in front of him.

Of the still extant depositions sworn before the grand jury, four of the five are in the handwriting of Thomas Putnam, and the fifth—the testimony of Rev. Parris' niece Abigail Williams—is written in the hand of Parris. The evidence written by Putnam used similar language to describe afflictions—they include the phrases "grievously afflicted" or "grievously tortured."[103] Also, it was Putnam who signed the names of the accusers at the bottom of the depositions because many of the afflicted, being women who were not always taught to write, did not know how to sign their own names. There is a clear conflict of interest here on the part of Putnam. Not only were his own wife, daughter, maid, and other family members very involved in the accusations, but he personally filed complaints against some of the accused. His name appears on half of the legal complaints filed with the magistrates before July 1.[104]

After the attorney general presented the evidence against Nurse, her family and others presented evidence for her defense. Her husband Francis Nurse had served as a grand juror just the previous year, and was therefore familiar with the process and had prior experience at these sessions.[105] Of the statements presented (or possibly presented) as evidence for the defense, two call into question evidence submitted by the prosecution while two others that may have been entered are character witnesses for Nurse. Unlike the prosecution evidence that was sworn before the court and dated, the defense evidence was not sworn and therefore does not have a date written on the bottom of the document. Due to this lack of a date, it is not entirely clear which pieces of defense evidence in the court records were entered this day and which were entered at Nurse's trial.

Rebecca Nurse's daughters, Rebecca Preston and Mary Tarbell, entered a statement that disputed the conclusion of her physical examinations the previous day, "We whose names are underwritten can testify if called to it that Goody Nurse has been troubled with an infirmity of body for many years, which the jury of women seem to be afraid it should be something else." There are references to a previous illness of Nurse's and to her difficulty giving birth in two documents written by Nurse or her family in 1692.[106] Given the location of the alleged witch's mark, it could very well be related to such difficulties.

Another piece of testimony that calls into question part of the prosecution's evidence was entered by Clement Coldum. The document itself does not state exactly at what part of the judicial process it was entered as evidence, but it was likely used at Nurse's grand jury session.[107] Coldum was about sixty years old and from Gloucester, but he attended services in the village the previous Sunday—perhaps to see the afflicted first-hand.[108] He gave accuser Elizabeth Hubbard a ride home on the back of his horse after services at the village meetinghouse, and in court he revealed an incriminating remark of Hubbard's.

Coldum testified that while they were riding to Hubbard's home, she suddenly asked him to ride faster. He asked why he should go faster, and Hubbard told him that "the woods are full of devils" and she pointed to different places and said "there!" and "there they be!" Perhaps Hubbard was trying to impress an out-of-town spectator. Coldum rode faster for a while to escape from the described invisible devils and then slowed down. Now that they were away from the supposed threat, he asked Hubbard "if she was not afraid of the Devil," to which she answered him "no" and told Coldum that "she could discourse with the Devil as well as with [him]."[109] This was a shocking reply.

Coldum's evidence is interesting because it cast suspicion on Hubbard herself. Being able to casually converse with the Devil was witch-like behavior, not something God-fearing Puritans did. This description of her claimed close relationship with the Devil was likely meant to instill questions as to whether Hubbard herself might actually be a witch, for not only did she describe conversing with the Devil but she seemed to brag about it.

There are two other documents that were possibly entered by the Nurse family that day: the petition of thirty-nine people who supported Rebecca Nurse, and the statement by Daniel Andrew, Peter Cloyce, Israel Porter, and Elizabeth (Hathorne) Porter that recounted their bedside visit to inform Nurse that she had been accused. Both documents were attested to by, among others, Daniel Andrew, who was currently on the run from the law as an accused witch. Potentially these pieces of evidence were now tainted and not entered, but this cannot be determined with any certainty.[110]

The grand jury, after it heard testimony from the prosecution and defense, departed to consider the evidence. Each of the four indictments—for witchcraft against Ann Putnam Jr., Abigail Williams, Mary Walcott, and Elizabeth Hubbard—was judged individually since they were separate charges. After the jury returned from deliberations, the foreman John Ruck stood as each indictment was read by the clerk, Stephen Sewall. Ruck announced the grand jury's findings for each one: All four were returned as "*billa vera*," credible charges, and bear Ruck's signature certifying the verdicts.

The accusers were convincing, and the defense evidence was insufficient to overcome the burden of assumed guilt. The guards took Rebecca Nurse back to the Salem jail. She would be tried on all four charges.

NINE

TRIAL

Moreover they of all the Sons of Men
That rule, and are in highest Places set,
Are most inclin'd to scorn their Bretheren,
And God himself (without great Grace) forget.

For as the Sun doth blind the gazers' eyes
That for a time they nought discern aright:
So Honour doth befool and blind the Wise,
And their own lustre 'reaves them of their sight.
—Rev. Michael Wigglesworth, "Day of Doom," 1662

REBECCA NURSE RETURNED to the miserable Salem jail for more than three weeks, awaiting her trial day. The grand jury hearings on June 3 ended the first sitting of the court, which adjourned until June 28.

Although Nurse was indicted the day after Bridget Bishop, her trial did not happen immediately as Bishop's had. This decision was the attorney general's, and it is suggested that this was in part due to the evidence Nurse's family gathered for her defense.[1] Given Nurse's pious reputation and status as a visible saint, her case was far more difficult for the prosecution than Bishop's.

During these intervening weeks, accusations continued as did hearings for the newly accused, conducted locally by magistrates Jonathan Corwin, John Hathorne, and Bartholomew Gedney.[2] Some hearings occurred at Samuel Beadle's Tavern in Salem Town, just a short way down Prison Lane from the jail.[3] The smallness of the jail ensured that Nurse and the others confined there saw the comings and goings of their fellow prisoners, hauled out in chains to appear before the magistrates, and presumably also heard them recounting the details of their hearings.

One of the other accused, Job Tookey, was questioned before the magistrates on June 4. At Tookey's hearing he declared that he was not the Devil's servant, but rather that the Devil was *his* servant. The magistrates were not impressed. Additionally, he was accused of being able to "raise the Devil as he pleased"—despite the fact that on the previous day at Nurse's grand jury session Caleb Coldum pointed out that Elizabeth Hubbard, one of Nurse and Tookey's accusers, bragged about her own ability to easily converse with the Devil.[4] Somehow this accusation was damning when said by the usual accusers but did not have the same result when lodged against an accuser.

Later that week, the constables arrested recently accused Ann Dolliver and brought her before the magistrates. She was the daughter of senior Salem Town minister Rev. John Higginson, who described her as suffering from "overbearing melancholy, crazed in her understanding."[5] One of the claims leveled against Dolliver was that she "had been at Goodwife Nurse's."[6] This was an attempt to connect her to Nurse, whose case was determined to be legitimate enough to go to trial.

Dolliver replied that she was at the Nurse farm only once, because she was lost and "missed her way by going around because she would not go over with the ferryman."[7] There were two ways to get from Salem Town to Beverly and points north at that time: One was to take the ferry across the mouth of the river, and the other was to travel inland to where the river narrows and then head north. After the road turned north it came to a fork near the edge of the Nurse family's farm. If one went right they continued along the Ipswich Road heading north, but if they went left they passed by John Tarbell's house, the Nurse homestead, and then reached the village center. Dolliver apparently went left instead of right.[8] After her hearing that day, Dolliver was sent to Nurse's new home, the Salem jail.[9]

On June 8, Chief Justice William Stoughton was at the Boston Town House for the opening of the new General Court. As lieutenant governor, he had a formal role in the opening of the legislature and walked in the procession with the other officers of Their Majesties' Province, including Gov. William Phips, who was surrounded by six attendants carrying swords and halberds as an honor guard.[10] At some point during the pomp, Stoughton slipped away to sign Bishop's death warrant, ordering her to be "hanged by the neck until she be dead."[11]

Two days later, the guards came for Bishop. Entering the Salem jail that morning and walking among the other accused, they took her in chains out of the main room of the jail under the eyes of the other prisoners. They led her to the site of execution, and hanged her.

At Rebecca Nurse's hearing in March, Judge John Hathorne had told her that if the accusers were lying in their witchcraft accusations she "must look upon them as murderers," for their accusations could lead to killing.[12] Now that Bishop was dead, the accusers were indeed murderers. According to the original colony laws that were brought back into force, if one used "false witness" to take away someone's life, the penalty was death.[13] The accusers now could not recant or change their stories without opening themselves up to being put on trial for their own lives. There was no going back.

IT WAS SOMETIME around Bishop's execution that Judge Nathaniel Saltonstall quit the Court of Oyer and Terminer.[14] A contemporary writer states that Saltonstall resigned because he was "very much dissatisfied with the proceedings."[15] He likely resigned from the court over its use of English witch-hunting methods that were not previously accepted in Massachusetts, such as the reliance on spectral evidence and the physical examinations of the accused. The other judges—particularly those from Boston—were aware that since Massachusetts was now a royal province the court's methods would be scrutinized in London and supported these English practices.[16] Additionally, Phips' original order establishing the court instructed the judges to use English law along with Massachusetts law—even though they were different.[17] Saltonstall's resignation was one brave yet isolated display of disapproval among the political class of Massachusetts.

When accusations later began in Saltonstall's hometown of Haverhill, where he was the local magistrate, he refused to sign the legal complaints—but the accusers simply went to Andover and had that town's magistrate sign them instead.[18] Due to his opposition to the witch-hunt, Saltonstall was later accused of being a witch, but he was never formally charged or arrested.[19] Because of his dissent, he feared that his long career of public service—which included his patriotic defense of traditional Massachusetts rights and liberties in opposition to the prior Dominion government—was now over.[20] Saltonstall drank heavily after leaving the court, missed at least one meeting of the General Court, and Judge Samuel Sewall recorded that during the following winter Saltonstall showed up drunk to a council meeting with the governor. He was passed over for a seat on the permanent Massachusetts Superior Court of Judicature established that winter, and he feared losing his position as major of the North Regiment of the Essex County militia.[21] Despite such a high-profile figure quitting the court and attempting to slow the accusations in his own town, the witch hunt continued unabated.

As THE FULL MOON rose on June 18, Rev. Samuel Parris and John Putnam Sr. (of the Topsfield dispute) were at his son Jonathan Putnam's house, who was "very ill."[22] Jonathan Putnam was one of the men who filed the legal complaint of witchcraft against Nurse in March, though afterward he signed the petition in her defense.[23] Parris and John Putnam Sr. later stated that they sent for Mercy Lewis so she could determine whether there were any specters present, clearly suspecting that Jonathan Putnam's illness was not natural. The afflicted accusers seem to have become oracles, and could supposedly see what regular villagers could not.

When Lewis arrived, according to Parris and Putnam's later testimony, "she was presently struck dumb." So the two men asked her to hold up a hand if she saw any specters afflicting Jonathan Putnam, and she did so raise her hand. Later, the two men recount that "when Mercy came to herself" she stated that "she saw Goody Nurse and Goody Carrier"[24] Even while wasting away in jail under irons, Nurse was accused of impossible attacks.

That same day nine other prisoners were sent to the Salem jail from Boston, including Rev. George Burroughs, George Jacobs Sr., and Nurse's sister Sarah Cloyce.[25] The Salem jail was already overcrowded, sweaty, and stinking. Adding nine more prisoners during the hot season further exacerbated the inhospitable and unsanitary conditions.

In MID-JUNE, there was a pause in the local hearings, grand jury sessions, and trials. During this time, the government consulted with several leading ministers about the evidence used in court. These men were a cadre of well-educated elites and were the academic intelligentsia of New England.[26]

Among those consulted were president of Harvard College Rev. Increase Mather, vice president of Harvard and minister of Boston's Third Church Rev. Samuel Willard, Rev. James Allen of Boston's First Church (who sold the Nurse family their farm), Rev. Cotton Mather of Boston's

Second Church, renowned poet Rev. Michael Wigglesworth of Malden, and eleven other ministers from the Boston area and parts north, including two ministers of towns that bordered Salem Village: Rev. Joseph Capen of Topsfield and Rev. Joseph Gerrish of Wenham.[27] Neither of the two Salem Town ministers nor Rev. Parris were involved. As these leading lights met on June 15 in the library of Harvard College, there was a real possibility that the witch hunt could take a different path.

After their discussion at the college, the ministers made several recommendations in a document sent to the Massachusetts government, the "Return of Several Ministers Consulted."[28] Rev. Cotton Mather wrote and submitted the final report on behalf of the gathered group.[29] Though the ministers believed broadly that witchcraft was afoot, their conclusions urged caution regarding the weight that spectral evidence should be given in court.

Spectral evidence, allowing accusers to enter as legal evidence in court their claims of affliction caused by specters that bystanders could not see, was admissible under English law since 1593, and continued to be used in English courts during the 1690s.[30] Attorney General Thomas Newton along with his later replacement Anthony Checkley, both English lawyers, approved of the court's treatment of spectral evidence since they used it in their prosecution of the accused.[31] In Salem Village, Rev. Parris' sermons show that he likewise believed in the use of spectral evidence.[32] Five days prior to the ministers' meeting, Bridget Bishop was convicted and executed based on such flawed evidence.

In contrast to English law, the views of the court, and the views expressed by Parris in his sermons, the consulted ministers stated that spectral evidence alone was not sufficient to convict an accused person of witchcraft: "Presumptions whereupon persons may be committed, and, much more, convictions whereupon persons may be condemned as guilty of witchcrafts, ought certainly to be more considerable than barely the accused person being represented by a specter unto the afflicted, inasmuch as 'tis an undoubted even notorious thing that a demon may, by God's permission, appear, even to ill purposes, in the shape of an innocent, yea, and a virtuous man."[33] Here the intellectual elite of Massachusetts reject as unreliable the very evidence by which the court had recently convicted and killed Bishop.

Puritan theology considered spectral evidence sufficient to arrest and question a suspect, but not to convict them at trial—which required additional physical evidence. But English law accepted spectral evidence as sufficient not just to arrest a suspect but also to convict and execute them.[34] The religious authorities were more cautious with this supposedly religious crime than the judicial authorities.

Regarding spectral evidence, the ministers further recommended "that all proceedings thereabout be managed with an exceeding tenderness towards those that may be complained of, especially if they have been persons formerly of an unblemished reputation."[35] This statement applied to individuals such as Nurse, who lived devoted lives and were respected in their community but suddenly found themselves accused of witchcraft.

Despite the note of caution the "Return of Several Ministers" sounded, its last paragraph complicates this message. The document concludes, "Nevertheless, we cannot but humbly recommend unto the Government the speedy and vigorous prosecution of such as have rendered themselves obnoxious, according to the direction given in the laws of God, and the wholesome statutes of the English nation for the detection of witchcrafts."[36] This statement appears to recommend that the court continue with the course that it was on, despite the serious criticism of its practices earlier in the document.

Historians interpret this last paragraph in different ways. It is suggested by those who fault Cotton Mather for his later support of the court that perhaps the final paragraph was written by him alone, without input from the gathered council of ministers.[37] Another interpretation is that the magistrates were reluctant to entirely repudiate the court because to do so would pit them against the new royal government, and in particular the magistrates—some of whom were leading members of their churches—which therefore led to this final ambiguous message sent to the court.[38] In the end, the judges effectively ignored the ministers' criticisms of their flawed practices.[39]

In addition to writing the "Return" in June, over the summer several Puritan ministers testified in support of the accused and spoke out in sermons against the methods of the court. By supporting the accused and publicly questioning the methods of the court these ministers opened themselves up to being accused of witchcraft—and with Rev. Burroughs in jail and then executed later that summer, it is clear that not even ministers were off limits to such accusations. Despite this danger, over the course of 1692 Rev. Samuel Phillips and Rev. Edward Payson of Rowley testified in defense of Elizabeth Howe, Rev. James Allen of Salisbury testified in defense of Mary Bradbury, Rev. William Hubbard of Ipswich testified in defense of Sarah Buckley, Rev. John Wise of Ipswich started a petition (and signed his name at the top) in defense of John and Elizabeth Proctor, and Rev. Francis Dane of Andover signed a petition along with fifty-two others that revealed how the false confessions from some of the accused were coerced and obtained by promising accused individuals that they would escape execution if they falsely confessed.[40]

One prominent example of a minister speaking out against the methods of the trials, not just testifying in an individual case, was Rev. Samuel Willard's sermon on June 19, only days after the "Return," that he was consulted for. Willard's sermon to Boston's Third Church was significant not just because he openly stated that the spectral evidence used in court was inconsistent with Puritan beliefs, but even more so because three of the judges—Samuel Sewall, Wait-Still Winthrop, and Peter Sergeant—sat in his congregation.[41]

Rev. Willard announced to his church, "I do assert that the Devil may represent innocent, nay a godly person, doing a bad act," and further declared that the devil could "persuade the person afflicted that it is done by the person thus represented."[42] One can imagine the judges squirming as Willard refuted the way that they used spectral evidence—which they relied on to condemn and kill Bridget Bishop.

There was a strong reaction to Willard's criticism of the methods used in the witch hunt. Thomas Brattle, a critic of the witch hunt, wrote of Willard in the fall of 1692, "I am fully persuaded, that had his notions and proposals been hearkened to, and followed, when these troubles were in their birth, in an ordinary way, they would never have grown unto that height which they now have. He has as yet met with little but unkindness, abuse, and reproach from many men; but I trust that, in after times, his wisdom and service will find a more universal acknowledgement."[43] In reaction to Willard's rejection of the court's methods, chronicler Robert Calef notes that Willard was accused of witchcraft later that summer during a trial.[44]

On June 28, the Oyer and Terminer Court met again in Salem Town. During this session Rebecca Nurse was put on trial, along with several other accused. It was the first sitting of the court since the ministers were consulted, and the first since several of the judges heard Rev. Willard decry their flawed methods.

The guards led Sarah Good out of jail for her nine o'clock trial.[45] In addition to the accusers still being permitted to enter flawed spectral evidence, there was another attempt at producing false physical evidence of witchcraft—such as when previously bite marks were produced at Nurse's hearing and when Ann Putnam Jr. somehow produced chain marks on her arm and claimed that Nurse's specter hit her with a chain.[46] Perhaps the recent questioning of spectral evidence motivated the accusers to buttress their claims with new false physical evidence.

At Good's trial, one of the afflicted accusers went into a wild fit. When the unnamed accuser eventually regained her composure, she had a broken knife blade in her hand. She presented this to the court and claimed that Good's specter tried to stab her. After the broken knife was produced the story was initially believed, but then a young man came forward who had with him the other half of the broken knife. The man told the court "that yesterday he happened to break that knife, and he cast away the upper part" in the presence of the accuser who now claimed a spectral origin of the broken knife. The lying accuser was "bidden by the Court not to tell lies," but was allowed to testify in subsequent trials when the accused were on trial for their lives.[47]

The same day that this courtroom fraud occurred, Nurse wrote a petition to the judges concerning her physical examination four weeks prior. She argued that although a mark on her body was reported during the first search, one of the women who examined her disagreed with the conclusion that it was an unnatural mark. Nurse's petition states, "One of the said women which is known to be the most ancient, skillful, prudent person of them all as to any such concerned, did express herself to be of a contrary opinion from the rest and did then declare the she saw nothing in or about Your Honors' poor petitioner but what might arise from a natural cause." The document then states that she told the women of the examining jury about medical issues related to childbirth that caused the mark, "I then rendered the said persons a sufficient known reason as to myself of the moving cause thereof: which was by exceeding weaknesses descending partly from an overture of nature and difficult exigencies that hath befallen me in the times of my travails."[48]

Despite the humiliation of the two strip-searches, in this petition Nurse offered to submit herself to the indignity of yet another search by a different group of women to prove that the allegedly suspicious mark was not diabolical in nature. For examiners, she suggested Mary Higginson, wife of the senior Salem Town minister, and three other women, two of whom were known to have aided in the birth of children, along with "such others as may be chosen on that account."[49] Suggesting the minister's wife for the examination would ensure that it would be respected, and suggesting women who had experience in childbirth and its effects was a strategy to have her allegedly suspicious mark refuted as being childbirth-related.

The petition finished with Nurse stating, "I hope your honors will take into your prudent consideration and find it requisite so to do, for my life lies now in your hands under God, and being conscious of my own innocency, I humbly beg that I may have liberty to manifest it to the world partly by the means aforesaid. And your poor petitioner shall evermore pray as in duty bound."[50] At the bottom of the paper is a squiggle where Nurse made her mark in place of a signature. There is no evidence that the court ever responded to her petition.

The next morning, June 29, Sarah Good's trial reconvened for day two and she was found guilty.[51] That same day, Susannah Martin appeared before a grand jury, went to trial, and was also found guilty.

Next to appear before the court that had a perfect conviction record was Rebecca Nurse. That morning her family and supporters likely lingered around the town house until the previous trials ended. Her extended family came from far and wide, including her daughter-in-law Sarah (Craggen) Nurse—and presumably Francis Nurse Jr., her husband, too—who came from Reading.[52] They would have heard about the two guilty verdicts from the gathered crowds before walking through the town house doors to await Rebecca Nurse's trial. The Nurse family's prepared defense for her, with many witnesses and submitted written testimony, was far superior to that presented on behalf of Good and Martin.

One street over, the guards entered the main room of the jail to take Nurse away. Chained, she was taken down Prison Lane, turned right onto the main road, and passed the meetinghouse of the Salem Town church of which Nurse remained a covenant member.[53] At the meetinghouse the procession took a right turn and continued up Town House Lane. Outside of the town house were several tools of justice: the stocks, pillory, and a whipping post standing among the gathered crowd.[54]

In addition to providing shingles for the town house years earlier to pay his debt to the town, Francis Nurse had previously sat on several trial juries here for the Essex County Quarterly Court. Also, he himself appeared before the county court several times during the many lawsuits relating to the boundary disputes of the Nurse farm. As with the grand jury session, he had practical legal knowledge to use in preparing the Nurse family's defense for Rebecca. Compared to her grand jury appearance, at her trial there was far more defense evidence and many witnesses to testify on her behalf.

According to Massachusetts law, a prisoner could have someone present to assist them in their defense, though it could not be a professional lawyer who practiced law for payment.[55] Rebecca's husband Francis Nurse collected the signatures for the petition attesting to her good character, and her son Samuel later wrote in a petition to the government that her family "spent much time and made many journeys to Boston and Salem and other places in order to have vindicated her innocency" and that her family "produced plentiful testimony that my honored and dear mother had led a blameless life from her youth up."[56] A challenge for the defense was that typically in English criminal trials the accused person was not told ahead of time what evidence the prosecution would bring forth, so the Nurse family had to guess which of her accusers would be chosen to testify against her.[57]

No defense lawyers were permitted because under the English legal system the supposedly neutral judges were responsible for intervening and defending the rights of the accused in court. This practice was used in both England and the English colonies.[58] Massachusetts law did not allow defense lawyers to practice for fees until 1705, and English law did not allow defense lawyers until 1836.[59] Though possibly this procedure may have been effective under ordinary circumstances in the trial of typical offenses, contemporary accounts during the witch hunt paint a far less benevolent picture of the judges. In the fall of 1692 Thomas Brattle wrote of Chief Justice Stoughton, "The chief judge is very zealous in these proceedings, and says, he is very clear as to all that has as yet been acted by this Court, and, as far as ever I could perceive, is very impatient in hearing anything that looks the other way."[60]

In another contrast to today's legal system, neither in England nor Massachusetts was the jury required to assume that a prisoner was innocent until proven guilty. As the legal historian J. M. Beattie writes of English trials in the seventeenth and early eighteenth centuries, "if any assumption was made in court about the prisoner himself, it was not that he was innocent until the case against him was proved beyond a reasonable doubt, but that if he *were* innocent he ought to be able to demonstrate it for the jury by the quality and character of his reply to the prosecutor's evidence. That put emphasis on the prisoner's active role. He was very much in the position of having to prove that the prosecutor was mistaken."[61] The burden of proof in court was on the accused, similar to how in the court of public opinion the accused was assumed guilty.

As to the jurors who decided Rebecca Nurse's fate that day, their identities are mostly unknown. The jury was all-male, and it was not until 1951 that the first women were seated on juries in the Commonwealth of Massachusetts.[62] Under the new 1692 royal charter, the requirements for a man to be eligible to sit on a jury were financial, not religious.[63] Of the forty-eight potential jurors chosen by the sheriff, twelve served at each trial, and the foreman for Nurse's jury was Thomas Fisk, a sixty-year-old man from Wenham.[64]

The jury trial was a hallmark of English justice and dates back a thousand years to the time following the Norman conquest of England in 1066. Interestingly, the first jury trial in English history was also the first to declare a false verdict. It was discovered that at least one of the jurors at this first jury trial was pressured by the local sheriff into entering a false verdict and the twelve jurors were severely punished.[65] In 1692, there is no evidence of the sheriff meddling and the jury theoretically had the power to independently come to its own conclusions, but the twelve jurors at the Salem Town House were not immune to outside pressures such as fear and the endemic presumption of guilt.

THE PROCEEDINGS BEGAN when the guards brought Rebecca Nurse into the courtroom and up to the bar to be arraigned on the four charges of witchcraft against her. There she stood before the court, pale, chained, bedraggled, and stinking. This visible saint of spotless reputation now had a malign appearance from the months she spent in the hellish, dung-filled jails.

The courtroom on the second floor of the town house was most likely arranged with an elevated table and seats at the front where the justices of the court sat. The clerk sat at a table below the judges' bench, and there was a bar or other dividing feature that separated the judicial area up front from the spectators, who sat on benches throughout the floor and in a gallery up above.[66] There was a separate location before the bar, likely a seat, for witnesses when they gave testimony.[67]

The first part of the proceedings was Nurse's arraignment on the charges that the grand jury endorsed. During this arraignment, and for the full trial afterward, she stood at the bar wearing shackles.[68] Nurse's name was called, and she held up her hand to identify herself as the accused, as she stood facing the judges, with her back to a wall of eyes in the courtroom.[69] Clerk Stephen Sewall then read each of the indictments against Nurse, for afflicting Ann Putnam Jr., Mary Walcott, Elizabeth Hubbard, and Abigail Williams.

Still at the bar, facing the judges, Nurse was asked how she pled to each charge. She answered that she pled not guilty, and was then asked "Culprit, how will you be tried?"[70] This was a formulaic question, to which she gave the required response, "By God and the Country."[71] At trials, the twelve jurors represented "the Country."[72]

After Nurse entered her pleas, she had the opportunity to challenge jurors.[73] Though there are no records of whether or not she used this right, it is likely that her husband's experience serving on juries would have led her to take full advantage of this opportunity. Once the jurors were seated and sworn, the trial began.

Court clerk Sewall transcribed the trial but no transcripts survive, unlike those for Rebecca Nurse's initial hearing. In fact, there are no transcripts for *any* of the Oyer and Terminer trials—only the documents entered as evidence and later statements by several people who were present at the trials. There is historical evidence from a later petition to the Massachusetts government by Abigail Faulkner that as late as 1700 a "Record Book" of the trials existed and indeed such records were required to be kept. The government responded to Faulkner's petition by "reading her trial," so there must have been some sort of transcripts for them to read over.[74]

There is another reference to a court record book in 1841, when historian Peleg W. Chandler wrote, "It is believed that the original record book of these trials is lost. A copy of it was made several years ago for Ichabod Tucker, Esq., of Salem, but this also is lost or misplaced."[75] Tucker was the Essex County clerk of courts in Salem for over thirty years, in addition to being president of the Essex Historical Society and president of the Salem Athenaeum, so he had access to the original court documents.[76] It is unclear exactly what year his copy was made, but it was sometime in the first part of the nineteenth century.

Charles W. Upham, who published his history of the witch hunt in 1867 (but did much of his research over the preceding decades) noted that no record book of the trials could be found at that time. However, he assumed that Thomas Hutchinson had access to the record book when he wrote his *History of the Province of Massachusetts-Bay* in the 1760s, because Hutchinson seems to draw upon documents that were no longer available to Upham—or to present-day historians. Upham mentions the possibility that some of those involved in the witch hunt may have destroyed written records while "trying to conceal their errors."[77]

A similar assertion is made by historian Mary Beth Norton, who claims that although there was not an organized purge of the documents related to 1692, some participants and their descendants individually destroyed written records of the trials to save their reputations or that of their family. She specifically states a belief that Rev. Parris later burned some of his notes, and that some in official positions during the witch hunt likewise destroyed other documents.[78]

It was suggested that some trial documents were destroyed when an anti-Stamp Act mob overran historian and then-Lt. Governor Thomas Hutchinson's Boston mansion in 1765 and threw many of his papers into the street.[79] It does appear that Hutchinson had access to the record book, but since Chandler mentioned a copy of the trial transcripts was made sometime during the early nineteenth century, these transcripts must not have been destroyed at Hutchinson's house, nor by participants in the trials who were long dead by that point. The most likely conclusion is that the record book was stored at the Salem courthouse, with other 1692-related documents known to have been there, at least until the nineteenth century and was then misplaced or damaged and subsequently lost to history.

As to the documents entered as evidence during Nurse's trial, clerk Sewall wrote in 1692 that there were twenty written pieces of evidence in total for her case.[80] Written evidence was the norm in Massachusetts, so that it could easily be referred back to at a later date in case of an appeal or similar situation.[81] However, in addition to these twenty written documents, Clerk Sewall notes that some evidence for both the prosecution and the defense was given *viva voce*—spoken aloud and not submitted as written evidence.

The below account of Nurse's trial therefore can only draw on the written pieces of evidence entered at the trial and accounts written by contemporaries. We are left wondering as to what evidence was entered *viva voce*, and also potentially what written documents have by now been lost to the ages.

AFTER THE clerk recorded Rebecca Nurse's plea on each charge, the prosecution entered its evidence to the court. The clerk read the notes from her initial hearing in March, which included descriptions of her accusers' fits that day, and then he individually read depositions from her accusers who were present to swear to their written testimony under oath.[82]

As to the evidence presented by the accusers, the prosecution needed to convince the jury that Nurse used witchcraft to afflict the four individuals named in the indictments approved by the grand jury: Ann Putnam Jr., Mary Walcott, Elizabeth Hubbard, and Abigail Williams. Several pieces of evidence were entered by these accusers and several were entered by witnesses to their claimed afflictions.

One of the depositions entered for the prosecution was from Sarah Bibber, a thirty-six-year-old Salem Town woman who was one of the first adults to claim to be afflicted early in the witch hunt.[83] She approached the bar, and her deposition was read to the court. In the document, written by Thomas Putnam, Bibber claimed that on May 2 she saw Nurse's specter "most grievously torture and afflict the bodies of Mary Walcott, Mercy Lewis, and Abigail Williams by pinching them and almost choking them to death." Bibber's written evidence also states that although she saw Nurse's specter during the alleged incident described above, Nurse's specter did not hurt her until two days prior to the trial, at which time she asserted that it "did most grievously torment me by pinching me and almost choking me several times."[84] The word "grievously" appears in many of the depositions that Thomas Putnam transcribed, and therefore was likely added by him to embellish her testimony.

Either while her testimony was being read or later in the trial, Bibber pretended to have a violent fit. During her convulsions she sneakily took pins from her clothes, "held them between her fingers and clasped her hands around her knees and then she cried out and said that Goody Nurse pricked her"—presumably with the blood to prove it.[85] Nurse's daughter-in-law Sarah (Craggen) Nurse watched this fraud take place, and either during or after the trial she wrote out a piece of testimony describing Bibber's actions and submitted it to the court.

This pin episode is yet another example of fraudulent physical evidence being used against Rebecca Nurse. While the early fits of the afflicted could have been psychosomatic, the instances of intentionally fabricated evidence and overt lying indicate that not all of the actions can be attributed to suffering from a mental illness. There were malicious lies as well.

Once Bibber swore to her testimony, one of Nurse's neighbors, the younger Sarah Holten, was called to enter evidence against her. Holten was the widow of Benjamin Holten and she testified about the incident with her husband, Rebecca Nurse, and the pigs in 1689. As noted above, she is not the same Sarah Holten whose name is on the petition in support of Nurse—that is her mother-in-law. Holten's deposition is in the handwriting of Thomas Putnam.[86]

The widow Holten's deposition states that three years previously her "dear and loving husband Benjamin Holten, deceased, was as well as I ever knew him in my life," until the incident with the pigs. The document recounts that one Saturday morning "Rebecca Nurse, who now stands charged with witchcraft, came to our house and fell railing at him because our pigs got into her field." As to the conversation between Nurse and the Holtens that followed, Sarah Holten swore before the court that "Yet all we could say to her could in no way pacify her, but she continued railing and scolding a great while together calling to her son Benjamin Nurse to go and get a gun and kill our pigs and let none of them go out of the field."[87]

Up until this point in the testimony all that is described is a dispute between neighbors, but then Holten claims a link between this episode and witchcraft: "Within a short time after this, my poor husband, going out very early in the morning, as he was coming in again he was taken with a strange fit in the entry, being struck blind and struck down two or three times." Her testimony continues, "All summer after, he continued in a languishing condition being much pained at his stomach and often struck blind. But, about a fortnight before he died, he was taken with strange and violent fits acting much like to our poor bewitched persons when we thought they would have died." Also, like the afflicted in 1692, a doctor was consulted who "could not find what his distemper was." Benjamin Holten finally died "a cruel death" at midnight one night after violent seizures.[88] Though apparently not seen as suspicious in 1689, when viewed through the lens of 1692 the incident seemed similar to the alleged afflictions of the accusers.

This accusation by Sarah Holten also reveals how some families split over the witchcraft accusations. Three Holtens—deceased Benjamin's parents Joseph Holten Sr. and the elder Sarah Holten and the deceased's brother Joseph Holten Jr.—signed the petition in support of Nurse earlier that spring.[89] Yet here, the younger Sarah Holten, wife of the deceased, is on the opposite side of her in-laws. To add another family dimension to this testimony, Nathaniel and Hannah Ingersoll, aunt and uncle of the deceased Benjamin Holten, also entered a deposition at Nurse's trial.[90]

The Ingersolls—keepers of the Salem Village tavern just down the road from the Holtens—also testified for the prosecution and corroborated part of the younger Sarah Holten's testimony about her husband's illness, but they cast doubt on the supposed connection to witchcraft. In this instance, the Ingersolls may not have been present in court to swear to their testimony, for the document bears clerk Stephen Sewall's signature attesting that they had sworn to it in front of him, presumably on a different occasion. As in Holten's deposition, the Ingersolls' deposition connects Benjamin Holten's illness to that of the supposedly afflicted accusers with the same phrase referring to him as "acting much like to our poor bewitched persons when we thought they would have died."[91] This exact phrase is no coincidence, since Thomas Putnam wrote both documents, and from the language similarities it is clear that Putnam did not just merely transcribe both of these depositions for the prosecution, but instead took an active role in composing the documents.

The Ingersolls' deposition does not accuse Nurse of anything, but instead just supports the basic details of Benjamin Holten's death. The document notes that "he died a most violent death with dreadful fits and the doctor that was with him said he could not tell what his distemper was." But, unlike Holten, the Ingersolls state, "though then we had no suspicion of witchcraft."[92] It only became suspicious when filtered through the fear and paranoia of 1692.

Rev. Parris and John Putnam Sr. also came forward to swear to a deposition. Their document was written by Parris, and the editors of the published collection of witch trials documents note, "Parris likely prepared the body of the document in advance. Subsequently he completed it, filling in his and Putnam's names and ages."[93] It seems strange that he wrote down the evidence before writing at the top who was going to enter it in court.

Their deposition described what happened when Mercy Lewis was summoned to Jonathan Putnam's house when he was ill to ascertain whether his illness was natural or an affliction by witchcraft. Parris and John Putnam Sr. swore that Lewis "saw Goody Nurse and Goody Carrier holding Jonathan's head." This is an unlikely accusation because Jonathan Putnam was among Nurse's supporters who signed the petition back in May.[94] Why would Nurse use witchcraft to harm one of her supporters?

In this deposition, it is important to note that Parris and John Putnam Sr. testified about Lewis that "she *saw* Goody Nurse," instead of stating that she *said she saw* her, which is all they could really be sure of as witnesses. Obviously the only way for the two men to know what Lewis saw was for her to tell them, and they evidently believed what she said for there is no equivocation or question as to her reliability in their testimony.

Parris returned to the bar later in the trial and swore to another piece of testimony alongside Nathaniel Ingersoll and Thomas Putnam, father of Ann Putnam Jr. Similarly to Parris' evidence discussed above, here the three witnesses express a belief in the validity of the supposed witchcraft. Their deposition describes how the three men saw Mrs. Ann Putnam, Ann Putnam Jr., Mary Walcott, and Abigail Williams have fits during Nurse's initial hearing in March. It states that the afflicted "were several times and grievously tortured," and that when Nurse moved her hands, "some of the afflicted were pinched, and upon the motion of her head and fingers some of them were tortured."[95] Like in the previous deposition Parris swore to in court, these men do not write that the afflicted *appeared* to be tortured, but instead that they "*were* tortured" and pinched by Nurse. They do not state just what they objectively saw, but instead state what their opinion was: that it was all real, and Rebecca Nurse was using witchcraft against her accusers. Parris' biased testimony such as this was denounced by the Nurse family in the years following 1692.[96]

Later, Thomas Putnam swore to another deposition alongside his brother and neighbor Edward Putnam. The first part of their testimony attempts to add support to Ann Jr.'s claims that Nurse hurt her over the course of that spring. The two men, Ann Putnam Jr.'s father and uncle, "witness and say that having been several times present with Ann Putnam Jr., in and after her fits and saw her much afflicted, being bitten, pinched, her limbs distorted, and pins thrust into her flesh, which she charged on Rebecca Nurse, that she was the actor thereof and that she saw her do it."[97] The deposition then continues with another description of Nurse allegedly afflicting Ann Jr. at Nurse's initial hearing on March 24, which is the exact charge written in an indictment. Once their testimony was read, the two men swore to it and returned to their seats.

There was one other new deposition read that day. Constable John Putnam Jr. and his wife Hannah Putnam, whose infant died an unfortunate death two months prior, approached the bar. Their deposition, also written by Thomas Putnam, is against not just Nurse, but also her two sisters Sarah Cloyce and Mary Easty.[98] All three Towne sisters are mentioned because the testimony relates to what John Putnam Jr. said about their mother, Joanna Towne.

In the deposition, John Putnam Jr. said that he blamed his infant's death on the three Towne women because he "had reported something which I had heard concerning the mother of Rebecca Nurse, Mary Easty, and Sarah Cloyce," after which he himself had fits. While Putnam is entirely vague as to just what the "something" he said regarding Nurse's mother was, in a separate document Mrs. Ann Putnam noted that he accused Joanna Towne of being a witch.[99] Joanna died decades prior to 1692, and there is no evidence that she was ever accused of being a witch in her lifetime. It seems to be yet another baseless accusation, but one that was used as evidence against Nurse.

Then, their testimony states that Putnam recovered from his apparent illness, but his infant began having seizures of some kind. He called his mother to the house in the middle of the night, and it was she who told him that the child "had an evil hand upon it." Putnam and his wife Hannah then called upon a doctor, "but all he did give it could do it no good." The child eventually "departed this life by a cruel and violent death being enough to pierce a stony heart, for to the best of our understanding it was five hours in dying."[100] The grieving parents swore to their testimony, placing blame for this tragedy on Nurse, and then returned to their seats.

There were two more depositions against Rebecca Nurse that were sworn to that day, which were also previously sworn before the grand jury. One was entered by Edward Putnam, who swore to seeing bite marks on Ann Putnam Jr.'s arm, and the chain marks that kept appearing—one of the early examples of the afflicted using false physical evidence against Nurse. The other previously entered deposition was by Ann Jr. in which, among other things, she describes first seeing Nurse's specter and not knowing who it was, and also how she was afflicted during Nurse's initial hearing.[101] This testimony was yet again accepted despite her technically being too young to enter legal evidence in a capital felony case.[102]

The afflicted who testified at the trials, such as Ann Putnam Jr. and Sarah Bibber at Nurse's trial, caused great disturbances. Rev. Cotton Mather's descriptions of the afflicted's actions at Susannah Martin's trial, which took place the day before Nurse's, and at Rev. Burroughs' and Martha Carrier's trials, which took place in August, are presumably quite similar to Bibber and Ann Jr.'s actions at Nurse's trial. Mather wrote of Martin's trial the previous day, "there was an extraordinary endeavor by witchcrafts, with cruel and frequent fits, to hinder the poor sufferers from giving in their complaints; which the Court was forced with much patience to obtain, by much waiting and watching for it." Similarly, at Burroughs' trial, "It cost the Court a wonderful deal of trouble, to hear the testimonies of the sufferers; for when they were going to give in their depositions, they would for a long time be taken with fits, that made them incapable of saying anything." As to the severity of their fits, Mather wrote of the accused at Carrier's trial, "the poor people were so tortured that everyone expected their death upon the very spot."[103] Ann Jr.'s deposition was read and she likely fell into a similar fit before she swore to it.

It is likely that it was during the fits of the afflicted at Nurse's trial that the accusation of witchcraft was leveled publicly against Rev. Samuel Willard of Boston.[104] According to one contemporary, during a fit in the courtroom, "one of the accusers cried out publicly of Mr. Willard, minister in Boston, as afflicting her." Willard had publicly decried the judges' use of spectral evidence at his Sunday sermon only two weeks prior, after he had attended the meeting of the ministers in Boston that discussed the flaws of spectral evidence. After speaking out, he was targeted. But, perhaps because several of the judges were members of his congregation and knew him, the afflicted accuser was "sent out of the court, and it was told about [that] she was mistaken in the person."[105] The judges disagreed with—and ultimately ignored—Willard and the other ministers' criticisms of their methods, but they protected him from this accusation.

There was one other piece of testimony for the prosecution, from confessors Abigail Hobbs and her stepmother Deliverance Hobbs. The guards led them through the door at the back of the courtroom and up to the bar, to the surprise of Rebecca Nurse who did not seem to expect them to testify against her.[106]

The use of testimony from those who falsely confessed to witchcraft, the impossible crime of covenanting with the Devil, was viewed as suspect by critics of the court in 1692. In part, they thought that it was sacrilegious for a confessed "witch" to invoke God's name when they swore to their testimony. Thomas Brattle wrote in the fall of 1692, "The confessors do declare what they know of the said prisoner; and some of the confessors are allowed to give their oaths; a thing which I believe was never heard of in this world; that such as confess themselves to be witches, to have renounced God and Christ, and all that is sacred, should yet be allowed and ordered to swear by the name of the great God! This indeed seems to me to be a gross taking of God's name in vain."[107] How could the phrase "so help me God," uttered when they swore their evidence in court, have any meaning if they previously claimed that they renounced God and signed the Devil's book?

It is unclear exactly what the Hobbs women said in court that day, for when confessors testified against other accused at trial there was often not a written record of their testimony.[108] Or, if there was, it no longer survives.[109] In a written petition to the court after her trial, Nurse disputed the legality of the testimony from these two false confessors because they were fellow prisoners under the same charge. Nurse stated that she "did then, and yet do, judge them not legal evidence against their fellow prisoners."[110] In the end it was not their words at trial that were the most important, but instead what Nurse said upon seeing them that mattered most.

Abigail Hobbs had falsely confessed to covenanting with the Devil on April 19 and Deliverance falsely confessed on April 23, which Nurse appears not to have realized.[111] She did not expect them to be at her trial, and when she turned and saw the guards bring them into the courtroom she said either "What? Do you bring her? She is one of us," as reported by one chronicler, or "What? Do these persons give in evidence against me now? They used to come among us," as reported by the jury foreman Thomas Fisk.[112] In a later document Nurse stated that she referenced the two confessors as "of our company"—meaning fellow prisoners.[113]

Although she merely expressed her surprise that they came to testify against her, the words Nurse uttered were later interpreted to her detriment. Whatever the exact wording was, it was erroneously thought by some present that Nurse was counting herself among the witches, as that is what both of the Hobbses claimed to be. This remark was not forgotten.

AFTER THE PROSECUTION CONCLUDED, Rebecca Nurse and her family presented evidence for her defense. Although Nurse was in jail and unable to collect testimony herself, her family had almost a month since the grand jury appearance to prepare a case, and had previously collected other evidence, such as the petition, well before that.

The outside help by her family members was essential, and prisoners of that century who did not get outside help were often unable to prepare a defense simply due to their confinement in jail. The prepared defense for Nurse had witnesses reveal the accusers as dishonest and inconsistent liars, while other witnesses refuted specific accusations against her. Additionally, the defense evidence included supporters testifying about Nurse's good character, which in typical criminal trials at the time was seen as an especially important deciding factor for the jury.[114] Nurse's family presented the strongest and most comprehensive defense that was prepared for any of the accused in 1692.[115]

Far more defense evidence was gathered for Nurse's trial than was presented at her grand jury session, which shows dedication on the part of her family, and willingness on the part of those who testified for her to risk being accused themselves. Despite such well-prepared formal evidence, in that century great weight was also usually given to how defendants acted and responded off-the-cuff to the allegations against them during the flow of the trial.[116] Nurse, being elderly, ill, hard of hearing, and malnourished—not to mention covered in dirt and filth from the jail—was at a clear disadvantage. Also, as a woman, she did not have experience addressing a crowded courtroom—which was especially challenging with spectators and judges that were quite hostile.

Although one cannot be entirely confident as to which pieces of the defense evidence were used at each stage of the process, because defense evidence was not sworn and dated like the prosecution's evidence, it can be generally assumed that all of the defense evidence submitted to the court in 1692 was indeed presented at trial.[117] The earliest document submitted to the court that was likely used for Nurse's defense at the trial was

Samuel Nurse and John Tarbell's report of their visit to Thomas Putnam's house. Nurse's son and son-in-law visited the Putnams on March 28, four days after her initial hearing. Their aim was to discover who first accused Nurse of witchcraft by name, though after asking the women of that household, each one placed blame on the next, without a clear conclusion being reached.[118] None of those present wanted to take responsibility for first accusing Nurse, and possibly the Nurse family hoped that these deflections revealed the accusation against Nurse to be less certain.

Several pieces of testimony submitted to the court that were likely used for Nurse's defense at trial sought to discredit Sarah Bibber, the witness for the prosecution who lied about being stabbed with pins in court. Joseph Fowler, who knew Bibber well because she and her husband lived in his house for a while, submitted testimony questioning her character. According to Fowler, a middle-aged brick maker from Wenham, "Goodwife Bibber was a woman who was very idle in her calling, and very much given to tattling and tale-bearing, making mischief among her neighbors, and very much given to speak bad words and would call her husband bad names, and was a woman of a very turbulent spirit."[119] Such facts undermined her credibility as a witness.

Thomas and Mary Jacobs, of Ipswich, similarly attempted to discredit Bibber as an accuser.[120] As with Fowler, Bibber lived in the Jacobs' home for a while so they were well-acquainted with her past. According to them, Bibber "would be very often speaking against one and another very obscenely, and those things were very false, and wishing very bad wishes, and very often she wished that when her child fell into the river that she had never pulled her out."[121] A history of lying clearly made Bibber an unreliable witness. Most shockingly, wishing ill upon others was something that traditionally could get one accused of witchcraft—never mind wishing ill toward one's own child!

The last segment of the Jacobs' testimony is the most significant: "The neighborhood where she lived among us after she buried her first husband has told us that this John Bibber's wife could fall into fits as she pleased." On the same piece of paper as the Jacobs testimony is a very similar statement by Richard Walker, who likely also came from Ipswich. Walker told the court, "Goodwife Bibber, sometimes living near to me, I did observe her to be a woman of an unruly turbulent spirit, and would often fall into strange fits when anything crossed her humor."[122] Not only was Bibber's testimony called into question due to her previous lying, but so was the authenticity of her supposed fits, which she had performed in public over the past three months.

John Porter, a Wenham farmer and a maltster, and his wife, Lydia, also submitted evidence for Nurse's defense.[123] John Porter testified that Bibber "would often fall into strange fits when she was crossed of her humor," and Lydia Porter recalled that "Goodwife Bibber and her husband would often quarrel and in their quarrels she would call him very bad names, and would have strange fits when she was crossed, and [was] a woman of an unruly spirit, and double-tongued."[124] There were multiple accounts of Bibber having supposed fits whenever she was upset and of her lying often.

Salem Village potter James Kettle submitted another piece of defense testimony that sought to discredit Elizabeth Hubbard, an accuser named in one of the indictments against Nurse.[125] At Nurse's previous grand jury session, Clement Coldum likely submitted a piece of testimony that also impugned the credibility of Hubbard. Coldum's document stated that Hubbard "could intercourse with the Devil as well as with [him]." The implication was that one who conversed freely with Satan should not be trusted as a witness in court. At Nurse's trial, Kettle's testimony is very similar to Coldum's regarding an incident that occurred when he encountered Hubbard at her aunt and uncle's house, after Sunday services on the same day as Coldum's reported conversation with her.[126]

Kettle testified that "being at Dr. Griggs on a Sabbath day about the last of May 1692, having some discourse with Elizabeth Hubbard and I found her to speak several untruths in denying the Sabbath day and saying she had not been to meeting that day, but had only been up to James Holten's."[127] In addition to denying the Sabbath, bragging about not attending Sunday services called into question her credentials as an allegedly innocent Puritan. Communing with Satan, denying the Sabbath, and not attending religious services sounds just like some of the accusations lodged against the accused—not actions expected of the accusers, and certainly not actions countenanced by the Puritans.

Most strangely though, is that Hubbard actually *had* attended services that Sunday, and lied to Kettle when she said she had not. Coldum's aforementioned testimony that he submitted a month earlier at the grand jury specifically states that he gave Hubbard a ride home from services that day.[128] If Hubbard could not be trusted to answer whether she had gone to church services that morning, she certainly was not a credible enough witness to be testifying in a trial where Nurse's life was on the line.

In addition to testimony against the credibility of Bibber and Hubbard, three witnesses—William Bradford, Rachel Bradford, and William Rayment Jr.—sought to discredit Mercy Lewis, the maid in Thomas and Ann

Putnam's household and one of Nurse's main accusers. Rachel and William Bradford, a Beverly fisherman, once briefly shared their home with Lewis.[129] Rayment, also from Beverly, was one of those at Ingersoll's tavern when several accusers were joking about their witchcraft accusations and "seemed to make a jest of it."[130]

This document entered by the three Beverly witnesses is torn down the left side, cutting off several words. What can be gathered is that two and a half years prior to the witch hunt Lewis lived with the Bradfords for about a "quarter of a year." There is a sentence partially missing in which they claim that Lewis would "stand stiffly" to "untruth," meaning that she would not admit to lies. The document also contains the phrase "we did then judge that . . . [*missing*] . . . matter of conscience of speaking the truth," which might be their justification for coming forward and testifying for Nurse, but it is impossible to be certain of the context due to the damaged manuscript.[131] Although only part of the record survives, it is clearly an attempt to undermine Mercy Lewis' credibility.

Another piece of defense testimony submitted to the court and presumably entered at trial was from Robert Moulton Sr. of Salem Town, in which he points out an example of Susannah Sheldon changing her story. Moulton's testimony is signed by him and has an attestation at the bottom: "Samuel Nurse and Joseph Trumbull saw Robert Moulton sign this writing." Therefore, it seems as though Nurse's son and Joseph Trumbull of Salem Town were the ones that encouraged Moulton to testify. Sheldon once claimed that witches dragged her around her yard and over a stone wall "like a snake," but then claimed the incident never happened. Additionally, Moulton relates that he "heard her say that she did ride upon a pole to Boston and she said the Devil carried the pole."[132] Not only does this evidence portray Sheldon as changing her stories, but it also describes her as admitting to flying on poles with the Devil—just like witches supposedly did.

There is one final piece of discrediting testimony submitted to the court for Nurse's defense. Joseph Hutchinson, a fifty-nine-year-old Salem Villager who signed the petition for Nurse, entered testimony to the court regarding Abigail Williams, one of the four accusers named in an indictment. In this document, Hutchinson taints Williams' testimony by relating how she bragged of her relationship with the Devil—just as Coldum previously revealed similar statements by Hubbard. Hutchinson testified, "Abigail Williams, I have heard you speak often of a book that has been offered to you. . . I asked her who brought the books to her, she told me that it was the black man. I asked her who the black man was. She told me it was the Devil. I asked if she was not afraid to see the Devil. She said at first she was and did go from him, but now she was not afraid but could talk with him as well as she could with me."[133] Williams allegedly admitted to easily talking with the Devil. Nurse denied any involvement with him. Yet, it was Nurse who was on trial for witchcraft. Hutchinson's attack on Williams' credibility seriously damaged her reputation as an accuser, and after this session of the court Parris stopped writing depositions on her behalf.[134]

In addition to the previous defense evidence that tarnished the credibility of certain accusers, several defense witnesses also sought to refute specific accusations against Nurse. One piece of such testimony was submitted to the court by John Putnam Sr. and his wife Rebecca Putnam of Salem Village.[135] John and Rebecca Putnam were heads of one of the three branches of the Putnam family, and long-time church members. He previously had represented Salem in the General Court, and he was the Putnam opposite the Towne family in the Topsfield dispute.[136]

Since he and his wife were defending Nurse, and previously they both signed the petition in support of her, it is unlikely that the Topsfield feud was one of the main causes of her accusation. John Putnam Sr. did, however, also sign a deposition alongside Rev. Parris corroborating one of Mercy Lewis' fits in which she mentioned Nurse.[137] John Putnam Sr. and Rebecca Putnam's defense evidence for Nurse, as well as their names on the petition for her—along with the names of several other Putnams and inhabitants from across Salem Village—shows the enormous support that Nurse had from her friends and neighbors, some of whom were very well-respected and influential people. It also shows that her support was not from just one side of any supposed factional divide.

The two Putnams' testimony is primarily a refutation of their niece Mrs. Ann Putnam's accusation that Nurse used witchcraft to murder John Fuller and Rebecca Shepard, members of their family.[138] Rebecca Shepard was their daughter, and Fuller was her husband and their son-in-law. (After Fuller died, Rebecca Putnam Fuller remarried John Shepard of Rowley prior to her own death, which is why her last name is noted as Shepard.)[139] John and Rebecca Putnam testified that "our son-in-law John Fuller and our daughter Rebecca Shepard did most of them die a most violent death and did act very strangely at the time of their death. [We] further say that we did judge then that they both died of a malignant fever and had no suspicion of witchcraft of any[one], neither can we accuse the prisoner at the bar of any such thing."[140] Here the parents of the deceased, who surely knew the situation better than Mrs. Ann

Putnam, refute the claim that witchcraft caused the deaths of their family members.

Two previously discussed pieces of evidence arguing against the findings from the physical examination were submitted to the court and presumably entered at trial. The first was Nurse's own petition to the court, written the day before, in which she contested the findings of the jury of women who searched her and offered to submit herself to the humiliation of another examination. The second piece of prior evidence possibly entered again was the petition by her two daughters, Rebecca Preston and Mary Tarbell, who stated that they believed the mark found by the jury of women was natural.[141]

The final group of documents submitted to the court for Nurse's defense describe her good character and impeccable credentials as a visible saint. In addition to new testimony, the petition signed by thirty-nine supporters was presumably entered for her defense along with the statement written after Nurse's brother-in-law Peter Cloyce, Israel Porter, Elizabeth (Hathorne) Porter, and Daniel Andrew visited her at her sickbed before she was formally charged with witchcraft.[142]

One witness who entered new testimony to the court about Nurse's good character was elderly Nathaniel Putnam, head of one branch of the Putnam family and deputy to the General Court for Salem.[143] He was Thomas Putnam's uncle and John Putnam Sr.'s brother. Nathaniel Putnam was the Nurse family's neighbor who was involved in the land dispute with the Endicotts. He was also the father of Constable John Putnam Jr., who accused Nurse of killing his infant after he spread a rumor about her mother being a witch.[144]

Nathaniel Putnam's testimony speaks more to Nurse's character than that of his brother John Sr., whose testimony only refuted one particular charge against her. Nathaniel Putnam's testimony states that he was "desired by Francis Nurse to give information of what I could say concerning his wife's [*here the paper is ripped*] and conversation" to the court. Putnam states the he had known Rebecca Nurse for fourteen years (since the Nurse family moved to the village), and that "I have observed of her, human frailties excepted, her life and conversation have been according to her profession [of faith], and she has brought up a great family of children and educated them well so that there is in some of them apparent signs of Godliness." His testimony continued, possibly alluding to the Holten incident, "I have known her to differ with her neighbors, but I never knew nor heard of any that did accuse her of what she is now charged with."[145] Thomas Putnam wrote many of the depositions against

Nurse, his wife and daughter made wild and fantastic accusations against her such as spectral torture to spectral murder, but in this testimony we see Thomas Putnam's uncle give a strong endorsement of Nurse's good character. His statements about Nurse raising and educating her children as to religion are particularly high praise, and make her an unlikely witch.

AFTER REBECCA NURSE's family and neighbors presented their defense evidence for her, Chief Justice William Stoughton addressed the jury and gave them instructions before they left to deliberate. Although it is not known what Stoughton's exact words were at Nurse's trial, his instructions at Bridget Bishop's trial—which were likely very similar to those at Nurse's trial—were recorded by Thomas Brattle in 1692: "I remember that when the chief Judge gave the first jury their charge, he told them, that they were not to mind whether the bodies of the said afflicted were really pined and consumed [by witchcraft], as was expressed in the indictment; but whether the said afflicted did not suffer from the accused such afflictions as naturally *tended* to their being pined and consumed, wasted, etc. This, (said he,) is a pining and consuming in the sense of the law. I add not."[146] Stoughton's instructions demonstrate a very loose interpretation of the law on witchcraft and how the accusers' fits were to be perceived. Overall, these instructions lowered the threshold required to find the accused guilty.

Stoughton based his instructions on the 1604 English Witchcraft Act and, in essence, what he told the jury was that it was not necessary for them to be convinced that the afflicted were "really pined or consumed"—truly permanently bewitched and made to suffer pain—directly by the accused, as their testimony claimed. Instead, the jury was to consider whether the accusers "tended," or appeared, as if they were hurt by witchcraft according to the jury's observations of the accusers' behavior in the courtroom and the descriptions of their fits that witnesses swore to in court.[147]

Brattle, in the quote above, points out that what Stoughton required of the jury was not what the law actually required in order for one to be found guilty of witchcraft. The key muddying word Stoughton added in his instructions, "tended," is not in the indictments or the death warrants, which state that the accused were charged with actually causing permanent harm through witchcraft.[148] Stoughton's remarks also defied legal authorities of the time, which focused on whether the accused signed a contract with the Devil. One legal work consulted in 1692 was Richard Bernard's *A Guide to Grand-Jury Men*. Bernard wrote that if a covenant with the Devil could not be proved, "all the strange fits, apparitions, naming of the suspected in trances, sudden falling down at the sight of the suspected, the ease at which some receive when the suspected are executed, be no good grounds for to find them guilty of witchcraft and to hang them."[149] Under Stoughton's direction, the witch trials court separated itself from the previous tradition of skepticism in Massachusetts toward the crime of witchcraft, ignored legal authorities of the day, and killed innocents based on the accusers' unsubstantiated claims of spectral affliction.

Once Stoughton finished his flawed instructions, the jury withdrew to deliberate. Just as today, a jury's verdict needed to be unanimous to convict. But, the jury did not require a higher burden of proof, such as "guilty beyond a reasonable doubt," to determine a verdict, as our current legal system does.[150]

Some time passed, and the jury slowly filed back into the courtroom, every eye in the room surely upon them. The room was crowded with people eager to hear the jury's decision, and others gathered outside the building to hear the news.[151]

Thomas Fisk, the foreman of the jury, rose. Chief Justice Stoughton looked down toward him from the judges' bench and asked him what verdict the jury found. Fisk responded that they found Rebecca Nurse not guilty.

Not guilty! The first and only not guilty verdict of the Oyer and Terminer Court. The Nurse family and the brave witnesses who testified before the court swayed the jury and broke the perfect conviction record of the court. They successfully defended Rebecca Nurse, an innocent, elderly grandmother against the wild claims—and outright lies—of her accusers.

Then a shriek punctuated the air.

Then another "hideous cry."[152]

And another.

Suddenly some of the accusers writhed on the floor, screaming, and the tempest crescendoed to the point that not only the spectators but even the judges of the court—who previously had seen many of the accusers' fits—were shocked at the scene.

The court briefly recessed amid the chaos. One judge, as he exited the bench, declared his dissatisfaction with the verdict, and another said they would indict Nurse again.[153] Perhaps one of these two frustrated judges was Wait-Still Winthrop, grandson of Governor John Winthrop. This was his City Upon the Hill, and the eyes of all in the courtroom were upon the judges to see what would happen next.

The court eventually resumed, and the judges took their places before the now stunned and confused crowd. One can imagine Nurse's family waiting on every word the chief justice was to utter. Stoughton addressed the jury and, according to Robert Calef, he "said he would not impose upon the jury; but intimated as if they had not well considered one expression of the prisoner when she was upon trial."[154] That "expression" was the words Nurse spoke when the guards brought Abigail and Deliverance Hobbs into the courtroom to testify. Stoughton wanted the jury to redeliberate.

The accusers' sudden outburst when the verdict was announced shows that their fits were at least sometimes intentional and on-demand, though it was not likely that the fits were the reason for Stoughton to ask the jury to reconsider. The judiciary had not been swayed by fits of the accusers previously, such as when obviously fake evidence was introduced like the broken knife at Sarah Good's trial, or when accusations touched someone they knew to be innocent such as Rev. Willard.[155] So, Stoughton likely did not ask the jury to reconsider because he was intimidated by the accusers' uproar, but rather did so on his own accord, because he believed strongly that the court was following the correct course in its hardline approach to the witch hunt.

As to Stoughton's request to the jury, it is true that occasionally judges did ask juries to reconsider a verdict. But in Massachusetts witchcraft cases, the judiciary had previously intervened only on the side of defendants and asked juries to reconsider guilty verdicts, and had not before asked a jury to reconsider a not-guilty verdict in a witchcraft case. Faced with this request, the jury either could refuse or could accept his request and redeliberate. If they refused, or redeliberated but found the same verdict, the judges could officially reject the verdict and throw the case to the General Court, the lower house of the legislature in Boston, for that body to conduct a retrial. This is the situation that arose in 1656 when Ann Hibbens was found guilty of witchcraft by a jury but the judges refused to accept the verdict.[156]

At Nurse's trial, because of the imposing judges and the "clamors of the accusers," the jurors apparently debated among themselves whether to redeliberate. A later document by the foreman notes, "several of the jury declared themselves desirous to go out again, and thereupon the honored Court gave leave."[157] The jury departed to reconsider Rebecca Nurse's fate.

Some time passed, as the spectators sat in the courtroom waiting on that June day. After this anxious pause, the jurors appeared in the doorway and walked to their seats. The crowd listened for a verdict to be announced, but instead the foreman Thomas Fisk walked over to Nurse at the bar and posed some questions to her. The twelve jurors were still not convinced of Nurse's guilt and wanted to hear her own interpretation of her supposedly suspicious remarks.

In a subsequent document, Fisk described his views at this moment. He wrote that the jury returned to the courtroom the second time because he "could not tell how to take her words, as an evidence against her, till she had a further opportunity to put her sense upon them, if she would take it."[158] Jurors in the late seventeenth century often deferred to the foreman, which makes his view particularly significant.[159] Thomas Fisk doubted, and perhaps other jurors did too.

Fisk then questioned Nurse—weak, ill, and standing at the bar after this long ordeal. He repeated her previous utterance to her, and asked "one of the Court" to confirm that these were indeed the words she spoke previously. The judge confirmed that it was so. Fisk then asked Nurse to explain her remark. Apparently, she did not make a reply to the foreman's questions. Fisk later wrote, "she being then at the bar, but made no reply, nor interpretation of them; whereupon these words were to me a principal evidence against her." Her lack of response was likely due to her being hard of hearing, and the strain on her—an ill and elderly woman who had been standing for quite a while during her overwhelming trial. Nurse later justified her lack of a response, "being something hard of hearing, and full of grief, none informing me how the Court took up my words, and therefore [I] had not the opportunity to declare what I intended.[160] However, the jury saw her lack of a response as a sign of guilt.

The jury withdrew again. The Nurse family, along with Nurse's accusers, witnesses for both sides, judges, and all of the spectators gathered in the courtroom and outside, awaited the jury's response.

After a while, the jurors filed back into the room and took their seats. Fisk stood and Stoughton asked if the jury had reached a verdict. They had. *Guilty.*

The guards approached Rebecca Nurse and led her out of the courtroom with her chains dragging behind her. Based on a few offhand remarks, a well-respected woman and a visible saint was condemned to die.

TEN

BODY AND SOUL

For we must consider that we shall be as a city upon a hill. The eyes of all people are upon us. So that if we shall deal falsely with our God in this work we have undertaken, and so cause Him to withdraw His present help from us, we shall be made a story and by-word throughout the world.
—John Winthrop, en route to Salem, 1630

THE PUNISHMENT FOR A CHURCH MEMBER found guilty of witchcraft was the death of both body and soul. If one signed an accord with the Devil, one sinned against God and forsook their place among the saints in Heaven. As such, church members condemned for witchcraft suffered a spiritual death through excommunication from Christ's church, and then bodily death through hanging as an enemy of the commonwealth.

Although Rebecca Nurse was found guilty, her family's belief in her innocence—bolstered by the strong supporting testimony of her friends and neighbors, and the unusual way in which the verdict was reached—led them to prepare a petition to the royal governor. In seeking to demonstrate how the final verdict hinged on a misunderstanding, the Nurse family collected their own testimony in the days after Nurse's trial and also sought a statement from the foreman of the jury, Thomas Fisk.

While her family gathered documents, Nurse remained in the Salem jail. By early July there were several others found guilty at the same session of the court in jail, along with others yet to be tried. Those found guilty at the court's second session in addition to Nurse were Sarah Good of Salem Village, Susannah Martin of Amesbury, Elizabeth Howe of Ipswich, and Sarah Wilds of Topsfield. These other convicted women knew that their executions were imminent, but of these condemned only Nurse, as a church member, died two deaths.

On the afternoon of July 3, the first Sacrament Sunday after her trial, the guards took Nurse from prison and brought her to the Salem Town meetinghouse, her home parish. That morning after the public service, the church members—Nurse's fellow visible saints—remained in the meetinghouse to celebrate the Lord's Supper, while the less worthy of the congregation left. After these Puritan saints ate and drank to their own salvation, Salem Town's junior minister Rev. Nicholas Noyes asked the church members to vote for Nurse's excommunication.[1]

Nurse first attended services with the Salem Town church around 1635 as a young girl who fled persecution in England, where Puritans suffered greatly under the king's religious diktats. She and her family risked their lives voyaging over three thousand miles across turbulent seas in the hope of being part of the New Jerusalem of the Puritans, where they could practice what they believed was the true, uncorrupted faith in peace.

It was her coreligionists, her fellow church members and visible saints whom she referred to as brothers and sisters, who brought humiliation and betrayal upon her in her old age. Her case was now before Salem's Sanhedrin. After Noyes announced Nurse's supposed sins to the church members, the issue was put to a vote. The saints voted unanimously to cast out one of their own.[2] She was falsely accused of taking the Devil's sacrament as part of the witch accusations, but it was those participating in the Lord's Supper that caused her damnation.

The guards brought Rebecca Nurse into the meetinghouse after the vote and took her to the front, as her chains dragged behind her. What happened next was the most shocking and scandalous of Puritan ceremonies, and 1692 was the last year that the Salem Town church ever performed the excommunication rite.[3]

The Puritans viewed those cast out of the church as irredeemable, and subject to all the cruelties of hell. Jonathan Edwards, a generation later, described the afterlife that awaited those locked out of heaven: "Their heads, their eyes, their tongues, their hands and feet and loins; their vitals shall forever be full of glowing melting fire, fierce enough to melt the very rocks and elements, and also shall eternally be full of the most quick and lively sense to feel the torment. . . . They shall know that they shall never cease restlessly to plunge and roll in that mighty ocean of fire. They will know that those billows of fire, that are greater than the highest waves, will never cease to roll over them, one following another, forever and ever."[4] This was the fate the church members unanimously decided for Nurse.

The Puritan rite of excommunication was normally a medicinal act—it was done to force the sinner to confess and repent their sin, after which the individual was allowed back into the church.[5] In Nurse's case, this excommunication was simply another punishment, for there was no possibility of confessing and then retaking her place at the table. She was set to be publicly executed in a matter of days, whether she "confessed" or not, and falsely confessing was also a grave enough sin to jeopardize her status in the church.

While Nurse stood in the meetinghouse, Rev. Noyes sat in front of her below the pulpit, the lay elders and church deacons sat on either side, and the church members were behind her back in the pews.[6] Noyes rose from his seat, walked toward Nurse, and stood facing her—his portly figure standing between her and the candles up front, overshadowing the frail yet steadfast old woman who stood before him.[7]

Although the exact words spoken by Noyes are not recorded, the transcripts of a previous seventeenth-century Puritan excommunication for one convicted of witchcraft reveals the typical procedure. While the minister stood in front of the person to be cast out, he listed their supposed sins, and then declared:

> For these and many more foul and sinful transgressions, I do here, in the name of the whole church and in the name of Lord Jesus Christ and by the virtue of that power and authority which He hath given to His church, pronounce you to be a leprous and unclean person, and I do cast you out and cut you off from the enjoyment of all those blessed privileges and ordinances which God hath entrusted His church withal, which you have so long abused. . . . And I do exclude you not only from the fellowship of the church in all the public ordinances of the same, but also from all private fellowship and communion with any of the servants of God in this church, except only in those relations in your own family. . . . And for the greater terror and amazing of you, I do here, in the name of Christ Jesus and His Church, deliver you up to Satan and to his power and working, that you who would not be guided by the council of God may be terrified and hampered by the snares and power of Satan—for the destruction of your proud flesh [and] for the humbling of your soul, that your spirit may be saved in the day of the Lord Jesus, if it be His blessed will. And so as an unclean beast

and unfit for the society of God's people, I do from this time forward pronounce you an excommunicated person from God and
his people.[8]

Once the minister said his part, one of the church elders at the front rose
and announced: "Then, Goodwife Nurse, you are to depart the congregation as one deprived worthily of all the holy things of God."[9]

To the faithful, Nurse was now no longer deserving of their sympathy.
She was no longer one of the elect, the visible saints, but instead a repro-
bate sinner, who was owed nothing and doomed for eternity. The guards
escorted Nurse out of the meetinghouse and back to the jail, until the
time came for her earthly end.

THERE SHE SAT, in the Salem jail, damned and dead in the eyes of her
church. The furnace-like summer weather she endured while ill in the
sweaty, cramped jail was just a taste of what her eternal fate was believed
to be.

Her family, undiscouraged by the excommunication, hurriedly collected papers for one final appeal. It was unclear how much time they had
before an execution warrant was signed, and they needed to act quickly.

On July 4, the day after Nurse's excommunication, one of her relatives
approached Stephen Sewall, clerk of the Court of Oyer and Terminer, to
ask for copies of all records relating to her trial. Although he was intimately involved in the court's prosecutions, Sewall complied with the
Nurse family's request. This might reveal a sympathetic view toward
Nurse's case on his part, because several months later when asked for trial
documents by Cotton Mather, who was writing a defense of the court's
actions, he stalled for weeks.[10]

Sewall turned over copies of at least twenty documents relating to
Nurse's case. He noted that there were other pieces of testimony that were
delivered orally to the court, and as such he had no written records of
those pieces of evidence to hand over.[11] In addition to helping the Nurse
family this day, Sewall also aided them again two decades later after the
witch hunt ended.

That same day, Nurse's family requested and received a statement from
Thomas Fisk, foreman of the jury at her trial. In his statement, Fisk writes
that he was "desired by some of the relations to give a reason why the jury
brought her in guilty, after her verdict of not guilty." He notes that it was
the judges who showed "dissatisfaction" with the verdict, but that it was

"several of the jury" who decided to redeliberate. Fisk takes credit for the decision to give Nurse a chance to explain herself regarding the phrase in question, but also states that she "made no reply, nor interpretation" of her words when given the chance. Finally, he admits that in his view Nurse's misconstrued phrase was "a principal evidence against her."[12] He does not mention that the jury examined any other evidence against her when they redeliberated, only the phrase wrongly interpreted as a possible admission of guilt. It was those words that swung her fate.

Once the copies of the court records were received from Sewall, and the statement from Fisk was received, Nurse and her family wrote a petition to the court. As she could not write, it was presumably written by a family member. The original document has been lost to history, but it was reprinted in an account of the trials published in 1700.

Before writing the petition, Nurse's family appears to have explained the situation to her and asked why she did not respond to the jury's questions in court, explaining that her lack of response was a major reason why she was found guilty. On the day of her trial she did not seem to understand the situation, and her statement reveals her confusion in that moment:

> These presents do humbly show, to the honored Court and Jury, that I being informed that the Jury brought me in Guilty upon my saying that Goodwife Hobbs and her Daughter were of our Company; but I intended not otherwise than they were Prisoners with us, and therefore did then, and yet do, judge them not legal Evidence against their fellow Prisoners. And I being something hard of hearing, and full of grief, none informing me how the Court took up my words, and therefore had not opportunity to declare what I intended, when I said they were of our Company.
> Rebecca Nurse[13]

This petition, though addressed to the Court, was added to the bundle of documents from Sewall along with Fisk's statement. The collection of documents almost certainly included Sarah (Craggen) Nurse's statement about Sarah Bibber stabbing herself with pins during Rebecca Nurse's trial and then falsely claiming that Nurse's specter did it. This testimony was written the day of the trial and possibly even submitted during the trial itself and reveals how fraudulent evidence was accepted by the court. Also likely to have been included among the documents is Nurse's daughters' statement explaining that her supposed witch's mark discovered during her physical examination a few weeks prior was merely natural.[14]

These documents reached Gov. William Phips in Boston in the days immediately following July 4. Presumably Francis Nurse or their sons delivered them. Charles W. Upham suggests that perhaps Rev. James Allen, the well-connected minister at the First Church of Boston and the man from whom the Nurse family purchased their farm, aided the family in requesting a reprieve, but there are no documents from the time that mention any role of his in this appeal.[15]

Upon review, Gov. Phips issued a reprieve for Rebecca Nurse. A reprieve is a temporary suspension in carrying out a sentence, not a pardon or a change of sentence. Therefore, she remained in jail and her verdict was technically still in effect. But, her execution was deferred. Previously the scales of justice were weighted against her, but now she had hope.

However, elsewhere in either Salem Town or Salem Village a counterplot unfolded, and others worked against her appeal. Robert Calef, a contemporary who wrote an account of the trials, relates that as soon as the reprieve was granted, "the accusers renewed their dismal outcries against her," and that the governor was persuaded by "some Salem gentlemen" to revoke the reprieve.[16]

It is not clear who these "Salem gentlemen" were, though since judges Jonathan Corwin, Bartholomew Gedney, and John Hathorne of Salem Town were also members of the Council of Assistants—and it was the judges who asked the jury to reverse their not-guilty verdict—it is possible that they persuaded Gov. Phips to change his mind. If Nurse's initial acquittal had stood as the verdict, it could have entirely undermined the credibility of the evidence admitted to the court, and the court's process overall. A reprieve from the governor did not have quite the same effect, though with the governor acting to prevent Nurse's verdict and sentence from being acted upon, it could still raise questions about the validity of the other guilty verdicts reached by the court.

The three Salem Town judges saw Gov. Phips that week. The council met on July 4 at the Boston Town House, while on July 6 Phips and most of the council were at Harvard's commencement in Cambridge, and then on July 8 the council met again, primarily to discuss a military expedition to Maine, which was to be led by Gov. Phips himself.[17] There were therefore many opportunities for Corwin, Gedney, Hathorne, and the other Oyer and Terminer judges to steal the governor's ear and discuss the reprieve.

It has also been suggested that Thomas Putnam was involved in lobbying Gov. Phips alongside the magistrates. His previous actions make this quite plausible, not to mention that his wife and daughter were

Nurse's main accusers, though there is no contemporary record of him intervening at this juncture.[18]

Besides the reprieve, according to the Massachusetts Body of Liberties—the colony's bill of rights, theoretically back in force since June 8 when the General Court revived the prior colonial laws, Nurse had the right to appeal her case to the General Court. The colony law stated: "It shall be in the liberty of every man cast, condemned, or sentenced in any cause in any Inferior Court, to make their appeal to the Court of Assistants," as long as they paid a security deposit and did so within six days. And, if one was tried initially before the Assistants (as witchcraft cases previously were), the law stated that "every man shall have liberty to complain to the General Court of any injustice done to him in any Court of Assistants or other."[19] Francis Nurse would have known of these possibilities, because the land dispute cases between him and the Endicotts were several times appealed to the General Court. Also, the usual intention of granting a reprieve in death penalty cases is for the purpose of allowing time for such an appeal. But there is no record of Nurse's case being appealed in such a manner.

There are several reasons that likely prevented an appeal. First, in a practical sense, the General Court was technically out of session beginning July 5 (the day after Nurse wrote her statement) and did not reconvene until October.[20] Second, the status of Massachusetts' appeal laws was questionable, since although Massachusetts law was back in force, the Oyer and Terminer Court was a special court that was ordered to take into account the laws of England as well. Next, the General Court had not yet established a permanent court system, so it may not have been clear which legal body was empowered to hear such an appeal at that time. Many unanswered questions remain. There just is not enough surviving documentation to determine many of the facts of the Nurse family's petition, the reprieve, and its withdrawal.

In Boston on the morning of July 12, 1692, Lt. Governor and Chief Justice William Stoughton signed a warrant for the execution of Rebecca Nurse, along with Sarah Good, Susannah Martin, Elizabeth Howe, and Sarah Wilds. Nurse's reprieve was withdrawn sometime before this date, and her death sentence was back in effect. She was to hang.

Court clerk Stephen Sewall, who the week before delivered copies of the trial records to the Nurse family for their petition to the governor, wrote out the death warrant:

To George Corwin, Gentleman High Sheriff of the County of Essex, Greeting,

Whereas Sarah Good, wife of William Good of Salem Village, Rebecca Nurse, wife of Francis Nurse of Salem Village, Susannah Martin of Amesbury, widow, Elizabeth Howe, wife of James Howe of Ipswich, Sarah Wilds, wife of John Wilds of Topsfield, all of the County of Essex in Their Majesties' Province of the Massachusetts Bay in New England, at a Court of Oyer and Terminer held by adjournment for Our Sovereign Lord and Lady King William and Queen Mary for the said County of Essex at Salem in the said County on the 29th day of June last were severally arraigned on several indictments for the horrible crime of Witchcraft by them practiced and committed on several persons, and pleading not guilty did for their trial put themselves on God and Their Country, whereupon they were each of them found and brought in Guilty by the Jury that passed on them according to their respective indictments, and sentence of death did then pass upon them as the Law directs, execution whereof yet remains to be done:

These are therefore in their Majesties' Names, William and Mary now King and Queen over England etc., to will and command you that upon Tuesday next, being the 19th day of this instant July, between the hours of Eight and Twelve in the forenoon the same day, you safely conduct the said Sarah Good, Rebecca Nurse, Susanna Martin, Elizabeth Howe, and Sarah Wilds from Their Majesties' Jail in Salem aforesaid to the place of execution and there cause them and every of them to be hanged by the necks until they be dead, and of your doings herein make return to the Clerk of the said Court and this precept and hereof you are not to fail at your peril, and this shall be your sufficient warrant given under my hand and seal at Boston the 12th day of July in the fourth year of the reign of Our Sovereign Lord and Lady William and Mary King and Queen, etc.

Anno Dom. 1692
Wm Stoughton[21]

The warrant, once written, was presented to Stoughton in Boston. He signed the bottom in indelible ink, and sealed the five women's fate with a bright red circle of wax at the top of the document. Rebecca Nurse had seven days to live.

FOR ANOTHER WHOLE WEEK after the warrant was signed, Nurse and the other condemned awaited their doom in the sweltering jail. One evening, as the end neared, the moon glowed red and was almost entirely eclipsed, an ominous sign during a time of heightened fear and suspicion.[22]

Strange signs in the skies were long assumed to announce great tragedies and misfortunes. Similar signs portended the Fall of Jerusalem at the hands of the Roman army in 70 A.D., and now the Puritans—who believed that signs in the heavens revealed God's Providence—saw an apocalyptic sign appear as their own City upon a Hill was in the throes of collapsing in on itself, though it was the Puritans' own doing.[23]

On the morning of July 19, the guards arrived at the prison. They came at an early hour, for the warrant required the killing to be done between the hours of 8 o'clock and noon.[24] The guards removed the shackles from Nurse and the other condemned and took them outside to Prison Lane. Once there, they hoisted the prisoners one by one into a waiting horse-drawn cart that had high sides like prison bars. Sheriff George Corwin led the doleful cortège mounted on his horse while lesser officers walked beside the cart.[25] Other executions featured a minister riding on a horse, so it is possible that Rev. Noyes rode alongside the procession as well.[26]

After the column departed the jail, the cart rocked back and forth as it traveled over bumps, rocks, and ruts on the dirt roads of Salem Town. The journey from Prison Lane to the execution site was just over a mile and took about twenty minutes; all the while the ill and aged Nurse remained standing as she bumped around in the crowded cart.

Such an occasion—not one execution like on June 10, but five together—drew much attention. People thronged into town to see the spectacle, just as so many out-of-towners came to the village to see firsthand the flailing and wailing of the afflicted during the initial hearings. Some spectators came to see the show of it all, while others believed that they were in a war against the Devil and wanted to witness what they believed was a glorious victory over the Kingdom of Darkness. Others came to see their beloved—innocent!—relatives and friends murdered by their neighbors and their government. People from all of these categories, along with those who were simply going about their morning routines in the town center, stared at the creaking cart as it rolled toward the edge of town.

The procession went south down to the end of Prison Lane, and took a right on the main road through the town center. It traveled west on this road through the main crossroads with Town House Lane. To the right of the prisoners lay the wide lane with the Town House in the center, the site of their conviction. To the left, at this same intersection, was the meetinghouse, where Nurse was cast out and damned by the other saints. Near the meetinghouse Judge John Hathorne's house was within sight, and down the road the cart passed the home of Stephen Sewall, who aided the Nurse family in their appeal to the governor and who took in Betty Parris to isolate her from the other afflicted and help treat her fits.

The prison column continued west along the main road, and at the next cross street the condemned passed by the windows of Judge Jonathan Corwin's house. They traveled with their backs to the rising sun, until they reached a fork in the road and took the country highway west out of town. They passed the site of the former palisade meant to defend against Satan's supposed French and Native allies, and crossed over the two-hundred-foot-long causeway and town bridge at the bend of the North River. They thus passed what was commonly considered the town limits, beyond which Rebecca Nurse met her mortal end.[27]

As TO THE EXACT LOCATION of the hangings in 1692, there is a long-standing misconception that they took place on so-called Gallows Hill. Prior to 1692, the Court of Assistants in Boston was the only court empowered to try capital crimes, and so all executions took place in Boston. Therefore, there was no traditional execution place in Salem Town.[28] Stoughton's warrant told Sheriff Corwin to take Nurse and the others "to the place of execution," without specifying the location—presumably the spot where he had previously hanged Bridget Bishop, though her warrant is no more specific.[29]

The likely location of the hangings is known as Proctor's Ledge.[30] It was common land (owned by the Town of Salem) until 1718, and it was uninhabited and undeveloped in 1692. Part of the reason that this land was not yet settled is because it was craggy, rocky, useless land. Executions were typically conducted right outside the settled areas of towns, and this spot was the closest patch of common land outside of town on the main road.[31]

The executions were likely conducted on this lower ledge, and not the taller hill mistakenly known for over two centuries as Gallows Hill. In 1692 the taller hill was wild land, not cleared, and not easily accessible by road. It was not a likely or practical spot for a public execution. The misleading moniker was not applied to the taller hill until a century after the hangings, when no witnesses were still alive.[32]

JUST AS REBECCA NURSE'S SOUL was believed to remain outside the gates of heaven due to her excommunication, so were she and the other condemned women taken outside the limits of Salem Town, never to return. Although the road to the village lay ahead of them, the cart took a quick left turn after crossing the bridge. The hills, trees, craggy rocks, and unfeeling ledge lay before them. The horse pulled the cart to the top of the ledge, where the hangman waited with a ladder and an ample supply of rope.[33]

The prisoners were either executed from a tree or possibly a simple gallows—a horizontal beam supported by posts at either end—though there is no exact record of which method of hanging was used. One contemporary mentions that a ladder was used, but a ladder would have been used for either a tree or for a simple beam gallows.[34] The later tradition was that a tree was used, and there are subsequent undocumented (and conflicting) claims about the type of tree.[35] But, one document that mentions Bridget Bishop's prior execution uses the word "gallows," supporting the theory that it was a simple gallows and not a tree that was used.[36]

From atop the ledge, to the east the town lay below and the sea beyond that. To the northeast, Nurse's childhood home of the Northfields stretched out between two rivers, and to the west lay the road to her Salem Village farm.[37] As they stood on the rocky outcrop overlooking the city below the hill, the eyes of all were upon them.

Nurse and the other condemned were led toward the waiting ladder, as the crowd gathered around. At another execution, Judge Samuel Sewall described "a very great number of spectators being present."[38] Few other public events in colonial America drew larger crowds than hangings, and it was considered a good experience for children to attend—to show them an example of what happened when one broke the law. For a 1686 hanging in Boston, spectators came from fifty miles away.[39] Sewall's note also reveals that the judges themselves attended some of the executions. As to important personages present on July 19, Rev. Cotton Mather later described the execution of Nurse and the others on that day in a letter, but it's not clear if he was actually present. He did attend a later round of executions in August.[40]

As the women lined up before the ladder, Rev. Noyes came forward and said a prayer. Quite possibly, he spoke from the saddle of his horse, towering over the condemned, as Mather later did in August.[41] It was Noyes who had officiated Nurse's spiritual death two weeks prior, and he was to be one of the chief witnesses to her bodily death.

After Noyes finished his prayer, he accused the condemned women of being witches and implored them to confess, so as not to die in sin. It is not known exactly what Nurse said in response to him, though she unwaveringly maintained her innocence until the end. In Robert Calef's account of the trials, he describes Nurse's "Christian behavior" when "at her death."[42] Similarly, Mather described those executed that day as "impudently demanding of God a miraculous vindication of their innocency."[43]

However, there was a slightly different reaction by one of the women about to be hanged with Nurse. One account describes Sarah Good as rebuking Noyes after he asked them to confess. When Noyes told her that she was a witch, Good replied, "You are a liar. I am no more a witch than you are a wizard, and if you take my life away God will give you blood to drink!"[44] Her comments were taken from the Book of Revelation, which in describing the Apocalypse states: "For they shed the blood of the saints and prophets, and therefore thou hast given them blood to drink."[45] Years later Noyes died of a hemorrhage, bleeding profusely from the same mouth he used to curse Good, Nurse, and all the wrongfully condemned.[46]

The five women were given an opportunity to speak their last words, with the hope that they would use them to confess. On one of the other execution days, the hangman stood next to those about to be killed while "smoking tobacco."[47] The smoke blew into the faces of the condemned, causing them to choke, interrupting their last words. Nathaniel Cary, whose wife was accused in 1692, wrote of the treatment of the condemned on their execution day, "but to speak of their usage of the prisoners, and their inhumanity shown to them, at the time of their execution, no sober Christian could bear. They had also trials of cruel mockings; which is the more, considering what a people for religion, I mean the profession of it, we have been; those that suffered being many of them church-members, and most of them unspotted in their conversation, till their adversary the Devil took up this method of accusing them."[48] Such was the lack of respect shown to the alleged witches.

Typically, executions in colonial Massachusetts were a ritual whereby peace was restored to the community after the condemned confessed and expressed penance and the community healed from the transgression of the condemned, whatever that might be.[49] Nurse and the others did not confess—since the crime was imaginary, and they were not guilty of it—which prevented a validation of the process, especially needed because Nurse was found guilty in a questionable way. With no confessions, the wound in the community only widened.

Sheriff Corwin then read the death warrant to the gathered crowd, which stated that Nurse and the others were to be "hanged by their necks until they be dead" for "the horrible crime of Witchcraft by them practiced and committed on several persons."[50] Once this was read, and made the murder legal, one by one the women's hands were tied behind them, their legs were tied together, and a noose placed around their necks.

Executions by hanging in those days were bloody, gruesome, and lengthy. The "modern hanging"—by which the condemned stood on a trap door with a noose around their neck, the trapdoor opened, and the condemned had a short drop into the next life as their neck immediately broke in the fall causing them to die instantaneously—was not implemented until 1874.[51] Nurse and the others executed in 1692 suffered a more terrible death: they were hanged but there was not enough of a drop to snap the neck. Instead, it could take upwards of half an hour for the condemned to die from strangulation—in excruciating pain.[52] Lungs heaved, the body convulsed, and blood poured forth from facial openings, dripping out from beneath the hood the condemned wore over their faces, and trickling down their clothes.[53] Then, the movement stopped, and the victim was dead. But the blood continued to drip.

The order of the executions is not known. Rebecca Nurse's turn came, she was carried up the ladder, the noose around her neck was tied to a branch or beam, and the hangman rolled her off the ladder. She was slowly strangled before the crowd of spectators.

In Salem Village, the Nurse family mourned. The day after Rebecca Nurse's execution, it rained for the first time after a long drought.[54] Rain lashed against the windows of her former home and, if tradition holds true, rain gathered on the mud of a fresh grave on the Nurse farm, in which she was buried.

In some places, bodies of criminals were left to hang for a while as a warning to would-be wrongdoers, but in Massachusetts bodies of the executed were required to be buried within twelve hours.[55] Nurse and the others killed that day were probably buried right near the execution site, at least temporarily.

Robert Calef's account of the witch hunt published in 1700 describes a victim executed later that summer being crudely buried after his execution: "When he was cut down, he was dragged by the halter to a hole, or grave, between the rocks, about two feet deep, his shirt and breeches being pulled off, and an old pair of trousers of one executed, put on his lower parts, he was so put in, together with Willard and Carrier, one of his hands and his chin, and a foot of one [of] them left uncovered."[56] Further evidence for the initial burial of those executed can be found in the sheriff's report after Bridget Bishop's execution: "hanged by the neck until she was dead ~~and buried in the place~~."[57] Historian Charles W. Upham proposed that because burial was not specified in the warrant, Sheriff Corwin crossed it out in his report right after he wrote it, and that this note showed that the victim was indeed buried—and therefore presumably subsequent victims were as well.[58]

Although Nurse's body was likely buried hastily in a shallow grave near the execution site, it was probably not her final resting place. A strong family tradition indicated that Nurse's sons took her body from her grave at the execution site and reburied her on the Nurse farm. This theory is entirely plausible, and likely.

After the executions there does not appear to have been any impediment to families claiming the bodies of their executed relatives. Historian David L. Greene notes that in the years following 1692 many petitions were sent to the government by the accused and their families listing grievances, but none mentioned their executed relatives' remains being treated improperly.[59] John Proctor, in the will he wrote later that summer prior to his execution, left "my body unto decent burial at the discretion of my executors."[60] His body was said to be reburied on his farm by his family, and similarly the body of George Jacobs Sr. (also executed later that summer) was reburied on his farm. Burying the deceased on farms was typical for those living outside of town centers, as the Puritans did not believe in burial in consecrated ground.

Jacobs' body is the only one ever discovered of those executed in 1692, and he was later reburied in 1992.[61] His burial on his family farm after his execution proves the concept that the Nurse family could have done likewise for Rebecca. Furthermore, her husband Francis Nurse and the rest of her family were the most involved and organized of all those whose loved ones were accused in 1692, and they went to great lengths to prepare her defense. If the Jacobs family, some of whom turned against George Sr. when he was accused and some of whom were either in jail or on the run from charges at the time of his death, were able to retrieve and rebury his body, it is even more likely that the large and devoted Nurse family did similarly for Rebecca.

The Nurse family tradition claims that her sons and sons-in-law retrieved her body and reburied her in the grove of pines west of the house, where the cemetery is located today.[62] It has been suggested both that

Nurse's body was taken from the ledge to the Nurse farm by land and that it was taken by boat.[63] Either method is plausible enough, since there was no prohibition on the Nurse family doing so. If her body was taken by boat, it went down the North River, passed by her childhood home in the Northfields where the rivers met, and then traveled up the Crane River which narrows and flows right near the family cemetery.

There are no known burials on the Nurse farm prior to 1692, and it is assumed that the Nurse family cemetery began around the spot where Rebecca was buried. Today, there are several graves either marked only with fieldstones or not marked at all, and possibly one of these belongs to her. Seventeenth-century farmers often used only rocks or wooden headstones to mark graves due to the great expense of carved stone headstones.[64] The family knew at the time who was buried in each of these now-anonymous graves, but it has since been lost to history.

Rebecca Nurse's likely grave in the Nurse family cemetery lies on the western side of the Nurse farm, and if one stands by her former house in the evening the bright sun sets directly over the graveyard, as the headstones of her descendants and a monument to her memory cast long shadows.

Part III

ELEVEN

AFTERMATH

The ages will not wear off that reproach and those stains which these things will leave behind them upon the land.—Thomas Brattle, 1692

AFTER REBECCA NURSE'S BURIAL, the severe summer drought returned, and the witchcraft accusations continued.[1] Rev. Cotton Mather wrote to his uncle about the executions of Nurse and four other women on July 19: "Our good God is working miracles. Five witches were lately executed, impudently demanding of God a miraculous vindication of their innocency."[2] But, unlike Nurse and the others who hanged, not all of the accused continued to claim innocence.

Two days after Nurse's death, accused witch Mary Lacey Sr. was brought before magistrates Jonathan Corwin, Bartholomew Gedney, John Hathorne, and John Higginson Jr. at Beadle's Tavern, not far from the Salem jail. This was the fourth time that she was questioned, and she had previously falsely confessed to witchcraft.[3]

At this hearing, Lacey elaborated on her confession, claiming that "about three or four years ago she saw Mistress Bradbury, Goody Howe, and Goody Nurse baptized by the old serpent at Newbury Falls, and that [the Devil] dipped their heads in the water and then said they were his and he had power over them." Lacey said that there were "near about a hundred" witches. Lacey's daughter, another falsely confessed witch, had also mentioned Nurse and reported that there were about seventy witches in the area, and therefore many more to be caught.[4]

By mentioning Nurse specifically in this story of evil baptism, Lacey and her daughter connected themselves with one who was convicted and hanged, thereby making their false confessions seem credible. At this point, it was becoming clear that false confessors would escape the hangman's noose for the time being—after all, Tituba, the first false confessor, still lived, unlike those who claimed innocence like Nurse—and alleged satanic baptisms such the one Lacey describes were mentioned in previous examinations, making it appear as a credible claim.[5]

False confessions spurred the witch hunt on, because they appeared to be further evidence that witchcraft was indeed happening. Critic of the witch hunt Thomas Brattle wrote in 1692 of how the false confessions were used as a potent counterargument against the skeptics of the trials: "The great cry of many of our neighbors is, 'What, will you not believe the confessors? Will you not believe men and women who confess that they have signed to the Devil's book? That they were baptized by the Devil?; and that they were at the mock-sacrament once and again? What! Will you not believe that this is witchcraft, and that such and such men are witches, although the confessors do own and assert it?"[6] These false confessions lent further legitimacy to the deluded witch hunt, and the claims that there were many more alleged witches yet to be caught led to more accusations. There was no end in sight.

The day after Mary Lacey Sr. made the allegations of Nurse's evil baptism, another false confessor, Richard Carrier, also mentioned Nurse's diabolical dip in Newbury Falls.[7] After being accused, sixteen-year old Carrier initially maintained his innocence. He later falsely confessed, but not for the reasons that several previous false confessors did: He confessed due to torture.

John Proctor, himself in jail, wrote in a letter that Carrier and his brother were "tied . . . neck and heels till the blood was ready to come out of their noses, and 'tis credibly believed and reported that this was the occasion of making them confess."[8] This torture consisted of tying Carrier's head to the chains around his ankles, thereby pulling his head down below his body, which caused excruciating pain as the blood rushed to his head and eventually out his nose.

Torture such as this was forbidden by Massachusetts law, though there could be exceptions for someone who was already found guilty at trial and refused to name their accomplices, but Carrier had not been tried yet.[9] Carrier's use of Nurse's name was another attempt to tie himself to the case of one convicted, making his false confession believable and thereby freeing him from the throbbing, bloody pain inflicted upon him by his jailers. Even in death, Rebecca Nurse's name was marked.

AROUND THE BEGINNING OF AUGUST, Gov. Phips and his fleet departed for Maine to build a fort and bolster Massachusetts' defense against the French and Indians.[10] While Phips was away fighting a physical enemy, doubts grew back home about the conduct of the war against Massachusetts' alleged spiritual foes.

On August 1, eight ministers including Rev. Increase Mather, father of Rev. Cotton Mather, held a conference at Harvard College. These gathered ministers unanimously confirmed their previous belief that the Devil could appear in the shapes of innocent people, which they expressed to the government in June, and maintained their skepticism about the validity of spectral evidence used in court. But, just like in June, the court ignored the ministers' conclusions and continued using the same flawed rules of evidence.[11]

Further doubts were raised when John Foster, a member of the Council of Assistants who was not part of the Court of Oyer and Terminer, wrote to Cotton Mather, requesting advice on spectral evidence.[12] There was beginning to be an uneasiness, at least among some in the Massachusetts government, about the evidence used in court. Mather wrote back on August 17, once again confirming—as his father and seven other ministers did two weeks prior—that specters were unreliable, and it was possible for the Devil to appear in the shape of innocent people.[13] Rebecca Nurse stated as much at her initial hearing in March, when she said, "I cannot help it, for the devil may appear in my shape."[14] When Nurse and other accused individuals stated this view, it was not seriously considered by the magistrates. The councils of ministers made this same point in both June and August with no immediate effect on the court. The trials continued, relying on spectral evidence that ministers and some common people saw as flawed and easily manipulated.

Cotton Mather, in his letter to the council member, also advised that cases which relied primarily on spectral evidence should not go forward, as other more reliable evidence was needed. Mather referenced a 1645 Court of Oyer and Terminer trying witchcraft cases in England that did not convict a single person of the crime. This English court included clergymen, unlike in Massachusetts where ministers did not hold political or judicial office. In an interesting juxtaposition, the religious authorities on this previous court were more cautious in prosecuting and executing those who were accused of a supposed religious crime than the Massachusetts political-judicial authorities in 1692.

On August 9, Salisbury magistrate Robert Pike wrote a letter to fellow member of the Council of Assistants Jonathan Corwin expressing concerns about the court's use of spectral evidence. He wrote Corwin, a member of the Oyer and Terminer Court, that the Devil is "the father of lies" and "a liar and a mur[d]erer (John vii. 44), and may tell these lies to murder an innocent person," so therefore apparitions should not be believed. Pike proposed, because it was difficult to determine what testimony was true or not, "it may be more safe, for the present, to let a guilty person live till further discovery, than to put an innocent person to death. . . . Because a guilty person may afterward be discovered, and so put to death; but an innocent person to be put to death cannot be brought again to life." Corwin's response to this letter is unknown, but he kept the letter which shows that he valued it to some degree.[15]

Hesitations sprung up back in Salem in early August as well. After Rev. George Burroughs was found guilty he told the judges and jury that he understood why they convicted him: there were after all many witnesses against him. But, Burroughs told them that he "died by false witnesses."[16] This accusation by a fellow minister that the accusers had lied worried Rev. John Hale of Beverly. In his *Modest Enquiry* (1702), Hale recounts that after he heard Burroughs' claim of fraud he visited several of the false confessors in jail who testified against Burroughs, and told one of them: "You are one that bring this man to death, if you have charged anything upon him that is not true, recall it before it be too late."[17] But the false confessor maintained her story.

This is the first time the claim that witnesses were lying is recorded as having been taken seriously, likely because the claim was made by a minister—for when Nurse and others denied the accusations, their words were not heeded. Contrary to Hale's view, Rev. Increase Mather, usually seen as more critical of the proceedings than his son Cotton, found the testimony against Burroughs quite convincing. He wrote later that fall, "had I been one of his judges, I could not have acquitted him."[18] Hale's growing uneasiness was not shared by all, and executions continued.

Exactly one month after Nurse's execution, Burroughs, Martha Carrier, John Willard, George Jacobs Sr., and John Proctor were hanged for the same alleged crime. The first six people executed for witchcraft in 1692 were women, but as the victims of August 19 show, members of both sexes were killed during the witch hunt.

After the execution, according to local tradition, the spectators gathered at a tavern near the execution site for drink and merriment, celebrating their most recent victory in the war against the invisible world.[19]

By the summer of 1692, Rebecca Nurse's family stopped attending the Sabbath services at the village church, and those relatives who were church members had stopped attending the Lord's Supper several months prior. They could not bring themselves to participate in a congregation that presumed Nurse's guilt, and several of its leading members and their relatives had directly accused Nurse and her two sisters of witchcraft. Beginning in August, the church began to investigate her family's absence from the monthly Lord's Supper.

On August 14, Rev. Samuel Parris held the village church members after the sacrament and told them, "Brethren, you may all have taken notice that several Sacrament days past our brother Peter Cloyce, Samuel Nurse and his wife, and John Tarbell and his wife have absented from Communion with us at the Lord's Table, [and] have very rarely, except our brother Samuel Nurse, have been with us in common public worship." Parris then asked the church to "express [them]selves" on this issue.[20]

Only the absences of Nurse's relatives who were covenant members were mentioned by name at this church meeting. It is interesting that Samuel Nurse, Rebecca's son, was one of the last to continue attending the weekly sermons (though not the monthly sacrament), even after his family members mentioned above boycotted the village church. Perhaps he remembered his aunt Sarah Cloyce's actions on the sacrament Sunday in March that led to the accusations against her, and in his own self-interest sought to prevent a similar situation from happening to him.

The village church chose Nathaniel Putnam, Rev. Parris, Deacon Edward Putnam and Deacon Nathaniel Ingersoll to meet with the absent church members. They reported back that Tarbell was "sick, unmeet for discourse," Cloyce was "hard to be found at home, being often with his wife in prison at Ipswich for witchcraft," and that Samuel Nurse and his wife Mary sometimes attended services. The church decided "to wait further" before taking any other action.[21]

With the witch hunt still raging, Parris targeted the family of Rebecca Nurse, who had been executed, and Sarah Cloyce her sister, who was jailed for the same alleged crime. Parris was attempting to publicly discipline a bereaved family whose reasons for not attending worship were very obvious to all. This was an attempt by Parris to shore up support for his ministry in the face of dissension, and perhaps to cast suspicion on other members of the Nurse family. Historian Benjamin C. Ray describes Parris' actions against the Nurse family as "a deliberate act of confrontation."[22]

Over the next few months Parris alluded to the Nurse family's absence several times, and also preached sermons that appeared to be thinly veiled attempts to bolster his own support. After all, it was his church community that was the weak spot that supposedly allowed Satan into Massachusetts. As the spiritual leader of the community, Parris was in a precarious place—even more so when opponents of the trials also began to oppose his ministry.

In response to this threat, on September 11 he preached on Revelation 17:14, "These shall make war with the Lamb, and the Lamb shall overcome them: For He is the Lord of Lords, and King of Kings; And they that are with him, are called and chosen, and faithful."[23] Parris uses "the Lamb" to represent not just Jesus, but also the Puritan church and commonwealth. Through this verse Parris is rallying the congregation to the side of the Lamb—his side—in the war against the Devil and his supposed allies: the French Catholics, Natives, and alleged witches.

He makes this connection explicit, "In our days, how industrious and vigorous is the bloody French monarch and his confederates against Christ and his interest? Yes, and in our land (in this, and in some neighboring places) how many, what multitudes, of witches and wizards has the Devil instigated with utmost violence to attempt the overthrow of religion?"[24] Those on the side of the accused witches—Nurse's family and others who opposed the trials—are portrayed as not only on the side of the Devil in his spiritual war against the church, but also on the side of the French Catholics in their temporal war against the commonwealth.

Toward the end of the sermon, Parris preached against disobedience to laws and magistrates: "Disobedience towards Christ's ordinances is rebellion against Christ, and making war with him. As warring against magistrates, opposing them in their duties. In this sense Korah and his company are called rebels. 17. Num. 10. And the mutinous and murmuring Israelites are called rebels. 20. Num. 10. Hence resisters to authority are resisters of God, because they resist the ordinance of God."[25] For the congregation, the connection to the present could not be clearer: To resist the magistrates and authority—Parris himself—was to resist God.

WHILE PARRIS attempted to silence critics such as the Nurse family, Rebecca's sisters Mary Easty and Sarah Cloyce awaited their fates. In jail, they wrote a petition—likely on September 9, the day of Easty's trial and Cloyce's grand jury appearance. In the petition the two sisters state, "We are not conscious to ourselves of any guilt in the least degree of that crime, whereof we are now accused (in the presence of the Living God we speak it, before whose awful Tribunal we know we shall ere long appear)." They also asked for legal advice from the judges, who—since defense lawyers were not permitted—were supposed to safeguard the interests of the accused in court: "Seeing that we are neither able to plead our own cause, nor is counsel allowed to those in our condition, that you who are our judges would please be of counsel to us."[26] They received no such aid.

After finding Easty and eight others guilty, the court adjourned on September 17 and was not scheduled to meet again until November 1. Unbeknownst to the judges at that time, the witch court never sat again.

Later that month, Giles Corey was pressed to death in a field near the Salem jail. Corey had a checkered past, and he was accused of savagely beating his mentally challenged neighbor years before. Francis Nurse, along with son-in-law Thomas Preston, served on the coroner's jury for that case in 1676.[27]

Pressing, known as *peine forte et dure* ("strong and long-lasting pain"), was not legal under Massachusetts law, but was used in England.[28] At his trial, Corey pled "not guilty" but then refused to say the formulaic phrase agreeing to be put on trial "by God and the Country."[29] In those days, a common-law court could not proceed until the defendant consented by saying this phrase, and if they refused, pressing was used to compel them to consent so that the trial could continue. The reason often given for Corey "standing mute" is that he was afraid of losing his land, but his land was in no danger of being taken away.[30] However, standing mute meant that one's personal goods—but not land—were forfeited, so this principled stand against the court actually jeopardized the goods he owned rather than being a move to secure his property.[31]

A board was placed upon Corey as he lay in the field and rocks were stacked upon him, while a crowd of spectators gathered around. At one point the weight forced his tongue to push out of his mouth, and Sheriff George Corwin used his cane to push it back in. This stacking of rocks upon him continued until, according to tradition, he gasped a defiant request for "more weight" and died. He was the first and last person ever pressed to death in Massachusetts.[32]

Three days later, Nurse's sister Mary Easty was executed along with Alice Parker, Ann Pudeator, Martha Corey (wife of Giles Corey), Margaret Scott, Wilmot Read, Mary Parker, and Samuel Wardwell.[33] After the execution, as their lifeless bodies hung before the crowd, Rev. Nicholas Noyes of Salem turned to look at them and said, "What a sad thing it is to see eight firebrands of hell hanging there!"[34] Out of the three accused

Towne sisters, only Sarah Cloyce remained alive—and awaited her own trial.

Notably *not* among those executed were Ann Foster, Mary Lacey Sr. (who claimed to have witnessed Nurse's satanic baptism at Newbury Falls), Rebecca Eames, and Abigail Hobbs. These four women who falsely confessed to being witches were convicted and sentenced to death, but none of the falsely confessed witches in 1692 was executed.[35] Samuel Wardwell, executed the same day as Easty, was in this same category until his conscience intervened and he recanted his false confession. Speaking the truth led him to be killed.

DESPITE THE RECENT HANGINGS, momentum was leaving the witch court and opinion began to turn against it in the fall of 1692. Toward the end of September, Gov. Phips returned from Maine and set in motion the series of events that ended the trials.[36] His reason for returning was that he received word of a possible French attack on Boston, but upon his return he discovered that his wife was now involved in the witch hunt. While the governor was away, Lady Mary Phips forged signatures to release a person accused of witchcraft from jail and was then herself informally named as a witch—though there is no evidence that she was formally charged.[37] Now, the witch hunt affected the governor personally.

In Boston and Cambridge, Rev. Increase Mather continued to speak out against the trials. On October 3, Mather's essay *Cases of Conscience Concerning Evil Spirits* was read to a gathering of ministers at Harvard College. The essay refutes the use of spectral evidence, arguing that the Devil could appear in the shape of innocent people. Additionally, Mather points out that Martin Luther was accused of being a "wizard" and Jesus a "magician," so therefore such accusations should be thoroughly scrutinized. He wrote that the afflicted might not really be bewitched, but instead could potentially be possessed by demons—in which case, their accusations could be the Devil's own words and their testimony should be considered no more reliable than the Devil's lies. The essay includes his famous assessment: "It were better that ten suspected witches should escape, than that one innocent person should be condemned."[38]

The seven ministers present for the reading of the essay, including Rev. James Allen (the previous owner of the Nurse farm), signed a statement agreeing with Mather's arguments.[39] Additionally, these ministers and yet seven other ministers signed onto an introduction to the published essay, including Rev. Joseph Capen of Topsfield and Rev. Joseph Gerrish of Wenham, whose parishes bordered Salem Village.[40] Copies of the text were printed and distributed around Massachusetts, with a copy presented to Gov. Phips. On Sunday, October 9, when churchgoers awoke to the first frost, the ministers who attended the Harvard conference read the essay to their congregations in meetinghouses across eastern Massachusetts.[41] Slowly, the fear began to wither.

In contrast, Rev. Increase Mather's son, Rev. Cotton Mather, was in the process of writing and circulating copies of his own work on the trials—in support of the judges and the government. His *Wonders of the Invisible World* notes the precedent from English witchcraft cases for the court's actions, and examined five of that summer's trials that provided the best evidence for his argument that the court proceeded correctly. Nurse's trial was not among them.[42]

Cotton Mather had the support of Gov. Phips and repeatedly requested trial records from court clerk Stephen Sewall, who seems to have taken his time in sending them.[43] Mather then met with the clerk, his brother Judge Samuel Sewall, Judge Hathorne, and Chief Justice Stoughton to discuss "publishing some trials of the witches," according to Samuel Sewall's diary.[44] The text was completed at least as early as October 11, when Judge Sewall and Chief Justice Stoughton signed a postscript endorsing the work. Stoughton also wrote an introduction, in which he described it as a "most seasonable discourse" and remarked that the forces of Satan were "coming in like a flood among us."[45] However, it was Increase Mather's essay that had the largest effect on steering discourse and opinion.

Three days after Increase Mather's *Cases of Conscience* was read to the several congregations, Gov. Phips wrote in a letter back to the government in London that he "found that the Devil had taken upon him the name and shape of several persons who were doubtless innocent and to my certain knowledge of good reputation." He also told Their Majesties' government in London that he forbade any more arrests for witchcraft and awaited "any particular directions or commands if Their Majesties please to give me any for the fuller ordering of this perplexed affair."[46]

Phips takes all credit for halting the prosecutions and portrays himself as a voice of caution and moderation in the witch hunt. He writes, "I hereby declare that as soon as I came from fighting against Their Majesties' enemies and understood what danger some of their innocent subjects might be exposed to, if the evidence of the afflicted persons only did prevail either to the committing or trying any of them, I did before any application was made unto me about it put a stop to the proceedings of the Court and they are now stopped until Their Majesties' pleasure be known."[47] Despite these reassuring and self-aggrandizing words to Their Majesties in which Phips appears cautious and merciful, he acted in no such way toward Rebecca Nurse that July. He revoked her reprieve despite evidence and information that she was of "good reputation," to use his phrase above. Also, despite telling Their Majesties' government that he stopped the Court of Oyer and Terminer, he had done no such thing at the time of writing.

Around the time of this letter, Phips forbade the printing of any "discourse" arguing either for or against the witch hunt.[48] Several works were circulating at this time criticizing the actions of the court and commonwealth, including a letter from Thomas Brattle and Rev. Samuel Willard's *Some Miscellany Observations on our Present Debates Respecting Witchcraft*, in circulation in October 1692.[49] Despite this ban, Cotton Mather's tract in support of the court and commonwealth, *Wonders of the Invisible World*, was still published, and the reverse side of the title page reads: "Published by Special Command of his Excellency, the Governor of the Province of Massachusetts-Bay in New-England."[50] Historian Emerson W. Baker refers to the publication of this text supporting the court and government while banning the publication of any criticism as "the first large-scale government cover-up in American history."[51]

On October 13, the day after Phips wrote his letter, the General Court passed an act declaring nine "general privileges" to guarantee the rights of the inhabitants of Massachusetts.[52] These included the rights of due process, trial by jury, access to justice by all (even for slaves and foreigners), and no taxation without representation. This act had a long-lasting influence on judicial and political developments in Massachusetts, but the jails remained clogged with innocents accused of witchcraft based on flawed evidence.

As opinions on spectral evidence changed, Rev. Increase Mather paid a visit to prisoners in the Salem jail on October 19. While there, one prisoner who had falsely confessed to witchcraft told him "that she had confessed against herself things which were all utterly false," and another told him that "she was frightened into" falsely confessing.[53] The false confessors, whose words convinced others that witchcraft was really occurring and the accusations of the girls were true, started to change their tune.

In Salem Village, Rev. Parris preached his October 23 sermon on reconciliation. The verse Parris chose for that day was "Let him kiss me with the kisses of his mouth: for thy Love is better than wine."[54] But he soon discovered that his actions during the witch hunt would prevent reconciliation in Salem Village.

The mood within the government in Boston continued to shift against the witch court. On October 26 a bill was introduced in the General Court calling for a fast day and convocation of ministers—who by now had several times denounced the evidence used by the court—to discuss the witch hunt. Samuel Sewall, one of the judges on the court, wrote in his diary of the bill, "The season and manner of doing it, is such, that the Court of Oyer and Terminer count themselves thereby dismissed."[55] This feeling was not held by all, though.

Two days later, on the morning of October 28, Chief Justice William Stoughton rode toward Boston. While he rode across the narrow causeway connecting the town to the mainland, the tide rose around him and nearly washed him away. Stoughton was drenched, and sent someone back to Dorchester to bring him dry clothes so that he could attend a Council of Assistants meeting that afternoon. Later that day, he approached the governor at the council meeting to discover whether the court would be dissolved. Sewall described the response to Stoughton's question among the Assistants as "great silence, as if to say do not go."[56] On October 29, after several judges who were away fighting in Maine had already returned to Boston in anticipation of the next court session, Phips finally announced to the Council that the court was finished.[57]

The following day, Thomas and Ann Putnam's newborn daughter, Abigail, was baptized by Rev. Parris alongside Rebecca Nurse's grandson Jonathan Tarbell (son of her daughter Mary and John Tarbell, who that spring had interrogated the Putnams over who first named Nurse as a witch).[58] Although this baptism appears like an occasion of unity as the witch hunt was ending, the Nurses and Tarbells were still boycotting regular services of the village church and had only made an exception for this special sacrament. Also, Putnam and his family remained convinced that the Devil threatened Salem Village and awaited the resumption of the trials and executions.[59]

THE OYER AND TERMINER COURT never met again, though the witch trials were not yet over. The jails remained full, the afflicted continued their fits, and more innocents were accused. Sarah Hale, wife of Beverly minister Rev. John Hale, who had doubts beginning back in August, was accused of witchcraft on November 5.[60] However, she never went to trial.

Now that the witch court was disbanded, Judge Samuel Sewall prayed for divine help as the General Court began the process of choosing judges for the new permanent provincial courts of justice. He records in his diary that on November 22 he "prayed that God would pardon all my sinful wanderings, and direct me for the future. That God would bless the Assembly [General Court] in their debates. And that would choose and assist our judges, etc., and save New England as to Enemies and witchcrafts."[61] Even at this time, though the previous court's process was recognized as flawed, he believed that witchcraft remained a threat.

On November 25, the General Court passed a law allowing counsel to defendants in court.[62] This was a step toward fixing the judicial flaws exposed during the witch trials. That same day, the General Court established a new permanent high court for Massachusetts: the Superior Court of Judicature, which remains today as the oldest appellate court in continuous existence in the Western Hemisphere (though its name changed to the Supreme Judicial Court after the American Revolution).[63] Following the high court's creation, the council elected Stoughton as chief justice, the same position he held on the Court of Oyer and Terminer. Similarly, Corwin, Gedney, and Hathorne were chosen for the reconstituted Essex County Court. Although the tide of opinion had shifted against the witch hunt, the judges still had the confidence of those in government.

In the village, the delusion subsided enough to hold a village meeting, the first since the witch hunt began. The issues at hand were electing a new village committee for the upcoming year, and again discussing the questionable conveyance of the parsonage and surrounding land to Rev. Parris.[64] This was the issue raised by the village committee upon which Francis Nurse served only a couple months before the fits of the afflicted began in the parsonage. Among the five men chosen for the new village committee was Joseph Putnam, opponent of the trials and supporter of Rebecca Nurse.[65] This committee did not serve long, and Parris soon brought the courts to bear on the village government over its lack of payment of his salary.

Back in Boston, the General Court passed "An Act Against Conjuration, Witchcraft and Dealing with Evil Spirits." The act clarified the law under which the remaining witchcraft suspects were to be tried by the new Superior Court of Judicature. It included the death penalty for those consulting or conjuring evil spirits, digging up corpses to use in witchcraft, and the use of witchcraft to cause someone to "be killed, destroyed, wasted, consumed, pined or lamed in his or her body."[66] However, it instituted lesser penalties if one used magic to find buried treasure, find lost goods, seduce someone, hurt cattle, or attempt to hurt someone via witchcraft but fail in the process. This law was vetoed by London, not because it punished supposed witches—witchcraft remained a crime in England until 1735—but rather the law was struck down because it provided more rights to those convicted than English law allowed.[67]

That same day, the General Court passed an act ensuring the right of habeus corpus to prisoners, though this too was struck down by Their Majesties' Privy Council in London. The English government claimed that traditional English rights such as habeus corpus, the opportunity to challenge unlawful imprisonment, did not extend to those living in the colonies.[68]

On December 27, towns across Essex County elected jurors for the first sitting of the Superior Court of Judicature in Salem on January 3, 1693. Those chosen included Rebecca Nurse's nephew Jacob Towne Jr. of Topsfield, and two from Salem Town and Village who signed the petition in support of Nurse that previous spring: Job Swinnerton and Jonathan Putnam.[69]

Meeting in Salem, the jurors asked the judges how much weight should be given to spectral evidence, and they were told to give it no weight at all.[70] Of the more than fifty cases heard, the grand jury rejected more than thirty of them for having insufficient evidence for a trial. Nurse's sister Sarah Cloyce had the case against her rejected in this manner.[71] Of the twenty-one cases that went to trial, only three of the accused were found guilty.[72] Chief Justice Stoughton signed a warrant for the "speedy execution" of these three, along with five others previously found guilty by the Court of Oyer and Terminer.[73] Graves were dug in Salem Town in preparation for another round of hangings.[74]

Before further tragedy occurred, Gov. Phips issued a reprieve preventing the executions until "Their Majesties' pleasure be signified and declared."[75] This action ended the largest witch hunt in American history.

Phips apparently did not tell his lieutenant governor of his decision in advance, for Stoughton heard about the reprieve for the first time while the Superior Court of Judicature sat in Charlestown. Phips wrote that when Stoughton heard the news, he "was enraged and filled with a passionate anger."[76] Stoughton reportedly declared, "We were in a way to have cleared the land of these [the witches], who it is [that] obstructs the course of justice I know not, the Lord be merciful to the country!"[77] No more witchcraft cases were brought to trial, though many of the accused remained in jail until they—even those found not guilty—paid their jail fees, such as the expenses for any food they had consumed. Some died in the dark jails before their families could raise the money needed.[78]

WITH THE WITCH HUNT OVER, Salem Village sought a return to normalcy. This was no easy task, as accusers sat in Sunday meeting with those they falsely accused, and those who falsely confessed to witchcraft were realized to be frauds. For Rebecca Nurse's family, normalcy could not be restored until Rev. Parris—who played a role in the death of their beloved mother—left and a new minister reconciled the village.

After the witchcraft accusations ceased, members of the village church met on December 26, 1692, and voted to file a petition with the Essex County Court against the previous year's village committee, upon which Francis Nurse served. The village government had not collected a tax to support the minister for over a year and a half, and even the tax before that went partially uncollected.[79]

In addition to blaming the village committee, the church's petition placed blame on Rebecca Nurse's family and others who stopped attending worship, describing "the great and long disquietments of a few, who in this hour of some tribulation and temptation have drawn away others."[80]

On January 17, the Essex County Court met at Ingersoll's tavern, where the magistrates often dined before and after witchcraft hearings, within sight of the meetinghouse where accusations flew and devils were raised. The judges ordered Salem Village to call a new village meeting and elect a fresh village committee to collect the money owed to Parris.[81] The village had already elected a new committee just one month prior, but it also challenged Parris' contract. Five new men were then elected to another new village committee, one of whom refused to serve. Two of the remaining four were sons-in-law of Rebecca Nurse: John Tarbell and Thomas Preston.[82] This newly elected committee called a village meeting to discuss repairing the meetinghouse—which had fallen into disrepair and was damaged by the overflow crowds at the hearings in 1692—but also to formally cancel Parris' contract because he was "not complying with it" and void the suspicious vote transferring the parsonage ownership from the village to Parris that came to light just before the witch hunt exploded.[83]

Before the next village meeting was held, the village church attempted to make amends with its absent members. Perhaps the show of strength by the anti-Parris contingent at the previous village meeting spurred this move. After the Sabbath services on February 5, the church chose Parris, Deacon Edward Putnam, Deacon Nathaniel Ingersoll, John Putnam Sr., and Bray Wilkins—whose bladder was supposedly controlled by a witch in 1692—"to discourse with Brother Thomas Wilkins, Brother Samuel

Nurse, and Brother John Tarbell about their withdrawing of late from the Lord's Table and public worship of God among us."[84] The next day the church committee met with each absentee at home. The Nurse family's reaction to seeing the black-clad figure of Parris walking up their dirt path, as the sheriff did on that March morning a year prior, can only be imagined. However, all of the absentees agreed to meet with the church delegation on the following day, February 7.

The meeting was scheduled for 1 P.M. at the parsonage, but Samuel Nurse, John Tarbell, and Thomas Wilkins arrived unannounced at around 11 A.M.[85] Each desired to meet with Parris individually first. He agreed and met with them upstairs in his study. Parris later recorded the conversations he had with both Tarbell and Nurse. He wrote that Tarbell accused him of idolatry for consulting with the afflicted. (If one believed that they were possessed, as Rev. Increase Mather proposed in *Cases of Conscience*, then it may have been the demons speaking.)[86] Also, Parris recorded that Tarbell said, "Had it not been for me his mother[-in-law] Nurse might have been still living" and that Tarbell called him "the great prosecutor" of the trials.[87] Tarbell refused to return to the village church until Parris admitted his errors.

Samuel Nurse spoke with Parris for about an hour, and made similar points as his brother-in-law. Even though opinions on spectral evidence had changed, Parris told Nurse that he "did not see yet sufficient grounds" to change his opinion that witchcraft truly happened in the village over the previous year. Parris claimed this view "was confirmed by known and ancient experience."[88] Before the conversation was finished—and before Wilkins had his chance to speak with Parris—the church committee arrived.

At 1 P.M. the meeting with the absentees and the church committee began, and the committee told Nurse, Tarbell, and Wilkins that they sought to know the reasons why they absented themselves from communion—as if it was not obvious. The three dissenting church members asked for time to prepare their official response, and all agreed to meet on February 16.[89] In the intervening days, however, the situation in the village escalated.

The day after the meeting at the parsonage, Peter Cloyce—husband of Rebecca Nurse's sister, fellow accused witch Sarah Cloyce—rode into town. He was another church member who now opposed Parris because of his role in the trials, but Cloyce and his family moved away from the village to Framingham, west of Boston. They settled on land owned by Thomas Danforth, former lieutenant governor and member of the new Superior Court of Judicature that released Sarah Cloyce after the grand jury refused to indict her. It is likely that Danforth had a direct role in helping to resettle the Cloyces in Framingham.[90] Rebecca Nurse's son Benjamin Nurse and family also later moved to Framingham, along with fifty other former Salem Villagers.[91]

After his return to the village, Peter Cloyce met with Parris, according to whom he repeated "the very same objections" as the other three dissenting church members.[92] Cloyce then left, but soon after returned with Nurse, Tarbell, and Wilkins. The four also brought William Way, another church member, to serve as a witness to their conversations.

Generally, to resolve disputes between members of a Puritan church the rule set forth in Matthew 18:15–16 was followed: "Moreover, if thy brother trespass against thee, go and tell him his fault between thee and him alone: if he hear thee, thou hast won thy brother. But if he hear thee not, take yet with thee one or two, that by the mouth of two or three witnesses, every word may be confirmed." Parris' opponents implemented the first part of these instructions the day before when each met with Parris alone (except for Wilkins, because time ran out). Now the dissenters moved on to the second phase and brought another church member so that each dissenter had three other members present as witnesses.

Parris realized this escalation and refused to concede that they followed the evangelical instructions properly. He claimed that William Way was the only one he considered a true witness, and that the others could not count for witnesses for each other since they were not neutral.[93] The complainants left, dissatisfied.

On February 16, Nurse, Tarbell, and Wilkins met with the church delegation again as previously scheduled. The three dissenters brought their arguments in writing, which Nurse read to the church committee. He began by describing himself and the others as "having a long time gone under the burden of great grievances by reason of some unwarrantable actings of Mr. Parris."[94] He then stated that they attempted to resolve their issues through the formal dispute resolution process by bringing witnesses and speaking with the minister directly, according to the "Rule of our Lord Jesus Christ laid down in Matth. 18. 15. 16." They asked permission to continue the resolution process described in the Gospel, for if not they would take their grievances to the full church membership. Parris records that at the meeting "these displeased brethren were told that they did ill reflect upon the church."[95] The issues remained unresolved.

Cloyce, Wilkins, and Tarbell next went to the parsonage on March 27, the anniversary of Sarah Cloyce slamming the door of the meetinghouse during Parris' sermon comparing Rebecca Nurse to Judas. This time the aggrieved church members brought three other church members so that there would be no question of technicalities: Joseph Hutchinson Sr., Joseph Putnam, and William Osborne of Salem Town. They presented a petition seeking reconciliation and recognized "those uncomfortable differences that are amongst us are very dishonorable to God, and a scandal to religion, and very uncomfortable to ourselves, and an ill example to those that may come after us." They stated that they desired that "a foundation may be laid for peace and truth that the gates of Hell may not prevail against it."[96] To reach this reconciliation, the dissenters requested a council of elders to serve as arbitrators in the dispute. They then asked Parris his opinion of their petition, but he refused to give an answer.

The next morning, Rebecca Nurse's sons-in-law John Tarbell and Thomas Preston along with the rest of the village committee appeared before the Essex County Court in Ipswich. They were sued by the village church for not collecting rates to pay Parris' salary. It was the second village committee to be sued by the village church in less than four months. Tarbell, Joseph Pope, and Preston were found guilty. The court ordered the committee to collect the tax along with the past two years' assessment that went uncollected, even though this overrode a decision made by the majority of voters in Salem Village.[97]

That night, Tarbell, Cloyce, and Wilkins returned to the parsonage to again ask for a response to their petition. Parris told them he "had not considered of it yet." They met again on April 14, when the three aggrieved church members brought old Francis Nurse with them as a witness along with Hutchinson. But Parris said he "had no time to talk."[98]

On April 20, the three village dissenters, along with Peter Cloyce who returned again to the village, met with Parris and a church delegation. For witnesses they brought Hutchinson and Israel Porter, who the previous March visited with Rebecca Nurse before her arrest to tell her she was accused, and signed the document attesting to her good character. At this meeting Parris told the aggrieved that their petition to him was a "libel," though in a show of strength the dissenters produced a second copy of their petition signed with forty-two names—more than the number of members of the village church.[99] The meeting ran until nightfall, and they agreed to reconvene the next morning.

An hour after sunrise, the two groups met at Ingersoll's tavern. Samuel Nurse read "a large scroll" with fifteen points written on it.[100] The first seven were reasons they did not attend services, and the last eight were grievances against Parris. This was the last private meeting, for in May the frustrated dissenters took their case to the full church membership.

On May 18, Nurse, Tarbell, and Wilkins attended a church meeting with Parris and twenty other church members. It was a heated encounter. Parris asked the dissenters why they requested to come to the meeting, and they responded: "to tell their charges against Mr. Parris and now they had witnesses to prove it." Parris recorded that this response caused "much agitation" among the church membership.[101] The church then voted that they did not recognize the dissenters' attempts to meet with Parris with witnesses as valid, and decided that the aggrieved should begin the process of private meetings from the beginning.

By this point, from Parris' notes, the petitioners were quite frustrated—though Parris is far from a neutral source. He wrote of their demeanor: "The general deportment of the said three displeased brethren was at this meeting exceedingly unchristian, both to minister and the other brethren; very irreverent towards him." As to the church deciding that the dissenters needed to start over meeting one-on-one with Parris, he records Samuel Nurse as replying that "he did not care to come to the house, nor to discourse with me alone."[102] The dispute continued.

FRANCIS NURSE was at home on June 13, 1694, when the deputy sheriff came walking up the dirt path leading to the Nurse homestead. After years of legal disputes and troubles—from defending his ownership of the land disputed with the Endicotts to aiding his sons and sons-in-law in their attempt to oust the minister—not to mention the bitter, gut-wrenching attempt to save Rebecca Nurse from the jaws of the witch hunt—surely he had seen officers of the court more times in his lifetime than he cared to. And now another approached him, as he lived out the final year of his life on the Nurse farm.

The man walking up the driveway was sheriff's deputy Jonathan Putnam, the man who in 1692 signed the initial legal accusation against Rebecca Nurse but who later also signed the petition in her defense. Putnam approached Francis Nurse and read a warrant signed by former witch trials judge Bartholomew Gedney: Nurse was being sued for debt by John Hadlock, the man who served as his son Benjamin's substitute when he was drafted into militia duty in 1691—only three years prior, but surely it felt like a previous age with all that had transpired since those simpler days. Until the debt suit was settled, Putnam announced that the court put a legal attachment on part of the Nurse farm.[103]

Hadlock had returned in December 1691 to collect the first twenty shillings that Francis Nurse owed him, and Daniel Andrew had helped the Nurse family pay the required amount. Hadlock returned sometime around the beginning of 1693 and asked for another seven shillings. Francis Nurse's daughter-in-law Thamsen Nurse and his hired servant Susannah Trevet both testified to this later in court.[104] Before Francis Nurse paid Hadlock, he wanted his weapons back that he had loaned Hadlock during his time in the service. He went with Hadlock to his house, just up the road, to collect them. John Tarbell happened to walk by and see his father-in-law at Hadlock's house, so he went in and joined the conversation. At the end of the discussion, Nurse apparently paid Hadlock part of what he was owed, and it was agreed that Hadlock was owed only four more shillings.

Hadlock returned again sometime in February to the Nurse farm and spoke to Benjamin Nurse, because Francis was not home. Hadlock told Benjamin that his father still owed him four shillings and then their debt would be finished. Benjamin paid him the four shillings on the spot, with Susannah Trevet as his witness. All appeared settled.

Then Hadlock sued Francis Nurse in June 1694 for nonpayment of debt in a suit that appeared designed to take advantage of the elderly widower. Hadlock's suit claimed that Nurse owed him a whopping £10s15. Hadlock claimed that he was owed this money for eighty-six weeks in militia service, but a document from the Massachusetts government certified Hadlock as being in the service for only thirty-three weeks. At a June 26, 1694, court session, Tarbell, Trevet, Benjamin Nurse, Tamsen Nurse, and others testified about the arrangement, contesting Hadlock's claims. Evidently Francis Nurse won the suit, because Hadlock had to pay the court costs. This episode was yet one more unnecessary hurdle for the Nurse family to overcome, and yet another show of solidarity in a courtroom by the extended family.[105]

THE NURSE FAMILY church members who opposed Parris attended a meeting of the church in November 1694 to deliver a statement of their complaints to the church members, in which they stated explicitly that their issues were with Parris only and not with the church as a whole. Their list of complaints gives the best insight into exactly what troubled them, including that Parris allowed "distracting and disturbing tumults and noises" to be made by the afflicted during the witch hunt that interfered with the church services, that the Nurse family thought it prudent to avoid church services for fear of being accused by the afflicted if they were present during their fits, Parris' belief that the witchcraft accusations were true, his belief in the validity of spectral evidence that was contrary to the leading ministers' views, his swearing to the truth of witchcraft accusations in court, bias in his notetaking during the initial hearings of the accused, and finally his failure to admit that he was mistaken and continuing to hold on to his belief that the witchcraft was real, which they said was "further offending and dissatisfying ourselves."[106] As to their issue with Parris swearing to the truth of witchcraft accusations in court, Parris did so for fourteen different depositions against ten of the accused in 1692, including Rebecca Nurse. The issue raised about his potential bias in notetaking likewise extended to many cases, for he was the official recorder for fifteen different initial hearings, including that of Nurse.[107]

Parris replied that in 1692 he did what he "apprehended was duty, however through weakness, ignorance, etc., that I may have been mistaken" and admitted that the Devil may indeed appear in the shape of innocent people, renouncing his prior belief in spectral evidence. Parris stated that he sought "all your forgiveness of every offence in this or other affairs, wherein you see or conceive I have erred and offended."[108] This was the closest Parris ever came to an apology, though he does not admit that he *actually* erred.

Several other parts of Parris' statement seem to dodge his responsibility in the matter. He categorized the witch hunt as part of God's will—which, therefore, would seem to absolve the human actors of responsibility—while the relatives of the innocent victims would never accept the killing described in such a way. He also claimed that likely both sides of the issue were fooled, because God "has suffered the evil angels to delude us on both hands, but how far on the one side or the other is much above me to say."[109] This leaves open the possibility that Rebecca Nurse was actually a witch, certainly to the displeasure of the Nurse family.

A few days later, Nurse's son Samuel and son-in-law John Tarbell told Parris that his statement was not sufficient.[110] The issue clearly could not be resolved within the village church, and it widened over the next few years.

Parris continued to preach sermons in which he took shots at the dissenters.[111] The dissenters wrote letters to neighboring churches, and neighboring ministers wrote to Parris.[112] Those who opposed Parris petitioned the General Court and Gov. Phips—who doomed Rebecca Nurse in 1692—for help multiple times, and one petition carried the names of fifty men.[113] Parris described the petitioners as "scandalizing the church and minister," and later described his opponents' actions in general as "extremely disturbing the peace of this church and many other good people among us, sadly exposing all unto ruin."[114] Though, the witch hunt of 1692 had already accomplished that.

In June 1696, after continued disputes and a church council, Parris delivered his last sermon and quit.[115] But, he remained in the parsonage demanding his back pay. Two weeks after his resignation, his wife Elizabeth died and was buried in Salem Village.[116] The village elected a committee to negotiate Parris' back pay with him, though no settlement was reached.

Parris remained in the parsonage for nine months, and sued the village in the spring of 1697, which alienated even his former supporters. In April 1697, the village voted unanimously to sue Parris for ownership of the parsonage, and chose a cross-community group of men to act as agents for the village in an arbitration process that followed.[117] Parris' disputed claim to ownership of the parsonage had caused sharp opposition when the suspicious transaction was revealed in 1691, and his actions during the witch hunt drove a deep wedge between the villagers, but now the community was united—in opposition to its former minister.

The committee appointed to sue Parris consisted of Rebecca Nurse's son Samuel, son-in-law John Tarbell, Joseph Putnam, and Daniel Andrew. They wrote a petition that states in no uncertain terms what the Nurse family and the families of other accused in 1692 thought of Parris' actions during the witch hunt. They describe Parris as "the beginner and procurer of the sorest afflictions, not of this village only, but to this whole country, that ever did befall them." They note Parris' "teaching such dangerous errors," "his oath against the lives of several, wherein he swears that the prisoners with their looks knock down those pretended sufferers," and "His believing the Devil's accusations, and readily departing from all charity to persons, though of blameless and godly lives, upon such suggestions." The committee concludes, "on behalf of ourselves, and of several others of the same mind with us (touching these things), having some of us had our relations by these practices taken off by an untimely death; others have been imprisoned and suffered in our persons, reputations, and estates, submit the whole to your honors' decision, to determine whether we are or ought to be any ways obliged to honor, respect, and support such an instrument of our miseries."[118] This savage indictment of Parris' conduct in 1692 was persuasive, and the three court-appointed arbitrators—two of whom previously served as judges on the witch trials court—ordered the village to pay Parris £79 s9 d6 that he was owed and ordered Parris to give the village a deed to the parsonage and associated land in the village.[119]

This ended the dispute. Parris deeded the parsonage back to the village and left the community on September 24, 1697, never to return.[120]

TWENTY-TWO-YEAR-OLD Rev. Joseph Green was the village's next minister, and he worked to bring about reconciliation between the bitterly divided inhabitants. Soon after his ordination, Rebecca Nurse's family attended services again. Green reassigned seats in the meetinghouse so as to bridge divides among the congregation, placing Thomas Putnam and Samuel Nurse together, and Samuel Nurse's wife Mary with Sarah Holten, who testified against Rebecca Nurse in 1692 about the incident with the Holtens' loose pigs. On February 5, 1699, church members Thomas Wilkins, John and Mary Tarbell, and Samuel Nurse's wife Mary returned to communion for the first time since the witch hunt.[121]

TWELVE

REDEMPTION

O Time the fatal wrack of mortal things,
That draws oblivions curtains over kings,
Their sumptuous monuments, men know them not,
Their names without a Record are forgot,
Their parts, their ports, their pomp's all laid in th' dust.
Nor wit nor gold, nor buildings scape times rust;
But he whose name is grav'd in the white stone
Shall last and shine when all of these are gone.
—Anne Bradstreet, "Contemplations," 1678

ON AUGUST 25, 1706, Ann Putnam Jr. rose in her pew in the new Salem Village meetinghouse. Built upon the hill where the watchtower once loomed, the new building was larger with many more windows, illuminating the services.[1] The eyes of the congregation were upon Ann, though, unlike in 1692, she was standing still and silent on this summer day.

Her parents had died seven years prior, within three weeks of one another, leaving her at nineteen to care for her seven younger siblings, the youngest of whom was only seven months old.[2] She struggled to maintain a household at a young age with no husband to help. One Putnam family historian writes, "Her health was broken by the excitements of 1692, and she sank into an early grave."[3]

While Putnam remained standing, Rev. Joseph Green announced to the congregation that she desired to become a covenant member of the Salem Village church, the very church she nearly tore apart in 1692. As with all Puritans desiring admittance as full covenant members of the church, her candidacy was announced and time was given for people to object. Perhaps due to objections, or in anticipation of objections, she rose on this day to apologize for her actions in the witch hunt.

While Putnam stood with all eyes upon her, including those of Rebecca Nurse's family and those of other families who she caused grief and death to visit in 1692, Rev. Green read her prepared statement aloud:

> I desire to be humbled before God for that sad and humbling providence that befell my father's family in the year about '92, that I then being in my childhood should by such a providence of God be made an instrument for that accusing of several persons of a grievous crime whereby their lives were taken away from them, whom now I have just grounds and good reason to believe they were innocent persons, and that it was a great delusion of Satan that deceived me in that sad time, whereby I justly fear I have been instrumental with others, though ignorantly and unwittingly, to bring upon myself and this land the guilt of innocent blood. Though what was said or done by me against any person I can truly and uprightly say before God and man I did it not out of any anger, malice, or ill-will to any person for I had no such thing against one of them; but what I did was ignorantly being deluded by Satan. And particularly as I was a chief instrument of accusing of Goodwife Nurse and her two sisters I desire to lie in the dust and to be humbled for it in that I was a cause with others of so sad a calamity to them and their families, for which cause I desire to lie in the dust and earnestly beg forgiveness of God and from all those unto whom I have given just cause of sorrow and offence, whose relations were taken away or accused.[4]

According to this statement, Putnam's responsibility is entirely voided because it was Satan who deluded her and thus Satan who was at fault. According to Puritan beliefs, those who falsely accused another of witchcraft were damned to hell.[5] Therefore, this statement does not admit that her accusations were intentionally false, for if it did she would not be eligible for church membership, as such a sin was unforgivable. Similarly, she says her actions in 1692 were done "ignorantly and unwittingly." Bearing false witness "wittingly" was one of the original capital crimes in Massachusetts, based on the biblical commandment.[6] Therefore, the word "unwittingly" in her statement specifically avoided religious and possibly legal responsibility.

Rebecca Nurse is the only victim of Putnam's actions mentioned by name in the statement. Historian Charles W. Upham wrote in the nineteenth century that Samuel Nurse, as the head of the aggrieved family, was consulted and approved of the statement before it was read.[7] It is not clear what Upham's source for this claim is, but Putnam did need the other church members to vote her in, so it is likely that those in the Nurse family who were church members, and the church members related to others accused in 1692, needed to be satisfied in order for her to get a favorable vote.

Putnam admits that she was the "chief instrument" of accusing Rebecca Nurse, but by using the word "instrument" the implication is that someone else—the Devil—was merely using her as a tool, and therefore she lacked culpability. Despite never directly admitting guilt, Putnam was admitted as a church member. Her reputation remained one of infamy, however, and the name "Ann" all but disappeared from use in local branches of the Putnam family in the following centuries.[8]

More contrite and willing to admit his own responsibility was Judge Samuel Sewall, former justice of the Court of Oyer and Terminer. Nine years prior to Ann Putnam Jr.'s apology, Sewall wrote a resolution in the General Court calling for a day of prayer and fasting throughout the Province of Massachusetts Bay on January 14, 1697.[9] Although Sewall's resolution asks God to "pardon all the errors" that those in Massachusetts committed, the resolution attributes the initial cause to the actions of Satan.[10] This was as far as the government was willing to go in admitting some responsibility, but Sewall personally went much further.

It was on the fast day called by this resolution that Sewall made a personal apology similar in form to Putnam Jr.'s, but far more repentant in substance. Sewall stood in Boston's South Meetinghouse and handed a document to Rev. Samuel Willard as he passed by his pew. Rev. Willard himself was an early critic of the trials and his *Some Miscellany Observations on our Present Debates Respecting Witchcraft*, in circulation in October 1692, partly led to the ban on publications criticizing the witch hunt.[11]

Sewall remained standing as Willard read his apology to the congregation, "that as to the guilt contracted upon the opening of the late Commission of Oyer and Terminer at Salem . . . he is, upon many accounts, more concerned than any that he knows of, desires to take the blame and shame of it, asking pardon of men, and especially desiring prayers that God, who has an unlimited authority, would pardon that sin and all other [of] his sins."[12] After the minister finished reading, Sewall bowed and sat down.[13] Two other judges were members of this congregation and were

likely present in the pews on that day, but they never made public acknowledgment of the wrongs they committed.[14] Sewall's apology is immortalized
in *The Dawn of Tolerance in Massachusetts, Public Repentance of Judge
Samuel Sewall for His Action in the Witchcraft Trials* (1942), one of the mu-
rals in the House of Representatives chamber of the Massachusetts State-
house. However, it is not clear how the event relates to "tolerance."

During the remainder of his life Sewall observed an annual private day
of humiliation and prayer for his role in 1692.[15] In June 1700, he wrote
one of the first anti-slavery pamphlets ever written in English, *The Selling
of Joseph*. In the text, he argues against the idea that, due to one warped
interpretation of Genesis, Africans were cursed by God to be slaves and
therefore slavery was God's will. He writes: "Of all offices, one would not
beg this . . . to be an executioner of the vindictive wrath of God."[16] He
knew that role well in 1692.

On the same fast day in 1697 that Sewall apologized, twelve jurors also
came forward to beg forgiveness. Their declaration states that they too
were deluded by Satan, but also suffered from a lack of information—
probably referencing the incorrect instructions to the jury from Chief
Justice William Stoughton regarding spectral evidence. The jurors wrote,
"We fear, we have been instrumental with others, though ignorantly and
unwittingly, to bring upon ourselves and this people of the Lord, the guilt
of innocent blood; which sin, the Lord saith in Scripture, he would not
pardon. . . . We do, therefore, hereby signify to all in general (and to the
surviving sufferers in special) our deep sense of, and sorrow for our errors, in acting on such evidence to the condemning of any person." They
concluded, "And do hereby declare, that we justly fear that we were sadly
deluded and mistaken, for which we are much disquieted and distressed
in our minds; and do therefore humbly beg forgiveness."[17]

The first signature on the statement is "Foreman, Thomas Fisk," who
previously wrote to Rebecca Nurse's family describing why the jury re-
considered her verdict at her trial. The other names are Thomas Pearly
Sr., William Fisk, John Peabody, John Batcheler, Thomas Perkins, Thomas
Fisk Jr., Samuel Sayer, John Dane, Andrew Elliott, Joseph Evelith, and
Henry Herrick Sr. These men decided life and death in 1692.

Although some involved in the witch hunt later apologized (to varying
degrees) for their actions in 1692, most guilty in the prosecution of the
trials did not. Some, such as Chief Justice Stoughton, were promoted,
showing that he bore no social or political consequences for his actions.
He continued to serve prominently in the provincial government as lieutenant governor, and then acting governor.[18] By order of the king

Stoughton first became acting governor in 1694 because Gov. William Phips was ordered to return to London to face charges leveled by his political enemies. Phips was arrested as soon as he stepped foot in England on a £20,000 lawsuit lodged by political rival Joseph Dudley. Phips came down with influenza, and died in jail soon after his arrest.[19]

Stoughton, the man who asked the jury to reconsider their verdict against Rebecca Nurse and signed her death warrant, became the leader of the province for several years and thereby also commander of its militia. Nurse's male family members, like all adult men, were automatically required to be in the militia and under his command. Similarly to Stoughton, former Oyer and Terminer judges John Hathorne and Bartholomew Gedney were colonels in the militia and led troops in Maine during the years following 1692, continuing to fight against Massachusetts' perceived enemies, without any apparent stain on their reputations.[20]

ANGER AND HARD FEELINGS remained in Salem Village, Salem Town, and throughout the Province of Massachusetts Bay after the witch hunt.

Wealthy Salem Town merchant Philip English, who was accused of witchcraft in 1692 but fled to New York, was part of a controversy due to what he said about a leading figure in the witch hunt, Salem Town minister Rev. Nicholas Noyes, who excommunicated Rebecca Nurse in 1692. Noyes died in 1718 from a sudden brain hemorrhage and, according to local legend, Sarah Good's declaration that he would die drinking blood came true.[21]

Four years after Noyes' sanguinary death, English was prosecuted for saying that Noyes murdered Rebecca Nurse and John Proctor in 1692, and he went as far as to call the Salem Town church the "Devil's church." Even one as influential as English could not speak thus about an important figure in the witch hunt without consequences. Tradition says that on English's deathbed he forgave Noyes and the others who caused him harm in 1692. However, at the end of his statement English supposedly added: "But if I get well, I'll be damned if I forgive them."[22]

The strongest reaction against criticism of officials involved in the witch hunt came in the choppy wake of Salem Town resident Thomas Maule publishing *Truth Held Forth and Maintained According to the Testimony of the Holy Prophets, Christ and his Apostles Recorded in the Holy Scriptures* in 1695.[23] Maule was a known rabble-rouser and a Quaker, who coincidentally was previously arrested by constable Francis Nurse for offenses related to the practice of his faith in 1682.[24] His *Truth Held Forth* challenged the ban on publications critical of the government's actions during the witch trials, though there is some evidence that Maule actually supported the witchcraft accusations against Bridget Bishop.[25] The Council of Assistants ordered copies of the pamphlet burned in Boston and Salem, and arrested him.[26]

Maule was indicted before a Superior Court grand jury in the Salem Town House for "diverse slanders against the Churches and Government of the Province" by the attorney general who prosecuted the witchcraft cases in the latter part of 1692, and in front of two judges who had ties to the witch hunt.[27] Despite the above similarities to 1692, one significant change was that Maule had legal counsel during his time in court, and was acquitted.[28] Maule's acquittal in 1696 effectively ended the publication ban, and in the following years other writers published their own accounts of 1692.[29]

In 1700, Boston merchant Robert Calef published his scathing account of the witch hunt, sarcastically entitled *More Wonders of the Invisible World* (1700), which clearly targeted Cotton Mather's *Wonders of the Invisible World*, which was written in the fall of 1692 in support of the actions of the court and government. Calef's *More Wonders* was publicly burned in Harvard Yard by Cotton's father Increase Mather, president of the college.[30]

Rev. John Hale, the minister in neighboring Beverly, wrote *A Modest Enquiry Into the Nature of Witchcraft* in 1698, though it wasn't published until 1702, after his death. He was one of the first ministers called by Rev. Samuel Parris to examine the afflicted in 1692, and the one who later began to doubt the accusers' testimony against fellow minister Rev. George Burroughs. *A Modest Enquiry* gives his account of 1692, and calls for the names of at least some of the innocent victims to be cleared. He writes, "I would humbly propose whether it be not expedient, that for some, what more should be publicly done than yet has, for clearing the good name and reputation of some that have grounds for charity for them more convincing. And this (in order to our obtaining from the Lord further reconciliation to our land), and that none of their surviving relations, may suffer reproach upon that account."[31] It took years before this call was heeded.

Although it appears that views toward witchcraft were changing, belief in witches continued in North America, and around the world. The 1692 witch hunt was not the last time alleged "witches" were killed in the area that is now the United States, it was merely the last time that they were killed *legally*. Historian Owen Davies' investigation into alleged witchcraft in the following centuries reveals that more "witches" were killed in the area that is now the United States post–1692 than before it. The only difference is that these innocents were killed extrajudicially.[32]

One infamous post–1692 example of continued belief in witchcraft in America occurred in Philadelphia, during a supposedly more enlightened age, as the Constitutional Convention met in 1787 to draft a new governing system for the young United States. While the Founding Fathers deliberated, a woman known only as "Korbmacher" was attacked by a mob. She was carried through the streets of Philadelphia, was cut, and had items hurled at her, all because she was accused of using witchcraft to kill a child. She died of her wounds while those at the Convention were forming their "more perfect union."[33]

It was in the midst of the remaining fear, anger, and crackdown on criticism that the families of the innocent victims began to seek justice and redemption for their loved ones. The influence of William Stoughton, the chief justice of the Oyer and Terminer Court who later served terms as both lieutenant governor and acting governor, is seen as preventing any successful attempts at clearing the names of the victims until his death in 1701.[34]

In a petition dated March 2, 1703, relatives of Rebecca Nurse and other victims who were jailed and executed wrote to the governor and the General Court to clear the names of their loved ones. Among the twenty-one people who signed the petition were Nurse's son Samuel, daughter Rebecca Preston, son John, son-in-law John Tarbell, brother-in-law Peter Cloyce, brother-in-law Isaac Easty Sr., and nephew Isaac Easty Jr., whose mother Mary was also executed.[35]

In the document, the petitioners reference the flawed use of spectral evidence as the basis for their request: "The invalidity of the aforesaid evidence and the great wrong which (through errors and mistakes on those trials) was then done, has since plainly appeared, which we doubt not but this Honored Court is sensible of." Based on these "errors," the signers describe their request: "being dissatisfied and grieved that (besides what the aforesaid condemned persons have suffered in their persons and estates) their names are exposed to infamy and reproach, while their trial and condemnation stands upon the public record. We therefore humbly pray this Honored Court that something may be publicly done to take off infamy from the names and memory of those who have suffered aforesaid, that none of their surviving relations, nor their posterity may suffer reproach upon that account."[36] The petitioners look backward to remove the taint from the memory of their loved ones, but also forward to ensure that they and future generations are not affected by the negative association with the executed alleged witches.

Several months later, a group of ministers from Essex County addressed the General Court in a similar petition. The twelve local ministers who signed the petition included Rev. Green of Salem Village but notably not Rev. Noyes of Salem Town, who excommunicated Rebecca Nurse. The ministers directly endorse the previous petition by the victims' relatives and also express their belief that the trials were flawed: "Since it is apparent and has been acknowledged that there were errors and mistakes in the aforesaid trials ... there is a great reason to fear that innocent persons then suffered, and that God may have a controversy with the land upon that account."[37] Their fear that God was punishing Massachusetts for its actions was not without reason because another war, known to the English as Queen Anne's War (also known as the War of the Spanish Succession), spread from Europe to North America in 1702. Once again New England was fighting off attacks from Satan's supposed allies, the French Catholics and the Natives.[38] To avoid divine retribution for killing their innocent neighbors, the ministers requested government action "to clear the good name and reputation of some who have suffered as aforesaid, against whom there was not as is supposed sufficient evidence to prove the guilt of such a crime, and for whom there are good grounds for charity."[39]

In response to these petitions, and several other petitions about the cases of several victims from Andover, in 1703 the General Court ordered that a bill be drawn up to prevent the use of spectral evidence ever again.[40] The General Court did not at this time offer any compensation to the victims or their relatives who petitioned the provincial government.

One likely cause of this delay is that the provincial government was predisposed in organizing the conduct of the war against the French and Natives, which had devastating effects on Massachusetts. At one point during the war, the governor of New France reported back to Paris that two-thirds of all fields north of Boston were left untended because of French and Native raids on Massachusetts.[41] In 1708 French and Native raiders attacked Haverhill, less than twenty miles from Salem Village. Militiamen from Salem Village answered the alarm and raced north, with Rev. Green even carrying a musket, to defend against Massachusetts' enemies.[42]

Six years after the previous petitions, and only one year after the attack on Haverhill, another petition was sent to the General Court in May 1709 while the war still raged. This document was written by those who "had their near relations either parents or others who suffered death in the dark and doleful times that passed over this Province in the year 1692." It was signed by twenty-two people, including Rebecca Nurse's sons John, Samuel, Benjamin, and Francis Jr., along with son-in-law John Tarbell, grandsons John Preston, Samuel Nurse Jr., and George Nurse. Rebecca Nurse's brother-in-law Isaac Easty Sr. and two of his sons also signed the petition for the case of Mary Easty. These petitioners wanted the government to "restore the reputations to the posterity" of those who were killed in 1692, and described themselves and/or their relatives as having "been imprisoned, impaired, and blasted in our reputations and estates by reason of the same."[43] The stain of having an alleged witch in the family smeared the reputations of the victims' descendants, as well as the victims' themselves.

It was not for another year that the General Court finally acted on the many petitions from the relatives of the witch hunt victims and established a five-man committee to hear the petitions of restitution for the victims and their families. Stephen Sewall, the clerk of the Oyer and Terminer Court who gave the Nurse family copies of Rebecca Nurse's trial documents for their appeal to Gov. Phips, was on the committee that met in Salem Town in September 1710.[44]

On September 13, 1710, Samuel Nurse petitioned this committee in his own name and in the name of his siblings and presented five grievances on behalf of the family.[45] First, he noted that the family provided for Rebecca Nurse when she was in jail in Salem Town and Boston for almost four months. Second, the family made "many journeys to Boston and Salem and other places" in order to prepare her defense. Third, the family produced "plentiful testimony" that his "honored and dear mother had led a blameless life from her youth up—yet she was condemned and executed upon such evidence as is now generally thought to be insufficient." Fourth, he notes that Rebecca Nurse's "name and the name of her posterity lies under reproach, the removing of which reproach is the principle thing wherein we desire restitution." Fifth, he concludes by requesting restitution without putting a monetary value on the damage done to her and the Nurse family: "And as we know not how to express our loss of such a mother in such a way; so we know not how to compute our charge but shall leave it to the judgement of others, and shall not be critical but ready to receive such a satisfaction as shall be by the Honorable [General] Court judged sufficient—so praying God to guide unto such methods as may be for His Glory and the good of this land."[46]

Although Samuel Nurse's petition did not put a monetary value on the pain and suffering caused by the government, a monetary sum was later written at the bottom of the petition in another hand. Perhaps it was legally necessary to request an amount in order to receive restitution from the government. The note added to the petition reads: "Although forty pounds would not repair my loss and damage in my estate, yet I shall be satisfied if may be allowed five and twenty pounds, provided the attainder be taken off."[47] Although a monetary sum is added, the note clearly states that removing the attainder—her legal status of being convicted of a capital crime—is more important to Rebecca Nurse's descendants than the monetary compensation.

The committee recommended that the General Court reverse attainders for those who had family members petition on their behalf, including some of the executed and those found guilty but never executed.[48] But the relatives of Rebecca Nurse and the other condemned victims waited another year before the General Court finally acted.

On October 2, 1711, two weeks before the General Court met to decide on the requests to overturn convictions, a fire raged through Boston and burned the neighborhood of the Boston jail and the Town House, the meeting place of the General Court. In the nick of time, Queen Anne's portrait was saved from the Town House, as the flames raged around it, and as the war which bore her name continued to rage across New England.[49] The inferno was so huge that it was visible on the horizon in Salem Village.[50]

After picking through the charred rubble, the General Court met elsewhere in Boston on October 17, 1711, and passed "An Act to Reverse the Attainders of George Burroughs and Others for Witchcraft." In the act, the legislature recognized that "in the year of our Lord one thousand six hundred ninety two, several towns within this province were infested with a horrible witchcraft or possession of devils."[51] This statement by the Massachusetts government almost two decades after the trials still claimed that witchcraft (or possession) did indeed happen in 1692.[52] At least officially, some views had not changed in the years since the tragedy.

As to the cause of the act, the legislature credits the "humble petition and suit of several of the said persons and of the children of others of them whose parents were executed," and states, "Be it declared and enacted by His Excellency, the Governor's Council, and Representatives in General Court assembled, and by the authority of the same, that the several convictions, judgements, and attainders against the said George Burroughs, John Proctor, George Jacobs, John Willard, Giles Corey and [ ] Corey, Rebecca Nurse, Sarah Good, Elizabeth Howe, Mary Easty, Sarah

Wilds, Abigail Hobbs, Samuel Wardwell, Mary Parker, Martha Carrier, Abigail Faulkner, Ann Foster, Rebecca Eames, Mary Post, Mary Lacey, Mary Bradbury, and Dorcas Hoar and every of them be and hereby are reversed, made and declared to be null and void. . . as if no such convictions, judgments or attainders had ever been had or given."[53] Legally, Nurse and the others listed in the act were now clear and no longer considered witches.

However, only thirteen out of the twenty killed had their attainders reversed by this act. The other victims probably were not mentioned simply because no one petitioned on their behalf. Ann Pudeator, one of those left out of the 1711 act, was not cleared until 1957, and the final eight were not cleared until 2001.[54] The lobbying of Nurse's family, which always maintained her innocence, is why Nurse's conviction was overturned nearly three hundred years before some of the other victims of 1692.

In the act, the government places the blame for the tragedy of 1692 squarely at the feet of the accusers, "Several of the principal accusers and witnesses in those dark and severe prosecutions have since discovered themselves to be persons of profligate and vicious conversation." Perhaps these words against the accusers were meant to deflect blame from the government itself, for at the end of the act the General Court affirms "that no sheriff, constable, jailer, or other officer shall be liable to any prosecutions in the law for anything they then legally did in the execution of their respective offices."[55]

In December, the petitioners chose Stephen Sewall, whose committee recommended the government overturn the convictions, to act as their agent in dealing with the provincial government in Boston.[56] Governor Joseph Dudley signed the order to pay the damages to the individuals and families that suffered during 1692, and Rebecca Nurse's children designated Samuel Nurse to be the one to receive the funds and then distribute them among the siblings.[57] In total, Rebecca Nurse's eight children received £24 s8 d6.[58] This compensation was for financial losses, such as prison fees and expenses, not reparations for the lives lost.[59]

Although legally cleared, Rebecca Nurse remained excommunicated from the Salem Town church and therefore believed to be eternally damned. The same spring that Samuel Nurse received the compensation on behalf of his family, he petitioned the Salem Town church to void his mother's excommunication.[60] At 2 P.M. on March 6, 1712, the members of the Salem Town church gathered in Rev. Noyes' house, across the street from the courtroom where Rebecca Nurse was convicted, to consider "whether the record of the excommunication of our Sister Nurse, (all things considered) may not be erased and blotted out."[61] The church record notes that they were urged to act by Samuel Nurse, and that the church took into account that "the testimony on which she was convicted being not now so satisfactory to ourselves, and others as it was generally in that hour of darkness and temptation."[62]

The church members voted to "consent that the record of said Sister Nurse's excommunication be accordingly erased and blotted out; that it may no longer be a reproach to her memory, and an occasion of grief to her children, humbly requesting that the merciful God would pardon whatsoever sin, error, or mistake was in the application of that censure and of the whole affair."[63] In removing this ecclesiastical punishment, the final official stain on the family's reputation was cleared, and the believed barrier to the repose of Rebecca Nurse's soul removed.

SALEM VILLAGE, long seeking independence from Salem Town, finally became an independent self-governing district named Danvers in 1752. As a district, it had all the powers of a town except the right to send representatives to the General Court. Five years later, this odd halfway situation was remedied, and the legislature incorporated Danvers as a full town with representation, despite a veto from King George II in London. The veto was either received and ignored, or news of the veto never made it to Massachusetts. Either way, it shows the king's loosening grip on the Province of Massachusetts Bay, and the words of the royal veto, "The King Unwilling," appear on the Danvers town seal.

The year that Danvers was incorporated, Rebecca Nurse's great-grandson Sgt. Francis Nurse served as a selectman—alongside a Preston and a Southwick.[64] While his namesake and great-grandfather failed in his petitions for the independence of the village sixty years earlier, full independence from Salem was finally attained. The inhabitants were likely quite happy to shed the name "Salem Village"—which is forever marked with the scarlet letter of shame due to the events of 1692—and adopt "Danvers," a name with no local historical baggage.[65]

Although the name changed, the faces remained the same. The descendants of the accused and the descendants of the accusers lived side by side and continued to worship with each other at what was formerly known as the village church, now renamed the First Church of Danvers. Rebecca Nurse's great-grandson lived in the same house that she did, and descendants of other families involved in 1692 continued to live on their ancestral lands as well. Descendants of Joseph Putnam, Nurse's supporter in 1692 and father of Revolutionary War General Israel Putnam, lived in their family farmhouse until it was donated in 1991.

Around nine o'clock in the morning on April 19, 1775, the tolling of the bells at the church, the beating of drums, and the firing of muskets alerted Sgt. Francis Nurse to leave the Nurse homestead and gather with the militia.[66] He was a sergeant in the militia company of Capt. John Putnam, and the other sergeant was a Tarbell cousin.[67]

After joining up, the company hurried sixteen miles to cut off the British retreat from Lexington to Boston. They met the Redcoats at the Jason Russell House in Menotomy (present-day Arlington, Mass.), which was the site of the bloodiest fighting of the day—not Lexington or Concord as one would assume. Danvers lost seven men that day, more than any town except Lexington.[68]

The next day, Sgt. Francis Nurse and Capt. John Putnam marched back to Danvers in a mournful procession of militiamen escorting a cart with the bodies of the Danvers dead. Among the deceased were a Southwick and a Putnam.[69] Danvers militiamen later joined in the siege of Boston, leading up to the battle of Bunker Hill. On that day, General Israel Putnam purportedly told the gathered patriots not to fire at the Redcoats until they saw "the whites of their eyes."[70]

In 1780, Sgt. Francis Nurse died and was laid to rest in the family cemetery. He is buried beside his wife, Eunice Putnam, a descendant of Nathaniel Putnam, who was involved in the boundary disputes with the Nurses and Endicotts and who testified in support of Rebecca Nurse in 1692. Tradition has it that Sgt. Francis requested to be buried near where Rebecca and Francis Nurse were buried in the 1690s.

Sgt. Francis Nurse left the Nurse homestead to his son Benjamin, who sold it in 1784 to Phineas Putnam, a cousin of his mother Eunice.[71] Phineas' son Matthew, who fought with Sgt. Nurse and the other patriots on the first day of the Revolution, lived on the land after his father bought it and was buried not far from Nurse.[72] Beginning with this Revolution generation, both Nurses and Putnams were buried in the same cemetery at the Nurse homestead.[73]

BY THE MID-NINETEENTH CENTURY, the witch hunt was rarely talked about locally, as many inhabitants were still descendants of those on either side (or both) of the tragedy. Salem historian Charles W. Upham wrote in 1867: "This general desire to obliterate the memory of the calamity has nearly extinguished tradition. It is more scanty and less reliable than on any other event at an equal distance in the past. A subject on which men avoid to speak soon died out of knowledge."[74] The specters of the past largely remained buried.

The first local exception was Nathaniel Hawthorne, but he wrote about 1692 as a mournful, shameful memory. He was a descendant of John Hathorne, one of the judges who presided over Rebecca Nurse's first hearing and then her trial. Unlike Sewall, Hathorne never repented. In 1835 Nathaniel Hawthorne wrote in "Alice Doane's Appeal" that the witch hunt of 1692 "disgraced an age, and dipped a people's hands in blood."[75]

The late nineteenth century was a period of increased interest in colonial history. Around the U.S. Centennial in 1876, there was widespread media coverage of commemorative events, and local history came into vogue.[76] In 1889 the Danvers Historical Society was established—and its first president was a Putnam, the family whose ancestors played important roles on both sides of the witch hunt in 1692.[77]

It was during this period of renewed interest in early American history that the first efforts were made to memorialize Rebecca Nurse's legacy. In December 1875, a group of Nurse's descendants formed the Nourse Monument Association, using a spelling of the name that became common in later years. The association's officers included Nurse descendants from as near as Danvers and Salem, and as far as Chicago. The association held a "basket picnic" in the fields of the Nurse homestead in July 1883, which was both a family reunion and a fundraiser for a monument to Nurse.[78] It was reported in the *New York Times* that over two hundred descendants, aged as young as one to as old as eighty-five, gathered in the fields of her former farm. William P. Upham, son of the famed witch hunt historian, was present and addressed the crowd along with leaders of the association and Danvers minister Rev. Charles B. Rice.[79]

The association held a second fundraising family reunion at the Nurse homestead on July 19, 1884, and then the following year accomplished its mission of constructing a monument.[80] These gatherings on the grounds of the Nurse homestead became increasingly publicized, and the 1884 event was reported a great distance from Danvers, including a mention in a Vermont newspaper and in the German-language newspaper *Der Nordstern* in St. Cloud, Minnesota.[81] The nation took interest in the first attempt in the United States of memorializing someone accused of and executed for witchcraft.

Prior to the monument's completion, the Nurse family and the branch of the Putnam family that lived on the former Nurse farm inked an agreement to jointly build a fence around the cemetery.[82] Both families worked together to establish the area's permanent status as a burying ground set aside from the rest of the farm for both families to use, fittingly preserved and delineated with a dignified stone and iron rail fence.

The association dedicated the memorial to Rebecca Nurse on July 30, 1885, a fair summer day that saw a crowd arrive by steam trains, street-cars, and "horse-cars."[83] There were even carriages scheduled to leave each hour from downtown Salem near the train station to take visitors directly to the Nurse farm.[84] In total, around six hundred attended the dedication, which was the first remembrance service for any person ever executed for witchcraft in the United States.[85]

First, the attendees gathered a short ways down the road from the Nurse homestead in the meetinghouse of the First Church of Danvers, formerly known as the Salem Village church. The minister of the First Church of Danvers, Rev. Charles B. Rice, addressed the crowd along with Rev. Fielder Israel of the First Church of Salem, of which Rebecca Nurse had been a covenant member.[86] Following the addresses in the church, a banquet was served, after which the gathered crowd processed down what was once the main road in Salem Village to the cemetery on the Nurse farm for the dedication.[87]

At the dedication ceremony, Benjamin P. Nourse, one of Rebecca's descendants and vice president of the Monument Association, said of Rebecca's execution in 1692: "The tragic act cannot be wiped out from the book of record: then let the record be extended, and show that the people of Massachusetts, tardy as it may seem, condemn this act of her rulers of that day, by honoring all in a like manner, as we honor her to whom this monument has been erected."[88]

The monument itself is a polished granite obelisk designed by a Nurse descendant who was a partner at a Worcester, Mass., architectural firm. Danvers resident John Greenleaf Whittier, described at the time as "one of the most eminent and beloved poets of the present age," was enlisted to craft an inscription for the memorial. Whittier asked that his name not appear on the monument below the inscription he drafted, and insisted to the association that only Nurse's name should be on such a monument. In a letter, he expressed confidence to the committee that even without his name on the granite his contribution would not be lost to history.[89] Whittier's words are carved on one face of the obelisk:

O Christian Martyr! who for Truth could die,
When all about thee owned the hideous lie!

The world, redeemed from Superstition's sway
Is breathing freer for thy sake to-day.

On another face is carved Nurse's statement of her innocence:

Accused of Witchcraft
She declared
'I am innocent and
God will clear
My innocency'

The monument still stands in silent witness, among the tall pine trees in the family burial ground.

That night, the *Boston Globe* dedicated almost half of the front page of its evening edition to the dedication of the monument, including images of both the Nurse homestead and the monument itself.[90] It republished Danvers minister Rev. Rice's address, recounted the story of Rebecca Nurse during the witch hunt, and described the dedication of the monument. A briefer version of the article also appeared in the next morning's edition with the same image of the Nurse house.[91]

Brief articles or mentions of the memorial also appeared in the *New York Times* and newspapers in Delaware, Kansas, Kentucky, Louisiana, Mississippi, Oregon, Pennsylvania, Tennessee, and the Dakota Territory.[92] Worldwide, the monument's dedication was reported in Australian, British, Dutch, and French newspapers.[93] Although the dedication was a local event organized and attended by Nurse's descendants and members of the Danvers community, its prominent and continued presence in national and international media shows that the significance of the event was widely recognized.

Nurse's descendants did not stop there. At the time of the monument's dedication, the association recognized the need to also memorialize those brave neighbors in 1692 who signed the petition in support of her. They desired to mention each signer by name, but decided that due to space constraints on the obelisk a monument to the petitioners needed to be a separate project.[94] They continued holding family reunions, and accomplished their second goal in 1892, the bicentennial of the witch hunt.[95]

On July 30, 1892, a stone tablet was dedicated in "the little pine grove burial place" on the Nurse farm, as reported in the *New York Times*.[96] This event also featured a family reunion as descendants from many branches of the family gathered to listen to poems, sermons, and speeches from family members and ministers. This second monument memorialized those who stood with Nurse in 1692, and therefore is a reflection of her legacy just as it also commemorates those whose names are inscribed upon the stone.

This memorialization of Nurse and her supporters was the first step in commemorating the 1692 witch hunt, and it occurred in Danvers— formerly Salem Village, the community most affected by the witch hunt— instead of the city of Salem. The inclusion of the local Danvers community in this process, most prominently the First Church of Danvers and its minister Rev. Rice, who gave a key address at the 1885 dedication, is very significant when comparing the process of memorializing the witch hunt in Danvers and Salem.

It was long claimed that Salem, rather Danvers, was first able to confront its legacy of involvement with the witch hunt. One historian writes, "While the people of Danvers were the main participants in the witchcraft-related events of their community, it was to Salem that they turned for leadership and resolution—and it is now in Salem where the most persistent myths of witchcraft were and are made, remade, and sold."[97] However, the memorialization of Nurse shows that it was actually Danvers that provided the "leadership and resolution" in first confronting the tragedy of the witch hunt. Salem only led Danvers in the commercialization of this legacy, and undoubtedly it is where its legacy is sold.

The sermons that the Danvers and Salem ministers gave on the dedication day in 1885 give a clear comparison between attitudes on the memory of the witch hunt within the two communities. One historian rightly describes the power of Danvers minister Rev. Rice's sermon at the dedication of the 1885 memorial compared to that of Salem minister Rev. Fielder Israel: "Accordingly, he offered a striking testament, which contrasted uncomfortably with Israel's gentle platitudes. . . . It was Rice's extraordinarily pointed speech that set the tone of the day and embodied the association's endeavors over the previous decade." However, due to a simple misidentification of which minister was from which town, Rice's speech has been erroneously used to claim that Salem confronted its legacy first.[98]

Rice, as leader of the Danvers church, declared, "There is sufficient reason for our coming thus together today—or on any like occasion. The children of any of those who have suffered grievous injury in the former generations may properly take redress from mankind in the following ages . . . there is a public interest also with every man demanding that public errors of the past should stand in the light and be reproved." Rice was also invited to speak at the initial fundraiser for the monument in

1883, showing his early involvement in the effort as a leader of the local Danvers community supporting Nurse's descendants.[99]

It was in Danvers, the former Salem Village, scene of the outbreak of the witch hunt and the community that suffered most in 1692, that locals first supported and accomplished any form of memorialization of the witch hunt, led by the descendants of a witch hunt victim, with a desire to let old errors "stand in the light and be reproved," as Rice stated. It was in Danvers that Nurse and her supporters during the witch hunt were enshrined in stone. Despite a developing trade in witch-related souvenirs during the following decade, Salem did not dedicate a memorial to any of the witch hunt victims until 1992, over a century after the dedication of the monument to Nurse.

IN THE FORMER SALEM VILLAGE, the twentieth century began with the celebration of the 150th anniversary of the Town of Danvers in 1902. The events featured a six-mile-long parade, which took two hours to pass by the entrance to the Nurse homestead.[100] Rebecca Nurse was present in an historical address delivered by local historian Ezra D. Hines at the Peabody Institute for the anniversary.

Hines declared, "It is well that the relatives of and friends of one whose life was sacrificed have erected a monument to her memory. . . and have placed beside it another monument upon which they have caused to be inscribed the names of her friends and neighbors who stood by her in that hour when true friendship cost something and was of untold worth to her. How fitting to have done this deed! And when these monuments shall have crumbled to dust, character, for which they stand, will be remembered in the hearts and minds of generation after generation, to the last syllable of recorded time."[101] Locally, Nurse's memory continued to be foremost among the victims of 1692.

The preeminence of her legacy was shown again in 1907, when Sarah E. Hunt, curator of the Danvers Historical Society, purchased the Nurse homestead in her own name to preserve it as a historic site. Hunt was truly a trailblazer for her age as a single woman who was a leader in the local community. She purchased the Nurse farm with a sizable mortgage. The following year she transferred ownership of the property to the newly incorporated Rebecca Nurse Memorial Association.[102]

Fundraising to establish the museum came from local donors and many of Nurse's descendants. The newly preserved site was open to the public and used for important events, including celebrations marking

Massachusetts' Tercentennial in 1930 during which descendants of many figures from 1692 gathered and read documents that their ancestors wrote during that dark year.[103]

The Rebecca Nurse Homestead was then, and continues to be today, the only home of a victim of the witch hunt preserved and open to the public. Other homes of victims of 1692 still stand today, but only Nurse's memory was influential enough to spur local citizens to purchase a victim's home and preserve it as a historic landmark and museum. In addition to being the only home of a victim of 1692 open to visitors, it was for decades also the only 1692-related site of any sort in Danvers open to the public, in sharp contrast to Salem, which was already developing as a tourist destination.[104] This difference remains today.

Nationally, the 1950s brought Rebecca Nurse and the other personages of 1692 into the spotlight due to Arthur Miller's *The Crucible* (1953). This play appeared on countless stages over the following decades from Broadway to high school cafeterias, and was adapted for television, opera, and film, including a French-language film adapted by Jean-Paul Sartre, and the 1996 film starring Daniel Day-Lewis. *The Crucible*, more than any other work about 1692, has impressed the witch hunt onto popular culture.

Miller visited Salem and Danvers in the spring of 1952 doing research for the play. His first stop was the courthouse in Salem, where he asked for the legal records from 1692. He recounts in an article published after the play debuted on Broadway that when he first began reading the court records, it was Rebecca Nurse's initial hearing conducted by John Hathorne that jumped off the page at him.[105]

He later visited the Nurse homestead, and described "a feeling of love at seeing Rebecca Nurse's house on its gentle knoll; the house she lay in, ill, when they came, shuffling their feet, ashamed to ask her to come to court." When he visited the believed site of the hangings he again called Nurse to mind: "The sense of a terrible marvel again; that people could have such a belief in themselves and in the righteousness of their consciences as to give their lives rather than say what they thought was false. . . . Yet, Rebecca said, and it is in the record, 'I cannot belie myself.' And she knew who they were."[106] It was Nurse's story that Miller references most in describing his local visit. Although he fictionalized, romanticized, and merged historical figures into blended characters for the play, Nurse's story was so compelling that her character was left without much embellishment.

Many of its local historical figures now graced stage and screen, and then in the 1970s Nurse's former community uncovered the foundation of the original Salem Village parsonage, where Rev. Parris lived in 1692 and where the first fits of the afflicted began. A Nurse descendant, Alfred Hutchinson, owned the field off Centre Street in Danvers where the parsonage was once located, though the minister's house no longer existed, and the open grassy space was used by local neighborhood kids to play ball. Hutchinson allowed the site to be excavated and remain open to visitors.[107] Richard B. Trask led the search for the parsonage, and the day after it was announced that the parsonage foundation had been discovered, five hundred local residents showed up to volunteer their time excavating the site, which shows the enormous local interest it generated.[108] The parsonage site was later purchased by the Town of Danvers to become a permanent public historic site.

Also during the 1970s, the U.S. Bicentennial in 1976 renewed interest in the Nurse Homestead, just as the U.S. Centennial in 1876 led to interest in the early settlers in the years before the Rebecca Nurse Memorial was built. In the 1970s, the Danvers Bicentennial committee became alarmed that the Society for the Preservation of New England Antiquities was going to sell the Nurse farm property that it had been given by the Nurse Memorial Association decades earlier. In response, the Danvers Alarm List Company—a group of Revolutionary War reenactors formed during the Bicentennial that is named after the original town militia—was officially incorporated in order to lease and then eventually purchase the Nurse Homestead to preserve the nationally significant historic site as a museum.[109] Today, Danvers is perhaps the only town in America where each year all of the third graders take a field trip to the home and purported grave site of an accused witch.

In the 1980s, Academy Award-winning actress Vanessa Redgrave filmed a movie about the witch hunt on-site in Danvers, bringing further publicity about Salem Village's role in the events of 1692. The film, *Three Sovereigns for Sarah* (1985), was made by PBS as part of its American Playhouse series. It starred Redgrave as Nurse's sister Sarah Cloyce, Phyllis Thaxter as Rebecca Nurse, and Kim Hunter as Nurse's sister Mary Easty. The film follows the story of the three sisters during the witch hunt.

The movie was filmed in large part at the Nurse Homestead, and an exact copy of the Salem Village meetinghouse was constructed there for use in the film.[110] Originally, Nurse was to be the central character of the film, but instead producer and writer Victor Pisano decided to focus on Sarah Cloyce, the only one of the three sisters who survived 1692. This change was made so the film could also include the family's attempts to clear the names of the three women after the trials ended.[111] As with *The Crucible*, this PBS feature brought Nurse and her family's story into living rooms across the United States, and encouraged further study of the witch hunt.

IN 1992, Arthur Miller returned to Salem to dedicate a memorial in the center of the city, constructed after an international design contest.[112] This event was for a nationwide audience rather than a local one, and one writer notes, "The stated purpose of all this was to honor the innocents who had died and to remind the world of the danger of such atrocities happening again. The unstated purpose was to boost Salem's tourism."[113] In contrast, Danvers' commemorations focused on the local aspects and were for a local audience made up of many descendants of the original Salem Villagers.

A 1692 Tercentennial Committee was established by the Town of Danvers, which ran commemorative community events and built a memorial to the victims of 1692.[114] The tercentennial events began in 1990 with a dedication of the excavated parsonage site after the installation of informational signs and site modifications to prepare for an influx of visitors.[115] This work was followed by several years of educational community events, including lectures and exhibits on Salem Village history, which included the original Salem Village record book and a seventeenth-century copy of Rebecca and Francis Nurse's 1678 deed to the Nurse homestead.[116]

The defining moment of the tercentennial was the construction of the Salem Village Witchcraft Victims Memorial. The memorial was entirely funded by donations from private citizens and local civic groups. An important fundraiser was a 1991 walk-a-thon beginning at the Nurse homestead, which included more than two hundred walkers in both seventeenth-century and twentieth-century attire, and raised $10,000.[117]

This community-wide effort came to fruition on the morning of May 9, 1992, as a crowd of about eight hundred people stood in silence while the bells of nearby churches rang out for several minutes in the misty air, in memory of the innocents who died in 1692.[118] Standing along Hobart Street, once known as Meetinghouse Lane in Salem Village, they gathered to dedicate the first and only memorial to honor all of the known victims of 1692, directly across the way from the meetinghouse's original location.[119] When the meetinghouse was dismantled, it was moved across the road where the wood "decayed and became mixed with the soil."[120] It was on this site that the people gathered.

The Town of Danvers, as the successor to Salem Village, declared May 9, 1992, to be "a day of remembrance" and instructed all flags to be flown

at half-staff in honor of the victims of the witch hunt.[121] The memorial
dedication program featured tributes and the laying of flowers by a multitude of civic, religious, historical, and genealogical groups, including
many descendants of the victims of 1692. The ceremony ended with a
benediction by the minister of the First Church of Danvers, formerly the
Salem Village church.

The memorial features a stone sarcophagus of light-colored granite,
with a Bible box atop it.[122] The book placed on the Bible box is inscribed
with the words "The Book of Life." This image of the book serves two
purposes. First, this feature references the Book of Revelation, in which
it is said that all those granted eternal life have had their names inscribed
in the Book of Life.[123] Those executed for witchcraft were alleged to have
signed their names in the Devil's book and they refused to falsely confess
to such a crime, a lie that they believed would cause their names to be
blotted out of the Book of Life. In March 1692, while Mrs. Ann Putnam
prayed with Rev. Deodat Lawson before Rebecca Nurse was officially
charged, she accused Nurse of signing the Devil's book and yelled at her
alleged specter, "Your name is blotted out of God's Book, and it shall never
be put in God's book again!"[124] In 1992, the names of Rebecca Nurse and
the other victims were restored to the Book of Life.

Second, the book by which the victims are judged is also meant to
symbolize the historical record, which after 1692 redeemed the good
names of the innocent victims. On either side of the Book of Life are
metal shackles in the style of those worn by the accused in 1692. The
shackles are divided by the book and smashed open to symbolize truth
conquering falsehood. [125]

The final feature of the memorial is a wall behind the Book of Life inscribed with the names of the twenty-five men, women, and children who
were killed during the witch hunt or died in jail. Nurse's name is carved
along with her words: "I can say before my Eternal Father that I am innocent, & God will clear my innocency." The granite wall of quotes by the
innocent is topped by the image of a man grasping an open book, which
can be interpreted as a seventeenth-century judge with a law book or a
seventeenth-century minister with a Bible. As the visitor stands before
the Book of Life, facing the minister or judge, confronted with quotes by
the innocent dead, they are left wondering how they would have acted if
they lived during the witch-hunt.[126]

On July 19, 1992, a commemoration was held at the Rebecca Nurse
homestead in honor of Nurse, Sarah Good, Elizabeth Howe, Susannah
Martin, and Sarah Wilds who were executed three hundred years prior

on that date. More than three hundred people from as far away as California attended the commemoration, which culminated in the laying of wreaths at the 1885 memorial to Nurse.[127] Whereas Nurse was the only victim grandly memorialized before the tercentennial, with the 1885 monument and the preserved Nurse farm, she was also the only victim of 1692 to be individually recognized through a large event on the 325th anniversary of the trials, in 2017.

At the request of the directors of the Danvers Alarm List Company, custodians of the Nurse homestead, Massachusetts Governor Charles D. Baker proclaimed July 19, 2017, as "Rebecca Nurse Day" in the Commonwealth of Massachusetts. This proclamation added to a commemoration held at the Nurse homestead on that day, exactly 325 years after her execution, which featured seventeenth-century music and a historical address by Richard B. Trask in the reproduction Salem Village meetinghouse on the property.[128] Trask said of Nurse, "She, and the other occupants of the execution cart, whatever their weaknesses and flaws, all shared one common, precious, and in 1692 rare commodity: the belief in standing up and proclaiming the truth. This was a simple and yet for them deadly truth: that they were not witches."[129]

In 1692 villagers gathered around the original meetinghouse peering in windows to see Rebecca Nurse interrogated, but on that day in 2017 a crowd of several hundred gathered in the crowded reproduction meetinghouse and around its doors and windows in order to hear the commemorative program. After Trask's address, the governor's proclamation was read aloud to those gathered next to the Nurse house:

Commonwealth of Massachusetts
A Proclamation
WHEREAS This year we commemorate the 325th anniversary of the death of Rebecca Nurse, and all those innocents who lost their lives during the 1692 Salem Village Witchcraft Hysteria; and

WHEREAS As a young girl, Rebecca Nurse came to Massachusetts with her family fleeing persecution and became one of the earliest inhabitants of Essex County; and

WHEREAS On March 23, 1692, Rebecca Nurse was arrested on charges of witchcraft, and subsequently forty of her neighbors signed a petition to the Court of Oyer and Terminer attesting to her good character; and

WHEREAS Rebecca Nurse, at age 71, was unjustly convicted of the crime of witchcraft, and was executed on July 19, 1692; and

WHEREAS in October 1711 a Reversal of Attainder was Read & Accepted in the House of Representatives clearing Rebecca Nurse and others of the crime of witchcraft.

WHEREAS Rebecca Nurse's house and family cemetery in Danvers—included in the National Register of Historic Places Salem Village Historic District—has become an everlasting memorial to her legacy; and

WHEREAS Rebecca Nurse was memorialized in Arthur Miller's 1953 play, "The Crucible," and Massachusetts poet John Greenleaf Whittier wrote of Rebecca Nurse: "O Christian Martyr who for Truth could die / When all about thee owned the hideous lie! / The world redeemed from Superstition's sway / Is breathing freer for thy sake today;"

Now, Therefore, I, Charles D. Baker, Governor of the Commonwealth of Massachusetts, do hereby proclaim July 19th, 2017, to be, REBECCA NURSE DAY.

And urge all the citizens of the Commonwealth to take cognizance of this event and participate fittingly in its observance.

Given at the Executive Chamber in Boston, this Eleventh Day of July, in the year two thousand and seventeen, and of the independence of the United States of America, the two hundred forty-first.

By His Excellency
Charles D. Baker
Governor of the Commonwealth
Karyn E. Polito
Lt. Governor of the Commonwealth
William Francis Galvin
Secretary of the Commonwealth
God save the Commonwealth of Massachusetts[130]

After the proclamation was read, the crowd processed down to the Nurse cemetery in the direction of the then-setting sun. The commemoration culminated in a seventeenth-century-style prayer service among the Nurse family graves, where Rebecca Nurse is traditionally said to be buried, and descendants laid a wreath at the tall granite monument to Nurse in front of a large outpouring of members of the community and descendants who traveled thousands of miles to attend.

The large crowd that gathered from across the nation to honor Rebecca Nurse's memory and the official recognition of the day shows the influence her legacy still has in American culture. A first generation New Englander who was rejected in her later years and accused of an impossible crime by the very community that previously declared her to be a saint is one of the first American mysteries, and her seemingly impossible attempt to prove her innocence from this baseless accusation that culminated in her gruesome killing in the summer of 1692 is one of the earliest American tragedies, even a horror story.

The actions of later generations that memorialized her legacy in 1885, 1992, and 2017, however, reveal that this story is also something quite different. It is one of a community coming together to confront the past, and honor those of previous ages who did what was right and told the truth even if—or most especially if—their words were not heeded during their lifetime. Though Rebecca Nurse was killed in 1692, the spirit of quiet truth that she embodied still lives.

Notes

PREFACE

1. The importance of chronology in understanding the events of 1692 is noted in Mary Beth Norton, *In the Devil's Snare: The Salem Witchcraft Crisis of 1692* (New York: Vintage, 2003), 6–7.
2. Elizabeth Porter Gould, "The Home of Rebecca Nurse," *Essex Antiquarian* 4, no. 9 (September 1900): 135.

INTRODUCTION

1. For the total number accused and how it is calculated, see Emerson W. Baker, *A Storm of Witchcraft: The Salem Trials and the American Experience* (New York: Oxford University Press, 2015), 126–127.
2. See James E. Kences, "Some Unexplored Relationships of Essex County Witchcraft to the Indian Wars of 1675 and 1689," *Essex Institute Historical Collections* 120 (1984): 179–212.
3. David Thomas Konig, *Law and Society in Puritan Massachusetts: Essex County, 1629–1692* (Chapel Hill: University of North Carolina Press, 1979), 181.
4. For "unblemished reputation," see Baker, *Storm of Witchcraft*, 21; for "very model of Christian piety," see Paul Boyer and Stephen Nissenbaum, *Salem Possessed: The Social Origins of Witchcraft* (Cambridge, Mass.: Harvard University Press, 1974), 117; for "most conspicuously innocent," see Chadwick Hansen, *Witchcraft at Salem* (New York: George Braziller, 1969), 131.
5. Boyer and Nissenbaum, *Salem Possessed*, 149.
6. Charles W. Upham, *Salem Witchcraft: With an Account of Salem Village and a History of Opinions on Witchcraft and Kindred Subjects* (1867; repr. Mineola, N.Y.: Dover, 2000), 56.
7. Boyer and Nissenbaum, *Salem Possessed*, 92–93, 114–116, 185.
8. See Richard Latner, "Salem Witchcraft, Factionalism, and Social Change Reconsidered: Were Salem's Witch-Hunters Modernization's Failures?," *William and Mary Quarterly* 65, no. 3 (July 2008): 423–48; Benjamin C. Ray, "The Geography of Witchcraft Accusations in 1692 Salem Village," *William and Mary Quarterly* 65, no. 3 (July 2008): 449–478.
9. Upham, *Salem Witchcraft*, 612–613.
10. For a full discussion and refutation that actual attempted witchcraft occurred, see Tony Fels, *Switching Sides: How a Generation of Historians Lost Sympathy for the Victims of the Salem Witch Hunt* (Baltimore: Johns Hopkins University Press, 2018), 42–48.
11. Quoted in Christopher Bigsby, "Introduction," in *The Crucible*, by Arthur Miller (New York: Penguin, 2003), ix.

CHAPTER 1: EXODUS

Epigraph: Edward J. Lupson, St. Nicholas Church, Great Yarmouth: Its History, Organ, Pulpit, Library, Etc. (Yarmouth: Edward J. Lupson, 1881), 219.

1. *The Book of Common Prayer: King James Anno 1604, Commonly Called the Hampton Court Book* (London: William Pickering, 1844), "Baptism."

2. "Great Yarmouth Parish Registers, St. Nicholas Church," 1558–1653, Norfolk Records Office PD28/1. Baptism was usually performed shortly after birth, and although Rebecca Nurse's exact birthdate is unknown it was likely only a few days before this baptism. See P. M. Kitson, "Religious Change and the Timing of Baptism in England, 1538–1750," *Historical Journal* 52, no. 2 (2009): 273–274.

3. William White, *History, Gazetteer, and Directory, of Norfolk, and the City and County of the City of Norfolk* (Sheffield: W. White, 1836), 238.

4. Norfolk Historic Environment Service, "Site of Great Yarmouth Castle," Norfolk Heritage Explorer, accessed June 4, 2018, http://www.heritage.norfolk.gov.uk/record-details?MNF13375-Site-of-Great-Yarmouth-Castle&Index=12577&RecordCount=56734&SessionID=1f46896c-0e97-4368-97af-4d0a0e38e399.

5. Henry Manship, *The History of Great Yarmouth*, ed. Charles John Palmer (1619; repr., Great Yarmouth: Louis Alfred Meall, 1854), 9.

6. White, *History, Gazetteer, and Directory*, 238, 244.

7. Manship, *The History of Great Yarmouth*, 169.

8. Lois Payne Hoover, *Towne Family: William Towne and Joanna Blessing, Salem, Massachusetts, 1635* (Baltimore, MD: Otter Bay Books, 2010), 1–2.

9. Malcolm Thick, "Garden Seeds in England before the Late Eighteenth Century: I. Seed Growing," *Agricultural History Review* 38, no. 1 (1990): 60.

10. Hoover, *Towne Family*, 5.

11. White, *History, Gazetteer, and Directory*, 240, 253.

12. John Preston, *The Picture of Yarmouth: Being a Compendious History and Description of All the Public Establishments Within That Borough* (Yarmouth: John Preston, 1819), 255.

13. For an account of the English Reformation, see Roger Lockyer, *Tudor and Stuart Britain, 1471–1714* (London: Longman, 1964).

14. Roger Thompson, *Mobility and Migration: East Anglian Founders of New England, 1629–1640* (Amherst: University of Massachusetts Press, 1994), 19.

15. H. Hensley Henson, *Puritanism in England* (New York: Lenox Hill, 1972), 19.

16. John Coffey and Paul C. H. Lim, "Introduction," in *The Cambridge Companion to Puritanism*, ed. John Coffey and Paul C. H. Lim, Cambridge Companions to Religion (Cambridge: Cambridge University Press, 2008), 2.

17. Albert E. Dunning, *Congregationalists in America: A Popular History of Their Origin, Belief, Polity, Growth and Work* (New York: J. A. Hill and Company, 1894), xi; for a general introduction to Puritanism, see Francis J. Bremer, *Puritanism: A Very Short Introduction* (Oxford: Oxford University Press, 2009).

18. Coffey and Lim, "Introduction," 2.

19. Charles John Palmer, *The History of Great Yarmouth, Designed as a Continuation of Manship's History of That Town* (Great Yarmouth: Louis Alfred Meall, 1856), 109, 112, 114, 116.

20. White, *History, Gazetteer, and Directory*, 253.

21. Palmer, *The History of Great Yarmouth*, 124.

22. Palmer, *The History of Great Yarmouth*, 124–125.

23. Quoted in Henson, *Puritanism in England*, 54, 59.

24. Tom Webster, "Early Stuart Puritanism," in *The Cambridge Companion to Puritanism*, ed. John Coffey and Paul C. H. Lim, Cambridge Companions to Religion (Cambridge: Cambridge University Press, 2008), 56.

25. Edward Johnson, *Wonder-Working Providence of Sion's Saviour in New-England*, ed. J. Franklin Jameson, Original Narratives of Early American History (1654; repr., New York: Charles Scribner's Sons, 1910), 23 note.

26. Johnson, *Wonder-Working Providence*, 23.

27. Michael Walzer, *The Revolution of the Saints: A Study in the Origins of Radical Politics* (Cambridge, Mass.: Harvard University Press, 1965), 19, 300–320.

28. Johnson, *Wonder-Working Providence*, 50, 52.

29. Hoover, *Towne Family*, 2.

30. Marilynne K. Roach, *Six Women of Salem: The Untold Story of the Accused and Their Accusers in the Salem Witch Trials* (Boston: Da Capo, 2013), 8.

31. Samuel R. Gardiner, *History of England, From the Accession of King James to the Outbreak of the Civil War, 1603–1642*, vol. 8 (London: Longmans, Green, and Co., 1891), 169, 167.

32. Daniel Wait Howe, *The Puritan Republic of Massachusetts Bay in New England* (Indianapolis: Bobbs-Merrill Company, 1899), 9.

33. Johnson, *Wonder-Working Providence*, 58 and note.

34. Francis Higginson, *New-England's Plantation* (1630; repr., Salem, Mass.: Essex Book and Print Club, 1908), 121.

35. Johnson, *Wonder-Working Providence*, 61 and note.

36. Higginson, *New-England's Plantation*, 61.

37. Johnson, *Wonder-Working Providence*, 56.

38. Higginson, *New-England's Plantation*, 62.

39. John Dunton, *John Dunton's Letters from New-England.*, ed. William H. Whitmore, Prince Society Publications (Boston: Prince Society, 1867), 45–46, 47–48.

40. Leo Bonfanti, *The Massachusetts Bay Colony*, vol. 2, New England Historical Series. (Wakefield, Mass.: Pride Publications, 1980), 8.

41. Johnson, *Wonder-Working Providence*, 63.

42. Higginson, *New-England's Plantation*, 66.

43. Higginson, *New-England's Plantation*, 83.

CHAPTER 2: NEW JERUSALEM

Epigraph: First Church of Salem, *The Records of the First Church in Salem, Massachusetts, 1629–1736*, ed. Richard D. Pierce (Salem, Mass.: Essex Institute, 1974), 3.

1. Higginson, *New-England's Plantation*, 77.

2. Johnson, *Wonder-Working Providence*, 62.

3. Jeffrey K. Jue, "Puritan Millenarianism in Old and New England," in *The Cambridge Companion to Puritanism*, ed. John Coffey and Paul C. H. Lim, Cambridge Companions to Religion (Cambridge: Cambridge University Press, 2008), 269.

4. John Winthrop, "Model of Christian Charity," *Collections of the Massachusetts Historical Society*, 3, 7 (1838): 47.

5. Winthrop, "Model of Christian Charity," 47.

6. James Hastings, *A Dictionary of the Bible: Dealing with its Language, Literature, and Contents Including Biblical Theology*, vol. 2 (1898; repr., Honolulu: University Press of the Pacific, 2004), 584.

7. John Josselyn, *New England's Rarities Discovered in Birds, Beasts, Fishes, Serpents, and Plants of that Country* (1672; repr., Boston: William Veazie, 1865), 79; Higginson, *New-England's Plantation*, 26–27.

8. Josselyn, *New England's Rarities*, 48; Alan Taylor, *American Colonies: The Settling of North America* (New York: Penguin, 2001), 189–190.

9. Higginson, *New-England's Plantation*, 30–31, 33.

10. Higginson, *New-England's Plantation*, 41.

11. Taylor, *American Colonies*, 165, 179.

12. Josiah Henry Benton, *The Story of the Old Boston Town House, 1658–1711* (Boston, 1908), 147.

13. Harriet S. Tapley, *Chronicles of Danvers (Old Salem Village), Massachusetts, 1632–1923* (Danvers, Mass.: Danvers Historical Society, 1923), 10; Gardiner, *History of England*, 169.

14. Frank E. Moynahan, *Danvers, Massachusetts: A Resume of Her Past History and Future Progress* (Danvers, Mass.: Danvers Mirror, 1899), 81.

15. Richard Francis, *Judge Sewall's Apology: The Salem Witch Trials and the Forming of an American Conscience* (New York: HarperCollins, 2005), 271.

16. General Court of Massachusetts, *The Charters and General Laws of the Colony and Province of Massachusetts Bay* (Boston: T. B. Wait and Co., 1814), 195–196.

17. Joseph A. Conforti, *Saints and Strangers: New England in British North America* (Baltimore: Johns Hopkins University Press, 2006), 2, 55–56.

18. Tapley, *Chronicles of Danvers*, 3.

19. Sidney Perley, *The History of Salem Massachusetts*, vol. 1 (Salem, Mass.: Sidney Perley, 1924), 315.

20. Town of Salem, *Town Records of Salem, Massachusetts*, 3 vols. (Salem, Mass.: Essex Institute, 1868–1934), 1:108.

21. Perley, *History of Salem*, 316 and map opposite 315; Southern Essex Registry of Deeds, 1:35. The deed record books use two sets of page/folio numbers. The newer page numbers are given here, as that is how they can be accessed online.

22. Robert F. Rantoul, "Old Modes of Travel," in *History of Essex County, Massachusetts, with Biographical Sketches of Many of Its Pioneers*, ed. D. Hamilton Hurd, vol. 1 (Philadelphia: J. W. Lewis & Co., 1888), lxi.

23. Emerson W. Baker, "Salem as Frontier Outpost," in *Salem: Place, Myth, and Memory*, ed. Dane Anthony Morrison and Nancy Lusignan Schultz (Boston: Northeastern University Press, 2004), 25–26.

24. George Francis Dow, *Every Day Life in the Massachusetts Bay Colony* (1935; repr., New York: Dover, 1988), 16–17, 19.

25. Sidney Perley, *Historic Storms of New England* (Salem: Salem Press, 1891), 4, 5–6.

26. Dow, *Every Day Life*, 19–22, 39–40.

27. It was originally thought that Edmund Towne was apprenticed to Henry Skerry in Great Yarmouth and came to Salem in 1637 separately from his family, though Lois Paine Hoover concludes that based on age this was a different Edmund Towne. See Hoover, *Towne Family*, 103–4.

28. Roach, *Six Women of Salem*, 8.

29. Dow, *Every Day Life*, 39–40.

30. Description of the estate of William Googe of Lynn (1646) in Dow, *Every Day Life*, 37–38.

31. Francis Grose, *A Classical Dictionary of the Vulgar Tongue*, 3rd ed. (London: Hooper and Co., 1796), "pompkin."

32. Dow, *Every Day Life*, 41.

33. C. Dallett Hemphill, "Women in Court: Sex-Role Differentiation in Salem, Massachusetts, 1636 to 1683," *William and Mary Quarterly* 39, no. 1 (January 1982): 166–167; David Freeman Hawke, *Everyday Life in Early America* (New York: Harper & Row, 1989), 63.

34. Dow, *Every Day Life*, 42.

35. Harry S. Stout, *The New England Soul: Preaching and Religious Culture in Colonial New England* (New York: Oxford University Press, 1986), 31.

36. Dow, *Every Day Life*, 94.

37. Alice Morse Earle, *The Sabbath in Puritan New England* (New York: Charles Scribner's Sons, 1891), 1.

38. Howe, *Puritan Republic*, 198; Michael Martin and Leonard Gelber, *Dictionary of American History*, ed. Leo Lieberman, rev. and enl. ed. (Totowa, N.J.: Rowman & Littlefield, 1978), 44.

39. Thomas Hutchinson, *The History of the Province of Massachusetts-Bay*, 3 vols. (Boston: Thomas and John Fleet, 1765–1828),1:37–38; Howe, *Puritan Republic*, 100, 211–212.

40. Dunning, *Congregationalists in America*, 150–151; Howe, *Puritan Republic*, 169.

41. Earle, *Sabbath in Puritan New England*, 79, 81.

42. Salem, *Town Records*, 2:209–210.

43. Dunning, *Congregationalists in America*, 150–151; Horace E. Scudder, "Life in Boston in the Colonial Period," in *The Memorial History of Boston, Including Suffolk County, Massachusetts, 1630–1880*, ed. Justin Winsor, vol. 1 (Boston: Ticknor and Company, 1880), 481–520, 512.

44. Earle, *Sabbath in Puritan New England*, 11–12, 85.

45. Earle, *Sabbath in Puritan New England*, 247.

46. Howe, *Puritan Republic*, 160, 163.

47. Laurel Thatcher Ulrich, *Good Wives: Image and Reality in the Lives of Women in Northern New England, 1650–1750* (New York: Vintage, 1991), 138–139.

48. George Francis Dow, ed., *Records and Files of the Quarterly Courts of Essex County*, (Salem, Mass.: Essex Institute, 1911–1975), 1:7, 21, 37, 52, 60, 110, 113, 178, 220, 233, 286, 338, 447. Subsequent references will be cited as *EQC*.

49. Rebecca's marriage is too early to be recorded in the Salem records, though the marriages of her children are; see Salem, *Vital Records of Salem, Massachusetts, to the End of the Year 1849*, vol. 4 (Salem, Mass.: Essex Institute, 1924), 4:130, 131–132. Most authoritative sources list Rebecca's marriage as about 1645; see Clarence Almon Torrey, *New England Marriages Prior to 1700* (Baltimore: Genealogical Publishing Co., 1985), 541; Hoover, *Towne Family*, 7.

50. Philip J. Greven, Jr., *Four Generations: Population, Land, and Family in Colonial Andover, Massachusetts* (Ithaca, N.Y.: Cornell University Press, 1970), 33–35; For discussion of Francis' age, see Hoover, *Towne Family*, 9.

51. *EQC*, 1:16.

52. General Court of Massachusetts, *Charters and General Laws*, 151.

53. Alice Morse Earle, *Customs and Fashions in Old New England* (New York: Charles Scribner's Sons, 1894), 62.

54. Walzer, *Revolution of the Saints*, 193–194.

55. Alice Morse Earle, "Old-Time Marriage Customs in New England," *Journal of American Folklore* 6, no. 21 (June 1893): 101; General Court of Massachusetts, *Charters and General Laws*, 151; Dow, *Every Day Life*, 100.

56. William D. Northend, "Address Before the Essex Bar Association," *Essex Institute Historical Collections* 22 (1885): 169–170.

57. There is a report of a wedding ring being confiscated from the wife of an accused witch in Robert Calef, *More Wonders of the Invisible World: Or, The Wonders of the Invisible World Display'd in Five Parts* (London, 1700), excerpted in *Narratives of the New England Witchcraft Cases*, ed. George Lincoln Burr (1914; repr., Mineola, N.Y.: Dover, 2002), 364. For men not wearing wedding rings until the twentieth century, see Vicki Howard, "'Real Man's Ring': Gender and the Invention of Tradition," *Journal of Social History* 36, no. 4 (Summer 2003): 837–856.

58. General Court of Massachusetts, *Charters and General Laws*, 152. In an interesting and perhaps unexpected way, the Puritan view of marriage as a contract rather than a sacrament was later used in the 1990s as grounds for arguing that same-sex marriage should be legalized: Dwight J. Penas, "Bless the Tie That Binds: A Puritan-Covenant Case for Same-Sex Marriage," *Law & Inequality: A Journal of Theory and Practice* 8, no. 3 (1990): 533–565.

59. Earle, *Customs and Fashions*, 72–73, 168; Earle, "Old-Time Marriage Customs," 101.

60. Earle, "Old-Time Marriage Customs," 97.

61. Howe, *Puritan Republic*, 129.

62. Hemphill, "Women in Court," 167.

63. Samuel Sewall, *Diary of Samuel Sewall, 1674–1729*, 3 vols., Collections of the Massachusetts Historical Society 5 (Boston: Massachusetts Historical Society, 1878–1882), 2:93.

64. Cotton Mather, *Ornaments for the Daughters of Zion, Or The Character and Happiness of a Vertuous Woman: In a Discourse Which Directs the Female-Sex How to Express, the Fear of God, in Every Age and State of Their Life; and Obtain Both Temporal and Eternal Blessedness* (Boston: Samuel Phillips, 1692), 80.

65. Ulrich, *Good Wives*, 38–39.

66. Hoover, *Towne Family*, 9–10.

67. Greven, *Four Generations*, 30.

68. Cotton Mather, *Magnalia Christi Americana; or, The Ecclesiastical History of New-England, from Its First Planting in the Year 1620, unto the Year of Our Lord, 1698* (London: Printed for T. Parkhurst, 1702), book III, 165.

69. Dow, *Every Day Life*, 175.

70. Edward Shorter, *Women's Bodies: A Social History of Women's Encounter with Health, Ill-Health, and Medicine* (New Brunswick, N.J.: Transaction Publishers, 1997), 98.

71. Shorter, *Women's Bodies*, 98; United Health Foundation, "2016 Health of Women and Children Report," America's Health Rankings, accessed May 4, 2018.

72. Parnel Wickham, "Idiocy and the Construction of Competence in Colonial Massachusetts," in *Children in Colonial America* (New York: New York University Press, 2007), 142.

73. Upham, *Salem Witchcraft*, 53.

74. There are no deeds recorded for Francis Nurse owning land before 1662, confirmed by my search through all recorded Essex deeds for that time frame, though not all deeds were recorded in those times. Also, see "Christopher Waller to Francis Nurse (Deed, 1662)," reprinted in Paul Boyer and Stephen Nissenbaum, eds., *Salem-Village Witchcraft: A Documentary Record of Local Conflict in New England* (Boston: Northeastern University Press, 1993), 149. Perhaps they rented a home near Skerry, or possibly owned land but never recorded the deed. However, knowing that only five years before their marriage

Francis was in court accused of stealing food, and in the following years he repeatedly asked the town for land grants, it appears unlikely that he owned land at this time. Although no deed exists, a passage of court testimony Francis later gave shows that they likely did at some point live along the road to the ferry. In 1678 Francis testified about the location of certain property boundary lines in that section of town, and clearly knew the area very well. See *EQC*, 7:108. In this testimony, he also recounts something that one of the previous landowners in that area told him about how their property lined up with the main road. This is information that a neighbor would know.

75. Marilynne K. Roach suggests this in Roach, *Six Women of Salem*, 10.

76. *EQC*, 1:428.

77. General Court of Massachusetts, *Charters and General Laws*, 160.

78. Hoover, *Towne Family*, 9–10.

79. Bernard Rosenthal, ed., *Records of the Salem Witch-Hunt* (New York: Cambridge University Press, 2009), Docs. 31, 294.

80. Rosenthal, *Records of the Salem Witch-Hunt*, Doc. 340.

81. Salem, *Town Records*, 1:154, 2:16.

82. Today this area is in east Danvers, near the Bradstreet Open Space Area. "Christopher Waller to Francis Nurse (Deed, 1662)," 149.

83. Southern Essex Deeds, 3:45–46.

84. Salem, *Town Records*, 2:46.

85. Two months prior, a town meeting voted to authorize the selectmen to grant land near Humphrey's Hill and the Seven Men's Bounds, a point on the southwestern boundary of Salem along the main road heading inland (present-day Lowell Street in Peabody, Mass.). See Salem, *Town Records*, 2:43. The selectmen on April 11 were presumably acting on this authorization when they granted land to Francis and the others. One of the other grants made that day mentions the Seven Men's Bounds, so it is likely that the Nurse's grant was in this section of town as well. Also, a grant to another farmer in 1668 and a town meeting committee report in 1673 both mention the Nurse land in relation to other neighboring farms. Salem, *Town Records*, 2:93–94, 164. By comparing these records with Salem antiquarian Sidney Perley's research on landholding in the area, it appears that the location today is within the city of Peabody, somewhere in what are now the Salem Country Club and the Proctor Meadows conservation area. Sidney Perley, "'Groton,' Salem, in 1700," *Essex Institute Historical Collections* 51 (1915): frontispiece map and 261; Sidney Perley, "Ceder Pond Region, Salem, in 1700," *Essex Institute Historical Collections* 51 (1915): frontispiece map and 29–30.

86. John A. Wells, *The Peabody Story* (Salem, Mass.: Essex Institute, 1972), 47.

87. Southern Essex Deeds, 3:45–46; Salem, *Town Records*, 1:207.

88. Salem, *Town Records*, 3:22, 175.

89. A deed between Francis Nurse and George Jacobs describes Nurse as a "traymaker." See Southern Essex Deeds, 3:45–46.

90. Hoover, *Towne Family*, 10.

91. The records of nearby Andover, Mass., paint a picture of the health hazards the Puritans faced. Greven, *Four Generations*, 26–27.

92. Cotton Mather, *The Angel of Bethesda*, ed. Gordon W. Jones (Barre, Mass.: American Antiquarian Society and Barre Publishers, 1972), 272.

93. Cotton Mather, *Corderius Americanus, an Essay upon the Good Education of Children, in a Funeral Sermon upon Mr. Ezekiel Cheever, Master of the Free School of Boston* (Boston: John Allen, 1708), 18.

94. Sewall, *Diary*, 1:374.

95. This theory is put forward in Barbara Ehrenreich and Deidre English's non-historical interpretation of women and medicine. See Barbara Ehrenreich and Deirdre English, *Witches, Nurse, and Midwives: A History of Women Healers* (New York: Feminist Press, 1973).

96. Zerobabel Endecott, *Synopsis Medicinæ, or a Compendium of Galenical and Chymical Physick: Showing the Art of Healing According to the Precepts of Galen & Paracelsus (1677)*, ed. George Francis Dow (Salem, Mass., 1914), 23, 31, 33.

97. See David Harley, "Historians as Demonologists: The Myth of the Midwife-Witch," *Social History of Medicine* 3, no. 1 (April 1990): 1–26.

98. General Court of Massachusetts, *Charters and General Laws*, 196–197.

99. Johnson, *Wonder-Working Providence*, 199.

100. David D. Hall, *Worlds of Wonder, Days of Judgment: Popular Religious Belief in Early New England* (New York: Alfred A. Knopf, 1989), 34.

101. Calef, *More Wonders*, 360.

102. Francis J. Bremer, *Puritanism: A Very Short Introduction* (Oxford: Oxford University Press, 2009), 82.

103. Hall, *Worlds of Wonder*, 32–33.

104. Upham, *Salem Witchcraft*, 142. One such document Francis Nurse signed with his mark was the deed between him and George Jacobs: Southern Essex Deeds, 3:45–46.

105. See: Rosenthal, *Records of the Salem Witch-Hunt*, Doc. 340.

106. *EQC*, 1:45, 157, 272.

107. Southern Essex Deeds, 2:25–26.

108. *EQC*, 1:363.

109. Salem, *Town Records*, 1:218, 219.

110. For one example of Francis chosen to settle a land dispute: Salem, *Town Records*, 2:36, 37–38.

111. *EQC*, 5:117; Salem, *Town Records*, 2:149.

112. Scudder, "Life in Boston in the Colonial Period," 508.

113. General Court of Massachusetts, *Charters and General Laws*, 82–84.

114. General Court of Massachusetts, *Charters and General Laws*, 144.

115. Salem, *Town Records*, 2:195, 173.

116. Hoover, *Towne Family*, 11, 13, 10, 12, 17; Rosenthal, *Records of the Salem Witch-Hunt*, Doc. 1.

117. The Towne Farm in Topsfield was located near the present-day intersection of South Main Street and Salem Street. Southern Essex Deeds, 1:35; Hoover, *Towne Family*, 2; Topsfield Historical Society Historical Records Committee and Topsfield Witch Trials Tercentenary Committee, *Topsfield and the Witchcraft Tragedy* (Topsfield, Mass.: Topsfield Historical Society, 1992), 3.

118. George Francis Dow, *The Probate Records of Essex County, Massachusetts*, 3 vols. (Salem, Mass.: The Essex Institute, 1917), 2:358.

119. Hoover, *Towne Family*, 103, 183, 263, 327, 397, 398.

120. For use of the term "Puritan Revolution," see Bremer, *Puritanism*, 24.

121. Manship, *The History of Great Yarmouth*, 277.

122. Hutchinson, *The History of the Province of Massachusetts-Bay*, 1:136.

123. Philip Sidney, *The Headsman of Whitehall* (Edinburgh: G. A. Morton, 1905), 45.

124. Malcolm Gaskill, *Between Two Worlds: How the English Became Americans* (Oxford: Oxford University Press, 2014), 226.

125. Dunning, *Congregationalists in America*, 125.

126. Ulrich, *Good Wives*, 216.

127. Conforti, *Saints and Strangers*, 60.

128. Carol F. Karlsen, *The Devil in the Shape of a Woman: Witchcraft in Colonial New England* (New York: W. W. Norton, 1987), 193; Mather, *Ornaments for the Daughters of Zion*, 44–45.

129. Bremer, *Puritanism*, 69.

130. George Lee Haskins, *Law and Authority in Early Massachusetts: A Study in Tradition and Design* (New York: Macmillan, 1960), 86–87.

131. Daniel Appleton White, *New England Congregationalism in Its Origin and Purity: Illustrated by the Foundation and Early Records of the First Church in Salem* (Salem, Mass., 1861), 50.

132. Bremer, *Puritanism*, 42.

133. First Church of Salem, *The Records of the First Church in Salem*, 127.

134. Covenant reprinted in White, *New England Congregationalism*, 13–14.

135. Salem, *Town Records*, 2:219.

136. For age, see: Salem, *Vital Records*, 1:189.

137. *EQC*, 5:430. Thomas Clungen previously testified in court that he "unrigged a ship." *EQC*, 4:195.

138. *EQC*, 5:430.

139. Ulrich, *Good Wives*, 7.

140. *EQC*, 5:431.

141. Salem, *Town Records*, 2:196, 217.

142. James M. Caller and M. A. Ober, *Genealogy of the Descendants of Lawrence and Cassandra Southwick of Salem, Mass.* (Salem, Mass.: J. H. Choate, 1881), 71; *EQC*, 5:117; Salem, *Town Records*, 2:149.

143. First Church of Salem, *The Records of the First Church in Salem*, 8; Perley, *History of Salem*, 2:256.

144. Quoted in Taylor, *American Colonies*, 181.

145. Perley, *History of Salem*, 2:269.

146. *EQC*, 6:294.

147. For location of John Southwick's house, see: National Park Service, "National Register of Historic Places Nomination Form: Southwick House," 1983, File Unit: National Register of Historic Places and National Historic Landmarks Program Records: Massachusetts, 1964–2012, National Archives, https://catalog.archives.gov/id/63794661; Wells, *The Peabody Story*, 109.

148. Caller and Ober, *Descendants of Lawrence and Cassandra Southwick*, 71, 72; General Court of Massachusetts, *Charters and General Laws*, 44.

149. Christine Leigh Heyrman, *Commerce and Culture: The Maritime Communities of Colonial Massachusetts, 1690–1750* (New York: W. W. Norton, 1984), 112–113.

150. *EQC*, 8:225.

151. Marilynne K. Roach, *The Salem Witch Trials: A Day-By-Day Chronicle of a Community Under Siege* (Lanham, Md.: Taylor Trade, 2002), 159.

152. Perley, *History of Salem*, 2:252.

153. Francis, *Judge Sewall's Apology*, 25; Gaskill, *Between Two Worlds*, 293.

154. Perley, *History of Salem*, 3:91–92.

155. Salem, *Town Records*, 2:287–88.

156. It was at one time claimed that her nephew Thomas Towne served in the war, but recent research shows that he was conflated with another Thomas from Topsfield. Kyle F. Zelner, *A Rabble in Arms: Massachusetts Towns and Militiamen During King Philip's War* (New York: New York University Press, 2009), 91, 94, 267 note 138.

157. Town of Danvers, *Report of the Committee Appointed to Revise the Soldiers' Record* (Danvers, Mass.: Town of Danvers, 1895), 93; Eben Putnam, "Historical Sketch of Danvers," in *Danvers, Massachusetts: A Resume of Her Past History and Future Progress*, by Frank E. Moynahan (Danvers, Mass.: Danvers Mirror, 1899), 8.

158. Gaskill, *Between Two Worlds*, 283–284.

159. Taylor, *American Colonies*, 200.

160. Gaskill, *Between Two Worlds*, 278, 279, 287, 288.

161. Taylor, *American Colonies*, 201–202.

162. *EQC*, 6:191; Cotton Mather, *The Wonders of the Invisible World* (Boston: John Dunton, 1693), excerpted in *Narratives of the New England Witchcraft Cases*, ed. George Lincoln Burr (1914; repr., Mineola, N.Y.: Dover, 2002), 250.

163. *EQC*, 6:190.

164. *EQC*, 6:190–191.

CHAPTER 3: SALEM VILLAGE

Epigraph: Jeremiah Watts, "Letter to George Burroughs, April 11, 1682," in *Salem-Village Witchcraft: A Documentary Record of Local Conflict in Colonial New England*, ed. Paul Boyer and Stephen Nissenbaum (Boston: Northeastern University Press, 1993), 171.

1. Mortgage agreement in Suffolk County, *Suffolk Deeds*, 14 vols. (Boston: Rockwell and Churchill Press, 1880–1906), 11:10–13.

2. They were on the farm at least as early as June of that year, when Francis was sued for trespass as part of the boundary disputes. See *EQC*, 7:10.

3. Putnam, "Historical Sketch of Danvers," 3.

4. Upham, *Salem Witchcraft*, 30, 42.

5. Baker, *Storm of Witchcraft*, 77.

6. "Petition of Salem Farmers, 1667," reprinted in *Historical Collections of the Danvers Historical Society* 9 (1921): 116–119; Tapley, *Chronicles of Danvers*, 18. The training field still exists much as it did then, on Centre Street in Danvers.

7. Boyer and Nissenbaum, *Salem Possessed*, 39–40.

8. Tapley, *Chronicles of Danvers*, 16–17.

9. "Church Book Belonging to Salem Village 1689" (1689–1845), First Church of Danvers Congregational, deposited in the Danvers Archival Center, Danvers, Mass., 1–2, November 19, 1689. Hereafter "Salem Village Church Book." Both page number and date will be provided for each entry referenced.

10. Today, the former site of the meetinghouse is near the corner of Hobart St. and Forest St., across from the Salem Village Witchcraft Victims Memorial. Richard B. Trask, *The Meetinghouse at Salem Village* (Danvers, Mass.: Yeoman Press, 1992), 2.

11. "A Book of Record of the Severall Publique Transactions of the Inhabitants of Salem Village Vulgarly Called The Farmes" (1672–1712), Danvers Archival Center, Danvers, Mass., 20, September 11, 1684. Hereafter "Salem Village Record Book." Both page number and date will be provided for each entry referenced. Trask, *Meetinghouse*, 3–5, 11.

12. Trask, *Meetinghouse*, 5.

13. Earle, *Customs and Fashions*, 2.

14. Trask, *Meetinghouse*, 5.

15. Earle, *Sabbath in Puritan New England*, 19.

16. Tapley, *Chronicles of Danvers*, 21.

17. Danvers, *Soldiers' Record*, 94; Upham, *Salem Witchcraft*, 162; Rosenthal, *Records of the Salem Witch-Hunt*, Doc. 862.

18. Sidney Perley, "Endecott Land, Salem Village, in 1700," *Historical Collections of the Danvers Historical Society* 4 (1916): 118; Southern Essex Deeds, 31:227.

19. Dow, *Every Day Life*, 22–23.

20. There is no evidence that Rebecca Nurse's children John and Sarah ever lived on the village farm: both were married and had their own households before the family's move, and Sarah's children were born in Topsfield. Hoover, *Towne Family*, 13. Samuel Southwick presumably lived at the Nurse farm for about two years until he came of age and was able to claim his late father's estate: Caller and Ober, *Descendants of Lawrence and Cassandra Southwick*, 72. As to Nurse's other adoptee, little Elizabeth Clungen is absent from the historical record after she was left with the family in 1674. Rebecca's daughter Elizabeth lived on the farm only briefly, and moved out after her marriage in October 1678. Hoover, *Towne Family*, 14.

Those children who lived with Rebecca and Francis Nurse for longer periods of time include their son Francis Jr., who lived with them until his marriage in about 1685, after which he moved to Reading and had a son there in 1686: Hoover, *Towne Family*, 15. Their son Benjamin, along with his wife Tamsen after their 1688 marriage, lived with or near Rebecca and Francis until at least 1691 when their first child was born. Their first child was born in Salem Village, and sometime afterward they moved to Framingham. Salem, *Vital Records*, 2:116; Hoover, *Towne Family*, 17, 18.

21. Perley mentions the house, but on his map he places it on the wrong side of the Ipswich Road (present-day Ash Street), Perley, "Endecott Land, Salem Village, in 1700," map before page 99, 115; Town of Danvers, "103 Ash Street," Town of Danvers Property Assessment Data, accessed August 9, 2018, http://danvers.patriotproperties.com/Summary.asp?AccountNumber=7443.

22. Often incorrectly referred to as a lease, the payment agreement was a mortgage contract and the Nurses received the deed up front, something that a lessee would not receive. For mortgage agreement, see Suffolk County, *Suffolk Deeds*, 11:10–13. Records in these volumes are numbered by page number in the original deed book, not page number as reprinted. For transfer of deed, see Southern Essex Deeds, 4:643–646. For a contemporary handwritten copy, see "Copy of Deed to Nurse Farm" (April 29, 1678), Danvers Archival Center. Additionally, Francis subdivided the land to several family members by deed before the terms of the agreement were up, something a lessee also would not have had the power to do. See Deed to Thomas Preston, Southern Essex Deeds, 5:473–475; Deed to Samuel Nurse, Southern Essex Deeds, 5:475–477; Deed to John Tarbell, Southern Essex Deeds, 5:477–480.

23. Cotton Mather, *Memorable Providences Relating to Witchcrafts and Possessions* (Boston: Joseph Brunning, 1689), in *Narratives of the New England Witchcraft Cases*, ed. George Lincoln Burr (1914; repr., Mineola, N.Y.: Dover, 2002), 97.

24. Suffolk County, *Suffolk Deeds*, 11:10–13; Southern Essex Deeds, 4:643–646.

25. Salem, *Town Records*, 1:14–15; Copy of 1648 deed for the farm from Henry Chickering to John Endicott, which refers to a "mansion house" built by the first owner, Townsend Bishop, reprinted in *EQC*, 7:16. For information on how the Natives used the land prior

to the arrival of the settlers, see Jessica E. Watson, "Lithic Debitage and Settlement Patterns at the Rebecca Nurse Homestead," *Northeast Anthropology*, no. 81–82 (2014): 23–47.

26. Upham, *Salem Witchcraft*, 45.

27. Danvers, *Soldiers' Record*, 162.

28. Upham, *Salem Witchcraft*, 51–53.

29. Jonathan M. Chu, "Nursing A Poisonous Tree: Litigation and Property Law in Seventeenth-Century Essex County, Massachusetts: The Case of Bishop's Farm," *American Journal of Legal History* 31, no. 3 (July 1987): 224–238.

30. Chu, "Nursing a Poisonous Tree," 231.

31. Allen-Nurse Deed, Southern Essex Deeds, 4:644–646.

32. They were required to pay £7 per year for the first twelve years, then £10 per year for the remaining nine years. Suffolk County, *Suffolk Deeds*, 11:10–13.

33. Suffolk County, *Suffolk Deeds*, 11:12.

34. Upham, *Salem Witchcraft*, 56.

35. Rosenthal, *Records of the Salem Witch-Hunt*, Docs. 254, 373.

36. The misconception derives from two places. First, under the law in England at the time, executed felons' land would revert back to being owned by the king and could not be passed down to the next generation. But, English law had an exception forbidding this taking of land for convicted "witches," and most important, land forfeitures were illegal under Massachusetts law. Second, in 1692 Sheriff George Corwin did seize the personal property of eight men and women convicted of the felony charge of witchcraft, and from Giles Corey who stood mute at his trial and was killed under torture. Corwin also confiscated the personal goods of those who escaped from jail, though this was likely illegal under both English and Massachusetts law. David C. Brown, "The Forfeitures at Salem, 1692," *William and Mary Quarterly* 50, no. 1 (January 1993): 87–88, 91–96, 108.

37. Ulrich, *Good Wives*, 7.

38. Upham, *Salem Witchcraft*, 514.

39. Hoover, *Towne Family*, 14, 16.

40. Perley, "Endecott Land, Salem Village, in 1700," 113–115.

41. Dow, *The Probate Records of Essex County, Massachusetts*, 2:358.

42. This is the only inventory of Rebecca and Francis Nurse's belongings that exists, though it is very incomplete because the belongings of Francis in 1694, then an elderly widower, differ greatly from the family's belongings in 1678. Francis Nurse's will and his division of property in 1694 is reprinted in Boyer and Nissenbaum, *Salem-Village Witchcraft*, 153–154.

43. For more information on Sarah and her marriages, see Hoover, *Towne Family*, 397.

44. Dow, *The Probate Records of Essex County, Massachusetts*, 2:358.

45. Sarah Peabody Turnbaugh, "The Real Properties of Witches in the Salem Witchcraft Delusion of 1692," *Historical Collections of the Danvers Historical Society* 45 (1981): 25. Salem, for example, was required to perambulate its town boundaries annually since 1647, but did not actually do so until 1673, once land became scarce: Konig, *Law and Society*, 45.

46. Chu, "Nursing a Poisonous Tree," 223.

47. For case studies, see Konig, *Law and Society*, 55–63, and Chu, "Nursing a Poisonous Tree," 221–252; Upham, *Salem Witchcraft*, 57.

48. For this theory, see Konig, *Law and Society*, 55–57.

49. For this theory, see Chu, "Nursing a Poisonous Tree," 221–252.

50. Harold Putnam, *The Putnams of Salem Village*, 2nd ed. (Vero Beach, FL: Penobscot Press, 1997), 51.

51. *EQC*, 7:166.

52. Konig, *Law and Society*, 56.

53. *EQC*, 7:10.

54. *EQC*, 7:18–20, 10–11.

55. *EQC*, 7:11, 18.

56. John Noble, ed., *Records of the Court of Assistants of the Colony of Massachusetts Bay, 1630–1692*, vol. 1 (Boston: County of Suffolk, Mass., 1901), 1:120; Chu, "Nursing a Poisonous Tree," 234, 235; *EQC*, 8:120.

57. Chu, "Nursing a Poisonous Tree," 224–238; *EQC*, 8:116–121.

58. *EQC*, 9:5–6, 52–56.

59. Upham, *Salem Witchcraft*, 61.

60. *EQC*, 9:55.

61. Chu, "Nursing a Poisonous Tree," 240, 241.

62. Noble, *Records of the Court of Assistants*, 235–236; Chu, "Nursing a Poisonous Tree," 241.

63. Upham, *Salem Witchcraft*, 62.

64. *EQC*, 9:258.

65. The other two acres were in a far corner of the farm bordering Joseph Holten's land. Suffolk County, *Suffolk Deeds*, 13:238–239.

66. Rosenthal, *Records of the Salem Witch-Hunt*, Docs. 254, 373.

67. Southern Essex Deeds, 1:35; Hoover, *Towne Family*, 2.

68. Upham, *Salem Witchcraft*, 158–159.

69. Upham, *Salem Witchcraft*, 160.

70. Quoted in George Francis Dow, *History of Topsfield Massachusetts* (Topsfield, Mass.: Topsfield Historical Society, 1940), 49.

71. Topsfield Historical Society Historical Records Committee and Topsfield Witch Trials Tercentenary Committee, *Topsfield and the Witchcraft Tragedy*, 1–3.

72. Konig, *Law and Society*, 105.

73. Upham, *Salem Witchcraft*, 160; Dow, *History of Topsfield*, 323.

74. Howe, *Puritan Republic*, 111, 156.

75. Harriet S. Tapley, "Old Tavern Days in Danvers," *Historical Collections of the Danvers Historical Society* 8 (1920): 4; Howe, *Puritan Republic*, 104; Rosenthal, *Records of the Salem Witch-Hunt*, Doc. 862.

76. Roach, *The Salem Witch Trials*, 140.

77. Tapley, "Old Tavern Days in Danvers," 5–6.

78. *EQC*, 7:106.

79. *EQC*, 7:155.

80. Benton, *Town House*, 167–168.

81. *EQC*, 7:195; Salem, *Town Records*, 3:16, 165; *EQC*, 8:222–226.

82. "Salem Village Record Book," 19, April 17, 1684, and 21, December 18, 1684.

83. Upham, *Salem Witchcraft*, 141.

84. Salem, *Town Records*, 3: 97, 151, 170, 231. For other references to men being paid for their work and that of their "boy," see Salem, *Town Records*, 3:147, 166, 195, 219, 220, 221, 231, 264. These references to a "boy" likely refer to a hired hand and not a slave because of the high frequency of their mention in the town record book, whereas there were only very few slaves in the area at this time. Furthermore, with the Nurse family's financial trouble it is highly unlikely that they would be able to purchase a slave, a great expense

that only the wealthiest households could afford. Last, toward the end of Francis Nurse's life there was a female hired servant working in the household, so it is plausible that prior to that they had a male hired servant working in the fields with Francis.

85. *EQC*, 9:247. For their agreement with Rev. Allen, see Suffolk County, *Suffolk Deeds*, 11:10–13.

86. Salem, *Town Records*, 3:32.

87. Chu, "Nursing a Poisonous Tree," 242.

88. "Salem Village Record Book," 13, December 27, 1681.

89. "Salem Village Record Book," 18, January 17, 1683/4.

90. Benjamin C. Ray, *Satan and Salem: The Witch-Hunt Crisis of 1692* (Charlottesville: University of Virginia Press, 2015), 126.

91. Tapley, *Chronicles of Danvers*, 119.

92. Konig, *Law and Society*, 105.

93. "Salem Village Record Book," 6, November 11, 1672.

94. Baker, *Storm of Witchcraft*, 81.

95. Sidney Perley, ed., "Bailey-Bayley Genealogies," *Essex Antiquarian* 5 (1901): 123.

96. "Salem Village Record Book," 7–8, November 7, 1673; Baker, *Storm of Witchcraft*, 83; "Salem Village Record Book," 9, see receipts written by James Bailey below the entry dated January 15, 1673.

97. Roach, *The Salem Witch Trials*, xxviii.

98. Quoted in Upham, *Salem Witchcraft*, 164.

99. Baker, *Storm of Witchcraft*, 81.

100. "Salem Village Record Book," 12, April 6, 1680.

101. Upham, *Salem Witchcraft*, 168; Danvers, *Soldiers' Record*, 93.

102. Rosenthal, *Records of the Salem Witch-Hunt*, Doc. 96.

103. "Salem Village Record Book," 12, April 6, 1680; 10, November 25 and February 16, 1680, and 13, December 27, 1681. For Burroughs' background, see Baker, *Storm of Witchcraft*, 81–82.

104. *EQC*, 9:48, 30–32.

105. *EQC*, 9:48.

106. Rosenthal, *Records of the Salem Witch-Hunt*, Doc. 126.

107. *EQC*, 9:47–49.

108. "Salem Village Record Book," 18, January 17, 1683/4; 20, September 11, 1684.

109. "Salem Village Record Book," 22–23, February 2, 1684/5; 24, March 20, 1684/5.

110. "Salem Village Record Book," 26, June 3, 1685.

111. Tapley, "Old Tavern Days in Danvers," 5.

112. Earle, *Sabbath in Puritan New England*, 48.

113. "Salem Village Record Book," 26, June 3, 1685.

114. A. Whitney Griswold, "Three Puritans on Prosperity," *New England Quarterly* 7, no. 3 (1934): 477–483.

115. The records of Salem Town describe where Rebecca sat when she attended the services and Lord's Supper there each month. In 1686, she sat next to the wife of George Lockiar, who like Francis was appointed to many town positions. Salem, *Town Records*, 3:151. For some of Lockiar's elected roles, see Salem, *Town Records*, 3:182, 204, 215, 242.

116. Eben Putnam, *A History of the Putnam Family in England and America* (Salem, Mass.: Salem Press, 1891), 7; Rosenthal, *Records of the Salem Witch-Hunt*, Doc. 35; Putnam, *The Putnams of Salem Village*, 41.

117. First Church of Salem, *The Records of the First Church in Salem*, 39.
118. For Sarah Cloyce, see "Salem Village Church Book," 3, January 12, 1689/90; For Samuel Nurse, his wife Mary, John Tarbell, and Mary (Nurse) Tarbell, see "Salem Village Church Book," 4, March 2, 1689/90.

CHAPTER 4: THE FALL

Epigraph: Cotton Mather, *The Present State of New England Considered in a Discourse on the Necessities and Advantages of a Public Spirit in Every Man; Especially, at Such a Time as This* (Boston: Samuel Green, 1690), 35.
1. Conforti, *Saints and Strangers*, 99.
2. Kenneth Silverman, *Selected Letters of Cotton Mather* (Baton Rouge: Louisiana State University Press, 1971), 13.
3. Benton, *Town House*, 170.
4. Sewall, *Diary*, 1:70.
5. Dow, *History of Topsfield*, 323.
6. Rosenthal, *Records of the Salem Witch-Hunt*, Doc. 23.
7. For John Putnam owning the land, see Baker, *Storm of Witchcraft*, 83. For the petition, see Rosenthal, *Records of the Salem Witch-Hunt*, Doc. 254.
8. Rosenthal, *Records of the Salem Witch-Hunt*, Doc. 373.
9. Some historians over the decades have incorrectly noted Rebecca as being from Topsfield to further tie her into this dispute. For one example, see Boyer and Nissenbaum, *Salem Possessed*, 149. But, she married Francis Nurse and began her own family in Salem years before her parents and siblings moved to Topsfield. Additionally, it has been noted that on two occasions at village meetings members of Rebecca's family voted against pressing the village's land claims against Topsfield, ostensibly siding with their kin in Topsfield (Upham, *Salem Witchcraft*, 354). But, these votes occurred after the witch hunt. Thomas Preston and Samuel Nurse voted no in April 1694, and Francis Nurse, Samuel Nurse, John Tarbell, and Thomas Preston voted no in November 1694 ("Salem Village Record Book," 60, April 30, 1694, and 63, November 30, 1694). These votes could be a reaction to the events of the witch hunt, rather than a cause. Also, the specific vote at hand was for the village to sue the Topsfield landholders—the Nurses' cousins—so it is hardly a surprise that the family was unwilling to sue their own relatives. In both cases, the dissenting Nurse family members specifically asked the village clerk, Thomas Putnam Jr., to write in the village record book that they opposed the motions.
10. Topsfield Historical Society Historical Records Committee and Topsfield Witch Trials Tercentenary Committee, *Topsfield and the Witchcraft Tragedy*, 3–4, 7.
11. Rosenthal, *Records of the Salem Witch-Hunt*, Doc. 79.
12. Roach, *The Salem Witch Trials*, xxvii; Lockyer, *Tudor and Stuart Britain*, 430.
13. Carla Gardina Pestana, *Protestant Empire: Religion and the Making of the British Atlantic World* (Philadelphia: University of Pennsylvania Press, 2009), 152.
14. Taylor, *American Colonies*, 276.
15. Hutchinson, *The History of the Province of Massachusetts-Bay*, 1:353.
16. Conforti, *Saints and Strangers*, 118–119.
17. Edward Howland, *Annals of North America, Being A Concise Account of the Important Events in the United States, the British Provinces, and Mexico* (Hartford: J. B. Burr, 1877), 145.
18. Albert W. Matthews, "Notes on the Massachusetts Royal Commissions, 1681–1775," *Publications of the Colonial Society of Massachusetts* 17 (1915):7; Benton, *Town House*, x.

19. Roach, *The Salem Witch Trials*, xxviii.

20. Baker, *Storm of Witchcraft*, 58; Taylor, *American Colonies*, 277–278.

21. Emerson W. Baker and John G. Reid, *The New England Knight: Sir William Phips, 1651–1695* (Toronto: University of Toronto Press, 1998), 65.

22. Silverman, *Selected Letters of Cotton Mather*, 20.

23. Baker, *Storm of Witchcraft*, 55–56; Gaskill, *Between Two Worlds*, 346–347; Taylor, *American Colonies*, 277.

24. Baker, *Storm of Witchcraft*, 55.

25. Quoted in Taylor, *American Colonies*, 277.

26. William Cronon, *Changes in the Land: Indians, Colonists, and the Ecology of New England* (New York: Hill and Wang, 1983), 136.

27. Rosenthal, *Records of the Salem Witch-Hunt*, Doc. 358.

28. Rosenthal, *Records of the Salem Witch-Hunt*, Doc. 358.

29. General Court of Massachusetts, *Charters and General Laws*, 35.

30. Konig, *Law and Society*, 181.

31. Rosenthal, *Records of the Salem Witch-Hunt*, Doc. 358.

32. Cronon, *Changes in the Land*, 135.

33. Fels, *Switching Sides*, 25.

34. Upham, *Salem Witchcraft*, 179.

35. Quoted in Upham, *Salem Witchcraft*, 180.

36. Quoted in Upham, *Salem Witchcraft*, 180.

37. Fels, *Switching Sides*, 25–26.

38. Larry Gragg, *A Quest for Security: The Life of Samuel Parris, 1653–1720* (New York: Greenwood Press, 1990), 1–17, 33.

39. Gragg, *Quest for Security*, 46–49.

40. Upham, *Salem Witchcraft*, 191–192; Gragg, *Quest for Security*, 46.

41. "Salem Village Record Book," 45–46, June 18, 1689.

42. Quoted in Upham, *Salem Witchcraft*, 195.

43. Upham, *Salem Witchcraft*, 195; "Salem Village Record Book," 46, June 18, 1689.

44. Boyer and Nissenbaum, *Salem Possessed*, 153.

45. Samuel Parris, *The Sermon Notebook of Samuel Parris, 1689–1694*, ed. James F. Cooper, Jr. and Kenneth P. Minkema (Boston: Colonial Society of Massachusetts, 1993), 38.

46. "Salem Village Church Book," 1, November 19, 1689.

47. David A. Weir, *Early New England: A Covenanted Society* (Grand Rapids, Mich.: William B. Eerdmans, 2005), 166–167.

48. For Sarah Cloyce, see "Salem Village Church Book," 3, January 12, 1689/90. For Samuel Nurse, John Tarbell, and Mary (Nurse) Tarbell, see "Salem Village Church Book," 4, March 2, 1689/90. For Samuel Nurse's wife Mary, see "Salem Village Church Book," 4, March 23, 1689/90.

49. Boyer and Nissenbaum state: "There is a clear connection between membership in the Salem Village church and support for Samuel Parris." Boyer and Nissenbaum, *Salem Possessed*, 81. These members of the Nurse family joined the village church—and put their support for Parris and his church on record—even before Ann Putnam Sr., wife of Thomas Putnam Jr., who along with her daughter Ann Putnam Jr. were among the first and most vocal accusers of Rebecca Nurse in 1692. Ann Putnam Sr. did not join the village church until June 1691. "Salem Village Church Book," 6, June 4, 1691. This implicit support for Parris by members of the Nurse family is counter to Boyer and Nissenbaum's portrayal of the family as being opposed to Rev. Parris.

50. Ray, *Satan and Salem*, 22; "Salem Village Record Book," 47–48, below entry for December 17, 1689. Some historians caution about reading too much into this lack of payment; because of the difficulty of collecting taxes during this time of political turmoil at the colony level, not paying taxes on time was fairly common, and several of these non-paying individuals joined the church soon after and so were likely not opponents of Parris. See Roach, *The Salem Witch Trials*, xxxix; Fels, *Switching Sides*, 39 note 29.

51. It appears as though Parris omitted this part when reading it to the congregation. Parris, *Sermon Notebook*, 126 and note 26.

52. Roach, *The Salem Witch Trials*, xxxv.

53. The foundation is located at the Salem Village Parsonage Archeological Site, behind Centre St. in Danvers. For more on the parsonage, see Richard B. Trask, "Raising the Devil," *Yankee Magazine*, May 1972, 74–77, 190–201; Sharon S. McKern, "They're Digging up Witch Lore in Salem," *Science Digest*, May 1971, 27–28, 32–34.

54. Gragg, *Quest for Security*, 49; Upham, *Salem Witchcraft*, 194–198.

55. David D. Hall, *The Faithful Shepherd: A History of the New England Ministry* (Williamsburg, Va.: Institute of Early American History and Culture, 1972), 193.

56. "Salem Village Record Book," 46, June 18, 1689.

57. "Salem Village Record Book," 47, October 10, 1689.

58. Silverman, *Selected Letters of Cotton Mather*, 14; John Murrin, "Coming to Terms with the Salem Witch Trials," *Proceedings of the American Antiquarian Society* 110, no. 2 (2000): 322.

59. Taylor, *American Colonies*. 277.

60. Sewall, *Diary*, 1:175.

61. Lockyer, *Tudor and Stuart Britain*, 361–362.

62. Mather, *Memorable Providences*, 106–110.

63. Charles W. Upham, *Lectures on Witchcraft, Comprising a History of the Delusion in Salem in 1692*, 2nd ed. (Boston: Carter and Hendee, 1832), 182–183.

64. Peter Charles Hoffer, *The Devil's Disciples: Makers of the Salem Witchcraft Trials* (Baltimore: Johns Hopkins University Press, 1996), 60.

65. Mary Rezac, "Was the Last 'Witch' of Boston Actually a Catholic Martyr?," Catholic News Agency, accessed January 6, 2018, http://www.catholicnewsagency.com/news/was-the-last-witch-of-boston-actually-a-catholic-martyr–27747/.

66. Calef in Mather, *Memorable Providences*, 124 note 1.

67. Upham, *Lectures on Witchcraft*, 12–13; Dow, *Every Day Life*, 147.

68. Roach, *The Salem Witch Trials*, xxxv.

69. William Henry Whitmore, ed., *The Andros Tracts*, vol. 1 (Boston: Prince Society, 1868), 1:90.

70. Taylor, *American Colonies*, 280; Benton, *Town House*, 183.

71. Taylor, *American Colonies*, 278; Lockyer, *Tudor and Stuart Britain*, 361–364.

72. Baker and Reid, *New England Knight*, 74; Matthews, "Massachusetts Royal Commissions," 17:18, 19.

73. Boyer and Nissenbaum, *Salem Possessed*, 92–93, 114–116, 185.

74. Latner, "Salem Witchcraft, Factionalism, and Social Change Reconsidered," 434–435, 439–440, 444; Ray, *Satan and Salem*, 188; Ray, "Geography of Witchcraft Accusations," 453.

75. Even Boyer and Nissenbaum describe the area in which the Nurse family lived in the western part of Salem Town as agricultural: Boyer and Nissenbaum, *Salem Possessed*, 88 note 14.

76. Francis Nurse was elected to a committee to negotiate town status for Salem Village in August 1689 along with John Putnam Sr., Nathaniel Putnam, and others: "Salem Village Record Book," 46, August 23, 1689. The following year, Francis Nurse, along with John Putnam Sr., Thomas Putnam Jr., and two others, were chosen by a village meeting to write a petition to the General Court asking to eliminate the villagers' responsibility to pay taxes toward the maintenance of the Salem Town meetinghouse, because they had their own village meetinghouse to maintain: "Salem Village Record Book," 50, December 9, 1690. Last, prior to the witch hunt, the village named Francis Nurse, John Putnam Sr., Nathaniel Putnam, and two others to a committee to attend the all-Salem town meeting in January 1692 to petition for village independence: "Salem Village Record Book," 57, January 8, 1691/2.

77. Ray, "Geography of Witchcraft Accusations," 475.

78. Boyer and Nissenbaum list Preston as a "defender" in 1692. Boyer and Nissenbaum, *Salem Possessed*, 34. See also Benjamin C. Ray's georegistered version of Upham's map of Salem Village: Ray, "Geography of Witchcraft Accusations," 455.

79. Rosenthal, *Records of the Salem Witch-Hunt*, Doc. 1.

80. Boyer and Nissenbaum, *Salem Possessed*, 149.

81. Mather, *Magnalia*, book VII, 82.

82. Hoffer, *Devil's Disciples*, 57–58.

83. Roach, *The Salem Witch Trials*, 326 and 464.

84. Quoted in Stacy Schiff, *The Witches: Salem, 1692* (New York: Little, Brown, 2015), 389.

85. Samuel P. Fowler, ed., "Rev. Samuel Parris' Records of Deaths at Salem Village During His Ministry," *New England Historical and Genealogical Register* 36 (1847): 188; Danvers, *Soldiers' Record*, 96; Tapley, *Chronicles of Danvers*, 21.

86. Upham, *Salem Witchcraft*, 6.

87. Quoted in Konig, *Law and Society*, 167.

88. Norton, *In the Devil's Snare*, 102–103; Roach, *The Salem Witch Trials*, xxxix–xl.

89. The four men were Thomas Alsot, Edward Crocker, and George Bogwell. Fowler, "Rev. Samuel Parris' Records of Deaths at Salem Village during His Ministry," 188.

90. Baker and Reid, *New England Knight*, 84.

91. Baker, *Storm of Witchcraft*, 11.

92. United States Works Progress Administration and Archie N. Frost, eds., *Verbatim Transcriptions of the Records of the Quarterly Courts of Essex County Massachusetts, 1636–1694*, 57 vols., 1936, 57:65–2. This collection is numbered by volume, then by file (or so it appears), and then by page number.

93. Zelner, *Rabble in Arms*, 53.

94. Zelner, *Rabble in Arms*, 64.

95. "An Act to Authorize the President to Increase Temporarily the Military Establishment of the United States," Pub. L. No. 65–12, § 3, 40 U.S. Statutes at Large 76 (1917), 78.

96. United States Works Progress Administration and Frost, *Verbatim Transcriptions of the Records of the Quarterly Courts of Essex County*, 57:65–2.

97. Roach, *The Salem Witch Trials*, xliv; Cotton Mather, *Decennium Luctuosum: An History of Remarkable Occurrences, in the Long War, Which New-England Hath Had with the Indian Savages, from the Year 1688 To the Year 1698* (Boston: Samuel Phillips, 1699), 83; Lawrence Hammond, *Diary Kept by Capt. Lawrence Hammond of Charlestown, Mass., 1677–1694*, ed. Samuel A. Green (Cambridge, Mass.: John Wilson and Son, 1892), 157.

98. Richard B. Trask, *The Devil Hath Been Raised: A Documentary History of the Salem Village Witchcraft Outbreak of March 1692* (West Kennebunk, Me.: Phoenix, 1992), 123.

99. Samuel Nurse bought 50 acres of land worth £60s10, Preston bought 52 acres worth £63s15, and Tarbell bought 50 acres worth £60s10. Southern Essex Deeds, 5:473–475, 475–477, 477–480; Perley, "Endecott Land, Salem Village, in 1700," 113–114. For later payments to Allen, see James Allen, "Receipts, May 18, 1698 & April 24, 1699," Danvers Archival Center.

100. "Salem Village Record Book," 51, below entry for January 6, 1690/1.

101. Salem, *Town Records*, 3:218, 263.

102. "Salem Village Record Book," 45, April 7, 1687; Salem, *Town Records*, 3:223; James Savage, *A Genealogical Dictionary of the First Settlers of New England Showing Three Generations of Those Who Came before May, 1692, on the Basis of Farmer's Register*, 4 vols. (Boston: Little, Brown, and Company, 1862), 3:300.

103. "Salem Village Record Book," 49, September 23, 1690.

104. Salem, *Town Records*, 3:242 and 3:252.

105. Chu, "Nursing a Poisonous Tree," 245.

106. Chu, "Nursing a Poisonous Tree," 246 and note 97. Jonathan M. Chu points out that although the records and files of the court do not state who won or lost the 1690 suits, it appears as though Endicott lost both cases because he was charged court costs for them, which losers in civil suits were required to pay. See Chu, "Nursing a Poisonous Tree," 247 and note 101.

107. Chu, "Nursing a Poisonous Tree," 249, 250; Perley, "Endecott Land, Salem Village, in 1700," 112.

108. Boyer and Nissenbaum, *Salem Possessed*, 185.

109. Boyer and Nissenbaum describe Francis Nurse as an "anti-Parris leader" and the entire village committee elected in 1691 (of which Francis Nurse was a member) as "the anti-Parris Village Committee." Boyer and Nissenbaum, *Salem Possessed*, 149, chart on 184.

110. See Boyer and Nissenbaum, *Salem Possessed*, 114. For Parris testifying against Rebecca Nurse, see Rosenthal, *Records of the Salem Witch-Hunt*, Docs. 360, 361.

111. Boyer and Nissenbaum dismiss out of hand the idea that the witch hunt changed villagers' views on disputes in the village such as the controversy surrounding Parris. "The witchcraft episode did not generate the divisions within the Village, nor did it shift them in any fundamental way, but it laid bare the intensity with which they were experienced and heightened the vindictiveness with which they were expressed." This claim that the witch hunt—almost a year of chaos, upheaval, and fear, in which Parris played a key role—did not have a significant effect on villagers' views of Parris is just not plausible. Boyer and Nissenbaum, *Salem Possessed*, 69. Tony Fels discusses other ways that Boyer and Nissenbaum use evidence from after 1692 to support the factionalism theory: Fels, *Switching Sides*, 26–27.

112. Fels, *Switching Sides*, 29.

113. Upham, *Salem Witchcraft*, 191–192.

114. See Chapter 11.

115. Petition reprinted in Boyer and Nissenbaum, *Salem-Village Witchcraft*, 266.

116. Boyer and Nissenbaum, *Salem Possessed*, 182 note 1.

117. Nurse was noted in a court record as sitting in the same Village meetinghouse seat as Mary Veren Putnam. These seats were assigned for Sunday religious services, and therefore Rebecca Nurse must have attended Sunday services with the Village church. Rosenthal, *Records of the Salem Witch-Hunt*, Doc. 35.

118. "Salem Village Record Book," 49, October 28, 1690, and 51, January 6, 1691. For the deed being lost, see "Salem Village Record Book," 22–23, February 2, 1684/5.

119. "Salem Village Record Book," 13, December 27, 1681, and 47, October 10, 1689; Upham, *Salem Witchcraft*, 194.

120. See deed reprinted in Boyer and Nissenbaum, *Salem-Village Witchcraft*, 267–268.

121. Tony Fels places this revelation earlier, in 1690, because of how he dates a contentious meeting described in a later deposition that partly deals with that issue. Instead, I place that meeting as occurring in December 1691, which will be discussed below. If my interpretation of the timing of the contentious meeting holds true, then no action was taken on the issue of the parsonage conveyance until the fall of 1691, and therefore it is likely that sometime that fall the issue first became publicly known. Fels, *Switching Sides*, 26 and note 21.

122. "Salem Village Record Book," 54–55, April 3, 1691.

123. See "Salem Village Church Book," 5–11, June 8, 1690, through March 25, 1692. Boyer and Nissenbaum also consider this slowed rate of villagers seeking admittance to the church in the second half of 1690 and 1691 as showing a decline in support for Parris. Boyer and Nissenbaum, *Salem Possessed*, 66.

124. "Salem Village Church Book," 9, October 8, 1691.

125. Upham, *Salem Witchcraft*, 209.

126. "Salem Village Record Book," 55, October 16 and December 1, 1691; Robert Calef notes the issue of parsonage ownership as the key issue that caused opposition to Rev. Parris. See Calef, *More Wonders*, 341.

127. Fels, *Switching Sides*, 28, 39 note 29.

128. "Salem Village Record Book," 55, October 16, 1691.

129. "Salem Village Church Book," 9, November 2, 1691.

130. "Salem Village Church Book," 9, November 2 and 10, 1691.

131. For the call to meeting, see "Salem Village Church Book," 10, November 15, 1691.

132. "Salem Village Church Book," 10, November 18, 1691.

133. Parris, *Sermon Notebook*, 176.

134. James F. Cooper, Jr. and Kenneth P. Minkema, "Introduction," in *The Sermon Notebook of Samuel Parris, 1689–1694*, by Samuel Parris, Publications of the Colonial Society of Massachusetts 66 (Boston: Colonial Society of Massachusetts, 1993), 20; Gragg, *Quest for Security*, 100.

135. Boyer and Nissenbaum, *Salem-Village Witchcraft*, 163–167.

136. "Salem Village Record Book," 55, December 1, 1691.

137. Roach, *The Salem Witch Trials*, xlvi.

138. Marilynne K. Roach notes that this deposition might relate to the December 1, 1691, village meeting (Roach, *The Salem Witch Trials*, xlvi). Parris' biographer Larry Gragg instead connects this deposition to a meeting in 1690 (Gragg, *Quest for Security*, 96–97). Since the meeting deals with Parris' contract, in particular a mutual agreement between Parris and the village meeting that no contract existed any further between them, it likely references the December 1691 meeting. Up until this point there is no hint that Parris' contract was voided, and he was paid—or at least it was recognized that he was supposed to be paid—according to the original contract terms. Therefore, it is unlikely that his contract was cancelled prior to this point. Also, the men writing the deposition describing the village meeting were all on the 1691 village committee that called the December 1691 meeting. Finally, the deposition states that the described meeting occurred "a considerable time" after Parris' ordination, and placing it in 1690 as Gragg does, only one year after

the ordination, does not seem to fit with the amount of time that would have passed. Though "a considerable time" is certainly a vague reference point.

139. Deposition reprinted in Upham, *Salem Witchcraft*, 196–197, including quotation marks.

140. Deposition reprinted in Upham, *Salem Witchcraft*, 196–197.

141. This decline in baptisms and new church members continued even past the end of the witch hunt. See Gragg, *Quest for Security*, 89–90.

CHAPTER 5: THE DEVIL HATH BEEN RAISED

Epigraph: John Milton, *Paradise Lost: A Poem in Twelve Books* (London: J. M. Dent, 1904), 1.249–255.

1. Parris, *Sermon Notebook*, 183.

2. Parris, *Sermon Notebook*, 185.

3. Roach, *The Salem Witch Trials*, 7.

4. Baker, *Storm of Witchcraft*, 304 note 3.

5. Calef, *More Wonders*, 341–342.

6. Lawson, *A Brief and True Narrative*, excerpted in *Narratives of the New England Witchcraft Cases*, ed. George Lincoln Burr (Mineola, N.Y.: Dover, 2002), 162.

7. John Hale, *A Modest Enquiry Into the Nature of Witchcraft* (Boston: Benjamin Elliot, 1702), in *Narratives of the New England Witchcraft Cases*, ed. George Lincoln Burr (1914; repr., Mineola, N.Y.: Dover, 2002), 413.

8. Roach, *The Salem Witch Trials*, 7.

9. George Burroughs, "Rev. George Burroughs et al., to Governor and Council," in *Documentary History of the State of Maine*, ed. James Phinney Baxter, vol. 5, Collections of the Maine Historical Society 2 (Portland: Maine Historical Society, 1897), 316.

10. Roach, *The Salem Witch Trials*, 9.

11. Johnson, *Wonder-Working Providence*, 122.

12. Roach, *The Salem Witch Trials*, 9.

13. Sewall, *Diary*, 1:356.

14. Baker, *Storm of Witchcraft*, 136.

15. "Salem Village Church Book," 11, March 27, 1692.

16. For the theory of the witch hunt as a conspiracy, see Enders A. Robinson, *The Devil Discovered: Salem Witchcraft 1692* (New York: Hippocrene Books, 1991), 109, 110–116.

17. Hale, *Modest Enquiry*, 413.

18. Hale, *Modest Enquiry*, 413. See also: Calef, *More Wonders*, 341–342 and note.

19. Upham, *Salem Witchcraft*, 321.

20. John Putnam Demos, *Entertaining Satan: Witchcraft and the Culture of Early New England* (Oxford: Oxford University Press, 1982), 425 note 11.

21. Upham, *Salem Witchcraft*, 269–270; Peleg W. Chandler, *American Criminal Trials*, 2 vols. (Boston: Charles C. Little and James Brown, 1844), 1:97.

22. Hale, *Modest Enquiry*, 411.

23. Karlsen, *The Devil in the Shape of a Woman*, 2.

24. Bengt Ankarloo, Stuart Clark, and William Monter, *Witchcraft and Magic in Europe: The Period of the Witch Trials* (London: Athlone Press, 2002), 166.

25. Upham, *Lectures on Witchcraft*, 181.

26. Hansen, *Witchcraft at Salem*, 19–20; Sarah Rivett, "Our Salem, Our Selves," *William and Mary Quarterly* 65, no. 3 (2008): 500. In addition to Mather's use of empiricism when

examining the actions of the afflicted, Richard Weisman writes, "The Court of Oyer and Terminer had organized the most cautiously empirical and systematic investigation into witchcraft ever to occur in New England." See Richard Weisman, *Witchcraft, Magic, and Religion in 17th-Century Massachusetts* (Amherst: University of Massachusetts Press, 1984), 179.

27. Rivett, "Our Salem, Our Selves," 501–502.

28. John Wagstaffe, *The Question of Witchcraft Debated, or a Discourse Against Their Opinions That Affirm Witches* (London: Edward Millington, 1669).

29. Upham, *Lectures on Witchcraft*, 213.

30. Rosemary Ellen Guiley, *The Encyclopedia of Witches, Witchcraft & Wicca*, 3rd ed. (New York: Facts on File, 2008), 380.

31. Sadakat Kadri, *The Trial: A History from Socrates to O. J. Simpson* (New York: Random House, 2005), 125.

32. "Witchcraft," UK Parliament, accessed August 24, 2017, http://www.parliament.uk/about/living-heritage/transformingsociety/private-lives/religion/overview/witchcraft/.

33. Demos, *Entertaining Satan*, 11.

34. Rev. Parris, in a church record a few weeks later, only notes John Indian as being part of this supposed magic charm, see "Salem Village Church Book," 10–11, March 27, 1692. Rev. Lawson, writing later that spring, however, notes Tituba as also being involved, as does Rev. Hale writing several years later; see Lawson, *A Brief and True Narrative*, 162–163, and Hale, *Modest Enquiry*, 413.

35. One common misconception is that Tituba practiced fortune-telling and taught several young women in the village "voodoo" or similarly viewed magical practices. There is no evidence of this. For an examination of this misconception and how it was repeated over the centuries, see Bernard Rosenthal, *Salem Story: Reading the Witch Trials of 1692* (Cambridge: Cambridge University Press, 1995), 10–14. See also Norton, *In the Devil's Snare*, 23–24.

36. Upham, *Salem Witchcraft*, 339.

37. Rosenthal, *Records of the Salem Witch-Hunt*, Doc. 31.

38. Rosenthal, *Records of the Salem Witch-Hunt*, Docs. 11, 12.

39. Hale, *Modest Enquiry*, 414.

40. Roach, *The Salem Witch Trials*, 19 and note.

41. Hale, *Modest Enquiry*, 414.

42. Hale, *Modest Enquiry*, 414.

43. Rosenthal, *Records of the Salem Witch-Hunt*, Docs. 9, 345, 10.

44. Norton, *In the Devil's Snare*, 22.

45. Sewall, *Diary*, 1:357; Hammond, *Diary*, 19.

46. Richard B. Trask, "Legal Procedures Used During the Salem Witch Trials and a Brief History of the Published Versions of the Records," in *Records of the Salem Witch Hunt*, ed. Bernard Rosenthal (New York: Cambridge University Press, 2009), 45.

47. Baker, *Storm of Witchcraft*, 98.

48. Rosenthal, *Records of the Salem Witch-Hunt*, Docs. 1, 2.

49. Hammond, *Diary*, 19.

50. Higginson in Hale, *Modest Enquiry*, 400.

51. Roach, *The Salem Witch Trials*, 25.

52. "Salem Village Record Book," 57, January 28, 1691/2.

53. See Calef's description of Good and Osborne in *More Wonders*, 393.

54. For a discussion of several theories regarding Tituba's background, see Roach, *Six Women of Salem*, 62–75.

55. Rosenthal, *Records of the Salem Witch-Hunt*, Doc. 345; Roach, *The Salem Witch Trials*, 13–14.

56. Roach, *The Salem Witch Trials*, 20.

57. Rosenthal, *Records of the Salem Witch-Hunt*, Doc. 4.

58. Rosenthal, *Salem Story*, 16.

59. Rosenthal, *Records of the Salem Witch-Hunt*, Doc. 14.

60. Rosenthal, *Records of the Salem Witch-Hunt*, Doc. 4.

61. See Rosenthal, *Salem Story*, 16.

62. Rosenthal, *Records of the Salem Witch-Hunt*, Doc. 5.

63. Hale, *Modest Enquiry*, 415.

64. Calef, *More Wonders*, 343.

65. Ray, *Satan and Salem*, 38–39; Hoffer, *Devil's Disciples*, 114.

66. Rosenthal, *Records of the Salem Witch-Hunt*, Doc. 3.

67. Hale, *Modest Enquiry*, 415.

68. Upham, *Lectures on Witchcraft*, 46.

69. Hale, *Modest Enquiry*, 415.

70. Rosenthal, *Records of the Salem Witch-Hunt*, Docs. 3, 136.

71. Benjamin C. Ray notes this turning point in *Satan and Salem*, 115.

72. Rosenthal, *Records of the Salem Witch-Hunt*, Doc. 14.

73. Deodat Lawson, "Deodat Lawson's Narrative," in *Salem Witchcraft: With an Account of Salem Village and A History of Opinions on Witchcraft and Kindred Subjects*, by Charles W. Upham (1867; repr., Mineola, N.Y.: Dover, 2000), 685–686.

74. The Porter, Cloyce, and Andrew visit later in March shows that Rebecca knew of the afflicted villagers. Rosenthal, *Records of the Salem Witch-Hunt*, Doc. 31.

75. Calef, *More Wonders*, 342.

76. Hale, *Modest Enquiry*, 414.

77. Ray, *Satan and Salem*, 29.

78. Gragg, *Quest for Security*, 117.

79. Benjamin C. Ray posits that perhaps Williams' accusations were useful to Parris so he kept her in the village, but that apparently he was unwilling to risk his own daughter: Ray, *Satan and Salem*, 29.

80. Gragg, *Quest for Security*, 125.

81. Roach, *The Salem Witch Trials*, 37–39.

82. *EQC*, 6:191.

83. *EQC*, 7:147; Roach, *The Salem Witch Trials*, 41.

84. Roach, *The Salem Witch Trials*, 37.

85. Roach, *The Salem Witch Trials*, 39; Rosenthal, *Records of the Salem Witch-Hunt*, Doc. 21.

86. Rosenthal, *Records of the Salem Witch-Hunt*, Docs. 291, 35.

87. For the total number of afflicted, see Baker, *Storm of Witchcraft*, 11.

88. Karlsen, *The Devil in the Shape of a Woman*, 223.

89. Karlsen, *The Devil in the Shape of a Woman*, 224.

90. Marion L. Starkey, *The Devil in Massachusetts: A Modern Enquiry into the Salem Witch Trials* (1949; repr. New York: Anchor Books, 1989), 45. Among those in the latter category are Bernard Rosenthal: Rosenthal, *Salem Story*, 18; Mary Beth Norton, who suggests that

the original fits of the young early afflicted were genuine, but admits uncertainty as to what caused them: Norton, *In the Devil's Snare*, 307; Frances Hill, who describes the cause of the fits as "a mixture of hysteria, vengeful fury, evil mischief, and longing": Frances Hill, *A Delusion of Satan: The Full Story of the Salem Witch Trials*, 2nd ed. (Cambridge, Mass.: Da Capo, 2002), 109; and James Beard, who states, "the genuine symptoms of real disease were supplemented by malignity and crime; that, in short, unintentional deception was reinforced by intentional deception, both on the part of the 'afflicted children' and of those who co-operated with them": James Beard, *The Psychology of the Salem Witchcraft Excitement of 1692 and Its Practical Application to Our Own Time* (New York: G. P. Putnam's Sons, 1882), 49.

91. This discussion of conversion disorder relies heavily on Baker, *Storm of Witchcraft*, 98–105.

92. Baker, *Storm of Witchcraft*, 99–100; Laura Dimon, "What Witchcraft Is Facebook?" *Atlantic*, September 11, 2013, https://www.theatlantic.com/health/archive/2013/09/what-witchcraft-is-facebook/279499/.

93. Karlsen, *The Devil in the Shape of a Woman*, 227.

94. Baker, *Storm of Witchcraft*, 104; Frances Hill, *Hunting for Witches: A Visitor's Guide to the Salem Witch Trials* (Beverly, Mass.: Commonwealth Editions, 2002), 16–17.

95. Hoffer, *Devil's Disciples*, 65.

96. For smallpox, see Roach, *The Salem Witch Trials*, xlvi.

97. See Hoffer, *Devil's Disciples*, 91–95.

98. Hoffer, *Devil's Disciples*, 65.

99. Baker, *Storm of Witchcraft*, 100–101.

100. Baker, *Storm of Witchcraft*, 99–100; Susan Dominus, "What Happened to the Girls in Le Roy?" *New York Times*, March 7, 2012, sec. Magazine, https://www.nytimes.com/2012/03/11/magazine/teenage-girls-twitching-le-roy.html.

101. Ethan Forman, "Reports: Cause of Students' Vocal Tics May Never Be Known," *Salem News*, accessed November 26, 2019, https://www.salemnews.com/news/local_news/reports-cause-of-students-vocal-tics-may-never-be-known/article_75188abd-d671-5165-b69c-b60535a7e6a1.html; Robert E Bartholomew, "Public Health, Politics and the Stigma of Mass Hysteria: Lessons from an Outbreak of Unusual Illness," *Journal of the Royal Society of Medicine* 109, no. 5 (May 2016): 175–179.

102. Bureau of Environmental Health, Massachusetts Department of Public Health, "Investigation of Neurological Vocal Tics and Repetitive Hiccups Reported Among Students Attending Essex Agricultural and Technical High School and North Shore Technical High School, Essex County, Massachusetts" (Commonwealth of Massachusetts, November 2014), https://bloximages.chicago2.vip.townnews.com/salemnews.com/content/tncms/assets/v3/editorial/f/cf/fcf1196c-74ea-11e4-a6a9-2365eb13b147/5474f79712b88.pdf.pdf.

103. Bartholomew, "Public Health, Politics and the Stigma of Mass Hysteria," 175–176.

104. Bartholomew, "Public Health, Politics and the Stigma of Mass Hysteria," 175.

105. Dimon, "What Witchcraft Is Facebook?"

106. For the original theory, see Linnda R. Caporeal, "Ergotism: The Satan Loosed in Salem?," *Science* 192, no. 4234 (April 2, 1976): 21–26. For the rebuttal, see Nicholas Spanos and Jack Gottlieb, "Ergots and Salem Village Witchcraft: A Critical Appraisal," *Science* 194, no. 4272 (December 24, 1976): 1390–94.

107. For encephalitis, see Laurie Winn Carlson, *A Fever in Salem: A New Interpretation of the New England Witch Trials* (Chicago: Ivan R. Dee, 1999). For Lyme disease, see M. M.

Drymon, *Disguised as the Devil: A History of Lyme Disease and Witch Accusations* (Brooklyn: Wythe Avenue Press, 2008), 189–198.

108. Ray, *Satan and Salem*, 115.

109. Thomas Brattle, "Letter of Thomas Brattle, F.R.S., 1692," in *Narratives of the New England Witchcraft Cases*, ed. George Lincoln Burr (1914; repr., Mineola, N.Y.: Dover, 2002), 187.

110. Hoffer, *Devil's Disciples*, 64.

111. Rosenthal, *Records of the Salem Witch-Hunt*, Doc. 360.

112. Rosenthal, *Records of the Salem Witch-Hunt*, Doc. 21.

113. Rosenthal, *Records of the Salem Witch-Hunt*, Doc. 15.

114. Roach, *Six Women of Salem*, 45–46, 48, 60.

115. Rosenthal, *Records of the Salem Witch-Hunt*, Doc. 30.

116. Roach, *The Salem Witch Trials*, 42.

117. Deodat Lawson, "Deodat Lawson's Narrative," 685.

118. Lawson, *A Brief and True Narrative*, 153.

119. Lawson, *A Brief and True Narrative*, 153.

120. Lawson, *A Brief and True Narrative*, 153.

121. Rosenthal, *Records of the Salem Witch-Hunt*, Docs. 28, 31.

122. Lawson, *A Brief and True Narrative*, 154.

123. Lawson, *A Brief and True Narrative*, 154.

124. Rosenthal, *Records of the Salem Witch-Hunt*, Doc. 31.

125. Lawson, *A Brief and True Narrative*, 156.

126. Rosenthal, *Records of the Salem Witch-Hunt*, Doc. 16.

127. Ray, *Satan and Salem*, 54.

128. Rosenthal, *Records of the Salem Witch-Hunt*, Doc. 16.

129. Rosenthal, *Records of the Salem Witch-Hunt*, Doc. 30.

130. Roach, *The Salem Witch Trials*, 49; Upham, *Salem Witchcraft*, 355; William T. Davis, "Salem: Miscellaneous," in *History of Essex County, Massachusetts, with Biographical Sketches of Many of Its Pioneers*, vol. I (Philadelphia: J. W. Lewis & Co., 1888), 163.

131. Rosenthal, *Records of the Salem Witch-Hunt*, Doc. 31.

132. Rosenthal, *Records of the Salem Witch-Hunt*, Doc. 31. Rebecca Nurse later described a stomach illness on March 24: Doc. 28. For "pale-faced" see Doc. 35.

133. Rosenthal, *Records of the Salem Witch-Hunt*, Doc. 31.

134. Rosenthal, *Records of the Salem Witch-Hunt*, Doc. 31.

135. Lawson, *A Brief and True Narrative*, 157.

136. Lawson, *A Brief and True Narrative*, 157.

137. Lawson, *A Brief and True Narrative*, 157. The scripture is Revelation 3:1.

138. Rosenthal, *Records of the Salem Witch-Hunt*, Docs. 30, 244, 290.

139. Lawson, *A Brief and True Narrative*, 157.

140. Rosenthal, *Records of the Salem Witch-Hunt*, Doc. 23.

141. Rosenthal, *Records of the Salem Witch-Hunt*, Doc. 23.

CHAPTER 6: THE VISIBLE SAINT AGAINST THE INVISIBLE WORLD

Epigraph: Rosenthal, *Records of the Salem Witch-Hunt*, Doc. 28.

1. Rosenthal, *Records of the Salem Witch-Hunt*, Doc. 862. The report of Herrick's expenses mentions "his attendants," so others were present alongside him.

2. Rosenthal, *Records of the Salem Witch-Hunt*, Doc. 23.

3. Roach, *Six Women*, 133–134.

4. Rosenthal, *Records of the Salem Witch-Hunt*, Doc. 23.

5. Rosenthal, *Records of the Salem Witch-Hunt*, Doc. 373.

6. Calef, *More Wonders*, 360.

7. Conforti, *Saints and Strangers*, 60.

8. Karlsen, *The Devil in the Shape of a Woman*, xii, 47.

9. Karlsen, *The Devil in the Shape of a Woman*, 40–41, 48–51.

10. Karlsen, *The Devil in the Shape of a Woman*, 64–68.

11. Karlsen, *The Devil in the Shape of a Woman*, 115.

12. Demos, *Entertaining Satan*, 93–94.

13. Lawson, *A Brief and True Narrative*, 158.

14. Rosenthal, *Records of the Salem Witch-Hunt*, Doc. 862.

15. Roach, *The Salem Witch Trials*, 45.

16. Upham, *Salem Witchcraft*, 392.

17. Trask, "Legal Procedures," 46.

18. Norton, *In the Devil's Snare*, 25.

19. Trask, "Legal Procedures," 46.

20. Nathaniel Cary's firsthand account of another hearing describes this arrangement, and is recorded in Calef, *More Wonders*, 350.

21. Lawson, *A Brief and True Narrative*, 158.

22. Rosenthal, *Records of the Salem Witch-Hunt*, Doc. 23; Lawson, *A Brief and True Narrative*, 158; Trask, "Legal Procedures," 46.

23. Rosenthal, *Records of the Salem Witch-Hunt*, Docs. 23, 28, 30, 501 and note.

24. Lawson, *A Brief and True Narrative*, 155–156; Rosenthal, *Records of the Salem Witch-Hunt*, Doc. 17.

25. Karlsen, *The Devil in the Shape of a Woman*, 39.

26. Rosenthal, *Records of the Salem Witch-Hunt*, Doc. 30.

27. Trask, "Legal Procedures," 46.

28. Rosenthal, *Records of the Salem Witch-Hunt*, Doc. 28.

29. "Salem Village Church Book," 24, November 26, 1694.

30. Ray, *Satan and Salem*, 152–153.

31. Rosenthal, *Records of the Salem Witch-Hunt*, Doc. 28.

32. Rosenthal, *Records of the Salem Witch-Hunt*, Docs. 28, 32.

33. Rosenthal, *Records of the Salem Witch-Hunt*, Doc. 28.

34. See Mather, *Wonders of the Invisible World*, 203–252.

35. Rosenthal, *Records of the Salem Witch-Hunt*, Doc. 28.

36. Lawson, *A Brief and True Narrative*, 158.

37. Rosenthal, *Records of the Salem Witch-Hunt*, Doc. 28.

38. Hansen mentions the folk belief that a witch could not cry, see Hansen, *Witchcraft at Salem*, 49.

39. Rosenthal, *Records of the Salem Witch-Hunt*, Doc. 28.

40. One example of the girls fighting back against Rebecca's alleged specter is when Lawson records that Abigail Williams threw firebrands at it. See Lawson, *A Brief and True Narrative*, 153–154.

41. Rosenthal, *Records of the Salem Witch-Hunt*, Doc. 28.

42. Rosenthal, *Records of the Salem Witch-Hunt*, Doc. 28.

43. The charge of the Devil whispering in her ear was related by Parris earlier in the hearing above, and is also recorded in Lawson, *A Brief and True Narrative*, 159.

44. Rosenthal, *Records of the Salem Witch-Hunt*, Doc. 28.

45. Lawson, *A Brief and True Narrative*, 159.

46. Rosenthal, *Records of the Salem Witch-Hunt*, Doc. 28.

47. Lawson, *A Brief and True Narrative*, 159; Rosenthal, *Records of the Salem Witch-Hunt*, Doc. 29. It is not clear from Parris' transcript, Lawson's description, or Mrs. Ann Putnam's later deposition when her grand and final fit occurred. It is inserted here at this point in the hearing because Parris read the evidence about her right afterwards. The fit is unlikely to have occurred when Mrs. Putnam is mentioned earlier in the hearing (when she shouted questions at Rebecca about how often she ate and drank her own damnation, etc.), because right after these questions were shouted Hathorne asked Rebecca to answer them, without any lengthy interruption as the above-described fit would require. Though, the reasons for choosing this spot in the hearing are admittedly not conclusive.

48. Lawson, *A Brief and True Narrative*, 159.

49. Rosenthal, *Records of the Salem Witch-Hunt*, Doc. 30. Peter Charles Hoffer points out that this phrase about lions likely came from Lawson's sermon that afternoon: Hoffer, *Devil's Disciples*, 119.

50. Rosenthal, *Records of the Salem Witch-Hunt*, Docs. 28, 30.

51. Rosenthal, *Records of the Salem Witch-Hunt*, Doc. 30

52. Rosenthal, *Records of the Salem Witch-Hunt*, Doc. 28.

53. All early published copies of the transcriptions of Rebecca's hearing include this final phrase, though the otherwise-authoritative book of court records (Rosenthal, *Records of the Salem Witch-Hunt*, Doc. 28) omits it, and leaves Hathorne's final question "What do you think of this?" unanswered. See Upham, *Salem Witchcraft*, 362; Zachariah Atwell Mudge, *Witch Hill: A History of Salem Witchcraft: Including Illustrative Sketches of Persons and Places* (New York: Carlton & Lanahan, 1870), 111; George Francis Dow, "Witchcraft Records Relating to Topsfield," in *The Historical Collections of the Topsfield Historical Society*, vol. 13 (Topsfield, Mass.: Topsfield Historical Society, 1908), 45; Paul Boyer and Stephen Nissenbaum, eds., *The Salem Witchcraft Papers: Verbatim Transcripts of the Legal Documents of the Salem Witchcraft Outbreak of 1692*, 3 vols. (New York: Da Capo, 1977), 2:584–587. Upon examination of the original document, the phrase is indeed written on the backside, in the upper left corner. "Examination of Rebecca Nurse" (Manuscript, March 24, 1692), Essex County Court Archives, vol. 1, no. 72, Massachusetts Supreme Judicial Court, Judicial Archives, on deposit James Duncan Phillips Library, Rowley, Mass.

54. See Cotton Mather, "The Return of Several Ministers Consulted (June 15, 1692)," in *Salem-Village Witchcraft: A Documentary Record of Local Conflict in Colonial New England*, ed. Paul Boyer and Stephen Nissenbaum (Boston: Northeastern University Press, 1993), 117–118.

55. Rosenthal, *Records of the Salem Witch-Hunt*, Doc. 28.

56. "Salem Village Church Book," 24, November 26, 1694; Ray, *Satan and Salem*, 152–153.

57. Rosenthal, *Records of the Salem Witch-Hunt*, Doc. 31 note.

58. Rosenthal, *Records of the Salem Witch-Hunt*, Doc. 28.

59. Upham, *Salem Witchcraft*, 341.

60. Upham, *Salem Witchcraft*, 341.

61. Rosenthal, *Records of the Salem Witch-Hunt*, Doc. 1.

62. Rosenthal, *Records of the Salem Witch-Hunt*, Doc. 862.

63. Lawson, *A Brief and True Narrative*, 159.

64. "Salem Village Record Book," 20, September 11, 1684.

65. Deodat Lawson, "Christ's Fidelity the Only Shield Against Satan's Malignity," in *Salem-Village Witchcraft: A Documentary Record of Local Conflict in Colonial New England*, ed. Paul Boyer and Stephen Nissenbaum (Boston: Northeastern University Press, 1993), 127.

66. Lawson, "Christ's Fidelity the Only Shield Against Satan's Malignity," 128.

CHAPTER 7: PRISON AND PETITION

Epigraph: *EQC*, 8:335.

1. Marilynne K. Roach, *Gallows and Graves: The Search to Locate the Death and Burial Sites of the People Executed for Witchcraft in 1692* (Watertown, Mass.: Sassafras Grove, 1997), 4.

2. Esther I. Wik, "The Jailkeeper at Salem in 1692," *Essex Institute Historical Collections* 111, no. 3 (July 1975): 221.

3. Perley, *History of Salem*, 3:174.

4. Konig, *Law and Society*, 64 note 2.

5. *EQC*, 8:335.

6. *EQC*, 8:227.

7. Robert Ellis Cahill, *The Horrors of Salem's Witch Dungeon* (Peabody, Mass.: Chandler-Smith Publishing House, 1986), 50.

8. J. M. Beattie, *Crime and the Courts in England, 1660–1800* (Princeton, N.J.: Princeton University Press, 1986), 301.

9. Rosenthal, *Records of the Salem Witch-Hunt*, Doc. 715.

10. Rosenthal, *Records of the Salem Witch-Hunt*, Doc. 694.

11. Rosenthal, *Records of the Salem Witch-Hunt*, Doc. 712.

12. Edwin Powers, *Crime and Punishment in Early Massachusetts, 1620–1692: A Documentary History* (Boston: Beacon Press, 1966), 232, 234–239.

13. General Court of Massachusetts, *Charters and General Laws*, 132.

14. Lawson, *A Brief and True Narrative*, 159.

15. Rosenthal, *Records of the Salem Witch-Hunt*, Docs. 907, 612.

16. Lawson, *A Brief and True Narrative*, 159–160.

17. Rosenthal, *Records of the Salem Witch-Hunt*, Doc. 32.

18. Lawson, *A Brief and True Narrative*, 158.

19. Calef, *More Wonders*, 389.

20. Edward Ward, "Trip to New England," in *Boston in 1682 and 1699*, ed. George Parker Winship (Providence: Club for Colonial Reprints, 1905), 53.

21. See Rosenthal, *Salem Story*, 38–40.

22. Lawson, "Deodat Lawson's Narrative," 688.

23. Rosenthal, *Salem Story*, 38–40. Enders A. Robinson takes the notion of conspiracy several steps further and claims not just that the afflicted were possibly conspiring, but that they were directed and organized by their fathers and other leading village men. Robinson describes a core group of ten villagers—which supposedly included Parris, Nathaniel Ingersoll, Dr. Griggs, Jonathan Walcott, Thomas Putnam Jr., Nathaniel Putnam, and several other Putnams—that colluded and conspired to engineer the witch hunt for their own gain. However, several of these alleged conspirators signed a petition for Rebecca Nurse or entered other testimony in support of her. Their defense of Nurse casts doubt on Robinson's theory that they engineered the accusations against her. The only evidence from the time clearly describing coordinated actions against the accused are done by the afflicted accusers themselves, not their fathers or other nonafflicted family members. Robinson, *The Devil Discovered*, 109, 110–116.

24. See Hoffer, *Devil's Disciples*, 168.

25. Lawson, *A Brief and True Narrative*, 162.

26. Hoffer, *Devil's Disciples*, 168.

27. Upham, *Salem Witchcraft*, 510.

28. Hutchinson, *The History of the Province of Massachusetts-Bay*, 2:62.

29. For dating this day's events, see: Roach, *The Salem Witch Trials*, 58–59.

30. Parris, *Sermon Notebook*, 194.

31. Parris, *Sermon Notebook*, 194.

32. Lawson, *A Brief and True Narrative*, 161.

33. Calef, *More Wonders*, 346.

34. Parris, *Sermon Notebook*, 198, 196.

35. See James F. Cooper Jr. and Kenneth P. Minkema, "Introduction," in *The Sermon Notebook of Samuel Parris, 1689–1694*, by Samuel Parris, Publications of The Colonial Society of Massachusetts 66 (Boston: Colonial Society of Massachusetts, 1993), 21.

36. Parris, *Sermon Notebook*, 197.

37. Parris, *Sermon Notebook*, 198.

38. Rosenthal, *Records of the Salem Witch-Hunt*, Doc. 343.

39. Lawson, *A Brief and True Narrative*, 161.

40. "Salem Village Church Book," 10–11, March 27, 1692.

41. Ray, *Satan and Salem*, 61, 95.

42. John Demos, *The Enemy Within: 2,000 Years of Witch-Hunting in the Western World* (New York: Viking, 2008), 149.

43. Roach, *Six Women of Salem*, 60.

44. Rosenthal, *Records of the Salem Witch-Hunt*, Doc. 185.

45. Ray, *Satan and Salem*, 95; "Salem Village Church Book," 2, November 19, 1689, and 6, June 4, 1691.

46. Ray, *Satan and Salem*, 96.

47. Ray, *Satan and Salem*, 103. See Rosenthal, *Records of the Salem Witch-Hunt*, Doc. 82.

48. Rosenthal, *Records of the Salem Witch-Hunt*, Doc. 35.

49. Rosenthal, *Records of the Salem Witch-Hunt*, Doc. 35.

50. Rosenthal, *Records of the Salem Witch-Hunt*, Docs. 498, 500.

51. Rosenthal, *Records of the Salem Witch-Hunt*, Docs. 498, 500.

52. Rosenthal, *Records of the Salem Witch-Hunt*, Docs. 244, 49.

53. Lawson, *A Brief and True Narrative*, 160.

54. Rosenthal, *Records of the Salem Witch-Hunt*, Doc. 49.

55. Lawson, *A Brief and True Narrative*, 161. Lawson's dating is off for this remark, for March 27 was the sacrament Sunday when Cloyce left the meetinghouse, not April 3 as he writes. See Roach, *The Salem Witch Trials*, 58.

56. Lawson, *A Brief and True Narrative*, 161.

57. Lawson, *A Brief and True Narrative*, 161.

58. Revelation 5:9.

59. Rosenthal, *Records of the Salem Witch-Hunt*, Doc. 382.

60. Rosenthal, *Records of the Salem Witch-Hunt*, Doc. 39.

61. Rosenthal, *Records of the Salem Witch-Hunt*, Doc. 47.

62. Trask, "Legal Procedures," 45.

63. Roach, *The Salem Witch Trials*, 69.

64. Baker, *Storm of Witchcraft*, 22.

65. Baker, *Storm of Witchcraft*, 22.

66. Brattle, "Letter," 184; Sewall, *Diary*, 1:367.

67. Northend, "Address Before the Essex Bar Association," 258–259.

68. "Constitutional Reform Act 2005," §23 (2005), https://www.legislation.gov.uk/ukpga/2005/4/section/23.

69. Murrin, "Coming to Terms with the Salem Witch Trials," 317.

70. Sewall, *Diary*, 1:358.

71. Sewall, *Diary*, 1:358; Rosenthal, *Records of the Salem Witch-Hunt*, Doc. 47.

72. Rosenthal, *Records of the Salem Witch-Hunt*, Doc. 49.

73. Rosenthal, *Records of the Salem Witch-Hunt*, Doc 49.

74. Rosenthal, *Records of the Salem Witch-Hunt*, Doc. 49.

75. Baker, *Storm of Witchcraft*, 22.

76. Rosenthal, *Salem Story*, 30.

77. Ray, *Satan and Salem*, 67.

78. Konig, *Law and Society*, 168.

79. Rosenthal, *Salem Story*, 30.

80. Rosenthal, *Records of the Salem Witch-Hunt*, Docs. 47, 216, 612.

81. Rosenthal, *Records of the Salem Witch-Hunt*, Doc. 47.

82. Dan Gagnon, *Map of Sites in the Life of Rebecca Nurse*, 2018, https://spectersofsalemvillage.com/map-life-of-rebecca-nurse/; Upham, *Salem Witchcraft*, 7.

83. Dunton, *Letters*, 163.

84. Roach, *Six Women of Salem*, 155; Rosenthal, *Records of the Salem Witch-Hunt*, Doc. 65.

85. Benton, *Town House*, 205.

86. Dunton, *Letters*, 67.

87. Alf J. Mapp, Jr., *Three Golden Ages: Discovering the Creative Secrets of Renaissance Florence, Elizabethan England, and America's Founding* (Lanham, Md.: Madison Books, 1998), 300.

88. Edwin L. Bynner, "Topography and Landmarks of the Colonial Period," in *The Memorial History of Boston, Including Suffolk County, Massachusetts, 1630–1880*, ed. Justin Winsor, 4 vols. (Boston: Ticknor and Company, 1880), 1:534.

89. George R. Stewart, *Names on the Land: A Historical Account of Place-Naming in the United States* (Boston: Houghton Mifflin, 1958), 38.

90. Scudder, "Life in Boston in the Colonial Period," 1:499.

91. Bynner, "Topography and Landmarks of the Colonial Period," 1:535.

92. This street is present-day Hanover Street. The Winnisimmet ferry dock was located along what is today Commercial Street in front of the Coast Guard Station. See Samuel C. Clough, *Map of the Town of Boston, 1676* (Boston, 1920), MHS Collections Online, https://www.masshist.org/database/viewer.php?item_id=1737&img_step=1&br=1&mode=zoomify#page1; Gagnon, "Map of Sites in the Life of Rebecca Nurse."

93. Sewall, *Diary*, 1:10, 78, 97.

94. Hoffer, *Devil's Disciples*, 20; Josselyn, *New England's Rarities*, 33.

95. Hoffer, *Devil's Disciples*, 21.

96. Baker, *Storm of Witchcraft*, 22.

97. The book was sold by Benjamin Harris, whose shop was in the Old Meetinghouse at the corner of Prison Lane and Town House Square in Boston. Lawson, *A Brief and True Narrative*, 148, 152; Ray, *Satan and Salem*, 74.

98. Benton, *Town House*, xi.

99. This is present-day Court Street, and the jail was located at present-day Court-Square. Boston Street Commissioners, *A Record of the Streets, Alleys, Places, Etc., in the City of Boston* (Boston: City of Boston, 1910), 137; Benton, *Town House*, 3.

100. Quoted in Samuel G. Drake, *The History and Antiquities of Boston, the Capital of Massachusetts and Metropolis of New England, From Its Settlement in 1630 to the Year 1770* (Boston: Luther Stevens, 1856), 635.

101. Edward Randolph, "Letter from Edward Randolph to Robert Chaplin," October 28, 1689, CO 5/855 no. 46 PRO, National Archives (UK).

102. Mather mentions Mercy Short throwing shavings from the jail floor at Sarah Good. Mather, "Wonders of the Invisible World," 260.

103. Rosenthal, *Records of the Salem Witch-Hunt*, Doc. 612.

104. Calef, *More Wonders*, 352, 349 note 3; Rosenthal, *Records of the Salem Witch-Hunt*, Doc. 612.

105. Powers, *Crime and Punishment in Early Massachusetts*, 231.

106. Rosenthal, *Records of the Salem Witch-Hunt*, Doc. 698.

107. Quoted in Roach, *The Salem Witch Trials*, 361.

108. Dunton, *Letters*, 118–119.

109. Rosenthal, *Records of the Salem Witch-Hunt*, Doc. 61.

110. Rosenthal, *Records of the Salem Witch-Hunt*, Docs. 244, 362, 267.

111. Rosenthal, *Records of the Salem Witch-Hunt*, Doc. 362.

112. Rosenthal, *Records of the Salem Witch-Hunt*, Doc. 362.

113. Rosenthal, *Records of the Salem Witch-Hunt*, Doc. 62.

114. Roach, *The Salem Witch Trials*, 66.

115. Rosenthal, *Records of the Salem Witch-Hunt*, Doc. 80.

116. Rosenthal, *Records of the Salem Witch-Hunt*, Doc. 501.

117. Rosenthal, *Records of the Salem Witch-Hunt*, Doc. 75.

118. Hoffer, *Devil's Disciples*, 128.

119. Rosenthal, *Records of the Salem Witch-Hunt*, Doc. 28.

120. Baker, *Storm of Witchcraft*, 116.

121. Rosenthal, *Records of the Salem Witch-Hunt*, Doc. 75.

122. Rosenthal, *Records of the Salem Witch-Hunt*, Docs. 75, 78, 80, 145, 262.

123. Rosenthal, *Records of the Salem Witch-Hunt*, Docs. 150, 255.

124. Norton, *In the Devil's Snare*, 321–322.

125. Rosenthal, *Records of the Salem Witch-Hunt*, Doc. 85.

126. Rosenthal, *Records of the Salem Witch-Hunt*, Doc. 85.

127. Rosenthal, *Records of the Salem Witch-Hunt*, Doc. 85.

128. Marilynne K. Roach, "Biographical Notes," in *Records of the Salem Witch-Hunt*, ed. Bernard Rosenthal (New York: Cambridge University Press, 2009), 955.

129. Rosenthal, *Records of the Salem Witch-Hunt*, Doc. 85.

130. Rosenthal, *Records of the Salem Witch-Hunt*, Docs. 79, 88, 526.

131. Hale, *Modest Enquiry*, 418.

132. Rosenthal, *Records of the Salem Witch-Hunt*, Doc. 95.

133. Rosenthal, *Records of the Salem Witch-Hunt*, Docs. 428, 525, 527.

134. Rosenthal, *Records of the Salem Witch-Hunt*, Doc. 205.

135. Hale, *Modest Enquiry*, 420.

136. Rosenthal, *Records of the Salem Witch-Hunt*, Doc. 86.

137. Hoover, *Towne Family*, 263, 265.

138. Rosenthal, *Records of the Salem Witch-Hunt*, Doc. 86.

139. Rosenthal, *Records of the Salem Witch-Hunt*, Docs. 89, 95.

140. Rosenthal, *Records of the Salem Witch-Hunt*, Doc. 116.

141. Sewall, *Diary*, 1:360.

142. Haskins, *Law and Authority in Early Massachusetts*, 31.

143. Rosenthal, *Records of the Salem Witch-Hunt*, Doc. 270; Roach, *The Salem Witch Trials*, 110.

144. Savage, *Genealogical Dictionary of the First Settlers of New England*, 3:300.

145. For Willard's relation to Wilkins, see Roach, "Biographical Notes," 963.

146. Rosenthal, *Records of the Salem Witch-Hunt*, Doc. 488.

147. Rosenthal, *Records of the Salem Witch-Hunt*, Doc. 488.

148. Robinson, *The Devil Discovered*, 184.

149. Hoffer, *Devil's Disciples*, 70–71.

150. Rosenthal, *Records of the Salem Witch-Hunt*, Doc. 179.

151. Rosenthal, *Records of the Salem Witch-Hunt*, Doc. 612.

152. The child was born in December 1691, see Marilynne K. Roach, "Records of the Rev. Samuel Parris, Salem Village, Massachusetts, 1688–1696," *New England Historical and Genealogical Register* 157 (January 2003): 9.

153. Rosenthal, *Records of the Salem Witch-Hunt*, Doc. 907.

154. Rosenthal, *Records of the Salem Witch-Hunt*, Docs. 612, 326.

155. Rosenthal, *Records of the Salem Witch-Hunt*, Doc. 326.

156. Roach, "Biographical Notes," 960.

157. Rosenthal, *Records of the Salem Witch-Hunt*, Docs. 314, 166.

158. Rosenthal, *Records of the Salem Witch-Hunt*, Doc. 841.

159. Breslaw includes him as being accused of witchcraft, see Elaine G. Breslaw, *Tituba, Reluctant Witch of Salem: Devilish Indians and Puritan Fantasies* (New York: NYU Press, 1997), 183. But Roach does not, see Roach, *The Salem Witch Trials*, Appendix A. No documents could be found connecting him to the witch hunt.

160. Rosenthal, *Records of the Salem Witch-Hunt*, Docs. 114, 920.

161. The other accused who arrived that day were Bethia Carter of Woburn, Ann Sears of Woburn, and Sarah Dustin of Reading, whose aged mother Lydia arrived several days earlier. Rosenthal, *Records of the Salem Witch-Hunt*, Doc. 841.

162. The other accused sent to the Boston jail that day were William Hobbs of Topsfield, Edward and Sarah Bishop of Salem Village, Bridget Bishop of Salem Town, Sarah Wilds of Topsfield, Mary English of Salem Town, Alice Parker of Salem Town, and Ann Pudeator of Salem Town. Rosenthal, *Records of the Salem Witch-Hunt*, Doc. 146.

163. Boyer and Nissenbaum, *Salem Possessed*, 31.

164. Rosenthal, *Records of the Salem Witch-Hunt*, Docs. 97, 99, 152, 253.

165. Rosenthal, *Records of the Salem Witch-Hunt*, Doc. 97.

166. Rosenthal, *Records of the Salem Witch-Hunt*, Doc. 841.

167. Cotton Mather, "A Brand Pluck'd out of the Burning (1693)," in *Narratives of the New England Witchcraft Cases* (1914; repr., Mineola, N.Y.: Dover, 2002), 281–282.

168. Rosenthal, *Records of the Salem Witch-Hunt*, Docs. 921, 883, 841.

169. "Salem Village Church Book," 12, August 31, 1692.

170. Roach, *The Salem Witch Trials*, 123.

171. Nathaniel Cary in Calef, *More Wonders*, 351.

172. Rosenthal, *Records of the Salem Witch-Hunt*, Docs. 123, 351.

173. Hansen, *Witchcraft at Salem*, 78.

174. Upham, *Salem Witchcraft*, 573.

175. Roach, *The Salem Witch Trials*, 116.

176. For an examination of the cases and legacies of Nurse and Jacobs, see Daniel A. Gagnon, "Skeletons in the Closet: How the Actions of the Salem Witch Trials Victims' Families in 1692 Affected Later Memorialization," *New England Journal of History* 75/76, no. 2/1 (Spring/Fall 2019): 32–73.

177. Rosenthal, *Records of the Salem Witch-Hunt*, Docs. 133, 28.

178. Hansen, *Witchcraft at Salem*, 104.

179. Hoffer, *Devil's Disciples*, 110–111. For all known defamation cases related to witchcraft pre–1692 and their results, see Weisman, *Witchcraft, Magic, and Religion*, Appendix B.

180. Rosenthal, *Records of the Salem Witch-Hunt*, Doc. 254 and note.

181. Rosenthal, *Records of the Salem Witch-Hunt*, Doc. 254.

182. Rosenthal, *Records of the Salem Witch-Hunt*, Doc. 343.

183. Rosenthal, *Records of the Salem Witch-Hunt*, Doc. 358.

184. Marilynne K. Roach similarly differentiates these two Sarah Holtens, see Roach, "Biographical Notes," 945–946.

185. A. P. Putnam, *Rebecca Nurse and Her Friends: Address at the Dedication of a Tablet in Honor of Forty Friends of Rebecca Nurse of Salem Village* (Boston: Thomas Todd, 1894), 22.

186. Rosenthal, *Records of the Salem Witch-Hunt*, Doc. 373.

187. Putnam, *Rebecca Nurse and Her Friends*, 20, 24.

188. Rosenthal, *Records of the Salem Witch-Hunt*, Doc. 23.

189. Upham, *Salem Witchcraft*, 626; Tapley, *Chronicles of Danvers*, 28–29.

190. Rosenthal, *Records of the Salem Witch-Hunt*, Doc. 152.

191. Sewall, *Diary*, 1:360; Rif Winfield, *British Warships in the Age of Sail 1603–1714: Design, Construction, Careers and Fates* (Barnsley: Seaforth, 2009), 122.

192. Baker and Reid, *New England Knight*, xi.

193. Baker and Reid, *New England Knight*, 8–11, 21–22.

194. Sewall, *Diary*, 1:360.

195. Sewall, *Diary*, 1:360.

196. Benton, *Town House*, 187.

197. Matthews, "Massachusetts Royal Commissions," 87, 45.

198. Matthews, "Massachusetts Royal Commissions," 45; Roach, *The Salem Witch Trials*, 128–130.

199. Matthews, "Massachusetts Royal Commissions," 46; Baker and Reid, *New England Knight*, 127–128.

200. Mather, *Magnalia*, book II, 61.

201. Rosenthal, *Records of the Salem Witch-Hunt*, Doc. 612; Calef, *More Wonders*, 349 and note 3.

202. Roach, *The Salem Witch Trials*, 135.

203. Rosenthal, *Records of the Salem Witch-Hunt*, Doc. 187.

204. Rosenthal, *Records of the Salem Witch-Hunt*, Docs. 216, 612. For John Arnold's bill misdating the May 19 transfer, see: Roach, *The Salem Witch Trials*, 136.

205. Rosenthal, *Records of the Salem Witch-Hunt*, Doc. 841.

206. Roach, *The Salem Witch Trials*, 131, 141.

207. Roach, *The Salem Witch Trials*, 141.

208. Rosenthal, *Records of the Salem Witch-Hunt*, Doc. 253.

209. Rosenthal, *Records of the Salem Witch-Hunt*, Doc. 253.

210. Rosenthal, *Records of the Salem Witch-Hunt*, Docs. 612, 841.

211. Roach notes this passing of prisoners in Roach, *Six Women of Salem*, 222.

CHAPTER 8: OYER AND TERMINER

Epigraph: Rosenthal, *Records of the Salem Witch-Hunt*, Doc. 3.

1. Defense lawyers were not allowed to practice for fees in Massachusetts until 1705. Baker, *Storm of Witchcraft*, 25–26.

2. Rosenthal, *Records of the Salem Witch-Hunt*, Doc. 264.

3. Kadri, *The Trial*, 117.

4. Weisman, *Witchcraft, Magic, and Religion*, 14.

5. For 18 as the number of grand jurors, see: Rosenthal, *Records of the Salem Witch-Hunt*, Doc. 232. Kadri (*The Trial*, 117) uses 23 in his example, but this was not the number used in 1692.

6. Kadri, *The Trial*, 117.

7. Bernard Rosenthal, "General Introduction," in *Records of the Salem Witch-Hunt*, ed. Bernard Rosenthal (New York: Cambridge University Press, 2009), 22.

8. Lawrence A. Cremin, *American Education: The Colonial Experience, 1607–1783* (New York: Harper & Row, 1970), 212.

9. For change in juror requirements, see Baker, *Storm of Witchcraft*, 26.

10. For an example of this interpretation, see Roach, *The Salem Witch Trials*, 142; "The Charter of the Province of the Massachusetts Bay in New England, 1691," in *The Charters and General Laws of the Colony and Province of Massachusetts Bay* (Boston: T. B. Wait and Co., 1814), 31–32.

11. Ray, *Satan and Salem*, 75; Hoffer, *Devil's Disciples*, 135.

12. Commonwealth of Massachusetts, "About the Supreme Judicial Court," Massachusetts Court System, 2018, https://www.mass.gov/service-details/about-the-supreme-judicial-court. Historian John Murrin points out that the new General Court convened only two weeks after Phips created the Oyer and Terminer Court, and Phips could have asked the legislature to establish a special court at that point, instead of doing it through executive authority. Apparently Phips was unwilling to wait even two weeks before he acted. Murrin, "Coming to Terms with the Salem Witch Trials," 337 note 51.

13. Hoffer, *Devil's Disciples*, 136.

14. William Phips, "Letter of October 12, 1692, to William Blathwayt, Clerk of the Privy Council," in *Narratives of the New England Witchcraft Cases*, ed. George Lincoln Burr (Mineola, N.Y.: Dover, 2002), 196.

15. Rosenthal, *Records of the Salem Witch-Hunt*, Doc. 220.

16. Rosenthal, *Records of the Salem Witch-Hunt*, Doc. 220.

17. Demos, *Entertaining Satan*, 58.

18. General Court of Massachusetts, *Charters and General Laws*, 213.

19. Norton, *In the Devil's Snare*, 199–201.

20. Upham, *Salem Witchcraft*, 486; Baker, *Storm of Witchcraft*, 33.

21. Rosenthal, *Records of the Salem Witch-Hunt*, Doc. 220; Roach, "Biographical Notes," 936, 942, 944, 956, 957, 959, 963.

22. Robinson, *The Devil Discovered*, 202; Baker, *Storm of Witchcraft*, 164–165, 167.

23. Norton, *In the Devil's Snare*, 197 note 7.

24. Hansen, *Witchcraft at Salem*, 122.

25. Rosenthal, *Records of the Salem Witch-Hunt*, Doc. 220.

26. Charles Pastoor and Galen K. Johnson, *Historical Dictionary of the Puritans* (Lanham, Md.: Scarecrow Press, 2007), 311.

27. John Langdon Sibley, *Biographical Sketches of Graduates of Harvard University*, vol. 1 (Cambridge, Mass.: Charles William Sever, 1873), 194–196.

28. Hutchinson, *The History of the Province of Massachusetts-Bay*, 2:61.

29. Baker, *Storm of Witchcraft*, 162; For some of the witchcraft cases before the Assistants during these years, see: Noble, *Records of the Court of Assistants*, 11, 33, 159, 188, 228, 233.

30. Baker, *Storm of Witchcraft*, 172.

31. Baker, *Storm of Witchcraft*, 55.

32. Murrin, "Coming to Terms with the Salem Witch Trials," 322–323.

33. Baker, *Storm of Witchcraft*, 178–179.

34. Norton, *In the Devil's Snare*, 300. See also 226, 229.

35. Baker, *Storm of Witchcraft*, 185–186. The Superior Court of Judicature compensated Thomas Putnam £5 in 1693 for his work: Rosenthal, *Records of the Salem Witch-Hunt*, Doc. 866.

36. Rosenthal, "General Introduction," 30–31.

37. Trask, "Legal Procedures," 46.

38. Konig, *Law and Society*, 170.

39. See, Roach, *The Salem Witch Trials*, Appendix B.

40. Baker and Reid, *New England Knight*, 144–145.

41. Rosenthal, *Records of the Salem Witch-Hunt*, Docs. 221, 224, 225.

42. Michael Dalton, *The Countrey Justice, Containing the Practice of the Justices of the Peace out of Their Sessions* (London: Company of Stationers, 1661), 341–342.

43. Haskins, *Law and Authority in Early Massachusetts*, 61.

44. Cotton Mather, "Letter to John Richards, May 31, 1692," in *Selected Letters of Cotton Mather*, ed. Kenneth Silverman (Baton Rouge: Louisiana State University Press, 1971), 36.

45. Rosenthal, *Records of the Salem Witch-Hunt*, Docs. 28, 133.

46. Upham, *Salem Witchcraft*, 484; Roach, "Biographical Notes," 944.

47. Rosenthal, *Records of the Salem Witch-Hunt*, Doc. 232.

48. Roach notes where Hathorne and Corwin were that day in Salem Village, see Roach, *The Salem Witch Trials*, 147–152.

49. Rosenthal, *Records of the Salem Witch-Hunt*, Doc. 30.

50. Rosenthal, *Records of the Salem Witch-Hunt*, Doc. 255.

51. Rosenthal, *Records of the Salem Witch-Hunt*, Docs. 362, 259.

52. Konig, *Law and Society*, 123–126; Hoffer, *Devil's Disciples*, 163.

53. Konig, *Law and Society*, 164–165.

54. Hoffer, *Devil's Disciples*, 163.

55. Roach notes that it occurred in the jail, see Roach, *The Salem Witch Trials*, 156.

56. Rosenthal, *Records of the Salem Witch-Hunt*, Doc. 271; Upham, *Lectures on Witchcraft*, 40.

57. Dalton, *Countrey Justice*, 342.

58. Rosenthal, *Records of the Salem Witch-Hunt*, Doc. 271. Though identified in the record only by his last name, Marilynne K. Roach gives the surgeon's first name as "John": Roach, *The Salem Witch Trials*, 156.

59. Rosenthal, *Salem Story*, 78.

60. Rosenthal, *Records of the Salem Witch-Hunt*, Doc. 271.

61. Hill, *Delusion of Satan*, 160.
62. Rosenthal, *Records of the Salem Witch-Hunt*, Doc. 340.
63. Hale, *Modest Enquiry*, 411.
64. Brattle, "Letter," 175.
65. Baker, *Storm of Witchcraft*, 28. For more of Bishop's background, see Roach, *The Salem Witch Trials*, 156–157.
66. Mather, *Wonders of the Invisible World*, 223.
67. In addition to noting the uniqueness of the treatment of the confessors in 1692, Bernard Rosenthal notes that the biblical command regarding executing witches was ignored. Rosenthal, *Salem Story*, 28–29.
68. Rosenthal, *Records of the Salem Witch-Hunt*, Docs. 273, 274, 275 and note, 276.
69. Roach, *The Salem Witch Trials*, 156; Calef, *More Wonders*, 356.
70. Roach, *The Salem Witch Trials*, 156–160.
71. Rosenthal, *Records of the Salem Witch-Hunt*, Doc. 271.
72. Rosenthal, *Records of the Salem Witch-Hunt*, Doc. 271.
73. Norton, *In the Devil's Snare*, 205.
74. Rosenthal, *Salem Story*, 77.
75. Rosenthal, *Records of the Salem Witch-Hunt*, Doc. 340.
76. Rosenthal, *Records of the Salem Witch-Hunt*, Doc. 259.
77. Rosenthal, *Records of the Salem Witch-Hunt*, Doc. 267.
78. Rosenthal, *Records of the Salem Witch-Hunt*, Doc. 267.
79. Rosenthal, *Records of the Salem Witch-Hunt*, Doc. 267.
80. Perley, *History of Salem*, 3:76; Sidney Perley, "The Court Houses in Salem," *Essex Institute Historical Collections* 47, no. 2 (April 1911): 103.
81. Roach, *Six Women of Salem*, 228.
82. Roach, "Biographical Notes," 957; Rosenthal, *Records of the Salem Witch-Hunt*, Docs. 285, 286, 287, 288.
83. Trask, "Legal Procedures," 51.
84. Trask, "Legal Procedures," 50.
85. For an example of this, see the attestations at the end of Rosenthal, *Records of the Salem Witch-Hunt*, Doc. 30.
86. Hoffer, *Devil's Disciples*, 156; Beattie, *Crime and the Courts*, 350.
87. Rosenthal, "General Introduction," 21.
88. Trask, "Legal Procedures," 51.
89. Rosenthal, *Records of the Salem Witch-Hunt*, Doc. 285.
90. Rosenthal, *Salem Story*, 43.
91. Hoffer, *Devil's Disciples*, 149.
92. Rosenthal, *Salem Story*, 81.
93. Rosenthal, *Records of the Salem Witch-Hunt*, Docs. 271, 28; Roach, *Six Women of Salem*, 239.
94. Rosenthal, *Records of the Salem Witch-Hunt*, Doc. 30.
95. Rosenthal, *Records of the Salem Witch-Hunt*, Doc. 244.
96. Fels, *Switching Sides*, 95.
97. Rosenthal, *Records of the Salem Witch-Hunt*, Doc. 290.
98. Rosenthal, *Records of the Salem Witch-Hunt*, Doc. 291.
99. The court records also include another deposition against Rebecca by Susannah Sheldon, who was listed in the subpoena for witnesses that day, but for whatever reason it does

not appear that Sheldon's testimony was actually entered at the grand jury session. Additionally, Mercy Lewis' name was listed on the subpoena for witnesses but no testimony from her seems to have been entered on that day. If Lewis did testify that day, the document is now lost to history. Rosenthal, *Records of the Salem Witch-Hunt*, Docs. 259, 289, 292.

100. Roach, "Biographical Notes," 957.

101. Rosenthal, *Records of the Salem Witch-Hunt*, Doc. 120; Roach, *The Salem Witch Trials*, 229.

102. For Ann Putnam Jr.'s claim about Burroughs' wives, see Rosenthal, *Records of the Salem Witch-Hunt*, Doc. 125.

103. Rosenthal, *Records of the Salem Witch-Hunt*, Docs. 30, 290, 291, 292.

104. Rosenthal, "General Introduction," 31.

105. Salem, *Town Records*, 3:252.

106. Rosenthal, *Records of the Salem Witch-Hunt*, Docs. 294 and note, and 340.

107. Rosenthal, *Records of the Salem Witch-Hunt*, Doc. 293 and note.

108. Roach, *The Salem Witch Trials*, 146.

109. Rosenthal, *Records of the Salem Witch-Hunt*, Doc. 293.

110. Rosenthal, *Records of the Salem Witch-Hunt*, Docs. 31, 254 and note.

CHAPTER 9: TRIAL

Epigraph: Michael Wigglesworth, *The Day of Doom; Or, A Poetical Description of the Great and Last Judgment: with Other Poems* (New York: American News Company, 1867), 109.

1. Baker, *Storm of Witchcraft*, 31.

2. Roach, *The Salem Witch Trials*, 162, 163.

3. Rosenthal, *Records of the Salem Witch-Hunt*, Doc. 304; Roach, *The Salem Witch Trials*, 163; Roach, *A Time Traveler's Maps of the Salem Witchcraft Trials* (Watertown, Mass.: Sassafras Grove, 1991), 8.

4. Rosenthal, *Records of the Salem Witch-Hunt*, Docs. 304, 306.

5. Quoted in Roach, *The Salem Witch Trials*, 164.

6. Rosenthal, *Records of the Salem Witch-Hunt*, Doc. 309.

7. Rosenthal, *Records of the Salem Witch-Hunt*, Doc. 309.

8. Marilynne K. Roach, "A Map of Salem Village and Vicinity in 1692" (Watertown, Mass.: Sassafrass Grove, 1990).

9. Roach, *The Salem Witch Trials*, 165.

10. Scudder, "Life in Boston in the Colonial Period," 510.

11. Rosenthal, *Records of the Salem Witch-Hunt*, Doc. 313.

12. Rosenthal, *Records of the Salem Witch-Hunt*, Doc. 28.

13. General Court of Massachusetts, *Charters and General Laws*, 59.

14. Roach, *The Salem Witch Trials*, 166.

15. Brattle, "Letter," 184.

16. Konig, *Law and Society*, 171.

17. Rosenthal, *Records of the Salem Witch-Hunt*, Doc. 220.

18. Konig, *Law and Society*, 177.

19. Sewall, *Diary*, 1:373.

20. Baker, *Storm of Witchcraft*, 55–56.

21. Sewall, *Diary*, 1:373.

22. Rosenthal, *Records of the Salem Witch-Hunt*, Doc. 360. The full moon is mentioned in Roach, *The Salem Witch Trials*, 172.

23. Rosenthal, *Records of the Salem Witch-Hunt*, Docs. 23, 254.

24. Rosenthal, *Records of the Salem Witch-Hunt*, Doc. 360. Martha Carrier was another person accused of witchcraft.

25. Roach, *The Salem Witch Trials*, 172 and note, 173.

26. Hoffer, *Devil's Disciples*, 139; Ray, *Satan and Salem*. 181.

27. Roach, *The Salem Witch Trials*, 171 and note.

28. Mather, "Return of Several Ministers," 117–118.

29. Stephen L. Robbins, "Samuel Willard and the Spectres of God's Wrathful Lion," *New England Quarterly* 60, no. 4 (December 1987): 597.

30. Konig, *Law and Society*, 172.

31. Ray, *Satan and Salem*. 80.

32. For one example of Parris on spectral evidence, see Parris, *Sermon Notebook*, 198.

33. Mather, "Return of Several Ministers," 118.

34. Ray, *Satan and Salem*, 71.

35. Mather, "Return of Several Ministers," 118.

36. Mather, "Return of Several Ministers," 118.

37. Hoffer, *Devil's Disciples*, 150.

38. Ray, *Satan and Salem*, 79–80.

39. Baker, *Storm of Witchcraft*, 188.

40. Rosenthal, *Salem Story*, 192–193.

41. Ray, *Satan and Salem*, 81 and note 49.

42. Quoted in Mark A. Peterson, "'Ordinary' Preaching and the Interpretation of the Salem Witchcraft Crisis by the Boston Clergy," *Essex Institute Historical Collections* 129, no. 1 (January 1993): 99.

43. Brattle, "Letter," 187.

44. Calef, *More Wonders*, 360.

45. Roach, *The Salem Witch Trials*, 177.

46. See Rosenthal, *Records of the Salem Witch-Hunt*, Docs. 28, 32.

47. Calef, *More Wonders*, 357, 358.

48. Rosenthal, *Records of the Salem Witch-Hunt*, Doc. 340.

49. Rosenthal, *Records of the Salem Witch-Hunt*, Doc. 340.

50. Rosenthal, *Records of the Salem Witch-Hunt*, Doc. 340.

51. For dating Sarah Good's trial, see Rosenthal, *Records of the Salem Witch-Hunt*, 415.

52. For them living in Reading, see Hoover, *Towne Family*, 15–16.

53. Mather describes Bishop as passing the meetinghouse on her way to trial, so presumably Rebecca was brought along the same route, see Mather, *Wonders of the Invisible World*, 229.

54. Perley, "The Court Houses in Salem," 104; Upham, *Salem Witchcraft*, 487.

55. General Court of Massachusetts, "The Liberties of the Massachusets Colonie in New England, 1641," in *American Historical Documents, 1000–1904*, vol. 43, Harvard Classics (New York: P. F. Collier and Son Company, 1910), Article 26.

56. Rosenthal, *Records of the Salem Witch-Hunt*, Doc. 921.

57. Beattie, *Crime and the Courts*, 271–272.

58. Beattie, *Crime and the Courts*, 345; Kadri, *The Trial*, 132.

59. Baker, *Storm of Witchcraft*, 26; Hoffer, *Devil's Disciples*, 162.

60. Brattle, "Letter," 184.

61. Italics in original. Beattie, *Crime and the Courts*, 341.

62. Massachusetts Office of Jury Commissioner, "Learn about the History of the Jury System," Mass.gov, 2019, https://www.mass.gov/info-details/learn-about-the-history-of-the-jury-system.

63. Trask, "Legal Procedures," 51.

64. Rosenthal, *Records of the Salem Witch-Hunt*, Doc. 460; Roach, "Biographical Notes," 940. It is not clear which twelve jurors served at Rebecca's trial, but several trial jurors for the Oyer and Terminer Court later signed an apology, see their declaration reprinted in Calef, *More Wonders*, 387–388.

65. John M. Zane, "The Attaint. I," *Michigan Law Review* 15, no. 1 (1916): 5–6.

66. Perley, *History of Salem*, 3:76.

67. This courtroom layout is based on a description of the Salem Town House as arranged in the early 1700s, as described in Martha J. McNamara, "'In the Face of the Court . . .': Law, Commerce, and the Transformation of Public Space in Boston, 1650–1770," *Winterthur Portfolio* 36, no. 2/3 (Summer/Autumn 2001): 133–134.

68. Roach, *Six Women of Salem*, 234.

69. Beattie, *Crime and the Courts*, 335.

70. David C. Brown, "The Case of Giles Corey," *Essex Institute Historical Collections* 121, no. 4 (October 1985): 286.

71. Trask, "Legal Procedures," 51.

72. Beattie, *Crime and the Courts*, 339.

73. General Court of Massachusetts, *Charters and General Laws*, 199. This right was exercised by George Burroughs at his trial later that summer, see Lawson, "Deodat Lawson's Narrative," 694. For use of this right in England at the time, see Beattie, *Crime and the Courts*, 340.

74. Rosenthal, *Records of the Salem Witch-Hunt*, Doc. 875 and note; Rosenthal, "General Introduction," 40 note 143.

75. Chandler, *American Criminal Trials*, 1:426.

76. Essex Institute, *The Fifth Half Century of the Landing of John Endicott at Salem, Massachusetts: Commemorative Exercises by the Essex Institute, September 18, 1878* (Salem: Essex Institute, 1879), 192.

77. Upham, *Salem Witchcraft*, 182.

78. Norton, *In the Devil's Snare*, 13.

79. Schiff, *The Witches*, 364.

80. Rosenthal, *Records of the Salem Witch-Hunt*, Doc. 285.

81. Trask, "Legal Procedures," 46.

82. Mather, *Wonders of the Invisible World*, 223.

83. Roach, "Biographical Notes," 930; Rosenthal, *Records of the Salem Witch-Hunt*, Doc. 17.

84. Rosenthal, *Records of the Salem Witch-Hunt*, Doc. 357.

85. Rosenthal, *Records of the Salem Witch-Hunt*, Doc. 360. The pins used by Bibber and others during antics in court are, allegedly, the ones on display today at the Essex County Superior Court's law library at the Salem courthouse, along with the Essex County seal used to stamp the death warrants in 1692. These pins have been on display at the courthouse since at least the nineteenth century, see Edwin M. Bacon, *Boston: A Guide Book* (Boston: Ginn & Company, 1903), 165; Tapley, *Chronicles of Danvers*, 25; Carl Webber and Winfield S. Nevins, *Old Naumkeag: An Historical Sketch of the City of Salem, and the Towns of Marblehead, Peabody, Beverly, Danvers, Wenham, Manchester, Topsfield, and Middleton* (A. A. Smith, 1877), 83. However, a more likely theory as to the origins of these

so-called "witch-pins" at the courthouse is that they were simply used to clip the trial papers together, instead of being evidence themselves.

86. Rosenthal, *Records of the Salem Witch-Hunt*, Doc. 358. On the incident with the pigs, see Chapter 4. On the two Sarah Holtens, see Chapter 7.

87. Rosenthal, *Records of the Salem Witch-Hunt*, Doc. 358.

88. Rosenthal, *Records of the Salem Witch-Hunt*, Doc. 358.

89. Rosenthal, *Records of the Salem Witch-Hunt*, Doc. 254.

90. Roach, "Biographical Notes," 945.

91. Rosenthal, *Records of the Salem Witch-Hunt*, Doc. 359 and note.

92. Rosenthal, *Records of the Salem Witch-Hunt*, Doc. 359.

93. Rosenthal, *Records of the Salem Witch-Hunt*, Doc. 360 and note.

94. Rosenthal, *Records of the Salem Witch-Hunt*, Docs. 360, 254.

95. Rosenthal, *Records of the Salem Witch-Hunt*, Doc. 361.

96. "Salem Village Church Book," 24, November 26, 1694.

97. Rosenthal, *Records of the Salem Witch-Hunt*, Doc. 363.

98. Rosenthal, *Records of the Salem Witch-Hunt*, Doc. 362 and note.

99. Rosenthal, *Records of the Salem Witch-Hunt*, Doc. 362. For Mrs. Ann Putnam's statement, see Doc. 267.

100. Rosenthal, *Records of the Salem Witch-Hunt*, Doc. 362.

101. Rosenthal, *Records of the Salem Witch-Hunt*, Docs. 32, 291.

102. Fels, *Switching Sides*, 95.

103. Mather, *Wonders of the Invisible World*, 229, 217, 241.

104. Mary Beth Norton connects this accusation to Nurse's trial. Norton, *In the Devil's Snare*, 224–225.

105. Calef, *More Wonders*, 360.

106. Rosenthal, *Records of the Salem Witch-Hunt*, Doc. 417.

107. Brattle, "Letter," 175.

108. Trask, "Legal Procedures," 52.

109. Previously they entered a deposition before Attorney General Newton, though there is no evidence that this document was entered at Rebecca's trial. See Rosenthal, *Records of the Salem Witch-Hunt*, Doc. 417.

110. Rosenthal, *Records of the Salem Witch-Hunt*, Doc. 417.

111. Rosenthal, *Records of the Salem Witch-Hunt*, Docs. 67, 95.

112. Calef, *More Wonders*, 358; Rosenthal, *Records of the Salem Witch-Hunt*, Doc. 416.

113. Rosenthal, *Records of the Salem Witch-Hunt*, Doc. 417.

114. Beattie, *Crime and the Courts*, 350.

115. Norton, *In the Devil's Snare*, 218–219.

116. Beattie, *Crime and the Courts*, 341.

117. Norton, *In the Devil's Snare*, 209.

118. Rosenthal, *Records of the Salem Witch-Hunt*, Doc. 35.

119. Rosenthal, *Records of the Salem Witch-Hunt*, Doc. 364; Roach, "Biographical Notes," 941.

120. Roach, "Biographical Notes," 947.

121. Rosenthal, *Records of the Salem Witch-Hunt*, Doc. 365.

122. Rosenthal, *Records of the Salem Witch-Hunt*, Doc. 365.

123. Roach, "Biographical Notes," 954.

124. Rosenthal, *Records of the Salem Witch-Hunt*, Doc. 367.

125. Roach, "Biographical Notes," 948.

126. Rosenthal, *Records of the Salem Witch-Hunt*, Docs. 293, 368.

127. Rosenthal, *Records of the Salem Witch-Hunt*, Doc. 368.

128. Rosenthal, *Records of the Salem Witch-Hunt*, Doc. 293.

129. Roach, "Biographical Notes," 931; Rosenthal, *Records of the Salem Witch-Hunt*, Doc. 369.

130. Rosenthal, *Records of the Salem Witch-Hunt*, Doc. 498.

131. Rosenthal, *Records of the Salem Witch-Hunt*, Doc. 369.

132. Rosenthal, *Records of the Salem Witch-Hunt*, Doc. 370.

133. Rosenthal, *Records of the Salem Witch-Hunt*, Doc. 371.

134. Ray, *Satan and Salem*, 64.

135. Rosenthal, *Records of the Salem Witch-Hunt*, Doc. 372.

136. Upham, *Salem Witchcraft*, 560.

137. See Rosenthal, *Records of the Salem Witch-Hunt*, Docs. 254, 360.

138. For Mrs. Ann Putnam's accusation, see Rosenthal, *Records of the Salem Witch-Hunt*, Doc. 267.

139. Roach, "Biographical Notes," 958.

140. Rosenthal, *Records of the Salem Witch-Hunt*, Doc. 372.

141. Rosenthal, *Records of the Salem Witch-Hunt*, Docs. 340, 294.

142. Rosenthal, *Records of the Salem Witch-Hunt*, Docs. 254, 31.

143. Rosenthal, *Records of the Salem Witch-Hunt*, Doc. 373; Putnam, *Rebecca Nurse and Her Friends*, 20, 24.

144. Rosenthal, *Records of the Salem Witch-Hunt*, Doc. 362.

145. Rosenthal, *Records of the Salem Witch-Hunt*, Doc. 373.

146. Italics included in Burr's reprint of the original. Brattle, "Letter," 188.

147. Ray, *Satan and Salem*, 77–78.

148. Ray, *Satan and Salem*, 77–78; Rosenthal, *Salem Story*, 69.

149. Richard Bernard, *A Guide to Grand-Jury Men, Divided into Two Books*, 2nd ed. (London: Felix Kingston, 1627), 217.

150. Hoffer, *Devil's Disciples*, 157; Beattie, *Crime and the Courts*, 341.

151. Upham, *Salem Witchcraft*, 509. Calef mentions that there were afflicted persons outside of the courtroom, see: Calef, *More Wonders*, 358–359.

152. Calef, *More Wonders*, 358.

153. Calef, *More Wonders*, 358.

154. Calef, *More Wonders*, 358.

155. Bernard Rosenthal makes this argument in Rosenthal, *Salem Story*, 93–94.

156. Hansen, *Witchcraft at Salem*, 128–129.

157. Rosenthal, *Records of the Salem Witch-Hunt*, Doc. 416.

158. Rosenthal, *Records of the Salem Witch-Hunt*, Doc. 416.

159. Beattie, *Crime and the Courts*, 398.

160. Rosenthal, *Records of the Salem Witch-Hunt*, Docs. 416, 417.

CHAPTER 10: BODY AND SOUL

Epigraph: Winthrop, "Model of Christian Charity," 47.

1. First Church in Salem, *Records of the First Church in Salem*, 172. Rev. Higginson, the senior minister who presided over Rebecca's admittance into the church in 1672, was ill and not very involved in the events of 1692; see Hale, *Modest Enquiry*, 401.

2. First Church in Salem, *Records of the First Church in Salem*, 172.

3. David C. Brown, "The Keys of the Kingdom: Excommunication in Colonial Massachusetts," *New England Quarterly* 67, no. 4 (1994): 556.

4. Jonathan Edwards, "Sinners in Zion," in *Sermons and Discourses, 1739–1742*, ed. Harry S. Stout, 26 vols. (New Haven: Yale University Press, 1957), 22:277.

5. Brown, "The Keys of the Kingdom," 545.

6. For details of the rite, such as that the excommunicate was standing, see John Demos, ed., "Proceedings of Excommunication against Mistress Ann Hibbens of Boston," in *Remarkable Providences: Readings on Early American History* (Boston: Northeastern University Press, 1991), 263–282.

7. Upham describes Noyes as being "corpulent"; see Upham, *Salem Witchcraft*, 496.

8. Demos, "Proceedings of Excommunication," 281.

9. Demos, "Proceedings of Excommunication," 281.

10. Burr, *Narratives of the New England Witchcraft Cases*, 206.

11. Rosenthal, *Records of the Salem Witch-Hunt*, Doc. 285.

12. Rosenthal, *Records of the Salem Witch-Hunt*, Doc. 416.

13. Rosenthal, *Records of the Salem Witch-Hunt*, Doc. 417.

14. Rosenthal, *Records of the Salem Witch-Hunt*, Docs. 294, 366.

15. Upham, *Salem Witchcraft*, 524.

16. Calef, *More Wonders*, 359.

17. Roach, *The Salem Witch Trials*, 192–193, 194, 196.

18. Marilynne K. Roach suggests this possibility in Roach, *Six Women of Salem*, 273.

19. General Court of Massachusetts, "Body of Liberties," Article 47.

20. Roach, *The Salem Witch Trials*, 194.

21. Rosenthal, *Records of the Salem Witch-Hunt*, Doc. 418.

22. Hammond, *Diary*, 22.

23. Hall, *Worlds of Wonder*, 79–80.

24. Rosenthal, *Records of the Salem Witch-Hunt*, Doc. 418.

25. Sidney Perley, "Where the Salem Witches Were Hanged," *Historical Collections of the Danvers Historical Society* 9 (1921): 39.

26. Calef, *More Wonders*, 361.

27. Roach, *A Time Traveler's Maps of the Salem Witchcraft Trials*, 6; Sidney Perley, "Part of Salem in 1700 No. 7," *Essex Antiquarian* 5, no. 10–12 (December 1901): 145.

28. Although there were no prior executions in Salem, there were subsequent ones post–1692 on an entirely different spot. These four hangings took place between 1778 and 1821 on Winter Island, see Roach, *Gallows and Graves*, 8.

29. Rosenthal, *Records of the Salem Witch-Hunt*, Docs. 313, 418.

30. The current historical consensus rests on the research of early twentieth-century Salem historian Sidney Perley. See Perley, "Where the Salem Witches Were Hanged," 33–50. Marilynne K. Roach discovered further evidence to support Perley's theory, and the theory was again corroborated by a group of scholars in 2016 who determined that Perley's conclusion is the most plausible theory. See Roach, *Gallows and Graves*; and Emerson W. Baker, "Gallows Hill Project," Emerson W. Baker, History Dept., Salem State University, January 11, 2016, http://w3.salemstate.edu/~ebaker/Gallows_Hill#pressrelease. The memorial recently constructed on Pope St. does not mark the exact location where the victims were executed, but rather it marks the bottom of the small ledge. Perley actually placed the probable site of the executions higher up on the Proctor St. side at the top of

the ledge, above and behind the memorial. See Perley, "Where the Salem Witches Were Hanged," frontispiece.

31. Perley, "Where the Salem Witches Were Hanged," 33, 39, 45; Perley, "Part of Salem in 1700 No. 7," 149.

32. Perley, "Where the Salem Witches Were Hanged," 36–37, 42.

33. Calef, *More Wonders*, 367.

34. Calef describes a ladder at the executions: Calef, *More Wonders*, 367.

35. See Roach, *Gallows and Graves*, 14.

36. The author is indebted to Richard B. Trask for pointing out this piece of evidence. Rosenthal, *Records of the Salem Witch-Hunt*, Doc. 480.

37. Northfields visible, see Perley, "Part of Salem in 1700 No. 7," 148.

38. Sewall, *Diary*, 1:363.

39. Dunton, *Letters*, 118.

40. Cotton Mather, "Letter to John Cotton, August 5, 1692," in *Selected Letters of Cotton Mather*, ed. Kenneth Silverman (Baton Rouge: Louisiana State University Press, 1971), 40–41; For Mather being present at the August 19 executions: Calef, *More Wonders*, 360–361.

41. Calef, *More Wonders*, 361.

42. Calef, *More Wonders*, 360.

43. Mather, "Letter to John Cotton, August 5, 1692," 40–41.

44. Calef, *More Wonders*, 360.

45. Rev. 16:6. Emerson W. Baker makes this connection between Sarah Good's response to Rev. Noyes and the Book of Revelation in Baker, *Storm of Witchcraft*, 32.

46. Upham, *Salem Witchcraft*, 497.

47. Calef, *More Wonders*, 367.

48. Nathaniel Cary in Calef, *More Wonders*, 352.

49. Peter Charles Hoffer, *Devil's Disciples*, 177.

50. Rosenthal, *Records of the Salem Witch-Hunt*, Doc. 418.

51. Trina N. Seitz, "A History of Execution Methods in the United States," in *Handbook of Death and Dying*, ed. Clifton D. Bryant, vol. 1 (Thousand Oaks, CA: Sage, 2003), 358.

52. Seitz, "A History of Execution Methods in the United States," 358.

53. Keith D. Wilson, *Cause of Death: A Writer's Guide to Death, Murder, and Forensic Medicine* (Cincinnati, Ohio: Writer's Digest Books, 1992), 114, 126–129.

54. Sewall, *Diary*, 1:363.

55. A colony law from 1641 stated: "Nor shall the body of any man so put to death, be unburied twelve hours, unless it be in case of anatomy." See General Court of Massachusetts, *Charters and General Laws*, 80.

56. Calef, *More Wonders*, 361.

57. Crossed in original. Rosenthal, *Records of the Salem Witch-Hunt*, Doc. 313.

58. Upham, *Salem Witchcraft*, 494.

59. David L. Greene, "Salem Witches II: George Jacobs," *American Genealogist* 58, no. 2 (April 1982): 71.

60. Quoted in Baker, *Storm of Witchcraft*, 36.

61. Gagnon, "Skeletons in the Closet," 54–60.

62. Upham, *Salem Witchcraft*, 513–514. Potentially, Nurse's relative Caleb Buffum, who lived near the execution site, helped the Nurse family retrieve the body. This tradition, related by Salem historian Sidney Perley, claimed that the Buffums helped remove the bodies

of Nurse, George Jacobs Sr., and John Proctor by boat. See Perley, "Where the Salem Witches Were Hanged," 46; Perley, "Part of Salem in 1700 No. 7," 149. Caleb Buffum was a distant relative by marriage to one of Nurse's aunts, and as a carpenter he also made coffins and he may have assisted in that respect as well: Roach, *Six Women of Salem*, 281; Winfield S. Nevins, *Witchcraft in Salem Village in 1692: Together With Some Account of Other Witchcraft Prosecutions In New England and Elsewhere* (Salem, Mass.: North Shore Publishing, 1892),77 and note.

63. For land, see Upham, *Salem Witchcraft*, 513–514; for boat, see Perley, "Where the Salem Witches Were Hanged," 46.

64. Hill, *Hunting for Witches*, 89.

CHAPTER 11: AFTERMATH

Epigraph: Brattle, "Letter," 190.

1. Samuel Sewall noted in his diary the drought continuing later that summer, see Sewall, *Diary*, 1:363.

2. Mather, "Letter to John Cotton, August 5, 1692," 40.

3. Roach, *The Salem Witch Trials*, 205.

4. Rosenthal, *Records of the Salem Witch-Hunt*, Docs. 426, 428. Newbury Falls is along the Parker River in the present-day village of Byfield, near the intersection of Central and Orchard Streets.

5. For previous mentions of satanic baptisms, see Mather, *Wonders of the Invisible World*, 240.

6. Brattle, "Letter," 174.

7. Rosenthal, *Records of the Salem Witch-Hunt*, Doc. 428.

8. Calef, *More Wonders*, 363.

9. General Court of Massachusetts, "Body of Liberties," Article 45.

10. Roach, *The Salem Witch Trials*, 220.

11. Roach, *The Salem Witch Trials*, 219.

12. Roach, *The Salem Witch Trials*, 240–241.

13. Cotton Mather, "Letter to John Foster, August 17, 1692," in *Selected Letters of Cotton Mather*, ed. Kenneth Silverman (Baton Rouge: Louisiana State University Press, 1971), 41.

14. See note 47 in Chapter 6 about this line written on the back of Parris' transcript of Rebecca's hearing.

15. Upham, *Salem Witchcraft*, 618.

16. Hale, *Modest Enquiry*, 421.

17. Hale, *Modest Enquiry*, 421.

18. Mather, *Cases of Conscience*, 71.

19. Nevins, *Witchcraft in Salem Village*, 77.

20. "Salem Village Church Book," 12, August 14, 1692.

21. "Salem Village Church Book," 12, August 31, 1692.

22. Ray, *Satan and Salem*, 139.

23. Parris, *Sermon Notebook*, 199.

24. Parris, *Sermon Notebook*, 201.

25. Parris, *Sermon Notebook*, 206.

26. Rosenthal, *Records of the Salem Witch-Hunt*, Doc. 596 and note.

27. *EQC*, 6:191.

28. General Court of Massachusetts, "Body of Liberties," Article 45; Roach, *The Salem Witch Trials*, 293.

29. Brown, "The Case of Giles Corey," 287.

30. Brown, "The Case of Giles Corey," 282–283, 290.

31. Brown, "The Forfeitures at Salem, 1692," 103.

32. Calef, *More Wonders*, 367; Roach, *The Salem Witch Trials*, 297.

33. Roach, *The Salem Witch Trials*, 300.

34. Calef, *More Wonders*, 369.

35. Baker, *Storm of Witchcraft*, 190–191.

36. Hammond, *Diary*, 23.

37. Roach, *The Salem Witch Trials*, Appendix A; Burr, *Narratives of the New England Witchcraft Cases*, 201 note.

38. Increase Mather, *Cases of Conscience Concerning Evil Spirits Personating Men, Witchcrafts, Infallible Proofs of Guilt in Such as Are Accused with That Crime* (Boston: Benjamin Harris, 1693), 3–6, 9, 38–39.

39. Roach, *The Salem Witch Trials*, 309.

40. Mather, *Cases of Conscience*, A4.

41. Roach, *The Salem Witch Trials*, 313.

42. The trials he used as examples are those of George Burroughs, Bridget Bishop, Susannah Martin, Elizabeth Howe, and Martha Carrier.

43. Burr, *Narratives of the New England Witchcraft Cases*, 206; Mather, "Wonders of the Invisible World," 250.

44. Sewall, *Diary*, 1:365–366.

45. Mather, "Wonders of the Invisible World," 212–213, 250–251.

46. Phips, "Letter of October 12, 1692," 197.

47. Phips, "Letter of October 12, 1692," 197–198.

48. Phips, "Letter of October 12, 1692," 197.

49. Baker, *Storm of Witchcraft*, 195; Samuel Willard, *Some Miscellany Observations on Our Present Debates Respecting Witchcrafts, in a Dialogue between S. and B. By P. E. and J. A.* (Philadelphia: William Bradford for Hezekiah Usher, 1692).

50. Mather, "Wonders of the Invisible World," 209.

51. Baker, *Storm of Witchcraft*, 195.

52. Roach, *The Salem Witch Trials*, 317–318.

53. Increase Mather, "Recantation of Confessors of Witchcraft," *Collections of the Massachusetts Historical Society*, 2nd ser., 3 (1815), 224, 270.

54. Parris, *Sermon Notebook*, 207.

55. Sewall, *Diary*, 1:367.

56. Sewall, *Diary*, 1:368.

57. Roach, *The Salem Witch Trials*, 324–325.

58. Henry Wheatland, ed., *Baptisms at Church in Salem Village, Now North Parish, Danvers* (Salem, Mass.: Salem Press, 1880), 4.

59. Roach, *The Salem Witch Trials*, 327.

60. Roach, *The Salem Witch Trials*, 331.

61. Sewall, *Diary*, 1:369–370.

62. General Court of Massachusetts, *Charters and General Laws*, 222; Roach, *The Salem Witch Trials*, 338.

63. Commonwealth of Massachusetts, "About the Supreme Judicial Court," Massachusetts Court System, 2018, https://www.mass.gov/service-details/about-the-supreme-judicial-court.

64. "Salem Village Record Book," 58, December 7, 1692.
65. "Salem Village Record Book," 58, December 13, 1692.
66. Rosenthal, *Records of the Salem Witch-Hunt*, Doc. 721.
67. A section of the law prohibited the forfeiture of goods by those convicted of witchcraft. Forfeiture was traditionally prohibited under Massachusetts law, but allowed by English law, causing a discrepancy. Roach, *The Salem Witch Trials*, 347.
68. Roach, *The Salem Witch Trials*, 347.
69. Roach, *The Salem Witch Trials*, 355.
70. The exact phrase that the jury was told when asked how much weight they should give to spectral evidence was "as much as of chips in wort," meaning no weight at all. Calef, *More Wonders*, 382 and note 7.
71. Rosenthal, *Records of the Salem Witch-Hunt*, Docs. 809, 810, 811.
72. Roach, *The Salem Witch Trials*, 365.
73. William Phips, "Letter of February 21, 1693, to the Earl of Nottingham," in *Narratives of the New England Witchcraft Cases*, ed. George Lincoln Burr (Mineola, N.Y.: Dover, 2002), 201.
74. Roach, *The Salem Witch Trials*, 371.
75. Phips, "Letter of February 21, 1693," 201.
76. Phips, "Letter of February 21, 1693," 201.
77. Quoted in Calef, *More Wonders*, 382–383.
78. For one example, see Roach, *The Salem Witch Trials*, 388.
79. "Salem Village Church Book," 12–13, December 26, 1692.
80. "Salem Village Church Book," 13, December 26, 1692.
81. "Salem Village Church Book," 13–14, January 17, 1692/3.
82. "Salem Village Church Book," 14, January 25, 1693; Roach, *The Salem Witch Trials*, 369.
83. "Salem Village Record Book," 59, February 3, 1693.
84. "Salem Village Church Book," 14, February 5, 1692/3.
85. "Salem Village Church Book," 14–15, February 16, 1692/3.
86. See Mather, *Cases of Conscience*, 38–39.
87. "Salem Village Church Book," 15, February 16, 1692/3.
88. "Salem Village Church Book," 15, February 16, 1692/3.
89. "Salem Village Church Book," 14, February 7, 1692/3 and February 16, 1692/3.
90. Baker, *Storm of Witchcraft*, 238.
91. J. H. Temple, *History of Framingham, Massachusetts, Early Known as Danforth's Farms, 1640–1680* (Framingham, Mass.: Town of Framingham, 1887), 653; Baker, *Storm of Witchcraft*, 240.
92. "Salem Village Church Book," 15, February 16, 1692/3.
93. "Salem Village Church Book," 15, February 16, 1692/3.
94. "Salem Village Church Book," 14, February 16, 1692/3.
95. "Salem Village Church Book," 15, February 16, 1692/3.
96. "Salem Village Church Book," 15-16, March 27, 1693.
97. James Smith had refused election to the committee and so was let off, and likewise Joseph Holten Jr., who by reasons of health was unable to complete the responsibility. Roach, *The Salem Witch Trials*, 393.
98. "Salem Village Church Book," 16, March 28 and April 14, 1693.
99. "Salem Village Church Book," 16, April 20, 1693; Roach, *The Salem Witch Trials*, 397–398.

100. "Salem Village Church Book," 16–17, April 21, 1693.

101. "Salem Village Church Book," 17, May 18, 1693.

102. "Salem Village Church Book," 17, May 18, 1693.

103. United States Works Progress Administration and Frost, *Verbatim Transcriptions of the Records of the Quarterly Courts of Essex County*, 57:63–1.

104. Nothing further can be found of Susannah Trevet, though her deposition notes her as being "about 20" years old in 1694. United States Works Progress Administration and Frost, *Verbatim Transcriptions of the Records of the Quarterly Courts of Essex County*, 57:64–3.

105. For all of the records for this case, see United States Works Progress Administration and Frost, *Verbatim Transcriptions of the Records of the Quarterly Courts of Essex County*, 57:63–1 through 57:65–4.

106. "Salem Village Church Book," 23–24, November 26, 1694.

107. Ray, *Satan and Salem*, 151; Gragg, *Quest for Security*, 134.

108. "Salem Village Church Book," 25, November 26, 1694.

109. "Salem Village Church Book," 25, November 26, 1694.

110. "Salem Village Church Book," 25, November 30, 1694.

111. Parris, *Sermon Notebook*, 245–251, 263–272, 272–281.

112. "Salem Village Church Book," 18, October 23, 1695, and 27, February 7, 1695.

113. For two petitions, see Boyer and Nissenbaum, *Salem-Village Witchcraft*, 258–260.

114. "Salem Village Church Book," 26–27, February 7, 1695.

115. Roach, *The Salem Witch Trials*, 533.

116. Elizabeth Parris tombstone, Wadsworth Cemetery, Danvers, Mass.

117. "Salem Village Record Book," 77, April 27, 1697.

118. Petition reprinted in Boyer and Nissenbaum, *Salem-Village Witchcraft*, 265–267.

119. "Salem Village Record Book," 78, September 14, 1697.

120. Deed reprinted in Boyer and Nissenbaum, *Salem-Village Witchcraft*, 267–268.

121. Upham, *Salem Witchcraft*, 669.

CHAPTER 12: REDEMPTION

Epigraph: Anne Bradstreet, *To My Husband and Other Poems* (Mineola, N.Y.: Dover, 2000), 45.

1. See artist's rendition in Trask, *Meetinghouse*, 19.

2. Putnam, *History of the Putnam Family*, 38; Baker, *Storm of Witchcraft*, 234.

3. Putnam, *History of the Putnam Family*, 74.

4. "Salem Village Church Book," 46–47, August 25, 1706.

5. Baker, *Storm of Witchcraft*, 103.

6. General Court of Massachusetts, *Charters and General Laws*, 59.

7. Upham, *Salem Witchcraft*, 672.

8. According to Charles S. Tapley's genealogical research, described in Richard P. Zollo, *On the Sands of Time: The Life of Charles Sutherland Tapley* (Danvers, Mass.: Danvers Historical Society, 1990), 36.

9. Francis, *Judge Sewall's Apology*, 177.

10. Resolution printed in Calef, *More Wonders*, 385–386.

11. Baker, *Storm of Witchcraft*, 195.

12. Sewall, *Diary*, 1:445.

13. Roach, *The Salem Witch Trials*, 557.

14. Ray, *Satan and Salem*. 166.

15. Upham, *Lectures on Witchcraft*, 129–130.

16. Samuel Sewall, *The Selling of Joseph: A Memorial* (Boston: Bartholomew Green and John Allen, 1700), 2.

17. Declaration reprinted in Calef, *More Wonders*, 387–388.

18. Matthews, "Massachusetts Royal Commissions," 88.

19. Roach, *The Salem Witch Trials*, 459, 485; Baker and Reid, *New England Knight*, 247–248.

20. Roach, *The Salem Witch Trials*, 538.

21. Hutchinson, *The History of the Province of Massachusetts-Bay*, 2:55 and note.

22. Roach, *The Salem Witch Trials*, 572.

23. Thomas Maule, *Truth Held Forth and Maintained According to the Testimony of the Holy Prophets, Christ and His Apostles Recorded in the Holy Scriptures* (New York: William Bradford, 1695).

24. *EQC*, 8:222–226.

25. Baker, *Storm of Witchcraft*, 215–216.

26. Roach, *The Salem Witch Trials*, 514.

27. Konig, *Law and Society*, 190; Perley, "The Court Houses in Salem." 104.

28. Perley, "The Court Houses in Salem," 104; Baker, *Storm of Witchcraft*, 8.

29. Maule later demonstrated not just his bravery in contesting his right to publish his opinions, but also a great knack for puns when he published his second book, which included an account of his trial: Thomas Maule, *New-England Pesecutors (sic) Mauled With Their Own Weapons* (New York: William Bradford, 1697).

30. Burr, *Narratives of the New England Witchcraft Cases*, 293; Upham, *Salem Witchcraft*, 265.

31. Hale, *Modest Enquiry*, 427.

32. Owen Davies, *America Bewitched: The Story of Witchcraft After Salem* (Oxford: Oxford University Press, 2013), 3.

33. See Edmund S. Morgan, "The Witch & We, The People," *American Heritage* 34, no. 5 (September 1983).

34. Baker, *Storm of Witchcraft*, 248.

35. Rosenthal, *Records of the Salem Witch-Hunt*, Doc. 876.

36. Rosenthal, *Records of the Salem Witch-Hunt*, Doc. 876.

37. Rosenthal, *Records of the Salem Witch-Hunt*, Doc. 878.

38. Roach, *The Salem Witch Trials*, 568.

39. Rosenthal, *Records of the Salem Witch-Hunt*, Doc. 878.

40. Rosenthal, *Records of the Salem Witch-Hunt*, Doc. 879.

41. W. J. Eccles, *The Canadian Frontier, 1534–1760* (New York: Holt, Rinehart, and Winston, 1969), 139.

42. Tapley, *Chronicles of Danvers*, 32; Danvers, *Soldiers' Record*, 97.

43. Rosenthal, *Records of the Salem Witch-Hunt*, Doc. 881.

44. Roach, *The Salem Witch Trials*, 569.

45. Rosenthal, *Records of the Salem Witch-Hunt*, Doc. 921. The title of this document in *Records* lists the author as Samuel Nurse Jr., but it is Samuel Nurse Sr., Rebecca's son.

46. Rosenthal, *Records of the Salem Witch-Hunt*, Doc. 921.

47. Rosenthal, *Records of the Salem Witch-Hunt*, Doc. 921 and note.

48. Rosenthal, *Records of the Salem Witch-Hunt*, Doc. 929.

49. Benton, *Town House*, 206–207.

50. Sewall, *Diary*, 2:323–324. Sewall recounts that the fire was visible twenty leagues away.

51. Rosenthal, *Records of the Salem Witch-Hunt*, Doc. 931.

52. Rosenthal, *Salem Story*, 184.

53. Rosenthal, *Records of the Salem Witch-Hunt*, Doc. 931.

54. Roach, *The Salem Witch Trials*, 586; General Court of Massachusetts, "An Act Relative to the Witchcraft Trial of 1692," § Chapter 122 (2001), https://malegislature.gov/Laws/SessionLaws/Acts/2001/Chapter122.

55. Rosenthal, *Records of the Salem Witch-Hunt*, Doc. 931.

56. Rosenthal, *Records of the Salem Witch-Hunt*, Doc. 933.

57. Rosenthal, *Records of the Salem Witch-Hunt*, Doc. 934. Six of his seven siblings signed an authorization to this effect in February, 1712: Doc. 954. Benjamin Nurse, who moved from Salem Village to Framingham, signed a separate authorization three months later for Samuel Nurse to receive the funds on his behalf: Doc. 964.

58. Rosenthal, *Records of the Salem Witch-Hunt*, Docs. 958, 959.

59. Ray, *Satan and Salem*, 175.

60. First Church in Salem, *The Records of the First Church in Salem*, 218–219.

61. William W. K. Freeman, *Map of Salem in 1700* (Salem, Mass., 1933), Salem Witch Trials Documentary Archive, http://salem.lib.virginia.edu/perley.html; First Church in Salem, *The Records of the First Church in Salem*, 218–219.

62. First Church in Salem, *The Records of the First Church in Salem*, 218–219.

63. First Church in Salem, *The Records of the First Church in Salem*, 218–219.

64. Tapley, *Chronicles of Danvers*, 251.

65. Richard B. Trask, "The Creation of Danvers," Danvers Archival Center at the Peabody Institute Library, August 2013, http://www.danverslibrary.org/archive/?page_id=211.

66. Richard P. Zollo, *From Muskets to Missiles: Danvers in Five Wars* (Danvers, Mass.: R. P. Zollo, 2001), 38.

67. Danvers, *Soldiers' Record*, 110.

68. Tapley, *Chronicles of Danvers*, 70–71.

69. Putnam, "Historical Sketch of Danvers," 14.

70. Robert Ernst Hubbard, *Major General Israel Putnam: Hero of the American Revolution* (Jefferson, NC: McFarland and Company, 2017), 88.

71. Southern Essex Deeds, 137:194; Shirley Drury Patterson, "Sergeant Francis Nurse of the Nurse Homestead," *About Towne: Quarterly Newsletter of the Towne Family Association* 27, no. 3 (September 2007): 41.

72. Perley, "Endecott Land, Salem Village, in 1700," 119.

73. Putnam, *History of the Putnam Family*, 210–211.

74. Upham, *Salem Witchcraft*, 631.

75. Nathaniel Hawthorne, *Tales and Sketches: Including Twice-Told Tales, Mosses from an Old Manse, and The Snow Image* (New York: Library of America, 1982), 216.

76. Richard B. Trask, "Introduction," in *From Muskets to Missiles: Danvers in Five Wars*, by Richard P. Zollo (Danvers, Mass., 2001), 14.

77. Moynahan, *Danvers*, 78.

78. William P. Upham, "Account of the Rebecca Nurse Monument," in *Essex Institute Historical Collections*, vol. 23 (Salem, Mass.: Essex Institute, 1886), 151.

79. "Rebecca Nurse; Reunion of the Descendants of a Victim of the Witchcraft Delusion," *New York Times*, July 21, 1883, https://timesmachine.nytimes.com/timesmachine/

1883/07/21/102949018.pdf (accessed September 3, 2018); See also "The Descendants of Nurse; A Gathering at Danvers Which Recalled the Days of Witchcraft," *Boston Globe*, July 19, 1883, Boston Globe Archive.

80. Upham, "Account of the Rebecca Nurse Monument," 152.

81. "Witches," *News and Citizen* (Morrisville, Vt.), August 28, 1884, Chronicling America: Historic American Newspapers, Library of Congress, https://chroniclingamerica.loc.gov/lccn/sn97067613/1884-08–28/ed–1/seq–1/ (accessed February 19, 2019); "Inland," *Der Nordstern* (St. Cloud, Minn.), August 13, 1884, Chronicling America: Historic American Newspapers, Library of Congress, https://chroniclingamerica.loc.gov/lccn/sn83045350/1884-08–13/ed–1/seq–1/ (accessed February 19, 2019).

82. Southern Essex Deeds, 1155:57.

83. Upham, "Account of the Rebecca Nurse Monument," 225.

84. "A Martyr's Monument; Perpetuating the Memory of Rebecca Nurse - The False Charge of Superstition - Justice After Two Centuries," *Boston Globe*, July 26, 1885, Boston Globe Archive.

85. Upham, "Account of the Rebecca Nurse Monument," 225; Demos, *The Enemy Within*, 155.

86. Upham, "Account of the Rebecca Nurse Monument," 153; Nourse Monument Association, "Memorial Services at the Dedication of the Rebecca Nourse Monument" (July 30, 1885).

87. Upham, "Account of the Rebecca Nurse Monument," 211.

88. Upham, "Account of the Rebecca Nurse Monument," 222.

89. Upham, "Account of the Rebecca Nurse Monument," 212, 213, 214.

90. "Rebecca Nourse - Hanged as a Witch 200 Years Ago - Honored Today by Hundreds of Her Descendants," *Boston Daily Globe*, July 30, 1885, Evening edition, Boston Globe Archive.

91. "Rebecca Nourse; Hanged as a Witch Two Hundred Years Ago, Honored Yesterday by Hundreds of Her Descendants," *Boston Globe*, July 31, 1885, Morning edition, Boston Globe Archive.

92. "The Monument to Rebecca Nourse," *New York Times*, July 30, 1885; "News of The Week," *Dodge City Times* (Dodge City, Kan.), August 6, 1885, Chronicling America: Historic American Newspapers, Library of Congress, https://chroniclingamerica.loc.gov/lccn/sn84029838/1885-08-06/ed–1/seq–2/ (accessed February 19, 2019); "Miscellaneous News Notes," *Griggs Courier* (Cooperstown, Dakota Territory), August 7, 1885, Chronicling America: Historic American Newspapers, Library of Congress, https://chroniclingamerica.loc.gov/lccn/sn88076998/1885-08-07/ed–1/seq–2/ (accessed February 19, 2019); "Topics of the Day," *St. Landry Democrat* (Opelousas, La.), August 8, 1855, Chronicling America: Historic American Newspapers, Library of Congress, https://chroniclingamerica.loc.gov/lccn/sn88064537/1885-08-08/ed–1/seq–2/ (accessed February 19, 2019); "Told By the Telegraph," *Daily Morning Astorian* (Astoria, Oregon), August 1, 1885, Chronicling America: Historic American Newspapers, Library of Congress, https://chroniclingamerica.loc.gov/lccn/sn96061150/1885-08-01/ed–1/seq–3/ (accessed February 19, 2019); "Personal and General," *Grenada Sentinel* (Grenada, Miss.), August 8, 1885, Chronicling America: Historic American Newspapers, Library of Congress, https://chroniclingamerica.loc.gov/lccn/sn85034375/1885-08-08/ed–1/seq–2/ (accessed February 19, 2019); "Monument to Rebecca Nourse," *Hickman Courier* (Hickman, Ky.), June 5, 1885, Chronicling America: Historic American Newspapers, Library of Congress, https://chroni-

clingamerica.loc.gov/lccn/sn85052141/1885-06-05/ed–1/seq–1/ (accessed February 19, 2019); "Personal and General," *Milan Exchange* (Milan, Tenn.), August 8, 1885, Chronicling America: Historic American Newspapers, Library of Congress, https://chroniclingamerica.loc.gov/lccn/sn86053488/1885-08-08/ed–1/seq–6/ (accessed February 19, 2019); "Prudence Crandall," *Daily Republican* (Wilmington, Del.), January 22, 1886, Chronicling America: Historic American Newspapers, Library of Congress, https://chroniclingamerica.loc.gov/lccn/sn84038114/1886-01–29/ed–1/seq–3/ (accessed February 19, 2019); "The Town of Danvers, Mass.," *Cambria Freeman* (Ebensburg, Pa.), August 21, 1885, Chronicling America: Historic American Newspapers, Library of Congress, https://chroniclingamerica.loc.gov/lccn/sn83032041/1885-08–21/ed–1/seq–2/ (accessed February 19, 2019).

93. "Une Monument Funèbre à Une Sorcière," *Le Journal des Débats Politiques et Littéraires* (Paris), September 2, 1885, Bibliothèque nationale de France, https://gallica.bnf.fr/ark:/12148/bpt6k463309d (accessed February 19, 2019); "Une Sorcière Réhabilitée," *Le Petit Journal* (Paris), September 1, 1885, Bibliothèque nationale de France, https://gallica.bnf.fr/ark:/12148/bpt6k608779d (accessed February 19, 2019); "Gemengd Nieuws," *Het Nieuws van Den Dag* (Amsterdam), September 8, 1885, The European Library, http://www.theeuropeanlibrary.org/tel4/newspapers/issue/Het_nieuws_van_den_dag_:_kleine_courant/1885/9/8 (accessed February 19, 2019); "Local and General News," *Newcastle Morning Herald and Miners' Advocate*, September 7, 1885, Trove, National Library of Australia, http://nla.gov.au/nla.news-page15203570 (accessed February 19, 2019); "The Trials for Witchcraft at Salem," *London North News and Finsbury Gazette*, June 20, 1885, Newspaper Archive, https://newspaperarchive.com/london-north-news-and-finsbury-gazette-jun–20–1885-p–5/ (accessed February 19, 2019).

94. Upham, "Account of the Rebecca Nurse Monument," 216, 219–220.

95. Nourse Monument Association, "Nourse Reunion Broadside," 1889, Peabody Historical Society.

96. "Worthy Witch Memorial," *The New York Times*, July 31, 1892. https://timesmachine.nytimes.com/timesmachine/1892/07/31/104141987.pdf (accessed September 3, 2018).

97. Marion Gibson, *Witchcraft Myths in American Culture* (New York: Routledge, 2007), 66.

98. Gibson, *Witchcraft Myths in American Culture*, 61.

99. Upham, "Account of the Rebecca Nurse Monument," 204, 151.

100. Town of Danvers, *The Celebration of the One Hundred and Fiftieth Anniversary of the Establishment of the Town of Danvers, Massachusetts, as a Separate Municipality* (Boston: Fort Hill Press, 1907), 208.

101. Ezra D. Hines, "Historical Address," in *The Celebration of the One Hundred and Fiftieth Anniversary of the Establishment of the Town of Danvers, Massachusetts, as a Separate Municipality* (Boston: Fort Hill Press, 1907), 150.

102. Southern Essex Deeds, 1860:284–287; mortgage agreement in Southern Essex Deeds, 1860:288–292; Perley, "Endecott Land, Salem Village, in 1700," 120.

103. "Witch Goes to Trial at Danvers Pageant," *Daily Boston Globe*, July 1, 1930.

104. Roach, *The Salem Witch Trials*, 23.

105. Arthur Miller, "Journey to 'The Crucible'; Visit to Salem Recalled by the Author of the New Play," *New York Times*, February 8, 1953, New York edition.

106. Miller, "Journey to 'The Crucible.'"

107. For more on the parsonage excavation, see: Richard B. Trask, "Raising the Devil," *Yankee Magazine*, May 1972, 74–77, 190–201; McKern, "They're Digging up Witch Lore

in Salem," 27–28, 32–34; Richard B. Trask, "Letter: Danvers Educator Helped Shine Light on Origins of Witchcraft Hysteria," *Salem News*, April 27, 2010, sec. Opinion; Dan Gagnon, "The Salem Village Parsonage," *Danvers Herald*, November 15, 2019—article also posted online at: https://spectersofsalemvillage.com/2019/11/11/the-salem-village-parsonage/.

108. Ron Agrella, "Witchcraft Site to Be Historic Landmark," *Beverly Times*, October 20, 1990, reprinted in Richard B. Trask, ed., *Danvers Remembers: The Commemoration of the 1692 Salem Village Witchcraft Delusion* (Danvers, Mass.: Salem Village Tercentennial Committee of Danvers, 1993), 3.

109. Saeed Naqvi, "Rebecca Nurse Land Earmarked for Model Farm," *Salem News*, June 19, 1977.

110. Fox Butterfield, "The Witches of Salem Get a New Hearing," *New York Times*, October 28, 1984, National edition, sec. Arts, https://www.nytimes.com/1984/10/28/arts/television-the-witches-of-salem-get-a-new-hearing.html.

111. "Commemoration in Danvers Marks Anniversary of Hangings," *Salem Evening News*, July 20, 1992, reprinted in Trask, *Danvers Remembers*, 40–41.

112. Roach, *The Salem Witch Trials*, 587; Alexander Stevens, "Which City Is Witch City?," *North Shore Sunday*, April 26, 1992, reprinted in Trask, *Danvers Remembers*, 24–26.

113. Frances Hill, "Salem as Witch City," in *Salem: Place, Myth, and Memory*, ed. Dane Anthony Morrison and Nancy Lusignan Schultz (Boston: Northeastern University Press, 2004), 290–291.

114. "Kin of Accused Witch on Salem Village Board," *Salem Evening News*, December 26, 1989, reprinted in Trask, *Danvers Remembers*, 1–2. Tercentennial Committee members included the Committee's chairman and Danvers Town Archivist Richard Trask, the minister of the First Church of Danvers Rev. Chris Anderson, and the president of the Danvers Alarm List Co. (the nonprofit that preserves the Nurse homestead), George J. Meehan.

115. Agrella, "Witchcraft Site to Be Historic Landmark."

116. Trask, *Danvers Remembers*, 7; Myrna Fearer, "Salem Village, Circa 1692, Hungered for Independence: New Exhibit by Danvers Historical Society At Tapley Memorial Hall," *Danvers Herald*, March 17, 1992, reprinted in Trask, *Danvers Remembers*, 15–16; Douglas W. Rendell, "Tercentennial Lecture Series," in Trask, *Danvers Remembers*, 20–21.

117. "Walk Brings Witch Monument 10,000 Giant Steps Closer," *Danvers Herald*, October 24, 1991, reprinted in Trask, *Danvers Remembers*, 11–12. One example of how local residents worked to ensure the success of the memorial effort is the story of Robert Osgood. He was an older volunteer who for many years helped maintain the Nurse homestead, but suffered a stroke several years prior and walked with a cane. Undaunted, he started along the walk-a-thon route three hours before the other participants, and it took him a total of five hours to reach the finish line.

118. Myrna Fearer, "Memorial Honors Victims of the Witchcraft Delusion," *Danvers Herald*, May 14, 1992, reprinted in Trask, *Danvers Remembers*, 32–33.

119. The memorial in downtown Salem does not mention any of those who died in the dungeon-like jails during the witchcraft delusion, deaths caused by the terrible conditions in which the prisoners were forced to live.

120. Danvers Preservation Commission, Salem Village meetinghouse historical marker.

121. Danvers Board of Selectmen, "Proclamation: Day of Remembrance, Victims of Witchcraft Delusion," April 22, 1992, reprinted in Trask, *Danvers Remembers*, 23.

122. Salem Village Witchcraft Tercentennial Committee of Danvers, "Dedication of the Witchcraft Victims' Memorial," May 9, 1992. The memorial was designed by Chairman

Trask, Danvers architect Robert D. Farley, and Danvers resident Marjorie C. Wetzel.

123. Revelation 20:12.

124. Lawson, *A Brief and True Narrative*, 157.

125. Salem Village Witchcraft Tercentennial Committee of Danvers, "Dedication of the Witchcraft Victims' Memorial," May 9, 1992.

126. Salem Village Witchcraft Tercentennial Committee of Danvers, "Dedication of the Witchcraft Victims' Memorial," May 9, 1992.

127. "Commemoration in Danvers Marks Anniversary of Hangings," *Salem Evening News*, July 20, 1992.

128. Mary Byrne, "Danvers Ceremony Honors 325th Anniversary of Rebecca Nurse's Execution," *Danvers Herald*, July 20, 2017; Ethan Forman, "Facing Death, Witch Trials Victim Spoke Truth to Injustice," *Salem News*, July 19, 2017; Danvers Alarm List Company, "Rebecca Nurse Commemoration Ceremony" (July 19, 2017), Rebecca Nurse Homestead.

129. Dan Gagnon, "A Proclamation: Rebecca Nurse Day," *Newsletter of the Rebecca Nurse Preservation Society*, October 2017.

130. This author had the honor of reading the proclamation that day. Commonwealth of Massachusetts, "Proclamation: Rebecca Nurse Day, July 19, 2017" (Boston, July 11, 2017), Rebecca Nurse Homestead.

Bibliography

MANUSCRIPTS

Danvers Archival Center, Danvers, Mass.

"A Book of Record of the Severall Publique Transactions of the Inhabitants of Salem Village Vulgarly Called The Farmes," 1672–1703.

Allen, James. "Receipts, May 18, 1698 & April 24, 1699,"

"Copy of Deed to Nurse Farm," April 29, 1678.

First Church of Danvers Congregational. "Church Book Belonging to Salem Village 1689," 1689–1845.

The National Archives, Kew, United Kingdom

Randolph, Edward. "Letter from Edward Randolph to Robert Chaplin," October 28, 1689. CO 5/855 no. 46 PRO.

Norfolk Records Office, Norwich, United Kingdom

"Great Yarmouth Parish Registers, St. Nicholas Church," 1558–1653. PD28/1.

Rebecca Nurse Homestead, Danvers, Mass.

Commonwealth of Massachusetts. "Proclamation: Rebecca Nurse Day, July 19, 2017." Boston, July 11, 2017.

Danvers Alarm List Company. "Rebecca Nurse Commemoration Ceremony," July 19, 2017.

Nourse Monument Association. "Memorial Services at the Dedication of the Rebecca Nourse Monument," July 30, 1885.

Southern Essex Registry of Deeds, Salem, Mass.

Essex County Deeds.

James Duncan Philips Library, Peabody Essex Museum, Rowley, Mass.

"Examination of Rebecca Nurse." Manuscript. Salem Village, March 24, 1692. Essex County Court Archives, vol. 1, no. 72.

United States Works Progress Administration, and Archie N. Frost, eds. *Verbatim Transcriptions of the Records of the Quarterly Courts of Essex County Massachusetts, 1636–1694*. 57 vols., 1936.

PUBLISHED SOURCES

An Act to Authorize the President to Increase Temporarily the Military Establishment of the United States, Pub. L. No. 65–12, § 3, 40 U.S. Statutes at Large 76 (1917).

Agrella, Ron. "Witchcraft Site to Be Historic Landmark." *Beverly Times*. October 20, 1990. Reprinted in *Danvers Remembers: The Commemoration of the Tercentennial of the 1692 Salem Village Witchcraft Delusion*, edited by Richard B. Trask, 3. Danvers, Mass.: Salem Village Tercentennial Committee of Danvers, 1993.

Ankarloo, Bengt, Stuart Clark, and William Monter. *Witchcraft and Magic in Europe: The Period of the Witch Trials*. London: Athlone Press, 2002.

Bacon, Edwin M. *Boston: A Guide Book*. Boston: Ginn & Company, 1903.

Baker, Emerson W. "Gallows Hill Project." Emerson W. Baker, History Dept., Salem State University, January 11, 2016. http://w3.salemstate.edu/~ebaker/ Gallows_Hill #pressrelease.

———. "Salem as Frontier Outpost." In *Salem: Place, Myth, and Memory*, edited by Dane Anthony Morrison and Nancy Lusignan Schultz, 21–42. Boston: Northeastern University Press, 2004.

———. *A Storm of Witchcraft: The Salem Trials and the American Experience*. New York: Oxford University Press, 2015.

Baker, Emerson W., and John G. Reid. *The New England Knight: Sir William Phips, 1651–1695*. Toronto: University of Toronto Press, 1998.

Bartholomew, Robert E. "Public Health, Politics and the Stigma of Mass Hysteria: Lessons from an Outbreak of Unusual Illness." *Journal of the Royal Society of Medicine* 109, no. 5 (May 2016): 175–79. https://doi.org/10.1177/0141076816 628866.

Beard, James. *The Psychology of the Salem Witchcraft Excitement of 1692 and Its Practical Application to Our Own Time*. New York: G. P. Putnam's Sons, 1882.

Beattie, J. M. *Crime and the Courts in England, 1660–1800*. Princeton, NJ: Princeton University Press, 1986.

Benton, Josiah Henry. *The Story of the Old Boston Town House, 1658–1711*. Boston, 1908.

Bernard, Richard. *A Guide to Grand-Jury Men, Divided into Two Books*. 2nd ed. London: Felix Kingston, 1627. http://name.umdl.umich.edu/A09118.0001.001.

Bigsby, Christopher. "Introduction." In *The Crucible*, by Arthur Miller, vii–xxv. Penguin, 2003.

Bonfanti, Leo. *The Massachusetts Bay Colony*. Vol. 2. New England Historical Series. Wakefield, Mass.: Pride Publications, 1980.

The Book of Common Prayer: King James Anno 1604, Commonly Called the Hampton Court Book. London: William Pickering, 1844.

Boston Street Commissioners. *A Record of the Streets, Alleys, Places, Etc., in the City of Boston*. Boston: City of Boston, 1910.

Boyer, Paul, and Stephen Nissenbaum. *Salem Possessed: The Social Origins of Witchcraft.* Cambridge, Mass.: Harvard University Press, 1974.

———, eds. *Salem-Village Witchcraft: A Documentary Record of Local Conflict in Colonial New England.* Boston: Northeastern University Press, 1993.

———, eds. *The Salem Witchcraft Papers: Verbatim Transcripts of the Legal Documents of the Salem Witchcraft Outbreak of 1692.* 3 vols. New York: Da Capo, 1977.

Bradstreet, Anne. *To My Husband and Other Poems.* Mineola, N.Y.: Dover, 2000.

Brattle, Thomas. "Letter of Thomas Brattle, F.R.S., 1692." In *Narratives of the New England Witchcraft Cases,* edited by George Lincoln Burr, 165–90. 1914. Reprint, Mineola, N.Y.: Dover, 2002.

Bremer, Francis J. *Puritanism: A Very Short Introduction.* Oxford: Oxford University Press, 2009.

Breslaw, Elaine G. *Tituba, Reluctant Witch of Salem: Devilish Indians and Puritan Fantasies.* New York: NYU Press, 1997.

Brown, David C. "The Case of Giles Corey." *Essex Institute Historical Collections* 121, no. 4 (October 1985): 282–99.

———. "The Forfeitures at Salem, 1692." *William and Mary Quarterly* 50, no. 1 (January 1993): 85–111. https://doi.org/10.2307/2947237.

———. "The Keys of the Kingdom: Excommunication in Colonial Massachusetts." *New England Quarterly* 67, no. 4 (1994): 531–66. https://doi.org/10.2307/366434.

Bureau of Environmental Health, Massachusetts Department of Public Health. "Investigation of Neurological Vocal Tics and Repetitive Hiccups Reported Among Students Attending Essex Agricultural and Technical High School and North Shore Technical High School, Essex County, Massachusetts." Commonwealth of Massachusetts, November 2014. https://bloximages.chicago2.vip.townnews.com/salemnews.com/content/tncms/assets/v3/editorial/f/cf/fcf1196c-74ea-11e4-a6a9-2365eb13b147/5474f79712b88.pdf.pdf.

Burr, George Lincoln, ed. *Narratives of the New England Witchcraft Cases.* 1914. Reprint, Mineola, N.Y.: Dover, 2002.

Burroughs, George. "Rev. George Burroughs et al., to Governor and Council." In *Documentary History of the State of Maine,* edited by James Phinney Baxter, 5:316–17. Collections of the Maine Historical Society 2. Portland: Maine Historical Society, 1897.

Butterfield, Fox. "The Witches of Salem Get a New Hearing." *New York Times,* October 28, 1984, National edition, sec. Arts. https://www.nytimes.com/1984/10/28/arts/television-the-witches-of-salem-get-a-new-hearing.html.

Bynner, Edwin L. "Topography and Landmarks of the Colonial Period." In *The Memorial History of Boston, Including Suffolk County, Massachusetts, 1630–1880,* edited by Justin Winsor, 521–56. Boston: Ticknor and Company, 1880.

Byrne, Mary. "Danvers Ceremony Honors 325th Anniversary of Rebecca Nurse's Execution." *Danvers Herald,* July 20, 2017. https://danvers.wickedlocal.com/

news/20170720/danvers-ceremony-honors-325th-anniversary-of-rebecca-nurses-execution.

Cahill, Robert Ellis. *The Horrors of Salem's Witch Dungeon*. Peabody, Mass.: Chandler-Smith Publishing House, 1986.

Calef, Robert. *More Wonders of the Invisible World: Or, The Wonders of the Invisible World Display'd in Five Parts*. London: Nathaniel Hillar, 1700. Excerpted in *Narratives of the New England Witchcraft Cases*, edited by George Lincoln Burr, 289–395. 1914. Reprint, Mineola, N.Y.: Dover, 2002.

Caller, James M., and M. A. Ober. *Genealogy of the Descendants of Lawrence and Cassandra Southwick of Salem, Mass*. Salem, Mass.: J. H. Choate, 1881.

Caporael, Linnda R. "Ergotism: The Satan Loosed in Salem?" *Science* 192, no. 4234 (April 2, 1976): 21–26.

Carlson, Laurie Winn. *A Fever in Salem: A New Interpretation of the New England Witch Trials*. Chicago: Ivan R. Dee, 1999.

Chandler, Peleg W. *American Criminal Trials*. 2 vols. Boston: Charles C. Little and James Brown, 1844.

"The Charter of the Province of the Massachusetts Bay in New England, 1691." In *The Charters and General Laws of the Colony and Province of Massachusetts Bay*, 18–37. Boston: T. B. Wait and Co., 1814.

Chu, Jonathan M. "Nursing a Poisonous Tree: Litigation and Property Law in Seventeenth-Century Essex County, Massachusetts: The Case of Bishop's Farm." *American Journal of Legal History* 31, no. 3 (July 1987): 221–52. https://doi.org/10.2307/845691.

Clough, Samuel C. "Map of the Town of Boston, 1676." Boston, 1920. MHS Collections Online. https://www.masshist.org/database/viewer.php?item_id=1737&br=1.

Coffey, John, and Paul C. H. Lim. "Introduction." In *The Cambridge Companion to Puritanism*, edited by John Coffey and Paul C. H. Lim. Cambridge Companions to Religion. Cambridge: Cambridge University Press, 2008.

"Commemoration in Danvers Marks Anniversary of Hangings." *Salem Evening News*. July 20, 1992. Reprinted in *Danvers Remembers: The Commemoration of the Tercentennial of the 1692 Salem Village Witchcraft Delusion*, edited by Richard B. Trask, 40–41. Danvers, Mass.: Salem Village Tercentennial Committee of Danvers, 1993.

Commonwealth of Massachusetts. "About the Supreme Judicial Court." Massachusetts Court System, 2018. https://www.mass.gov/service-details/about-the-supreme-judicial-court.

Conforti, Joseph A. *Saints and Strangers: New England in British North America*. Baltimore: Johns Hopkins University Press, 2006.

Constitutional Reform Act 2005, § 23 (2005). https://www.legislation.gov.uk/ukpga/2005/4/section/23.

Cooper, Jr., James F., and Kenneth P. Minkema. "Introduction." In *The Sermon Notebook of Samuel Parris, 1689–1694*, by Samuel Parris, 1–36. Publications of

Colonial Society of Massachusetts 66. Boston: Colonial Society of Massachusetts, 1993.

Cremin, Lawrence A. *American Education: The Colonial Experience, 1607–1783*. New York: Harper & Row, 1970.

Cronon, William. *Changes in the Land: Indians, Colonists, and the Ecology of New England*. New York: Hill and Wang, 1983.

Dalton, Michael. *The Countrey Justice, Containing the Practice of the Justices of the Peace out of Their Sessions*. London: Company of Stationers, 1661.

Danvers Board of Selectmen. "Proclamation: Day of Remembrance, Victims of Witchcraft Delusion," April 22, 1992. Reprinted in *Danvers Remembers: The Commemoration of the Tercentennial of the 1692 Salem Village Witchcraft Delusion*, edited by Richard B. Trask, 3. Danvers, Mass.: Salem Village Tercentennial Committee of Danvers, 1993.

Danvers, Town of. "103 Ash Street." Town of Danvers Property Assessment Data. Accessed August 8, 2018. http://danvers.patriotproperties.com/Summary.asp?AccountNumber=7443.

———. *The Celebration of the One Hundred and Fiftieth Anniversary of the Establishment of the Town of Danvers, Massachusetts, as a Separate Municipality*. Boston: Fort Hill Press, 1907.

———. *Report of the Committee Appointed to Revise the Soldiers' Record*. Danvers, Mass.: Town of Danvers, 1895.

Davies, Owen. *America Bewitched: The Story of Witchcraft After Salem*. Oxford: Oxford University Press, 2013.

Davis, William T. "Salem: Miscellaneous." In *History of Essex County, Massachusetts, with Biographical Sketches of Many of Its Pioneers*, 1:161–66. Philadelphia: J. W. Lewis & Co., 1888.

Demos, John. *The Enemy Within: 2,000 Years of Witch-Hunting in the Western World*. New York: Viking, 2008.

Demos, John, ed. "Proceedings of Excommunication against Mistress Ann Hibbens of Boston." In *Remarkable Providences: Readings on Early American History*, 263–82. Boston: Northeastern University Press, 1991.

Demos, John Putnam. *Entertaining Satan: Witchcraft and the Culture of Early New England*. Oxford: Oxford University Press, 1982.

"The Descendants of Nurse; A Gathering at Danvers Which Recalled the Days of Witchcraft." *Boston Globe*. July 19, 1883. Boston Globe Archive.

Dimon, Laura. "What Witchcraft Is Facebook?" *The Atlantic*, September 11, 2013. https://www.theatlantic.com/health/archive/2013/09/what-witchcraft-is-facebook/279499/.

Dominus, Susan. "What Happened to the Girls in Le Roy?" *New York Times*, March 7, 2012, sec. Magazine. https://www.nytimes.com/2012/03/11/magazine/teenage-girls-twitching-le-roy.html.

Dow, George Francis. *Every Day Life in the Massachusetts Bay Colony*. 1935. Reprint, New York: Dover, 1988.

———. *History of Topsfield Massachusetts.* Topsfield, Mass.: Topsfield Historical Society, 1940.

———. *The Probate Records of Essex County, Massachusetts.* 3 vols. Salem, Mass.: Essex Institute, 1917.

———, ed. *Records and Files of the Quarterly Courts of Essex County.* 9 vols. Salem, Mass.: Essex Institute, 1911.

———. "Witchcraft Records Relating to Topsfield." In *The Historical Collections of the Topsfield Historical Society,* 13:39–142. Topsfield, Mass.: Topsfield Historical Society, 1908.

Drake, Samuel G. *The History and Antiquities of Boston, the Capital of Massachusetts and Metropolis of New England, From Its Settlement in 1630 to the Year 1770.* Boston: Luther Stevens, 1856.

Drymon, M. M. *Disguised as the Devil: A History of Lyme Disease and Witch Accusations.* Brooklyn: Wythe Avenue Press, 2008.

Dunning, Albert E. *Congregationalists in America: A Popular History of Their Origin, Belief, Polity, Growth and Work.* New York: J. A. Hill and Company, 1894.

Dunton, John. *John Dunton's Letters from New-England.* Edited by William H. Whitmore. Prince Society Publications. Boston: Prince Society, 1867.

Earle, Alice Morse. *Customs and Fashions in Old New England.* New York: Charles Scribner's Sons, 1894.

———. "Old-Time Marriage Customs in New England." *Journal of American Folklore* 6, no. 21 (June 1893): 97–102. https://doi.org/10.2307/533294.

———. *The Sabbath in Puritan New England.* New York: Charles Scribner's Sons, 1891.

Eccles, W. J. *The Canadian Frontier, 1534–1760.* New York: Holt, Rinehart, and Winston, 1969.

Edwards, Jonathan. "Sinners in Zion." In *Sermons and Discourses, 1739–1742,* edited by Harry S. Stout, 266–84. New Haven: Yale University Press, 1957.

Ehrenreich, Barbara, and Deirdre English. *Witches, Nurses, and Midwives: A History of Women Healers.* New York: Feminist Press, 1973.

Endecott, Zerobabel. *Synopsis Medicinæ, or a Compendium of Galenical and Chymical Physick: Showing the Art of Healing According to the Precepts of Galen & Paracelsus (1677).* Edited by George Francis Dow. Salem, Mass., 1914.

Essex Institute. *The Fifth Half Century of the Landing of John Endicott at Salem, Massachusetts: Commemorative Exercises by the Essex Institute, September 18, 1878.* Salem: Essex Institute, 1879.

Fearer, Myrna. "Memorial Honors Victims of the Witchcraft Delusion." *Danvers Herald.* May 14, 1992. Reprinted in *Danvers Remembers: The Commemoration of the Tercentennial of the 1692 Salem Village Witchcraft Delusion,* edited by Richard B. Trask, 32. Danvers, Mass.: Salem Village Tercentennial Committee of Danvers, 1993.

———. "Salem Village, Circa 1692, Hungered for Independence: New Exhibit by Danvers Historical Society at Tapley Memorial Hall." *Danvers Herald.* March 17,

1992. Reprinted in *Danvers Remembers: The Commemoration of the Tercentennial of the 1692 Salem Village Witchcraft Delusion*, edited by Richard B. Trask, 15–16. Danvers, Mass.: Salem Village Tercentennial Committee of Danvers, 1993.

Fels, Tony. *Switching Sides: How a Generation of Historians Lost Sympathy for the Victims of the Salem Witch Hunt*. Baltimore: Johns Hopkins University Press, 2018.

First Church in Salem. *The Records of the First Church in Salem, Massachusetts, 1629–1736*. Edited by Richard D. Pierce. Salem, Mass.: Essex Institute, 1974.

Forman, Ethan. "Facing Death, Witch Trials Victim Spoke Truth to Injustice." *Salem News*. July 19, 2017. https://www.salemnews.com/news/facing-death-witch-trials-victim-spoke-truth-to-injustice/article_3dcd88a4-6cf4-11e7-a115-4b5b9d02a8a3.html.

———. "Reports: Cause of Students' Vocal Tics May Never Be Known." *Salem News*. https://www.salemnews.com/news/local_news/reports-cause-of-students-vocal-tics-may-never-be-known/article_75188abd-d671-5165-b69c-b60535a7e6a1.html.

Fowler, Samuel P., ed. "Rev. Samuel Parris' Records of Deaths at Salem Village During His Ministry." *New England Historical and Genealogical Register* 36 (1847): 187–89.

Francis, Richard. *Judge Sewall's Apology: The Salem Witch Trials and the Forming of an American Conscience*. New York: HarperCollins, 2005.

Freeman, William W. K. "Map of Salem in 1700." Salem, Mass., 1933. Salem Witch Trials Documentary Archive. http://salem.lib.virginia.edu/perley.html.

Gagnon, Daniel A. "Map of Sites in the Life of Rebecca Nurse." 2018. https://spectersofsalemvillage.com/map-life-of-rebecca-nurse/.

———. "A Proclamation: Rebecca Nurse Day." *Newsletter of the Rebecca Nurse Preservation Society*, October 2017, 1.

———. "The Salem Village Parsonage." *Danvers Herald*. November 15, 2019. https://spectersofsalemvillage.com/2019/11/11/the-salem-village-parsonage/.

———. "Skeletons in the Closet: How the Actions of the Salem Witch Trials Victims' Families in 1692 Affected Later Memorialization." *New England Journal of History* 75/76, no. 2/1 (Spring/Fall 2019): 32–73.

Gardiner, Samuel R. *History of England: From the Accession of King James to the Outbreak of the Civil War, 1603–1642*. Vol. 8. London: Longmans, Green, and Co., 1891.

Gaskill, Malcolm. *Between Two Worlds: How the English Became Americans*. Oxford: Oxford University Press, 2014.

"Gemengd Nieuws." *Het Nieuws van Den Dag* (Amsterdam). September 8, 1885. European Library. http://www.theeuropeanlibrary.org/tel4/newspapers/issue/Het_nieuws_van_den_dag_:_kleine_courant/1885/9/8.

General Court of Massachusetts. An Act Relative to the Witchcraft Trial of 1692, § Chapter 122 (2001). https://malegislature.gov/Laws/SessionLaws/Acts/2001/Chapter122.

————. *The Charters and General Laws of the Colony and Province of Massachusetts Bay*. Boston: T. B. Wait and Co., 1814.

————. "The Liberties of the Massachusets Colonie in New England, 1641." In *American Historical Documents, 1000–1904*, 43:66–85. Harvard Classics. New York: P. F. Collier and Son Company, 1910.

Gibson, Marion. *Witchcraft Myths in American Culture*. New York: Routledge, 2007.

Gould, Elizabeth Porter. "The Home of Rebecca Nurse." *Essex Antiquarian* 4, no. 9 (September 1900): 135–37.

Gragg, Larry. *A Quest for Security: The Life of Samuel Parris, 1653–1720*. New York: Greenwood Press, 1990.

————. *The Salem Witch Crisis*. New York: Praeger, 1992.

Greene, David L. "Salem Witches II: George Jacobs." *American Genealogist* 58, no. 2 (April 1982): 65–76.

Greven, Jr., Philip J. *Four Generations: Population, Land, and Family in Colonial Andover, Massachusetts*. Ithaca, N.Y.: Cornell University Press, 1970.

Griswold, A. Whitney. "Three Puritans on Prosperity." *New England Quarterly* 7, no. 3 (1934): 475–93. https://doi.org/10.2307/359674.

Grose, Francis. *A Classical Dictionary of the Vulgar Tongue*. 3rd ed. London: Hooper and Co., 1796.

Guiley, Rosemary Ellen. *The Encyclopedia of Witches, Witchcraft & Wicca*. 3rd ed. New York: Facts on File, 2008.

Hale, John. *A Modest Enquiry Into the Nature of Witchcraft*. Boston: Benjamin Elliot, 1702. In *Narratives of the New England Witchcraft Cases*, edited by George Lincoln Burr, 395–432. 1914. Reprint, Mineola, N.Y.: Dover, 2002.

Hall, David D. *The Faithful Shepherd: A History of the New England Ministry*. Williamsburg, Va.: Institute of Early American History and Culture, 1972.

————. *Worlds of Wonder, Days of Judgment: Popular Religious Belief in Early New England*. New York: Alfred A. Knopf, 1989.

Hammond, Lawrence. *Diary Kept by Capt. Lawrence Hammond of Charlestown, Mass., 1677–1694*. Edited by Samuel A. Green. Cambridge, Mass.: John Wilson and Son, 1892.

Hansen, Chadwick. *Witchcraft at Salem*. New York: George Braziller, 1969.

Harley, David. "Historians as Demonologists: The Myth of the Midwife-Witch." *Social History of Medicine* 3, no. 1 (April 1990): 1–26. https://doi.org/10.1093/shm/3.1.1.

Haskins, George Lee. *Law and Authority in Early Massachusetts: A Study in Tradition and Design*. New York: Macmillan, 1960.

Hastings, James. *A Dictionary of the Bible: Dealing with its Language, Literature, and Contents Including Biblical Theology*. Vol. 2. 1898. Reprint, Honolulu: University Press of the Pacific, 2004.

Hawke, David Freeman. *Everyday Life in Early America*. New York: Harper & Row, 1989.

Hawthorne, Nathaniel. *Tales and Sketches: Including Twice Told-Tales, Mosses from an Old Manse, and The Snow Image*. New York: Library of America, 1982.

Hemphill, C. Dallett. "Women in Court: Sex-Role Differentiation in Salem, Massachusetts, 1636 to 1683." *William and Mary Quarterly* 39, no. 1 (January 1982): 164–75. https://doi.org/10.2307/1923422.

Henson, H. Hensley. *Puritanism in England*. New York: Lenox Hill, 1972.

Heyrman, Christine Leigh. *Commerce and Culture: The Maritime Communities of Colonial Massachusetts, 1690–1750*. New York: W. W. Norton, 1984.

Higginson, Francis. *New-England's Plantation*. 1630. Reprint, Salem, Mass.: Essex Book and Print Club, 1908.

Hill, Frances. *A Delusion of Satan: The Full Story of the Salem Witch Trials*. 2nd ed. Cambridge, Mass.: Da Capo, 2002.

———. *Hunting for Witches: A Visitor's Guide to the Salem Witch Trials*. Beverly, Mass.: Commonwealth Editions, 2002.

———. "Salem as Witch City." In *Salem: Place, Myth, and Memory*, edited by Dane Anthony Morrison and Nancy Lusignan Schultz. Boston: Northeastern University Press, 2004.

Hines, Ezra D. "Historical Address." In *The Celebration of the One Hundred and Fiftieth Anniversary of the Establishment of the Town of Danvers, Massachusetts, as a Separate Municipality*. Boston: Fort Hill Press, 1907.

Hite, Richard. *In the Shadow of Salem: The Andover Witch Hunt of 1692*. Yardley, PA: Westholme Publishing, 2018.

Hoffer, Peter Charles. *The Devil's Disciples: Makers of the Salem Witchcraft Trials*. Baltimore: Johns Hopkins University Press, 1996.

Hoover, Lois Payne. *Towne Family: William Towne and Joanna Blessing, Salem, Massachusetts, 1635*. Baltimore: Otter Bay Books, 2010.

Howard, Vicki. "'Real Man's Ring': Gender and the Invention of Tradition." *Journal of Social History* 36, no. 4 (Summer 2003): 837–56.

Howe, Daniel Wait. *The Puritan Republic of Massachusetts Bay in New England*. Indianapolis: Bobbs-Merrill Company, 1899.

Howland, Edward. *Annals of North America, Being A Concise Account of the Important Events in the United States, the British Provinces, and Mexico*. Hartford: J. B. Burr, 1877.

Hubbard, Robert Ernst. *Major General Israel Putnam: Hero of the American Revolution*. Jefferson, NC: McFarland and Company, 2017.

Hutchinson, Thomas. *The History of the Province of Massachusetts-Bay*. 3 vols. Boston: Thomas and John Fleet, 1765–1828.

"Inland ('Domestic')." *Der Nordstern* (St. Cloud, Minn.). August 13, 1884. Chronicling America: Historic American Newspapers. https://chroniclingamerica.loc.gov/lccn/sn83045350/1884-08-13/ed-1/seq-1/.

Johnson, Edward. *Wonder-Working Providence of Sion's Saviour in New-England*. Edited by J. Franklin Jameson. Original Narratives of Early American History. 1654. Reprint, New York: Charles Scribner's Sons, 1910.

Josselyn, John. *New England's Rarities Discovered in Birds, Beasts, Fishes, Serpents, and Plants of that Country.* 1672. Reprint, Boston: William Veazie, 1865.

Jue, Jeffrey K. "Puritan Millenarianism in Old and New England." In *The Cambridge Companion to Puritanism*, edited by John Coffey and Paul C. H. Lim, 259–76. Cambridge Companions to Religion. Cambridge: Cambridge University Press, 2008.

Kadri, Sadakat. *The Trial: A History from Socrates to O. J. Simpson.* New York: Random House, 2005.

Karlsen, Carol F. *The Devil in the Shape of a Woman: Witchcraft in Colonial New England.* New York: W. W. Norton, 1987.

Kences, James E. "Some Unexplored Relationships of Essex County Witchcraft to the Indian Wars of 1675 and 1689." *Essex Institute Historical Collections* 120 (1984): 179–212.

"Kin of Accused Witch on Salem Village Board." *Salem Evening News.* December 26, 1989. Reprinted in *Danvers Remembers: The Commemoration of the Tercentennial of the 1692 Salem Village Witchcraft Delusion*, edited by Richard B. Trask, 1–2. Danvers, Mass.: Salem Village Tercentennial Committee of Danvers, 1993.

Kitson, P. M. "Religious Change and the Timing of Baptism in England, 1538–1750." *Historical Journal* 52, no. 2 (2009): 269–94.

Konig, David Thomas. *Law and Society in Puritan Massachusetts: Essex County, 1629–1692.* Chapel Hill: University of North Carolina Press, 1979.

Latner, Richard. "Salem Witchcraft, Factionalism, and Social Change Reconsidered: Were Salem's Witch-Hunters Modernization's Failures?" *William and Mary Quarterly* 65, no. 3 (July 2008): 423–48. https://doi.org/10.2307/ 2509 6806.

Lawson, Deodat. *A Brief and True Narrative of Some Remarkable Passages Relating to Sundry Persons Afflicted by Witchcraft at Salem Village.* Boston: Benjamin Harris, 1692. In *Narratives of the New England Witchcraft Cases*, edited by George Lincoln Burr, 152–164. 1914. Reprint, Mineola, N.Y.: Dover, 2002.

———. "Christ's Fidelity the Only Shield Against Satan's Malignity." In *Salem-Village Witchcraft: A Documentary Record of Local Conflict in Colonial New England*, edited by Paul Boyer and Stephen Nissenbaum, 124–28. Boston: Northeastern University Press, 1993.

———. "Deodat Lawson's Narrative." In *Salem Witchcraft: With an Account of Salem Village and A History of Opinions on Witchcraft and Kindred Subjects*, by Charles W. Upham, 685–97. 1867. Reprint, Mineola, N.Y.: Dover, 2000.

"Local and General News." *Newcastle Morning Herald and Miners' Advocate.* September 7, 1885. Trove, National Library of Australia. http://nla.gov.au/nla. news-page15203570.

Lockyer, Roger. *Tudor and Stuart Britain, 1471–1714.* London: Longman, 1964.

Lupson, Edward J. *St. Nicholas Church, Great Yarmouth: Its History, Organ, Pulpit, Library, Etc.* Yarmouth: Edward J. Lupson, 1881.

Manship, Henry. *The History of Great Yarmouth*. Edited by Charles John Palmer. 1619. Reprint, Great Yarmouth: Louis Alfred Meall, 1854.

Mapp, Jr., Alf J. *Three Golden Ages: Discovering the Creative Secrets of Renaissance Florence, Elizabethan England, and America's Founding*. Lanham, Md.: Madison Books, 1998.

Martin, Michael, and Leonard Gelber. *Dictionary of American History*. Edited by Leo Lieberman. Rev. and enl. ed. Totowa, N.J.: Rowman & Littlefield, 1978.

"A Martyr's Monument; Perpetuating the Memory of Rebecca Nurse—The False Charge of Superstition—Justice After Two Centuries." *Boston Globe*. July 26, 1885. Boston Globe Archive.

Massachusetts Office of Jury Commissioner. "Learn about the History of the Jury System." Mass.gov, 2019. https://www.mass.gov/info-details/learn-about-the-history-of-the-jury-system.

Mather, Cotton. *The Angel of Bethesda*. Edited by Gordon W. Jones. Barre, Mass.: American Antiquarian Society and Barre Publishers, 1972.

———. "A Brand Pluck'd out of the Burning (1693)." In *Narratives of the New England Witchcraft Cases*, edited by George Lincoln Burr, 259–87. 1914. Reprint, Mineola, N.Y.: Dover, 2002.

———. *Corderius Americanus, an Essay upon the Good Education of Children, in a Funeral Sermon upon Mr. Ezekiel Cheever, Master of the Free School of Boston*. Boston: John Allen, 1708. http://name.umdl.umich.edu/N01142.0001.001.

———. *Decennium Luctuosum: An History of Remarkable Occurrences, in the Long War, Which New-England Hath Had with the Indian Savages, from the Year 1688 To the Year 1698*. Boston: Samuel Phillips, 1699. http://name.umdl.umich.edu/N00725.0001.001.

———. "Letter to John Cotton, August 5, 1692." In *Selected Letters of Cotton Mather*, edited by Kenneth Silverman, 40–41. Baton Rouge: Louisiana State University Press, 1971.

———. "Letter to John Foster, August 17, 1692." In *Selected Letters of Cotton Mather*, edited by Kenneth Silverman, 41–43. Baton Rouge: Louisiana State University Press, 1971.

———. "Letter to John Richards, May 31, 1692." In *Selected Letters of Cotton Mather*, edited by Kenneth Silverman, 35–40. Baton Rouge: Louisiana State University Press, 1971.

———. *Magnalia Christi Americana; or, The Ecclesiastical History of New-England, from Its First Planting in the Year 1620, unto the Year of Our Lord, 1698*. London: Printed for T. Parkhurst, 1702. http://ebooks.library.cornell.edu/cgi/t/text/text-idx?c=witch;idno=wit112.

———. *Memorable Providences Relating to Witchcrafts and Possessions*. Boston: Joseph Brunning, 1689. In *Narratives of the New England Witchcraft Cases*, edited by George Lincoln Burr, 89–143. 1914. Reprint, Mineola, N.Y.: Dover, 2002.

———. *Ornaments for the Daughters of Zion, Or The Character and Happiness of a Vertuous Woman: In a Discourse Which Directs the Female-Sex How to Express, the Fear of God, in Every Age and State of Their Life; and Obtain Both Temporal and Eternal Blessedness.* Boston: Samuel Phillips, 1692. http://name. umdl.umich.edu/N00500.0001.001.

———. *The Present State of New England Considered in a Discourse on the Necessities and Advantages of a Public Spirit in Every Man; Especially, at Such a Time as This.* Boston: Samuel Green, 1690.

———. "The Return of Several Ministers Consulted (June 15, 1692)." In *Salem-Village Witchcraft: A Documentary Record of Local Conflict in Colonial New England*, edited by Paul Boyer and Stephen Nissenbaum, 117–18. Boston: Northeastern University Press, 1993.

———. *The Wonders of the Invisible World.* Boston: John Dunton, 1693. Excerpted in *Narratives of the New England Witchcraft Cases*, edited by George Lincoln Burr, 203–52. 1914. Reprint, Mineola, N.Y.: Dover, 2002.

Mather, Increase. *Cases of Conscience Concerning Evil Spirits Personating Men, Witchcrafts, Infallible Proofs of Guilt in Such as Are Accused with That Crime.* Boston: Benjamin Harris, 1693. http://salem.lib.virginia.edu/speccol/mather/ mather.html.

———. "Recantation of Confessors of Witchcraft." *Collections of the Massachusetts Historical Society*, 2nd ser., 3 (1815): 221–25.

Matthews, Albert W. "Notes on the Massachusetts Royal Commissions, 1681–1775." *Publications of the Colonial Society of Massachusetts* 17 (1915): 2–110.

Maule, Thomas. *New-England Pesecutors [Sic] Mauled With Their Own Weapons.* New York: William Bradford, 1697. http://ebooks.library.cornell.edu/cgi/t/text/ text-idx?c=witch;idno=wit123.

———. *Truth Held Forth and Maintained According to the Testimony of the Holy Prophets, Christ and His Apostles Recorded in the Holy Scriptures.* New York: William Bradford, 1695. http://ebooks.library.cornell.edu/cgi/t/text/text-idx?c=witch;idno=wit126.

McKern, Sharon S. "They're Digging up Witch Lore in Salem." *Science Digest*, May 1971.

McNamara, Martha J. "'In the Face of the Court . . .': Law, Commerce, and the Transformation of Public Space in Boston, 1650–1770." *Winterthur Portfolio* 36, no. 2/3 (Summer/Autumn 2001): 125–39.

Miller, Arthur. "Journey to 'The Crucible'; Visit to Salem Recalled by the Author of the New Play." *New York Times*, February 8, 1953, New York edition.

Milton, John. *Paradise Lost: A Poem in Twelve Books.* London: J. M. Dent, 1904.

"Miscellaneous News Notes." *Griggs Courier*. August 7, 1885. Chronicling America: Historic American Newspapers. https://chroniclingamerica.loc.gov/lccn/ sn88076998/1885-08-07/ed-1/seq-2/.

"Monument to Rebecca Nourse." *Hickman Courier*. June 5, 1885. Chronicling America: Historic American Newspapers. https://chroniclingamerica.loc.gov/ lccn/sn85052141/1885-06-05/ed-1/seq-1/.

"The Monument to Rebecca Nourse." *New York Times.* July 30, 1885.

Morgan, Edmund S. "The Witch & We, The People." *American Heritage* 34, no. 5 (September 1983). https://www.americanheritage.com/content/witch-we-people.

Moynahan, Frank E. *Danvers, Massachusetts: A Resume of Her Past History and Future Progress.* Danvers, Mass.: Danvers Mirror, 1899.

Mudge, Zachariah Atwell. *Witch Hill: A History of Salem Witchcraft Including Illustrative Sketches of Persons and Places.* New York: Carlton & Lanahan, 1870.

Murrin, John. "Coming to Terms with the Salem Witch Trials." *Proceedings of the American Antiquarian Society* 110, no. 2 (2000): 309–47.

Naqvi, Saeed. "Rebecca Nurse Land Earmarked for Model Farm." *Salem News,* June 19, 1977.

National Park Service. "National Register of Historic Places Nomination Form: Southwick House," 1983. File Unit: National Register of Historic Places and National Historic Landmarks Program Records: Massachusetts, 1964–2012. National Archives. https://catalog.archives.gov/id/63794661.

Nevins, Winfield S. *Witchcraft in Salem Village in 1692: Together With Some Account of Other Witchcraft Prosecutions In New England and Elsewhere.* Salem, Mass.: North Shore Publishing Company, 1892.

"News of The Week." *Dodge City Times.* August 6, 1885. Chronicling America: Historic American Newspapers. https://chroniclingamerica.loc.gov/lccn/sn 84029838/1885-08-06/ed-1/seq-2/.

Noble, John, ed. *Records of the Court of Assistants of the Colony of Massachusetts Bay, 1630–1692.* Vol. 1. Boston: County of Suffolk, Mass., 1901.

Norfolk Historic Environment Service. "Site of Great Yarmouth Castle." Norfolk Heritage Explorer. Accessed June 4, 2018. http://www.heritage.norfolk.gov. uk/record-details?MNF13375-Site-of-Great-Yarmouth-Castle&Index=12577 &RecordCount=56734&SessionID=1f46896c-0e97-4368-97af-4d0a0e38e399.

Northend, William D. "Address Before the Essex Bar Association." *Essex Institute Historical Collections* 22 (1885): 161–76, 257–78.

Norton, Mary Beth. *In the Devil's Snare: The Salem Witchcraft Crisis of 1692.* New York: Vintage, 2003.

Palmer, Charles John. *The History of Great Yarmouth, Designed as a Continuation of Manship's History of That Town.* Great Yarmouth: Louis Alfred Meall, 1856.

Parris, Samuel. *The Sermon Notebook of Samuel Parris, 1689–1694.* Edited by James F. Cooper, Jr. and Kenneth P. Minkema. Boston: Colonial Society of Massachusetts, 1993.

Pastoor, Charles, and Galen K. Johnson. *Historical Dictionary of the Puritans.* Lanham, Md.: Scarecrow Press, 2007.

Patterson, Shirley Drury. "Sergeant Francis Nurse of the Nurse Homestead." *About Towne: Quarterly Newsletter of the Towne Family Association* 27, no. 3 (September 2007): 41.

Penas, Dwight J. "Bless the Tie That Binds: A Puritan-Covenant Case for Same-Sex Marriage." *Law & Inequality: A Journal of Theory and Practice* 8, no. 3 (1990): 533–65.

Perley, Sidney, ed. "Bailey-Bayley Genealogies." *Essex Antiquarian* 5 (1901): 81–86, 110–20, 123–32.

———. "Ceder Pond Region, Salem, in 1700." *Essex Institute Historical Collections* 51 (1915): 23–40.

———. "The Court Houses in Salem." *Essex Institute Historical Collections* 47, no. 2 (April 1911): 101–23.

———. "Endecott Land, Salem Village, in 1700." *Historical Collections of the Danvers Historical Society* 4 (1916): 99–120.

———. "'Groton,' Salem, in 1700." *Essex Institute Historical Collections* 51 (1915): 257–70.

———. *Historic Storms of New England.* Salem: Salem Press, 1891.

———. *The History of Salem Massachusetts.* 3 vols. Salem, Mass.: Sidney Perley, 1924.

———. "Part of Salem in 1700 No. 7." *Essex Antiquarian* 5, no. 10–12 (December 1901): 145–92.

———. "Where the Salem Witches Were Hanged." *Historical Collections of the Danvers Historical Society* 9 (1921): 33–50.

"Personal and General." *Grenada Sentinel.* August 8, 1885. Chronicling America: Historic American Newspapers. https://chroniclingamerica.loc.gov/lccn/sn85034375/1885-08-08/ed-1/seq-2/.

"Personal and General." *Milan Exchange.* August 8, 1885. Chronicling America: Historic American Newspapers. https://chroniclingamerica.loc.gov/lccn/sn86053488/1885-08-08/ed-1/seq-6/.

Pestana, Carla Gardina. *Protestant Empire: Religion and the Making of the British Atlantic World.* Philadelphia: University of Pennsylvania Press, 2009.

Peterson, Mark A. "'Ordinary' Preaching and the Interpretation of the Salem Witchcraft Crisis by the Boston Clergy." *Essex Institute Historical Collections* 129, no. 1 (January 1993): 84–102.

"Petition of Salem Farmers, 1667." *Historical Collections of the Danvers Historical Society* 9 (1921): 116–19.

Phips, William. "Letter of February 21, 1693, to the Earl of Nottingham." In *Narratives of the New England Witchcraft Cases,* edited by George Lincoln Burr, 198–202. 1914. Reprint, Mineola, N.Y.: Dover, 2002.

———. "Letter of October 12, 1692, to William Blathwayt, Clerk of the Privy Council." In *Narratives of the New England Witchcraft Cases,* edited by George Lincoln Burr, 196–98. 1914. Reprint, Mineola, N.Y.: Dover, 2002.

Pike, Robert. "Letter from R. P. to Jonathan Corwin." In *Salem Witchcraft: With an Account of Salem Village and A History of Opinions on Witchcraft and Kindred Subjects,* by Charles W. Upham, 697–705. 1867. Reprint, Mineola, N.Y.: Dover, 2000.

Powers, Edwin. *Crime and Punishment in Early Massachusetts, 1620–1692: A Documentary History.* Boston: Beacon Press, 1966.

Preston, John. *The Picture of Yarmouth: Being a Compendious History and Description of All the Public Establishments Within That Borough.* Yarmouth: John Preston, 1819.

"Prudence Crandall." *Daily Republican* (Wilmington, Del.). January 22, 1886. Chronicling America: Historic American Newspapers. https://chroniclingamerica.loc.gov/lccn/sn84038114/1886-01-29/ed-1/seq-3/.

Putnam, A. P. *Rebecca Nurse and Her Friends: Address at the Dedication of a Tablet in Honor of Forty Friends of Rebecca Nurse of Salem Village.* Boston: Thomas Todd, 1894.

Putnam, Eben. *A History of the Putnam Family in England and America.* Salem, Mass.: Salem Press, 1891.

———. "Historical Sketch of Danvers." In *Danvers, Massachusetts: A Resume of Her Past History and Future Progress,* by Frank E. Moynahan, 1–32. Danvers, Mass.: Danvers Mirror, 1899.

Putnam, Harold. *The Putnams of Salem Village.* 2nd ed. Vero Beach, Fla.: Penobscot Press, 1997.

Rantoul, Robert F. "Old Modes of Travel." In *History of Essex County, Massachusetts, with Biographical Sketches of Many of Its Pioneers,* edited by D. Hamilton Hurd, 1:lx–lxxxvi. Philadelphia: J. W. Lewis & Co., 1888.

Ray, Benjamin C. *Satan and Salem: The Witch-Hunt Crisis of 1692.* Charlottesville: University of Virginia Press, 2015.

———. "The Geography of Witchcraft Accusations in 1692 Salem Village." *William and Mary Quarterly* 65, no. 3 (July 2008): 449–78. https://doi.org/10.2307/25096807.

"Rebecca Nourse-Hanged as a Witch 200 Years Ago-Honored Today by Hundreds of Her Descendants." *Boston Daily Globe.* July 30, 1885, Evening edition. Boston Globe Archive.

"Rebecca Nourse; Hanged as a Witch Two Hundred Years Ago, Honored Yesterday by Hundreds of Her Descendants." *Boston Globe.* July 31, 1885, Morning edition. Boston Globe Archive.

"Rebecca Nurse; Reunion of the Descendants of a Victim of the Witchcraft Delusion." *New York Times,* July 21, 1883.

Rendell, Douglas W. "Tercentennial Lecture Series." In *Danvers Remembers: The Commemoration of the Tercentennial of the 1692 Salem Village Witchcraft Delusion,* edited by Richard B. Trask, 20–21. Danvers, Mass.: Salem Village Tercentennial Committee of Danvers, 1993.

Rezac, Mary. "Was the Last 'Witch' of Boston Actually a Catholic Martyr?" Catholic News Agency. Accessed January 6, 2018. http://www.catholicnewsagency.com/news/was-the-last-witch-of-boston-actually-a-catholic-martyr-27747/.

Rivett, Sarah. "Our Salem, Our Selves." *William and Mary Quarterly* 65, no. 3 (2008): 495–502. https://doi.org/10.2307/25096811.

Roach, Marilynne K. "Biographical Notes." In *Records of the Salem Witch-Hunt*, edited by Bernard Rosenthal, 925–64. New York: Cambridge University Press, 2009.

———. *Gallows and Graves: The Search to Locate the Death and Burial Sites of the People Executed for Witchcraft in 1692*. Watertown, Mass.: Sassafrass Grove, 1997.

———. "A Map of Salem Village and Vicinity in 1692." Watertown, Mass.: Sassafrass Grove, 1990.

———. "Records of the Rev. Samuel Parris, Salem Village, Massachusetts, 1688–1696." *New England Historical and Genealogical Register* 157 (January 2003): 6–30.

———. *The Salem Witch Trials: A Day-By-Day Chronicle of a Community Under Siege*. Lanham, Md.: Taylor Trade, 2002.

———. *Six Women of Salem: The Untold Story of the Accused and Their Accusers in the Salem Witch Trials*. Boston: Da Capo, 2013.

———. *A Time Traveler's Maps of the Salem Witchcraft Trials*. Watertown, Mass.: Sassafrass Grove, 1991.

Robbins, Stephen L. "Samuel Willard and the Spectres of God's Wrathful Lion." *New England Quarterly* 60, no. 4 (December 1987): 596–603. https://doi.org/10.2307/365420.

Robinson, Enders A. *The Devil Discovered: Salem Witchcraft 1692*. New York: Hippocrene Books, 1991.

Rosenthal, Bernard. "General Introduction." In *Records of the Salem Witch-Hunt*, edited by Bernard Rosenthal, 15–43. New York: Cambridge University Press, 2009.

———, ed. *Records of the Salem Witch-Hunt*. New York: Cambridge University Press, 2009.

———. *Salem Story: Reading the Witch Trials of 1692*. Cambridge: Cambridge University Press, 1995.

Salem. *Vital Records of Salem, Massachusetts, to the End of the Year 1849*. 6 vols. Salem, Mass.: Essex Institute, 1924.

Salem, Town of. *Town Records of Salem, Massachusetts*. 3 vols. Salem, Mass.: Essex Institute, 1868.

Salem Village. "A Book of Record of the Severall Publique Transactions of the Inhabitants of Salem Village Vulgarly Called The Farmes." Edited by Harriet S. Tapley. *Historical Collections of the Danvers Historical Society* 13 (1925): 91–122, 14 (1926): 65–99, 16 (1928): 60–80, 17 (1929): 74–108.

———. "Petition of Salem Village to the General Court (December 1690)." In *Salem-Village Witchcraft: A Documentary Record of Local Conflict in Colonial New England*, edited by Paul Boyer and Stephen Nissenbaum, 237–38. Boston: Northeastern University Press, 1993.

Salem Village Witchcraft Tercentennial Committee of Danvers. "Dedication of the Witchcraft Victims' Memorial," May 9, 1992. Program.

Savage, James. *A Genealogical Dictionary of the First Settlers of New England Showing Three Generations of Those Who Came before May, 1692, on the Basis of Farmer's Register.* 4 vols. Boston: Little, Brown, and Company, 1862.

Schiff, Stacy. *The Witches: Salem, 1692.* New York: Little, Brown, 2015.

Scudder, Horace E. "Life in Boston in the Colonial Period." In *The Memorial History of Boston, Including Suffolk County, Massachusetts, 1630–1880,* edited by Justin Winsor, 481–520. Boston: Ticknor and Company, 1880.

Seitz, Trina N. "A History of Execution Methods in the United States." In *Handbook of Death and Dying,* edited by Clifton D. Bryant, 1:357–67. Thousand Oaks, Calif.: Sage, 2003.

Sewall, Samuel. *Diary of Samuel Sewall, 1674–1729.* 3 vols. Collections of the Massachusetts Historical Society 5. Boston: Massachusetts Historical Society, 1878.

———. *The Selling of Joseph: A Memorial.* Boston: Bartholomew Green and John Allen, 1700. https://www.masshist.org/database/viewer.php?item_id=53.

Shorter, Edward. *Women's Bodies: A Social History of Women's Encounter with Health, Ill-Health, and Medicine.* New Brunswick, N.J.: Transaction Publishers, 1997.

Sibley, John Langdon. *Biographical Sketches of Graduates of Harvard University.* Vol. 1. Cambridge, Mass.: Charles William Sever, 1873.

Sidney, Philip. *The Headsman of Whitehall.* Edinburgh: G. A. Morton, 1905.

Silverman, Kenneth. *Selected Letters of Cotton Mather.* Baton Rouge: Louisiana State University Press, 1971.

Spanos, Nicholas, and Jack Gottlieb. "Ergots and Salem Village Witchcraft: A Critical Appraisal." *Science* 194, no. 4272 (December 24, 1976): 1390–94.

Starkey, Marion L. *The Devil in Massachusetts: A Modern Enquiry into the Salem Witch Trials.* 1949. New York: Anchor Books, 1989.

Stevens, Alexander. "Which City Is Witch City?" *North Shore Sunday,* April 26, 1992. Reprinted in *Danvers Remembers: The Commemoration of the Tercentennial of the 1692 Salem Village Witchcraft Delusion,* edited by Richard B. Trask, 24–26. Danvers, Mass.: Salem Village Tercentennial Committee of Danvers, 1993.

Stewart, George R. *Names on the Land: A Historical Account of Place-Naming in the United States.* Boston: Houghton Mifflin, 1958.

Stout, Harry S. *The New England Soul: Preaching and Religious Culture in Colonial New England.* New York: Oxford University Press, 1986.

Suffolk County (Mass.). *Suffolk Deeds.* 14 vols. Boston: Rockwell and Churchill Press, 1880.

Tapley, Charles Sutherland. *Rebecca Nurse: Saint but Witch Victim.* Boston: Marshall Jones Company, 1930.

Tapley, Harriet S. *Chronicles of Danvers (Old Salem Village), Massachusetts, 1632–1923.* Danvers, Mass.: Danvers Historical Society, 1923.

———. "Old Tavern Days in Danvers." *Historical Collections of the Danvers Historical Society* 8 (1920): 1–32.

Taylor, Alan. *American Colonies: The Settling of North America*. New York: Penguin, 2001.

Temple, J. H. *History of Framingham, Massachusetts, Early Known as Danforth's Farms, 1640–1680*. Framingham, Mass.: Town of Framingham, 1887.

Thick, Malcolm. "Garden Seeds in England before the Late Eighteenth Century: I. Seed Growing." *Agricultural History Review* 38, no. 1 (1990): 58–71.

Thompson, Roger. *Mobility and Migration: East Anglian Founders of New England, 1629–1640*. Amherst: University of Massachusetts Press, 1994.

"Told By the Telegraph." *Daily Morning Astorian*. August 1, 1885. Chronicling America: Historic American Newspapers. https://chroniclingamerica.loc.gov/lccn/sn96061150/1885-08-01/ed-1/seq-3/.

"Topics of the Day." *St. Landry Democrat*. August 8, 1855. Chronicling America: Historic American Newspapers. https://chroniclingamerica.loc.gov/lccn/sn88064537/1885-08-08/ed-1/seq-2/.

Topsfield Historical Society Historical Records Committee, and Topsfield Witch Trials Tercentenary Committee. *Topsfield and the Witchcraft Tragedy*. Topsfield, Mass.: Topsfield Historical Society, 1992.

Torrey, Clarence Almon. *New England Marriages Prior to 1700*. Baltimore: Genealogical Publishing Co., 1985.

"The Town of Danvers, Mass." *Cambria Freeman*. August 21, 1885. Chronicling America: Historic American Newspapers. https://chroniclingamerica.loc.gov/lccn/sn83032041/1885-08-21/ed-1/seq-2/.

Trask, Richard B. "The Creation of Danvers." Danvers Archival Center at the Peabody Institute Library, August 2013. http://www.danverslibrary.org/archive/?page_id=211.

———, ed. *Danvers Remembers: The Commemoration of the 1692 Salem Village Witchcraft Delusion*. Danvers, Mass.: Salem Village Tercentennial Committee of Danvers, 1993.

———. *The Devil Hath Been Raised: A Documentary History of the Salem Village Witchcraft Outbreak of March 1692*. West Kennebunk, Me.: Phoenix Publishing, 1992

———. "Introduction." In *From Muskets to Missiles: Danvers in Five Wars*, by Richard P. Zollo. Danvers, Mass., 2001.

———. "Legal Procedures Used During the Salem Witch Trials and a Brief History of the Published Versions of the Records." In *Records of the Salem Witch Hunt*, edited by Bernard Rosenthal, 44–63. New York: Cambridge University Press, 2009.

———. "Letter: Danvers Educator Helped Shine Light on Origins of Witchcraft Hysteria." *Salem News*. April 27, 2010, sec. Opinion. http://www.salemnews.com/opinion/letter-danvers-educator-helped-shine-light-on-origins-of-witchcraft/article_b45a1f10-0448-5491-838f-83f5d8fffd1e.html.

———. *The Meetinghouse at Salem Village*. Danvers, Mass.: Yeoman Press, 1992.

———. "Raising the Devil." *Yankee Magazine*, May 1972.

"The Trials for Witchcraft at Salem." *London North News and Finsbury Gazette.* June 20, 1885. NewspaperArchive. https://newspaperarchive.com/london-north-news-and-finsbury-gazette-jun-20-1885-p-5/.

Turnbaugh, Sarah Peabody. "The Real Properties of Witches in the Salem Witchcraft Delusion of 1692." *Historical Collections of the Danvers Historical Society* 45 (1981): 22–38.

Ulrich, Laurel Thatcher. *Good Wives: Image and Reality in the Lives of Women in Northern New England, 1650–1750.* New York: Vintage, 1991.

"Une Monument Funèbre à Une Sorcière." *Le Journal des Débats Politiques et Littéraires* (Paris). September 2, 1885. Bibliothèque nationale de France. https://gallica.bnf.fr/ark:/12148/bpt6k463309d.

"Une Sorcière Réhabilitée." *Le Petit Journal* (Paris). September 1, 1885. Bibliothèque nationale de France. https://gallica.bnf.fr/ark:/12148/bpt6k608779d.

United Health Foundation. "2016 Health of Women and Children Report." America's Health Rankings. Accessed May 4, 2018. https://www.americashealthrankings.org/explore/2016-health-of-women-and-children-report/measure/maternal_mortality/state/MA.

Upham, Charles W. *Lectures on Witchcraft, Comprising a History of the Delusion in Salem in 1692.* 2nd ed. Boston: Carter and Hendee, 1832.

———. *Salem Witchcraft: With an Account of Salem Village and A History of Opinions on Witchcraft and Kindred Subjects.* 1867. Reprint, Mineola, N.Y.: Dover, 2000.

Upham, William P. "Account of the Rebecca Nurse Monument." In *Essex Institute Historical Collections*, 23:151–60, 201–28. Salem, Mass.: Essex Institute, 1886.

Wagstaffe, John. *The Question of Witchcraft Debated, or a Discourse Against Their Opinions That Affirm Witches.* London: Edward Millington, 1669.

"Walk Brings Witch Monument 10,000 Giant Steps Closer." *Danvers Herald.* October 24, 1991. Reprinted in *Danvers Remembers: The Commemoration of the Tercentennial of the 1692 Salem Village Witchcraft Delusion*, edited by Richard B. Trask, 11–12. Danvers, Mass.: Salem Village Tercentennial Committee of Danvers, 1993.

Walzer, Michael. *The Revolution of the Saints: A Study in the Origins of Radical Politics.* Cambridge, Mass.: Harvard University Press, 1965.

Ward, Edward. "Trip to New England." In *Boston in 1682 and 1699*, edited by George Parker Winship, 29–70. Providence: Club for Colonial Reprints, 1905.

Watson, Jessica E. "Lithic Debitage and Settlement Patterns at the Rebecca Nurse Homestead." *Northeast Anthropology*, no. 81–82 (2014): 23–47.

Watts, Jeremiah. "Letter to George Burroughs, April 11, 1682." In *Salem-Village Witchcraft: A Documentary Record of Local Conflict in Colonial New England*, edited by Paul Boyer and Stephen Nissenbaum, 170–71. Boston: Northeastern University Press, 1993.

Webber, Carl, and Winfield S. Nevins. *Old Naumkeag: An Historical Sketch of the City of Salem, and the Towns of Marblehead, Peabody, Beverly, Danvers, Wenham, Manchester, Topsfield, and Middleton.* Salem: A. A. Smith, 1877.

Webster, Tom. "Early Stuart Puritanism." In *The Cambridge Companion to Puritanism*, edited by John Coffey and Paul C. H. Lim. Cambridge Companions to Religion. Cambridge: Cambridge University Press, 2008.

Weir, David A. *Early New England: A Covenanted Society*. Grand Rapids, Michigan: William B. Eerdmans, 2005.

Weisman, Richard. *Witchcraft, Magic, and Religion in 17th-Century Massachusetts*. Amherst: University of Massachusetts Press, 1984.

Wells, John A. *The Peabody Story*. Salem, Mass.: Essex Institute, 1972.

Wheatland, Henry, ed. *Baptisms at Church in Salem Village, Now North Parish, Danvers*. Salem, Mass.: Salem Press, 1880.

White, Daniel Appleton. *New England Congregationalism in Its Origin and Purity: Illustrated by the Foundation and Early Records of the First Church in Salem*. Salem, Mass., 1861.

White, William. *History, Gazetteer, and Directory, of Norfolk, and the City and County of the City of Norfolk*. Sheffield: W. White, 1836.

Whitmore, William Henry, ed. *The Andros Tracts*. Vol. 1. Boston: The Prince Society, 1868.

Wickham, Parnel. "Idiocy and the Construction of Competence in Colonial Massachusetts." In *Children in Colonial America*, 141–54. New York: New York University Press, 2007.

Wigglesworth, Michael. *The Day of Doom; Or, A Poetical Description of the Great and Last Judgment: with Other Poems*. New York: American News Company, 1867.

Wik, Esther I. "The Jailkeeper at Salem in 1692." *Essex Institute Historical Collections* 111, no. 3 (July 1975): 221–27.

Willard, Samuel. *Some Miscellany Observations on Our Present Debates Respecting Witchcrafts, in a Dialogue between S. and B. By P. E. and J. A.* Philadelphia: William Bradford for Hezekiah Usher, 1692. http://salem.lib.virginia.edu/texts/willard/index.html.

Wilson, Keith D. *Cause of Death: A Writer's Guide to Death, Murder, and Forensic Medicine*. Cincinnati, Ohio: Writer's Digest Books, 1992.

Winfield, Rif. *British Warships in the Age of Sail 1603–1714: Design, Construction, Careers and Fates*. Barnsley: Seaforth, 2009.

Winthrop, John. "Model of Christian Charity." *Collections of the Massachusetts Historical Society*, 3, 7 (1838): 31–48.

"Witch Goes to Trial at Danvers Pageant." *Daily Boston Globe*, July 1, 1930. Boston Globe Archive.

"Witchcraft." UK Parliament. Accessed August 24, 2017. http://www.parliament.uk/about/living-heritage/transformingsociety/private-lives/religion/overview/witchcraft/.

"Witches." *News and Citizen* (Morrisville, Vt.). August 28, 1884. Chronicling America: Historic American Newspapers. https://chroniclingamerica.loc.gov/lccn/sn97067613/1884-08-28/ed-1/seq-1/.

"Worthy Witch Memorial." *New York Times*, July 31, 1892.

Zane, John M. "The Attaint. I." *Michigan Law Review* 15, no. 1 (1916): 1–20. https://doi.org/10.2307/1274691.

Zelner, Kyle F. *A Rabble in Arms: Massachusetts Towns and Militiamen During King Philip's War*. New York: New York University Press, 2009.

Zollo, Richard P. *From Muskets to Missiles: Danvers in Five Wars*. Danvers, Mass.: R. P. Zollo, 2001.

———. *On the Sands of Time: The Life of Charles Sutherland Tapley*. Danvers, Mass.: Danvers Historical Society, 1990.

Acknowledgments

A work such as this cannot be undertaken without the help of many individuals. I would like to thank Ron Gagnon, my father and dedicated editor, who aided both in revising the manuscript and in suggesting several areas of inquiry. I would also like to thank my mother Ann Gagnon, and Sarah Corley for reviewing early versions of the project and giving very helpful comments and perspective.

Richard Trask, Danvers Town Archivist, was beyond helpful in answering my many questions and pointing me in the right direction for sources. His knowledge of Salem Village and Danvers history is unsurpassed. I would also like to thank him and the Danvers Archival Center for permission to reprint several images in this book.

At Westholme, I would like to thank Bruce H. Franklin for his work in bringing this book to publication, Noreen O'Connor-Abel for her helpful edits, and Trudi Gershenov for the jacket design.

I am much indebted to the many historians over the centuries who have written of the 1692 Salem Village witch hunt previously, and especially to those whose research I have referenced in this work. As Joseph B. Felt aptly wrote at the beginning of his *Annals of Salem*: "To the memory of the dead, whose writings have assisted him; and for the kindness of the living, who have granted him the use of manuscripts—he would be long and sincerely thankful."

Finally, I would like to thank all of those in the Danvers community who continue to support and share local history, and the many people from all across the globe who support the Rebecca Nurse Homestead Museum—most especially my colleagues, the tireless volunteers of the Danvers Alarm List Company, who work to preserve this landmark historic site for future generations.

Index

on wife's management of family affairs, 20
Sewall, Stephen
  as agent for compensation funds, 257
  Betty Parris' stay with, 91, 94
  clerk of the court, 161
  Cotton Mather's request for trial records, 233
  death warrant, writing of, 214–215
  grand jury indictments, 177–178
  Ingersolls' deposition, 193
  Nurse family request for trial records, 211, 212
  oral evidence, 191
  Rebecca Nurse indictments, 189
  restitution committee, 255
  trial transcripts, 190
  witch cake incident, 86
  witness summons, 167
shackles, use of, 138, 154–155
Sheldon, Susannah, 93, 145, 146, 167, 201
Shelton, Godfrey, 67
Shepard, John, 202
Shepard, Rebecca, 170, 175, 202–203
Sibley, Mary, 85, 86, 127, 152
Sibley, Richard, 28–29
Sibley, Samuel, 140, 150, 152
sickness. *See* health issues
signs from God, Puritans' belief in, 216
Six Articles (1539), 5
slander lawsuits, 24, 252
slavery, 250
Soames, Abigail, 141
social status of accusers, 94, 128
Society for the Preservation of New England Antiquities, 266
Some Miscellany Observations (Willard), 234, 249
Southwick, John, 25, 29–30
Southwick, Samuel (adopted son), 29–30, 47
Southwick family descendant, 259
special court establishment. *See* Court of Oyer and Terminer
spectral duel, 141–142
spectral evidence
  as basis for Rebecca Nurse indictments, 173–174

bill to prevent use of, 254
government consultation with ministers on, 165, 183–185
Hathorne's doubts in, 112
importance of, in witch trials, 82
increase Mather's essay on, 232–233
jury instructions, 204–205
ministers' skepticism regarding, 164–165, 227
prosecution's trial evidence, 192, 194
Superior Court of Judicature, 237
See also specific accusers
spectral mock communions, 131, 143
spectral murder allegations, 91, 171, 174, 175, 202
St. Nicholas Church, 3, 4, 5, 6–7, 35
Starkey, Marion L., 93
Stoughton, William
  background, 161–162
  Bridget Bishop death warrant, 180
  Bridget Bishop trial, 170
  Court of Oyer and Terminer termination, 235
  death warrants, 214, 215, 217, 237
  grand jurors oath administration, 172
  as impediment to clearing victims' names, 253
  intervention in witch-hunt course, 160
  introduction to Cotton Mather work, 233
  jury instructions, 204–205
  post-trial life, 250–251
  prisoner transfer order, 156
  request for jury to reconsider verdict, 206, 207
  spectral evidence, 165
  Superior Court of Judicature, 236
  Thomas Brattle on, 188
Stout, Harry S., 16
stress and afflicted accusers, 93–94, 97
Stuart, James Francis Edward, 61
substitute military service, 68, 242–243
Suffolk County, 160
Superior Court of Judicature, 182, 236, 237, 239
supporters' evidence. *See* defense evidence
supporters' monument, 262–263